Crucible
The Battle of

Book Two of the Anglo-Zulu War

James Mace

Electronic Edition Copyright © 2017 by James Mace

All rights reserved as permitted under the U.S. Copyright Act of 1976, no part of this publication may be reproduced, distributed, or transmitted in any form or by any means, or stored in a database or retrieval system, without the prior permission of the publisher.

Characters and events portrayed in this book are based on actual persons and events, but are used fictitiously.

Legionary Books
Meridian, Idaho 83642, USA
http://www.legionarybooks.net

First eBook Edition: 2017

Published in the United States of America
Legionary Books

Cover Images by Radoslav Javor, copyright © 2017 by Radoslav Javor and Legionary Books

All photography and maps are used with the generous permission of the Royal Welsh Museum, and from the collection of Ian Knight, as well as the author's personal collection.

A man chosen to wield life and death on the battlefield must be an artist, for if he isn't, he is simply a murderer.

- Shaka Zulu

Dedicated in memory of

Lieutenant Colonel James Edward Harper III
1968 – 2017

and

First Sergeant Erin Rochelle Smith
1982 – 2017

Requiesce in Pace, Fraterno Militum

Rest in Peace, dear Brother and Sister-in-Arms

The Works of James Mace

Note: In each series or combination of series', all works are listed in chronological sequence

The Artorian Chronicles
Soldier of Rome: The Legionary
Soldier of Rome: The Sacrovir Revolt
Soldier of Rome: Heir to Rebellion
Soldier of Rome: The Centurion
*Empire Betrayed: The Fall of Sejanus
Soldier of Rome: Journey to Judea
Soldier of Rome: The Last Campaign

*Centurion Valens and the Empress of Death
*Slaves of Fear: A Land Unconquered

The Great Jewish Revolt and Year of the Four Emperors
Soldier of Rome: Rebellion in Judea
Soldier of Rome: Vespasian's Fury
Soldier of Rome: Reign of the Tyrants
Soldier of Rome: Rise of the Flavians
Soldier of Rome: The Fall of Jerusalem

Napoleonic Era
Forlorn Hope: The Storming of Badajoz
I Stood with Wellington
Courage, Marshal Ney

The Anglo-Zulu War
Brutal Valour: The Tragedy of Isandlwana
Crucible of Honour: The Battle of Rorke's Drift
Lost Souls: The Forgotten Heroes of Eshowe
Cruelty of Fate: The Fight for Khambula

* Stand-alone novel or novella

Table of Contents

Preface
Cast of Characters
Prologue: A Most Unremarkable Fellow
Chapter I: A Day Like Any Other
Chapter II: Something is Wrong
Chapter III: Our Chance for Glory
Chapter IV: The First Alarm
Chapter V: Prepare for Battle
Chapter VI: Nothing Remains but to Fight
Chapter VII: Is that all?
Chapter VIII: With Rifle and Bayonet
Chapter IX: The Tragedy of Isandlwana
Chapter X: Alright, Sir, We'll do it
Chapter XI: A Doctor's Bravery
Chapter XII: Loss of the Ramparts
Chapter XIII: Fight for the Hospital
Chapter XIV: Give it to them!
Chapter XV: As Bright as Day
Chapter XVI: Retaking the Camp
Chapter XVII: Night of Horror
Chapter XVIII: The Final Redoubt
Chapter XIX: The Sombre Return
Chapter XX: What are You Waiting for?
Chapter XXI: Dawn Riders
Chapter XXII: Overtures of Disaster
Chapter XXIII: Bitter Aftermath
Chapter XXIV: Blood of the Heroes
Chapter XXV: One Hell of a Day
Chapter XXVI: Tears for the Dead
Chapter XXVII: Oaths of the Fallen
Chapter XXVIII: The Queen's Colour
Chapter XXIX: A Crucible of Honour

Historical Afterward
Appendix A: Historical Requiem – B Company, 2nd Battalion, 24th Regiment
Appendix B: Historical Requiem – The Defenders of Rorke's Drift
Appendix C: List of Casualties
Appendix D: Glossary of Terms
Author's Final Thoughts
Bibliography

Preface

It is January of 1879. While three columns of British soldiers and their African allies cross the uMzinyathi River to commence the invasion of the Zulu Kingdom, a handful of redcoats from B Company, 2/24th Regiment are left to guard the centre column's supply depot at Rorke's Drift.

On the morning of 22 January, the main camp at Isandlwana, just ten miles to the east, comes under attack from the entire Zulu army and is utterly destroyed. Four thousand warriors from King Cetshwayo's elite Undi Corps remained in reserve and were denied any chance to take part in the fighting. Led by Prince Dabulamanzi, they disobey the king's orders and cross into British Natal, seeking their share in triumph and spoils. They soon converge on Rorke's Drift; an easy prize, with its paltry force of 150 redcoats to be readily swept aside.

Upon hearing of the disaster at Isandlwana, and with retreat impossible, the tiny British garrison readies to receive the coming onslaught. Leading them is Lieutenant John Chard, a newly-arrived engineer officer with no actual combat experience. Aiding him is B Company's previously undistinguished officer commanding, Lieutenant Gonville Bromhead, along with 24-year old Colour Sergeant Frank Bourne, and a retired soldier-turned civilian volunteer named James Dalton.

Unbeknownst to either the British or the Zulus, half of the centre column, under Lord Chelmsford's direct command, was not even at Isandlwana, but fifteen miles further east, at Mangeni Falls. However, with a huge Zulu force of over twenty-thousand warriors between them and the drift, their ammunition and ration stores taken or destroyed, and an impossible distance to cover, Chelmsford's battered column cannot possibly come to the depot's aid, and must look to their own survival. The defenders of Rorke's Drift stand alone.

Cast of Characters

At Rorke's Drift

Lieutenant John Chard – Royal Engineer subaltern, given temporary command of the garrison, due to seniority
Lieutenant Gonville Bromhead – Officer Commanding, B Company, 2/24th Regiment
Colour Sergeant Frank Bourne – Senior non-commissioned officer (NCO) of B Company
Sergeants Henry Gallagher, George Smith, Joseph Windridge – Section leaders
Corporal William Allan – Section leader, recently reduced from sergeant for drunkenness
Corporal John Lyons – Assistant section leader and friend of Allan
Privates Fred Hitch, Henry Hook, John Williams – Enlisted soldiers

At Mangeni

Lieutenant General Sir Frederic Thesiger, Lord Chelmsford – General Officer Commanding (GOC) of all forces in Southern Africa
Colonel Richard Glyn – Commanding Officer, No. 3 Column
Lieutenant Colonel Henry Degacher – Commanding Officer, 2nd Battalion, 24th Regiment. His brother, William, was killed at Isandlwana

The Zulus

Cetshwayo kaMpande – King of the Zulus and a former British Ally. He specifically orders his regiments not to cross the border into Natal, that he might show he is fighting a defensive war, and only wants to protect his kingdom.
Dabulamanzi kaMpande – One of Cetshwayo's brothers, and arguably his favourite. In open defiance of his sovereign, he goads the rest of the Undi Corps into launching a raid into Natal.

Zibhebhu kaMaphitha – A cousin of the king, and prince of the royal house. Given command of the elite Undi Corps, he willingly cedes control to the more popular Dabulamanzi when the warriors proclaim they will invade the British-held Natal.

Mandlenkosi – An *induna* in command of a company of warriors within the king's own uThulwana Regiment. His son, Kwanele, fought at Isandlwana, and Mandlenkosi fears for his safety.

27 January 1879

The War Office has today received the following telegram from Lord Chelmsford, General Officer Commanding of Her Majesty's forces in Natal Colony, South Africa:

I regret to have to report a very disastrous engagement which took place on the 22nd of January between the Zulus and a portion of No. 3 Column left to guard a camp at Isandlwana, about ten miles in front of Rorke's Drift. The Zulus came down in overwhelming numbers and, in spite the gallant resistance made by the six companies of the 24th Regiment, two guns, two Rocket-tubes, 104 mounted men and about 800 natives, completely overwhelmed them.

The camp, containing all the supplies, ammunition and transport of No. 3 Column, was taken, and but few of the defenders escaped. Our loss, I fear, must be set down at 30 officers and about 500 non-commissioned officers, rank-and-file of the Imperial troops, and 21 officers and 70 non-commissioned officers rank-and-file of the Colonial Forces.

A court-of-inquiry has been ordered to assemble to collect evidence regarding this unfortunate affair, and will be forwarded to you as soon as received.

Full particulars, as far as can be obtained, have been sent in my despatch of this day's date which will reach you by the next mail. It would seem that the troops were enticed away from their camp, as the action took place about one mile and a quarter outside it.

The effects of the reverse have already been very serious. Two whole regiments of Natives have deserted and, it is to be feared, that the rest will follow. A panic has been spreading over the Colony, which is difficult to allay.

Additional reinforcements must be sent out. At least three Infantry Regiments and two Cavalry Regiments with horses are required, and one more Company of Engineers. The Cavalry must be prepared to act as Mounted Infantry and should have their carbines slung on the shoulder, and a sword shorter than the regulation pattern fastened to the saddle.

Lieutenant General Frederic Thesiger, Lord Chelmsford

Prologue: A Most Unremarkable Fellow

Greytown, Natal, South Africa
16 January 1879

Lieutenant John Chard
Subaltern, No. 5 Field Company, Royal Engineers

It was a typical summer week in Southern Africa, the days alternating between blistering heat and torrential rainfall. What roads that did exist in British Natal were simple dirt tracks used by traders. These had been rendered into near-impassable quagmires, churned up by the passage of endless wagons and columns of imperial soldiers headed for the border with the Zulu Kingdom.

As the early morning rain continued to flatten the tall grass and turn the road into soupy mud, Captain Walter Jones, officer commanding of No. 5 Field Company, Royal Engineers, emerged from his tent. He held a tin cup of steaming coffee in one hand; the result of his batman's ingenuity. The young soldier managed to light a campfire in the soggy timber scraps, using his greatcoat to provide a makeshift lean-to, to sufficiently boil the water. The captain's helmet was cocked forward, shadowing his eyes. He reached into his pocket, seeking out his pipe, finding it filled with water. Both the pipe and tobacco pouch completely soaked.

He gave up on it and let out a resigned sigh. "Nasty habit, anyway," he muttered; disappointed at being denied one of the few pleasures to be found in the South African bush.

"A fine morning, sir," his senior subaltern, Lieutenant Richard Porter, called through the din of pouring rain.

"Beastly weather," the captain muttered. "Still, if we give it a few minutes, it will change on us."

As if his words held sway over the dark storm clouds, the downpour tapered off to a light drizzle before ceasing altogether a few minutes later.

"At least you have your hot coffee," Porter remarked, holding up his own mug. Its contents consisted of a cold brew with bits of ground up sludge on the surface. "I don't know how your batman does it."

"Neither do I." Jones added with a grin, "And I tend not to ask."

The lieutenant checked his watch in the pale glow of the early morning light. "Well, unless by some miracle Cetshwayo has ceded to the high commissioner's demands, we've been at war with the Zulus for five days now." He gazed around at their camp.

Soon the corporals and sergeants would form up their sections for morning parade. And as early as reveille sounded, officers and senior NCOs began their day at least an hour before their men were roused from their fitful slumber.

"A good morning to you, sir," the company's acting colour sergeant, James Ellis, said as he joined the two officers. He saluted the captain, while carrying a humble tin mug of cold coffee in his other hand.

"You've seen the movement orders, colour sergeant?" Jones asked.

"Already briefed my section leaders," Ellis replied. He motioned towards the wagon track. "But if you want my opinion, sir, I doubt we'll be getting very far today."

"It's the same everywhere," the captain remarked. "I spoke with a rider from Captain Wynne's company, who was carrying a despatch for Lord Chelmsford. They're making slightly better progress heading east towards Thukela, albeit just barely."

"They also have a much shorter journey than we do," Lieutenant Porter added. He then gazed around the landscape. There was nothing but rolling grass hills and the occasional stand of trees to be seen anywhere; no people, and only the occasional bird or meandering boar. "A pity we're a hundred miles from anywhere."

Among the few reinforcements Whitehall authorised sending to the Cape were two companies of engineers; No. 2 Field Company under Captain Warren Wynne, along with Jones' own No. 5 Field Company. Ostensibly, these forces were sent to Natal to be used for building roads and bridges, rather than conduct warfare. The pleas from Lord Chelmsford, General Officer Commanding (GOC) in Natal, for additional infantry battalions and some professional cavalry had thus far gone unheeded.

Despite covering nearly a third of the globe, with over 400-million souls under the rule of The Crown, the land component of Her Majesty's forces was surprisingly small. With the war in Afghanistan, and the Empire's military resources stretched to their limit, the Queen's government had made it clear in no uncertain terms to the high commissioner, Sir Henry Bartle-Frere; they wished for a diplomatic solution to what they viewed as a minor squabble with the Zulu Kingdom. What no one in London knew, least of all the Queen or her ministers, was how determined Bartle-Frere and Chelmsford were to have war with their former allies and trading partners.

Since their arrival in Southern Africa, No. 5 Field Company had slogged its way through the mud, managing just a few miles each day as wagons sunk in the muck and became stuck every few yards. Captain Wynne and No. 2 Company were heading due east to link up with Colonel Pearson's No. 1 Column at Thukela Drift. Jones' men were to take the much longer route to join up with Colonel Richard Glyn's No. 3 Column at Rorke's Drift. By the morning of 16 January, they'd made it no further than Greytown and were still 70 miles from their objective. Captain Jones was beginning to wonder if they'd even reach the crossing before the war was over!

With the predawn glow brightening the landscape, the officer commanding checked his watch. "Five minutes until reveille."

"The bugler's already posted, sir." Ellis came to attention and saluted. "And with your permission, I will conduct morning parade."

"Carry on, colour sergeant," Jones replied, returning the courtesy. As soon as Ellis was out of earshot, he turned to Porter. "Is Mister Chard even awake yet?"

"Oh, yes," the subaltern answered. "He's been fumbling in his tent for the last hour, trying to find a pouch of dry tobacco. I swear his pipe has become permanently fixed between his teeth."

"Yes, well, I can understand his dilemma." Jones scowled, recalling his own ruined pouch of soggy tobacco.

"I told him it's going to ruin his teeth and rot his tongue," Porter, who did not smoke, remarked. He then shook his head. "I still have not figured out what we should do with him. I mean, I know we're short on officers, but if there was anyone less remarkable that Aldershot could have assigned to us…" His voice trailed off.

"To be fair, he's not without talent," Jones remarked. "I saw some of his field fortification plans from Malta, and they were quite good. If only his ambition were even half his talent, he'd be a bloody major by now!"

The man he and Porter spoke of was Lieutenant John Chard, a career subaltern assigned to No. 5 Company just prior to their journey to the Cape. Thirty-one years of age, he was gazetted as a lieutenant upon graduation from Woolwich ten years prior. While in the Victorian Era it was certainly not uncommon for engineer officers to still be languishing as lieutenants after a decade, Chard seemed to have no ambition for promotion whatsoever. He was obviously intelligent and technically skilled. It grated on Captain Jones to no end that his junior subaltern possessed little, if any, initiative. He was hesitant to speak ill of one of his subordinates in front of a fellow officer, yet Richard Porter had become Jones' closest confidant during the past year.

The sound of the bugler's call to reveille echoed across the open plain and, like every morning since they'd arrived in South Africa, soldiers spilled forth from their tents, pulling on their tunics and trousers, slapping their foreign service helmets onto their heads, and shouldering their rifles as they sought out their section leaders. Captain Jones took his place with his junior officers on either side. As Lieutenant Chard made his way over, his pipe protruding between his teeth, a glaring look from Jones and he quickly extinguished it and stuffed it into his pocket. Colour Sergeant Ellis turned the formation over to Captain Jones, should he have anything he wished to brief the company. On this morning, there was nothing. He immediately exchanged salutes once more and left the colour sergeant and his section leaders to conduct morning inspection.

As he walked over to survey the soggy road, the captain heard a call from one of the sentries.

"Rider approaching, sir!" The horseman was only able to ride at a modest canter. His mount kicked up clods of thick mud as it struggled to maintain its footing. Porter recognised the man as Lord Chelmsford's staff engineer officer, Lieutenant McDowell.

"Well, bless me! Good to see you, Frances!" He called out to his old friend.

"And to you, Richard," McDowell replied. "His lordship dispatched me to find you. We heard you and Wynne's lot arrived in Durban on the 5th. I originally thought you would be further along by now, but having just come up the road from Rorke's Drift, I cannot say I'm surprised."

"If the column wishes to come and dig us out of this quagmire, they're welcome," Captain Jones interrupted curtly before returning McDowell's quick salute.

"Your pardon, sir," the lieutenant said. "And not to darken your day, but the road does not improve between here and Rorke's Drift, which is about seventy miles away."

"At the rate we've been progressing, it will take us at least another ten days to reach the drift," Porter reasoned.

"Did the GOC have any instructions for us?" Captain Jones asked.

"He did, sir. His lordship requires one officer and a team of sappers at the drift as soon as possible. The ponts may need some repair. But more importantly, he wants work on a fort overlooking the crossing to commence with all haste."

"*Haste* is not something that can be used to describe our rate of travel," Jones grumbled. He then asked McDowell, "Are the roads firm enough for one of our light wagons?"

"I would say so. A light engineer wagon with a minimal crew and only the essential tools…they could probably reach the drift in about three days."

Jones and Porter glanced at each other knowingly. The subaltern grinned and gave a short nod.

The captain then shouted over his shoulder, "*Mister Chard!* Do be a good fellow and come join us!"

Chard strolled over to them, lifting his feet high as he stepped through the muck. Despite suffering the same trials and tribulations as the rest of No. 5 Company, nothing seemed to ever phase him. "Can I be of assistance, sir?" he asked affably.

"I've got a mission for you," Walter explained. "Our light equipment wagons seem to be the only ones that don't get stuck every few feet in these swamps the locals dare to call a road. You are to take a team and make all haste for Rorke's Drift. Report to Major Spalding, conduct repairs on the ponts, and handle whatever immediate tasks the column may have for you. Most importantly, Lord Chelmsford wants a fort established overlooking the ponts."

"Right you are, sir."

"Once the rest of the company arrives, we will begin construction on the fort. I want all sketchings, as well as the basic outline fortifications, scraped and marked out by the time we arrive."

"Very good. How many men will I be taking with me?"

"I think six will suffice," Lieutenant Porter spoke up. "There's you and your batman, Driver Robson. I'll task Colour Sergeant Ellis with finding you an NCO and three volunteers."

"Splendid!" Chard replied, clapping his hands together.

Captain Jones turned to address McDowell. "Inform his lordship that Lieutenant Chard and a team of sappers will be at Rorke's Drift no later than the 20th."

"Very good, sir." As an engineer, Frances McDowell understood the difficulties Captain Jones and No. 5 Field Company were enduring. Having come from the main column, he also knew Lord Chelmsford's growing frustration at the ponderous pace of the invasion.

Since crossing into Zululand on the 11th, the No. 3 Column had gone no further than the far side of the river. Their only action thus far had been a raid upon the stronghold of a local *inkosi* named Sihayo.

His good humour returned, Captain Jones invited McDowell to join them for a cup of coffee and a hasty breakfast, which the lieutenant was grateful to oblige. Having been essentially blind to all that transpired since their arrival at the Cape, Captain Jones and his officers were anxious for any information they could glean from the column. What amazed them was that his lordship launched the invasion without waiting for all his forces to converge. In addition to the sappers, there were still at least two companies from 1/24th who had yet to arrive at Rorke's Drift.

"The GOC is anxious to engage the Zulus in a decisive engagement as soon as possible," Jones reasoned. "For the life of me, I cannot fathom why."

Unbeknownst to Jones, or indeed any outside of his lordship's inner circle, the desire for haste was borne out of Chelmsford's invading the Zulu Kingdom without the knowledge or consent from Her Majesty's government. Walter could only assume that the GOC was confident he could thrash the Zulus, like he had the Xhosa the previous year.

Having had a hasty breakfast and cup of cold coffee, Frances McDowell remounted his horse. No. 5 Field Company was nearly assembled, tents struck and wagons packed, ready to begin the drudgery of another day trekking through the mud. The engineer liaison exchanged salutes with Captain Jones and shook hands with Richard Porter. As Porter watched him ride away, a chill of premonition crept over him.

"Everything alright?" Walter asked.

"It's nothing, sir," Porter dismissed quickly.

There had been little difficulty finding volunteers for Lieutenant Chard's detachment. Given the chance to ride a light wagon all the way to Rorke's Drift, and not have to dig out the heavier ox wagons every few yards, perked the interest of every soldier within No. 5 Company. Sappers Cuthbert, Maclaren, and Wheatley were selected pretty much at random, along with a steady corporal named William Gamble, who Colour Sergeant Ellis privately told to, 'Keep an eye on Mister Chard'.

His pipe protruding between his teeth, Lieutenant John Chard eagerly called to Driver Robson and his team of sappers, ordering them to prepare their wagon for immediate departure. Charles Robson had just celebrated his twenty-fourth birthday a week prior, and was nearing the end of his six-year enlistment. Though his term of active service was set to end in April, he promised Lieutenant Chard that he would stay with him until the end of the war. He occasionally speculated that he might reenlist and make it a career with the Colours.

Over the past week, Robson became acquainted with the black African who actually drove the wagon, and who spoke just enough English so his white counterpart could convey basic instructions to him. The man's teenage son served as the wagon's *voorlooper*, who walked beside the wagon, guiding the draught animals with a long whip.

A pair of tents were quickly loaded, one for the sapper team and the other for Chard. Equipment was limited to their basic carpentry tools, spades and pickaxes, as well as a single wooden box of ammunition and a week's worth of biscuit's and tinned beef.

"I guess we'll have to make good time, if we want to keep eating, eh, sir?" Robson said with a grin as he held the reins of Chard's horse for him. The officer quickly mounted and the young driver climbed onto the bench seat, next to his African counterpart. With a signal from their officer, Robson gave the order to the black driver to move out, *'Phuma phandle!'* It was about the only local phrase he knew.

The rest of No. 5 Field Company watched with more than a touch of envy as the light equipment wagon bounded away, only occasionally sinking a few inches into the mud. The two remaining officers watched the 'Flying Sap' depart, bouncing along the rutted and churned up road, wobbling uneasily and nearly throwing one of the sappers over the side. Captain Walter Jones stood with his arms folded.

Lieutenant Porter articulated what both men were thinking. "And there goes the most unremarkable fellow to ever hold the Queen's Commission."

Chapter I: A Day Like Any Other

Rorke's Drift
22 January 1879
Dawn

Private Frederick Hitch
B Company, 2/24th Regiment

"Rather peaceful this morning," Fred said quietly. He stepped from his tent and buttoned his tunic. He stood tall, arched his back, and stretched his arms overhead, taking in a deep breath of the early morning dew.

For Private Frederick Hitch of B Company, 2/24th, the day began like any other. He always managed to rouse himself about ten minutes before the company bugler sounded reveille, just before dawn. This gave him a few moments of peace and reflection before the incessant rigours of the day. During the previous night, he'd had sentry duty from 1.00 to 3.00. Given how early dawn, and therefore reveille came, there was little point in trying to go back to sleep. He'd lain down on his bedroll for a few minutes, though he kept his tunic on, eyes wide open.

"Perhaps I can sneak away for a couple hours later." He yawned loudly. There had been little peace to be found during the past few weeks. Nearly 4,700 imperial redcoats and African auxiliaries from the No. 3 Column, along with all their draught oxen, mules, and horses, had covered the plain just east of the mission station at Rorke's Drift. Even when camped on the other side of the river, there was still the constant flow of messengers, commissariats, and other soldiers crossing the ponts. The neighs, braying, and groans of various draught animals never ceased. Then, on the 20th of January, the column at last departed. They bounded east towards what they hoped would be a decisive engagement with the Zulu *impi*, somewhere in the direction of the king's royal kraal at Ulundi. They had gotten as far as a mountain called Isandlwana, about ten miles east. Clearly visible from the river, it protruded like a giant sphinx on the horizon.

Soon after the main army's departure, Lieutenant Colonel Anthony Durnford arrived with his No. 2 Column, consisting almost entirely of mounted black Africans dressed in western-style hats and jackets, wielding Swinburne-Henry carbines. They were much fewer in number, at roughly 400 total troopers, with only a fraction of the wagons and baggage of No. 3 Column.

Fred recalled being impressed by the discipline and horsemanship displayed by the black troopers who, in his mind, conducted themselves with greater professionalism than their white counterparts from the European settler communities that made up the centre column's volunteer cavalry.

Durnford's stay would prove short-lived. As Fred Hitch enjoyed his few moments of solitude, a message from the main column was summoning No. 2 Column to Isandlwana.

"It would seem the war has moved on," a voice said from behind the young private.

He recognised the Irish brogue and turned to see his section leader, Sergeant Henry Gallagher. "That it has, sergeant. Some of the lads might be a bit unnerved by the silence, but I find it rather tranquil." He looked down at his tunic as he fumbled with one of the buttons, which came off in his hand. "Oh, bugger all."

Like most of the men in the 24th Regiment, Hitch's uniform was faded and in quite the state of disrepair. A second button was barely hanging on by a few threads. Both elbows had been patched several times over the nine months since their last uniform re-issue. The tunic was bunched up in places where he'd attempted to stitch tears closed. The private gave himself a quick look over, feeling it best to catch his own deficiencies, rather than having them brought to his attention by Sergeant Gallagher at morning parade.

"Two buttons need replacing, and I think I can feel the bottom coming out of my trousers again," Fred noted. "I swear it's the same story every morning."

"And it will be until April, Brickie, when Her Majesty sees fit to give each of her soldiers a fresh change of clothes."

'Brickie' was a nickname given to Hitch by his mates. He'd worked as a brick layer prior to joining the army, two years before, and the name stuck with him. Even Lieutenant Bromhead occasionally referred to him by it.

Gallagher added, "So long as your weapon and kit are serviceable."

"Sergeant, you know my bundook is always immaculate!" Hitch stressed; 'bundook' being a term picked up by soldiers in India to denote the Martini-Henry.

This elicited a chuckle from Gallagher, who understood just how much pride the soldier took in maintaining his rifle.

Being among their best shots, Fred Hitch was one of B Company's sharp-shooters and designated marksmen. He wore the crossed-rifle patch on his left cuff with immense pride. His long-distance vision was markedly superior to most of his mates, who claimed he could count the hairs on a giraffe's backside at a thousand yards without the need of field glasses. While most soldiers were prone to cringe under the fierce recoil of the Martini-Henry rifle, Hitch relished the savage kick; stating it made him feel alive, especially if the fellow on the other end of the barrel was dead!

Interestingly, Gallagher and Hitch had formed a type of friendship over the past two years; or at least as much as their differences in rank allowed. They never addressed each other by their given names, not even in private, and Gallagher was keen to show no sort of favouritism whatsoever within his section. For his part, Hitch had no idea why he had such a good rapport with his sergeant. Sure, they were very close in age; at twenty-three, Gallagher was scarcely a year older than Hitch. But then, most of the soldiers in B Company were of similar age. They weren't even from the same regions of Britain. Gallagher was born and raised in Tipperary, Ireland. Hitch was from London. Gallagher was well educated, the funds appropriated by the local Catholic parish after the death of his parents, and he'd worked as a clerk before joining the army. Conversely, Hitch was an illiterate labourer from a very poor family.

It was their passion for musketry that bonded the two soldiers. In addition to being one of the four section leaders in B Company, Henry Gallagher was given charge over the sharp-shooters. Like Hitch, he had a love of shooting, viewing marksmanship as a specialised art-form. When Colour Sergeant Bourne acquired some extra rounds for the sharp-shooters to showcase their skills, it had come down to Gallagher and Hitch for the final prize. Hitch won by scoring a pair of hits with his last two rounds at 800 yards, to Gallagher's one.

"So, glad you didn't give me extra duty for besting you," Fred said afterwards, garnering a knowing grin from the sergeant.

Reveille sounded as the bleary-eyed bugler, Drummer James Keefe, blared the notes from his tarnished and battered bugle. Hitch returned to his tent, grabbing his helmet and rifle left from near the main tent flap. The bugle notes continued to sound.

"Keefe's in rare form this morning," Hitch noted with a chuckle.

The grumbles and curses of more than a dozen soldiers crammed in the confined space resonated, as men struggled in the dark to find their boots, weapons, and other kit. It was the same story every morning; no matter how meticulous a soldier was in placing his equipment for the next morning, in the half-sleep mental fog, coupled with the enclosing darkness just before dawn, one's kit was never exactly where they thought it should be.

"Damn it, man, that's my sodding bundook!"
"No, it bloody well isn't!"
"Here, give me back my fucking boots, you twat!"
"Damn it all, why does my helmet smell like piss?"

Despite this disorganised chaos within each section tent, every soldier in B Company was dressed, kitted up, and ready for morning inspection within just a couple minutes.

"Company...'shun'!" came the booming voice of Colour Sergeant Bourne.

The deep bellow made one think of the tall, grizzled, barrel-chested, and much older senior non-commissioned officers who'd served a lifetime in the ranks. So, to hear such a powerful voice coming from one who was barely average in height, thin of build, and of such a youthful age that his soldiers referred to him as 'The Kid' was nothing short of astounding. At just twenty-four, and with most of his peers in their mid to late thirties, Frank Edward Bourne was in fact the youngest colour sergeant in the entire British Army.

The ninety soldiers of B Company stood tall, heels together, as the colour sergeant gave them their morning briefing before turning them over to their section leaders for inspection. The officer commanding, Lieutenant Gonville Bromhead, had intended to brief the men on the column's status. All were eager for news on the war just across the river. However, on that January morning, he knew no more than they did. Only that the column had reached Isandlwana and was still seeking out the main Zulu *impi*. There were also rumours that one of the companies en route from Natal was supposed to relieve them, allowing B Company to re-join the fight. However, this had not been confirmed, and the garrison commander, Major Spalding, refused to allow for any speculation.

"Section leaders, take charge of your men," Bourne directed.

Just like every morning, Sergeant Gallagher would walk the line of soldiers in his section. His assistant, Corporal John Lyons, kept his notebook ready and marked any deficiencies the sergeant found. At thirty-three years of age, Lyons was the oldest man in the section and ten years older than his sergeant. The two, however, had forged a strong rapport; Lyons' rather vulgar and brusque demeanour contrasting Gallagher's more amiable and gentlemanly deportment. The sergeant was keen to maintain proper bearing and almost never used coarse language. Lyons, on the other hand, could scarcely speak without dropping some form of profanity. Yet as different as the two men were, their leadership styles melded very well, and they prided themselves on having the most efficient and well-disciplined section in B Company.

"Two buttons unserviceable," the sergeant said, as he inspected Hitch. "Previous tear over right breast needs re-stitching."

"You slovenly soldier, Hitch," Lyons muttered, as he scribbled in his notebook. It was a phrase he said quite often.

Fred Hitch was never known for having an immaculate uniform, even on Home Service. Back in England, Hitch dreaded the days when Gallagher left inspections to Corporal Lyons, who seemed to single him out for extra duty for even the slightest flaw with his uniform.

Henry Gallagher was usually a mild-mannered and genial non-commissioned officer (NCO). However, he was also a stickler for detail and sharp with the rebuke and punishment if a soldier's kit was out of place. In addition to Hitch's buttons, two other uniforms required patching of the elbows or knees and many of the rest needed stitching. Another soldier, Private Thomas Cole, had a split sole on one of his boots.

Given the state of everyone's uniforms within the regiment, Sergeant Gallagher could be more forgiving than when on Home Service. That said, he had no tolerance whatsoever for unserviceable weapons or equipment. Since their arrival in South Africa, he'd made it clear that a soldier's helmet, waist belt, and ammunition pouches did not have to be pearly white; in fact, many had deliberately dyed them brown. *'But God help the man with a torn pouch or rust-pitted weapon!'* which he stated almost every morning during inspection.

Private Cole remembered all-too-well the morning his section leader gave his ammunition pouch a tug, only to have the stitching break and twenty loose rounds fell onto the ground. Sergeant Gallagher gave the unfortunate soldier such a thorough dressing-down, it left Cole trembling in his boots. Perhaps most poignant of all was Gallagher had scarcely raised his voice. Cole would later say the ten hours of extra duty awarded for this infraction had been a picnic by comparison. Needless to say, neither Private Thomas Cole, nor any other man in the section, ever had an issue with their ammunition pouches or weapons.

After nearly twenty minutes, the two NCOs finished with the morning inspection and dismissed their soldiers to breakfast. They returned to their tent where Private Henry Hook was stoking the coals from the previous night's fire.

"A sodding nightmare, keeping our uniforms from falling apart," one soldier muttered, noting the assortment of patches on his trousers. "Bloody beggars have better rags than these."

"And I'm sure there is many a beggar who would gladly trade places with you," Hook said reprovingly. Known as either 'Harry' or 'Hookie' to his friends, his own uniform was faded and patched, yet he was rarely called out for any deficiencies. Hook set about making the section's breakfast while Sergeant Gallagher and the other NCOs met with Colour Sergeant Bourne to review the day's duty rolls.

"So, Harry, what's for breakfast?" Private John Williams asked.

"Horse meat and axle grease." Hook gave a quick smile and wink.

There were no cooks assigned to the line companies. The men in each section were compelled to prepare their own meals. Hook's mates fancied him a decent cook; able to take the bland field rations given them, and turn it into something remotely palatable.

For Fred Hitch, his first task was finding his sewing kit and fixing his tunic button. Several of his mates joined him, conducting repairs to their own tunics or trousers.

"Every uniform in this company is a damned threadbare, patchwork mess," Private John Williams muttered, taking a needle and thread from Hook's sewing supply pouch. "Even Mister Bromhead's is looking a might ratty. And we've still got another three months until our next re-issue. How the bloody hell do they expect us to fight in the damned bush with only one sodding uniform issue per year?"

"*Benefit to the taxpayer*, as they say," Hitch replied. "Prime Minister Disraeli professes his love for the Empire in his flowering speeches, yet he is always looking to cut the expenses needed to maintain it."

"Typical Jew looking to pinch every penny," Cole bickered.

"I say sod the PM and the taxpayer," Williams ranted. "If the Queen saw us looking like this, she'd tell Disraeli to loosen the damned purse strings and buy us some new uniforms already."

"Remember that tunic what Captain Godwin-Austen got one of the locals to stitch together for him?" another soldier spoke up. "Looked like shit, but at least it got him wearing red again. They even put a blotch of green cloth on his collar."

"Well, I'm not paying for a locally made tunic out of me own pocket," Private Thomas Cole scoffed. "I'll fight the Zulus naked if I have to."

"Just make sure you wear your helmet," Hook laughed as he tossed some kindling onto the fire. "One needs to think about safety first!"

"I doubt the PM will give a damn if you choose to fight in the nude, Private Cole," Sergeant Gallagher said, walking over to the men. "But that pasty white skin of yours will, once it's turned redder than a lobster. The tics would probably love to make a feast out of your backside, as well." He then thumbed through his notebook. "Right, looks like we've got sentry duty today lads."

Before any of the privates could grumble, Corporal Lyons quickly added, "Any fucking complaints and you can join Sergeant Smith's section, digging the new latrine trench. There's also mounds of animal shit from the past few weeks that Major Spalding wants collected and disposed of. Don't think anyone wants *that* as an additional duty. And yes, I'm looking at you, Private Hitch."

Sergeant Gallagher's mouth twitched in a faint grin for a moment. "Once you finish sorting your uniforms and choke down a lovely breakfast of our Hookie's famous gruel, Fagan and Williams will join up with Lance Sergeant Williams to guard the ponts. Barry, Cole, Hitch, and Harris you're with Corporal Lyons watching the south road. The rest of you, except Hook, will take up two-man posts three hundred yards beyond the camp. We'll be rotating two-hour shifts with Sergeant Windridge's section."

"No sentry duty for our Hookie?" Private Fagan asked.

"Lucky Harry gets to keep emptying bed pans and making tea for the poor sods in the hospital," John Williams remarked.

"Thankfully, Surgeon Reynolds has orderlies for cleaning up shit," Hook noted. "I just provide what little comfort I can for the sick. Still, it's the best duty I've gotten since the column decided to leave us here."

At twenty-eight years of age, Harry had joined the regular army just two years prior; much later in life than many of his mates, who'd mostly enlisted between eighteen and twenty years old. Hook was also a lay preacher with a knack for bringing mental and spiritual comfort to those distressed souls lingering in the depot's makeshift hospital. There was one fellow who was an unrepentant atheist, yet even he found solace in Hooks spiritual counselling.

"You're a compassionate one, Harry," Gallagher noted with a touch of approval. "And yes, Surgeon Reynolds' senior orderly, Corporal Miller, has asked Mister Bromhead if he can keep you on as an assistant rather than deal with a new man every day."

"Just don't spend so much time in the hospital that you catch dysentery and give it to the rest of us," Private Williams scoffed.

Sergeant Gallagher allowed himself a soft chuckle and left to see about his own breakfast, which he usually took with his fellow section leaders; Sergeants Joseph Windridge, George Smith, and Corporal William Allan. John Lyons was a close friend of Allan's so he usually joined him as well. This morning, however, Allan was coming off a night-time guarding of the ponts and was waiting for his relief to arrive.

While Lieutenant Bromhead's B Company, 2/24th guarded the depot, the supply operations were overseen by a pair of commissariats and their assistants, with the infantrymen providing the muscle for labour as needed. The lack of sufficient wagons for the column meant supplies had to be sent forward in stages. Commissary Dunne was expecting a batch of empty wagons from Isandlwana that very morning, ready to fetch rations and mealie sacks for the column. The small field hospital was overseen by the doctor from 1/24th, Surgeon James Reynolds. In addition to the redcoats and commissaries, there were several hundred warriors from the Natal Native Contingent (NNC) under the command of a local volunteer captain named Stevenson. These were excess levies, left behind with little to do except provide menial labour.

The entire operation was overseen by Brevet Major Henry Spalding, the column's senior transportation officer. Because he was responsible for the lines of communication between Rorke's Drift and Helpmekaar, he spent much of his time between both depots. It was on that morning of 22 January that he decided to make for Helpmekaar to see what delayed two long overdue companies of reinforcements.

To the outside observer, it looked like complete chaos, yet for the garrison at Rorke's Drift, their daily life operated like a well-oiled machine.

Rorke's Drift had been built by its namesake, an Irish trader named Jim Rorke, decades before. Rorke had forged a friendship with the Zulu kings, with many of the *amakhosi* trading cattle for firearms and exotic goods from around the British Empire. The Zulus had named the homestead kwaJimu, or 'Jim's place'. Rorke died unexpectedly in 1873, the year after Cetshwayo became King of the Zulus. Two years later, his widow sold the outpost to a pair of families, who in turn sold it to Swedish missionaries. The current owner, Reverend Otto Witt, had sought in vain to use it as a bastion for converting Zulus to Christianity. When making his preparations for the pending invasion of Zululand, Lord Chelmsford had approached Witt about leasing the mission due to its ideal location as a supply depot near the drift. Witt, who blamed Cetshwayo for his inability to convert the Zulu populace and had expelled all missionaries from the kingdom, was happy to oblige.

The mission station itself consisted of just two buildings, along with a small cookhouse, and a latrine shack. A fruit orchard lay to the north, just beyond a field of brush and the road which led to the drift itself. An unfinished 5-foot high stone wall ran parallel to, and about thirty yards north of, the westernmost structure. The main buildings were long bungalows with thatched roofs and open verandas facing north. The exterior walls were made of dolerite bricks. The interior walls were mostly mud brick and plaster.

The eastern building had served as Witt's church and was twenty-five yards long and seven yards wide. The rooms were large with lofty ceilings. An attic was accessed via a step ladder outside the west wall. Because of its open layout, the church became the commissariat storehouse. Sacks of mealie, large crates of hard biscuits, and tins of bully beef were stacked from floor to ceiling. Excess biscuit boxes and mealie bags, each weighing two hundred pounds, were piled outside the storehouse under large tarps to keep off the rain. In addition to the food stores was B Company's reserve supply of ammunition; thirty-four heavy wooden boxes, each carrying sixty packets of ten cartridges each for a total of 20,400 rounds. A few yards off the northeast corner of the building was a large stone kraal for keeping cattle.

The western building was the smaller of the two. Prior to the war, it served as the home of Reverend Witt and his family. Since leasing the mission station to the British Army, Witt sent his wife and two young children to stay with friends at the town of Msinga, while he and a friend from their native Sweden stayed in a small tent. Witt had told Chelmsford that he felt obligated to remain and defend his home against the Zulus. Privately, he feared what the British might do to the homestead in his absence.

The house now served as the depot's hospital, ready to receive any sick or wounded evacuated from the main column. The interior layout of the house was very confusing, as there were no hallways. Some of the rooms could only be accessed from the outside and did not connect to any of the others. Witt explained that prior to his ownership, the house was shared by two families. They'd closed off some of the interior doors to give each other a measure of privacy.

Aside from the Witts' bedroom and a living room just off the veranda, the rooms were very cramped, especially for the approximately thirty patients housed there. While a handful were men who'd been wounded during a recent attack on the stronghold belonging to a Zulu *inkosi* named Sihayo, just across the river, most were suffering from severe cases of typhoid and dysentery. There were no actual beds for them, just pallets with straw for mattresses and a single blanket. It was here that Private Henry Hook reported after having breakfast with his mates.

"Morning, Corporal Atwood," Henry said. He walked over to the hospital veranda, a metal tea kettle and a string of tin cups hanging from his hand.

Sitting on the veranda was Second Corporal Francis Atwood; an NCO from the Army Service Corps who spent his days assisting at both the storehouse and hospital. He and Hook had aided Corporal Miller and the overworked orderlies when the wounded were evacuated following the skirmish at Sihayo's kraal. There was also the occasional influx of men who came down with the terrible fever that struck the column. The closest actual hospital was in the city of Ladysmith, nearly seventy miles to the west. With every wagon in the column dedicated to ferrying supplies to Isandlwana, plus the terrible state of the muddy roads, the wounded and gravely ill had to make do with what meagre care Surgeon Reynolds and his orderlies could provide. 'God help us if the column gets into a real scrap,' the doctor had said on more than one occasion.

"And a good morning to you, Private Hook," Atwood replied. "With as much time as you spend over here, I wonder why you haven't applied for a transfer to the Army Hospital Corps."

Hook simply shrugged. "With no supply wagons arriving lately and the rest of the column chasing after Zulus across the river, there isn't much for us to do. I figured I might as well make myself useful."

"Gets you out of sentry duty as well," the corporal added.

Harry grinned and shrugged. "Someone told Colour Sergeant Bourne that I can cook, so he assigned me to take care of the hospital meals. Of course, there are only so many ways one can dress up tinned bully beef and hard biscuits. I thought about growing my own vegetables here. But even if I could get the seeds, all the damned draught animals and goats would eat anything I planted."

Hook and Atwood shared a brief chuckle before the private's expression became serious. He looked towards the door that led into what had once been the private bedroom of Reverend and Mrs Witt. "How is he?" he asked.

"I'm afraid Surgeon Reynolds has done all he can for him," Atwood answered. "I'm sorry, man, but unless by some miracle his fever breaks within the next few days, I fear Sergeant Maxfield will not be with us much longer."

Robert Maxfield was a very young NCO from G Company. His elder brother had been a childhood friend of Hook's. Of all the patients suffering from typhoid fever, his case was by far the most serious. Hence, Surgeon Reynolds had given him the Witts' bed in a private room, rather than making him sleep on a pallet with the other patients.

Their thoughts were interrupted by the sound of muffled popping in the distance. The large hill of Shiyane towered over the camp to the east, making it impossible to see across the river to the column's main camp at Isandlwana, ten miles away. Hook instinctively pulled out his pocket watch; a gift from his wife during a happier time in their now estranged marriage. It was just after 11.00.

"Seems his lordship has found the Zulus," Harry speculated. He strained to hear the distant sound of rifle fire.

The deep boom of a cannon seemed to confirm his assessment.

"Yes, Mister Chard made mention of Lord Chelmsford taking most of the column east towards Mangeni Falls to attack the Zulu *impi*," the corporal recalled.

"Mister Chard?" Hook asked, momentarily confused. He then recalled the name and gave a quick nod. "Of course. That engineer officer what came up from Greytown three days ago. I thought he left this morning for the column?"

"He did, but I overheard him complaining to Commissary Dunne after he returned. Apparently, Colonel Pulleine sent him and his batman back, along with their equipment wagon. They kept Chard's sappers at the camp, though God only knows why. Without their tools, there's not much use for them. Damned officer logic. In my fifteen years in the ranks, I've never figured them out."

The two men laughed, though this was broken up by the distant thunder of a pair of cannons firing in quick succession.

"I thought Mangeni Falls was least thirty miles from here," Hook recalled. "There's no way we should be able to hear the reports of rifle and cannon fire from there. You don't suppose the Zulus are attacking Isandlwana, do you?"

"If they are, they must have a death wish," Atwood observed. "A few more of those cannon blasts, with some volleys from the Martini-Henry for good measure, and those bastards will be sorted out." He furrowed his brow. "Mind you, they've been banging away for some time now. Surgeon Reynolds left about an hour ago with Reverend Witt and Padre Smith to see if they could get a view of the action from atop Shiyane."

"Well, if it's anything to worry about, I'm sure Major Spalding will tell us."

"He's not even here," Atwood remarked. "Popped off to Helpmekaar this morning to find out where our damned reinforcements from 1st Battalion are. He left Mister Chard in command."

They could only assume this was because Chard had seniority over B Company's officer commanding, Lieutenant Bromhead. It felt absurd to Hook; an engineer officer with no combat experience, who had been in South Africa just two weeks and at Rorke's Drift a mere three days, was left in charge. But, Atwood noted that Spalding would only be gone a few hours and was supposed to return before nightfall.

"Hopefully with those damned reinforcements." The corporal's voice was casual, though the words took on an ominous tone as they heard the distant boom of cannon firing once more. These came not long after the last salvo, and the NCO quietly wondered if he should be impressed by the crews' rapid reloading skills, or alarmed that they were having to load and fire so quickly.

Harry simply nodded and walked into the hospital to make his rounds of bringing tea to the patients. Whatever fighting was going on at Isandlwana, Mangeni, or wherever Lord Chelmsford had found the Zulus, there was nothing he could do about it. His duty, at that moment, was to bring what little comfort could be found in freshly brewed tea to three dozen injured and terribly sick men.

He tried to spend as much time as was proper with Robert Maxfield. Though they had not seen each other in years, the young man was like a little brother to Harry. Only once during the past week had Robert briefly recognised him before succumbing to fits of delirium. As a lay minister, Hook prayed daily for the young man and the other lads in the hospital. On this day, he asked the Almighty: if he would not bring healing and recovery to Sergeant Robert Maxfield, might he be given a few lucid moments, so Private Henry Hook, the man he'd looked up to as a boy, could say just how proud he was of him.

Second Corporal Francis Atwood
Army Service Corps

Chapter II: Something is Wrong

Rorke's Drift
22 January 1879
11.00 a.m.

Lieutenant Gonville Bromhead
Officer Commanding, B Company, 2/24th Regiment

Fred Hitch had done his best to re-sew the buttons onto his ratty tunic, while choking down his reakfast. "Don't know why I even bother," he muttered, holding up the tunic and seeing the gaping hole where his buttons should have gone. The few sparse threads that remained seemed to mock him. Instead, he had to stitch them a couple inches further in, which made his tunic fit tight when buttoned up.

"Hey, you want to look all nice and smart, should Her Majesty come and visit us here in the armpit of hell," his mate, John Williams, chuckled.

"A visit from the Queen would be a Godsend," Hitch remarked. "You can bet the army would outfit us in brand new uniforms, with polished kit straight from the factory, were she to visit the far-flung corners of her domain. Sadly, I think this place is nothing but an insignificant backwater to Her Majesty, one the rest of the public back home could not even find on a bloody map."

Williams shrugged. "Perhaps after the lads across the river have slapped the Zulus around a bit, they'll take notice."

"Perhaps."

A voice shouted from outside, *"Relief detail, fall in!"*

"Come on, John," Private Fagan said to Williams. "That's us."

Near the cattle kraal, the two privates and four other soldiers assembled and made ready to march off; all glancing towards the east every time they heard another muffled volley of musketry in the distance.

"Somebody's gotten into a bit of a scrap," one of them said quietly.

"Fall in!" their NCO, a 22-year old lance sergeant named Thomas Williams, shouted. The six privates immediately came to attention. "Slope…arms!"

Originally from Walsall, just outside of Birmingham, England, Williams was now into the fifth of his six-year contract. Like many who joined the ranks, he enlisted as a means of escaping the workhouses, which seemed to be the fate of all young men and women of the poorer classes in industrial Britain.

'At least I can breathe the air here.' He was fond of saying this aloud whenever one of his soldiers decided to complain about the climate. His rank of lance sergeant was uncommon in the British Army. Wearing three white chevrons instead of the usual gold, lance sergeants were technically corporals who were either temporarily posted to a higher billet or appointed meritoriously while awaiting promotion to full sergeant.

"Left…turn!" he barked. "Quick…march!"

The NCO and his detail stepped off, their black boots and trousers splattered with mud as they followed the heavily rutted track down to the drift. It was about a half mile walk to the river crossing itself. As they marched in step, they saw a giraffe and a pair of zebras grazing in the tall grass just beyond where the rest of the column had bivouacked.

"Some of the locals come down to say 'hallo'," John Williams remarked.

The ponts were a pair of flat-bottomed barges attached to a rope pulley which spanned the entire width of the uMzinyathi River.

They were manned by a lone sergeant named Frederick Milne, who was one of the few redcoats at Rorke's Drift that was not a member of the 24th Regiment. Instead, he belonged to 2nd Battalion of the 3rd Regiment; more commonly known as 'The Buffs'. His battalion was actually part of Colonel Pearson's No. 1 Column, a hundred miles to the south. Though an infantryman, Milne had taken a course on construction and engineering early on in his career, receiving a certificate from the Royal Engineers for his efforts. With the centre column lacking in sappers, and Captain Jones' No. 5 Field Company not arriving in South Africa until well after Lord Chelmsford decided to make Rorke's Drift their crossing point, the hapless sergeant was taken from his company and detached to build and man the ponts.

Because the drift was the most likely place for an enemy incursion, once the column departed for Isandlwana, Major Spalding ordered a detail of fifty warriors from Stevenson's NNC, along with six British riflemen, to guard the crossing at all times. This was meant as a temporary measure, until such time as the depot was reinforced, with a proper fort overlooking the crossing.

On the morning of 22 January, the NNC were conspicuous by their absence. Lance Sergeant Williams halted his detail and walked briskly over to the NCO he was relieving, Corporal William Allan.

"What the bleeding hell?" he asked. "Where in the sodding fuck are those damned darkies?"

"Sleeping or buggered off for all I know," the corporal replied.

The two NCOs walked towards the river, while their men bantered amongst each other. "Their non-comm marched them off about an hour ago, even though their relief had not arrived. I shouted at him to stop, but that stupid Euro-twat either doesn't speak English or doesn't give two shits about performing his duty."

"Typical worthless mercenaries," Williams grumbled. "When you get back to camp, find Major Spalding and see if he'll give their officer, Stevenson, a swift kick in the arse."

"I may give him a boot up the backside myself," Allan spat.

"Yes, well, just don't be getting yourself into any more trouble," the lance sergeant chided, glancing at the corporal's right shoulder. One could readily see the fading and stitch marks from where his three gold chevrons had been replaced with two white ones.

"Oh, piss off, Tommy!" Allan retorted. "I already got an earful from the colour sergeant; right after Mister Bromhead took my stripes and my access to spirits. Try giving me a lecture, and I'll punch you square in the balls! And don't think just because they made you a lance sergeant that you'll be taking over my section."

"Enforced sobriety is making you irritable, old man," Williams remarked with a short laugh.

"Let's go a round of fisticuffs and I'll show you an 'old man'," Allan said. He, too, was grinning as he set the butt of his rifle on the ground and wrapped his hands around the end of the barrel.

At thirty-five years of age, Corporal William Allan was one of the oldest members of B Company, having first joined the regiment twenty years prior at the rank of 'Boy'. Like a number of troubled youths who joined the ranks, he had spent many a night in the military cells for drunken behaviour during his early years. He cleaned himself up while posted as an orderly at The Depot in Brecon, where he also taught himself to read, and began to rise through the ranks. In the spring of 1874, he received both his good conduct pay and permission from the regimental colonel to marry. His wife, Sarah Ann, was his pillar of support. The embarrassment of having to tell her that he'd succumbed to his former vice of the bottle and lost his sergeant stripes as a result shamed him far greater than any admonishments from either Lieutenant Bromhead or Colour Sergeant Bourne.

"Feels strange, seeing this place deserted," Thomas said, changing the subject as they scanned the slopes of trampled grass leading down to the ponts.

For weeks, they had been swarming with thousands of redcoats and African auxiliaries, along with several thousand draught animals and hundreds of horses. With their departure, the calm stillness seemed odd. There was a brief interlude the day prior, when Lieutenant Colonel Durnford's column of mounted troops arrived at the drift. Now, they, too, were gone.

"Nothing remains but Mister Chard's little camp," Allan observed, nodding towards the pair of tents and a lone wagon full of engineer equipment. He took a deep breath through his nose, noting the remnants of animal scat and other smells. "That wonderful stench of the column still lingers."

"I thought they were done fixing the ponts?" the lance sergeant asked, nodding towards Chard's tents and engineer wagon. "Shouldn't they be up with the rest of the column?"

"That's what I thought," Allan concurred. "But I also heard they were sent up here to lay out the foundations for a fort at the top of the drift. Bugger all, I have no idea what they're up to, nor do I particularly care. They all left early this morning. Then a couple hours later, Mister Chard and his batman returned with their wagon. Seemed all his lordship wanted was his sappers, and not him or their equipment."

"Typical," Williams remarked with a derisive snort. He paused, his brow furrowed. "You know, it was the strangest thing. Right before we came down here, we heard the muffled popping of musketry in the distance. We even heard the booming of a cannon at one point."

"Hmm, didn't hear a damned thing," the corporal noted. "But, we are down in a bowl. Any sounds coming from ten miles away could have simply travelled over our heads." He shrugged dismissively. "At least the boys in the column are getting a bit of live target practice in."

"Yes, a pity we're missing it all," Thomas added.

His nervous grin troubled Allan. Why would a few distant rifle pops in the distance unnerve him?

Despite his age, Thomas Williams was a seasoned veteran who, like the rest of B Company, saw a fair amount of action at the end of the Xhosa War. He had witnessed the fearful effects of the Martini-Henry against indigenous tribesmen armed with spears and shields. If the column was in contact with the Zulu *impi*, then perhaps the war would be over by supper.

"Well, at least we didn't end up like poor Sergeant Milne," Allan said, nodding towards the ponts, where the lone sergeant lay with his back against a rock, helmet over his face. The faint sound of snoring could be heard. "All of his mates from 'The Buffs' are with Colonel Pearson and the southern column, while he gets stuck here by himself, manning the ponts."

Unbeknownst to anyone at the mission station, The Buffs were at that moment fighting their own battle against several regiments from the Zulu *amabutho* at a place called Inyezane. Given his only enemy since being attached to No. 3 Column was extreme monotony, Frederick Milne would have doubtless been envious of his old mates, had he known they were putting the Zulus to flight.

"Does Major Spalding care that all he does is sit on his backside all day? All I ever see him doing is sleeping or playing cards with that fellow, Daniels." Williams looked at the civilian volunteer, who was also dozing nearby.

"If they are ready to work the ponts whenever men or wagons need to go over, the good major doesn't give a bucket of piss what they do. Between overseeing our little outpost, the depot at Helpmekaar, and with the roads from there to Greytown all soggy and shit, he has more important things to concern himself with; including where the hell our damned relief is! Oh, and speaking of which, I overheard Mister Bromhead mention that the major was heading off to Helpmekaar to see where the blazes those two companies from 1st Battalion are."

"Soggy roads or not, those slow bastards should have been here two days ago," the lance sergeant added derisively.

"Meanwhile, our engineer guest, Lieutenant Chard, is in command."

"Let's hope the responsibility of a few hours' command doesn't stress him too much," Williams said with a chuckle.

"Oh, he's alright...for an engineer officer," Allan added. "I helped him and his lads get sorted when they arrived three days ago. His sappers were anxious to get stuck in with the Zulus. Bunch of kids. Aside from their corporal, I don't think any of them are older than nineteen. Mister Chard was quick to remind them that if they had wanted to get 'stuck in' they should have joined the infantry. Still, you should probably check and see if he needs anything."

"Of course," the lance sergeant confirmed. He let out an exaggerated yawn. "Well, here's to another day of fighting that savage enemy known as 'boredom'."

It was not just the men of B Company who were feeling the tedium of doldrums while the main column got to fight the Zulus. Lieutenant John Chard was more than a little put out that he had been sent back to Rorke's Drift with his batman, rather than overseeing the detail his sappers were needed for. Last he knew, most of his No. 5 Field Company was still slogging through the muddy road from Greytown, seventy miles to the south. His own journey had been rather eventful. Even minimally loaded, his light equipment wagon still became stuck in the mud several times. They had only found the road reasonably clear once they reached Helpmekaar. Still, he rather enjoyed the relative solitude. He knew that once Captain Jones and the rest of the company arrived, their work would begin in earnest.

Thinking they might be needed to repair the ponts, the sappers had posted themselves near the drift itself. Their entire camp consisted of Chard's tent, one more for his men, and their equipment wagon. What repairs were to be had only took part of a day. Sergeant Milne had expressed his gratitude, as he seemed to be the only soldier at Rorke's Drift with any real carpentry skills. A couple of well-meaning privates were detailed to him, yet the sergeant found them more trouble than they were worth. When one accidentally dropped a hammer into the river, an exacerbated Milne shoved him in, not allowing him back ashore until he retrieved it. Afterwards, he informed Lieutenant Bromhead that he was better off working alone.

Ever since then, the 'Flying Sap' detachment, as they called themselves, waited anxiously to join the main column. Lieutenant Chard had not yet told them their primary task was to begin the layout of a stone fort which would overlook the drift. Most of the actual work would have to wait until the rest of No. 5 Field Company arrived, though Captain Jones instructed Chard to get the basic layout finished and marked before they arrived. Given the ponderous pace along the sodden roads, the engineer officer reckoned he had a day or two before he needed to begin his work in earnest. Besides, not much he could do while his sappers were with the column at Isandlwana. He had already surveyed the terrain, with a basic idea of what would be needed, and made a preliminary sketch. The entire task had taken just over an hour.

As he dug a sheaf of paper and a pencil from his saddlebags, he contemplated the events of that morning. It had been around the time he was having his morning coffee when Chard was informed by Major Spalding that his sappers were needed up at the main camp. Excited to finally be crossing into Zululand, and temporarily forgetting his mission to layout the stone fort, Chard accompanied his men and their tool wagon. He was to be disappointed when he arrived at Isandlwana and met with Lieutenant Colonel Pulleine of 1/24th, who was left in command while Chelmsford took half the column in pursuit of what they thought was the main Zulu *impi*. Pulleine informed the engineer officer that only his men were required. He could take his wagon back to the drift. In what was the closest thing to an adventure Chard experienced during his ten-year career, he spotted several hundred Zulus to the north of Isandlwana, who he feared might be making a dash for the ponts. On the road back to Rorke's Drift, he was relieved to come across Lieutenant Colonel Durnford and the mounted No. 2 Column. Though they had never served together, Chard felt a sense of kinship with Durnford as a fellow engineer officer.

He informed the colonel of the possible Zulu threat before continuing on his way. That had been around 7.00 in the morning. He reported back to Major Spalding, informing him of what he had seen, as well as the information he received from Lieutenant Colonel Pulleine about Lord Chelmsford's advance towards Mangeni with half the column. For his part, Spalding was extremely irritated at the tardiness of the relief companies from Helpmekaar, and he told Chard he was going to see what the delay was. In the meantime, as he had seniority, Chard was left in command of Rorke's Drift. As he departed, Spalding assured him that nothing would happen, and he would return by nightfall.

All had remained quiet, and he assumed Durnford had dealt with any threats the Zulus made towards the river crossing. John Chard and his batman, Driver Charles Robson, settled in for what promised to be a rather lazy day. He had first paid a courtesy visit to Lieutenant Bromhead, telling him of Spalding's directives and letting his fellow officer know where he could be found.

Chard then returned to his camp to find Robson fast asleep on his bedroll in the shade beneath their equipment wagon. Leaving him be, the engineer officer spent the morning lounging on a camp chair, smoking his favourite pipe, listening to the sound of the river as he penned a letter to his brother. Presumably, Captain Stevenson's NNC levies were tasked with guarding the ponts, yet the only persons he could see were six red-jacketed privates from Bromhead's company and Lance Sergeant Thomas Williams.

"Beautiful day, Mister Chard," Williams said, walking over to the officer, leaning against his rifle for a moment while he stretched out his lower back.

"That it is," Chard concurred. "I am glad to see the rains have stopped for the time being."

"Give it an hour or two, sir," the sergeant snickered.

"Yes. I haven't been in country long, but if I've learned anything, it's that the South African summer varies between days of stifling heat and torrential rains in equal measure."

"That it does, sir."

When Chard looked at the faces of the men in B Company, he first noticed how young most of them were. Lance Sergeant Williams looked more like a boy who should be studying at Eton than a non-commissioned officer of Her Majesty's imperial redcoats.

During the Army's most recent reforms, enlistments for other ranks were changed from a mandatory twelve years on active service to six, with the remaining six in the part-time reserves. Most of the men in B Company fell within this 'short-service' term, making their average age somewhere between eighteen and twenty-three years. Even the NCOs tended to be much younger than their peers in the regiment. The boyish lance sergeant who stood before Chard looked as if his face had never required a shave in his life.

"If you'll be needing anything, sir," Williams said, "me and the lads will be over by the ponts, keeping an eye on things."

"Yes, thank you, sergeant." Chard went back to his letter as Williams came to attention and saluted before returning to his post. He instinctively glanced eastward, where the sphinx-like mountain of Isandlwana stood out on the horizon.

View of Isandlwana in the distance, as seen from the river crossing at Rorke's Drift

As the morning rolled into afternoon, the soldiers at the mission station became more concerned about the increasing frequency of rifle fire coming from the direction of Isandlwana. Colour Sergeant Bourne and his section leaders decided to climb Shiyane Mountain to see if they could ascertain what was happening; however, they returned before they could reach the summit. Around 11.00, Surgeon Reynolds, accompanied by Reverend Witt and a civilian volunteer chaplain, Padre George Smith, decided to make their own trek to the very top of the mountain.

"There must be a spot of trouble at the camp, 'Gunny'," Commissary Walter Dunne said to his friend, Lieutenant Gonville Bromhead.

Bromhead was thirty-three, and had held his commission for over eleven years, spending his entire career with the 24th Regiment. While liked by his peers, his battalion commander, Lieutenant Colonel Degacher, viewed him as an only marginally capable officer. This was perhaps in part because Bromhead, who was called 'Gunny' by his friends, was partially deaf. He was only given command of B Company when their previous officer commanding, Captain Alfred Godwin-Austen, was gravely wounded during the closing stages of the Xhosa War, seven months prior. And though he'd held his commission a year longer than John Chard, his fellow officer had three years date-of-rank on him. This was due to engineers being gazetted as full lieutenants upon commissioning, thereby bypassing the ranks of ensign / 2nd lieutenant altogether. Bromhead understood this, and accepted Chard's assumption of command for the day with his usual professionalism. Albeit, he privately viewed the engineer as an inexperienced amateur.

"Wagons from Isandlwana were due to pick up supplies hours ago," the commissary continued. "Byrne, Dalton, Atwood and I even roused ourselves before reveille to have the next batch of mealie sacks and ration boxes sorted for them."

"It would seem young Horace has his hands full," Bromhead replied, referring to the column's deputy transportation officer, Lieutenant Horace Smith-Dorrien.

Smith-Dorrien had arrived at the drift around 7.00 with a message for Lieutenant Colonel Durnford and stayed to have coffee with Dunne and his assistant, James Dalton, before returning to Isandlwana to fetch his wagons. The youngest officer in the entire column, serving in his first campaign on active service, Horace had expressed concern to the two commissaries about his lack of pistol cartridges. Unfortunately, Dunne and Dalton did not have any in the storehouse. Bromhead gave the nervous officer a few of his own, just in case he ran into trouble. Little did 'Gunny' know just how much trouble Smith-Dorrien would find that day. By late morning, Horace was leading a detail consisting of a single donkey cart and a few volunteers, furiously trying to ferry ammunition boxes to the terribly stretched firing line to the north of Isandlwana. Unbeknownst to the small garrison at Rorke's Drift, the fighting was now becoming desperate.

The faint boom of cannon fire in the distance alerted Bromhead and Dunne. "Then again, perhaps there is a spot of bother going on at the camp after all," the infantry officer mused.

Despite the calm, deadpan tone in his voice, Dunne thought he saw Bromhead's face twitch slightly. All knew from Lieutenant Chard's morning report, Lord Chelmsford had taken over half the column and most of the cannon, in pursuit of what he thought was the main Zulu *impi*. After his conversation with Smith-Dorrien, Bromhead understood elements of the NNC had been in contact the night before at a place called Mangeni Falls, and Chelmsford was bringing his men in support. He then recalled taking a look at Major Spalding's map. Mangeni was about fifteen miles from Isandlwana, making it twenty-five from Rorke's Drift. The faint sound of cannon fire was therefore most likely not coming from Mangeni, but from Isandlwana. Another man who came to this conclusion was Dunne's assistant, an old retired soldier named James Dalton.

Forty-six years of age, Dalton stood six feet in height, with a powerful chest and arms, making him older and larger than any of Bromhead's garrison of redcoats. He'd served a full career in the ranks, retiring as quartermaster sergeant seven years prior. His adventurous spirit became restless, however, and he did not remain inactive for long. During the Xhosa War, he volunteered as a civilian and was given the post of acting assistant commissary, where he'd remained since. Though his was a non-combat role, the faint sound of musketry, accented by yet another cannon boom, shifted his mind back to that of the old senior non-commissioned officer.

"Mister Bromhead," he said. "Judging by the rate those guns are firing, I fear the camp may be in danger."

"A possibility, Mister Dalton," Gunny concurred. "But there's not much we can do about it, is there? Surgeon Reynolds and our two God-fearing pastors have taken a stroll to the top of Shiyane. I'm sure they'll let us know in due course if there is anything amiss. Although…" He paused for a moment before deciding to articulate his thoughts. "I confess I will feel much better once Major Spalding returns from Helpmekaar with our wayward reinforcements."

Both men felt uneasy as the cannon fired once more. Though clearly visible from down by the river, the distance to Isandlwana was deceptive. And because the fighting was taking place on the east side of the mountain, little could be seen, even from the very top of Shiyane. As the sound of distant musketry grew more intense, Bromhead paused for a moment, his thoughts turning to his friend, who had served with him in B Company over the past two years, Lieutenant Fred Godwin-Austen. The younger brother of Captain Alfred Godwin-Austen, Gunny had taken a liking to Fred and enjoyed having him as his subaltern after he assumed command.

Their working relationship had ended a few weeks prior, however. Once it was decided that B Company would remain at Rorke's Drift, Fred was reassigned to Charlie Pope's G Company. *'Better luck next time, old boy,'* had been his parting words to Gunny.

The Regiment was often referred to as a family, and in many cases the familial relations were literal, especially among the officers. It was not uncommon for a son to follow his father into the Regiment, or for brothers to serve together. Indeed, Gunny's elder brother, Major Charles Bromhead, was also a member of the 24th; though at the moment he was home on leave in England. And prior to Lieutenant Colonel Pulleine's return to assume command of the 1st, both battalions of the 24th were led by a pair of brothers, William and Henry Degacher.

A sense of unease came over the camp. The faint sound of musketry and cannon fire continued. It was past noon, and the heat of the midday sun threatened to bake the men in their wool tunics.

Fred Hitch glanced over his shoulder before undoing his buttons. "Ah, that's much better." He sighed.

He and Private Thomas Cole were currently on their second sentry shift of the day. Hitch had stepped away for a few moments to *'have a look at something in the brush'*. Cole made an off-colour remark about Hitch needing 'some alone time'. In truth, all he wanted was a few minutes to allow the faint breeze to cool the sweat that stuck his tunic and shirtsleeves to his body.

Having closed his eyes for a few moments, his thoughts were interrupted by the sound of galloping hooves. His jacket still open, Fred turned to see a dishevelled man in a red jacket riding towards camp from the south. He'd stopped once he saw Cole, and was speaking to him frantically. As far as Hitch knew, Rorke's Drift was the only crossing point for miles. He couldn't fathom where the man came from. Even from a distance, Hitch could tell the soldier was thoroughly soaked, as if he'd swum across the uMzinyathi. Though Fred couldn't hear their conversation, the soldier was gesticulating wildly, while pointing to the east. After a few moments, he kicked his horse into a gallop, and rode away in the direction of Helpmekaar to the west.

Hitch picked up his rifle and walked over to his friend, who was relaying the rider's frantic message to Sergeant Gallagher. Their section leader was making his rounds of the sentry posts, and had just missed the rider. Cole was speaking quickly, trying to remember all the soldier had said in his haste. He finished just as Hitch returned.

"Alright, carry on, Private Cole," Gallagher said, before giving Fred a reproving glare. "Hitch, do your tunic up. Where do you think you are, man?"

"Oh, bloody hell." Fred tried to suck in his chest as he complied, hoping the re-sewn buttons wouldn't pop loose again.

Gallagher shook his head, stating as he walked away, "If you don't sort yourself out, I may just you here for the rest of the day."

Hitch's discomfort with his threadbare jacket was forgotten when he saw the look of consternation on Cole's face. The young private was leaning against his rifle, his hands wrapped around the barrel, brow furrowed, eyes distant.

"What is it, Tommy? That madman got you all worked up? For all you know, he could have been a deserter."

"That was Sergeant Gallagher's first thought." Cole shook his head. "I doubt it, though. Why would he ride up here in the first place? He said the camp was under attack and in serious trouble."

"Well they've certainly been in a bit of a scrap," Hitch concurred. With all the sounds coming from birds and other wildlife in the direction of the river, the faint popping of musketry had faded into the background. It was only when he cocked his head to one side that he could hear what sounded like concentrated volleys. He looked at his watch. "Bugger all. They've been at it for at least the past couple hours. Don't tell me the Zulus are all at Isandlwana!"

Thomas seemed to not hear him and continued. "That rider wore the brass '24' and sphinx insignia. Since I didn't recognise him, I assume he was from 1st Battalion. He told me he was attached to the rocket battery from Lieutenant Colonel Durnford's column. They were overrun and cut off from the rest of the camp. He and the other survivors were headed for Helpmekaar."

"What did Sergeant Gallagher have to say about it?"

Cole shrugged. "He didn't seem too concerned. But, he never lets his emotions show. I recall last year, when a Xhosa musket ball knocked his helmet from his head, he scarcely batted an eye. Anyway, he reckoned if the man and his mates were headed for Helpmekaar, Major Spalding will sort them out."

The sound of footsteps walking through the tall grass alerted them to a pair of soldiers from Sergeant Windridge's section, coming to relieve them.

"A pity," Hitch said, "you two missed out on all the excitement!"

Thomas told their replacements about the rider and what he said about the camp being in danger. The men listened intently, interrupting frequently to ask questions. Afterwards, Hitch and Cole returned to their section's tent.

Fred rooted through his pack, finding a few crumbling biscuits and a tin of bully beef for his lunch. "Hot as a fucking oven in here." He let out a loud yawn; a reminder that his sleep was cut short by guard duty the night before.

"Didn't you say you were headed down to the ponts for a bit?" Cole asked, removing his tunic and sitting down on his bedroll.

"As soon as I've had a bite of this delectable sludge that the Army tells us is supposed to be beef. Then I would like to pop over to the ponts and soak my head in the river…sod that, I'm going to throw my whole body in! I'll tell you, Tommy, I would give me last shilling right now for a pint of ale that doesn't taste like warm piss, a vigorous bath, and a soft piece of flesh that hasn't rotting away at one of those fetid frontier brothels. Do you know when the last time I felt a woman's warmth was?"

"In London, just prior to when we left," Cole recalled quickly.

"Ah, so you heard about that."

"Come off it, Fred, everyone heard about it. I think even the officers knew."

"Well they was all out at some fancy gentleman's club, getting pissed up, while us lowly rankers were told to camp out on the cold and nasty train platform for the night." Hitch snorted and shook his head at the memory. "We was told not to wander off, and I'll never forget when Sergeant Gallagher caught me trying to sneak away."

"What exactly did you say to him?" Cole asked, being unfamiliar with the minute details of the story.

"I told him the truth. I said I needed some relief, that I knew London better than any man in the regiment, and there was the perfect place to go for a bit of 'companionship' not half a mile away."

"And he just let you?"

"Well, not exactly," Hitch confessed. "But the way he said, 'just don't let me see you sneaking off,' made it sound like he was giving his implied consent…provided I didn't get caught, of course. I said I could probably score a deal on any number of delightful young ladies who would just love his Irish accent. He thanked me, but then rather curtly reminded me that he was very much happily married."

The men shared a quick laugh and Hitch let out a sigh at the memory. He never told Thomas that he'd actually gotten lost trying to find a decent brothel, and had only managed to make his way back to the platform just prior to their train's arrival, before dawn. With all that had transpired over the past year since they arrived in Southern Africa, it may as well have been in another life.

A cannon fired in the distance, sending a chill up Fred's spine. Suddenly, he was no longer hungry.

Chapter III: Our Chance for Glory

Isandlwana
22 January 1879
2.30 p.m.

Prince Dabulamanzi kaMpande

The past few hours were a blur. Lieutenant Alfred Henderson paused to catch his breath, give his horse a few minutes' reprieve, and try to assess the disaster that had befallen. His ears rang from the incessant thunder of rifle and carbine fire.

"How?" a black sergeant said, using his slouch hat to wipe the sweat from his face. "How did the *inkosi* and Durnford allow this to happen?"

The lieutenant could only shake his head in dismay. Fearing the Zulu hordes were not far behind them, the African NCO kicked his exhausted horse into a gallop.

Commanding a troop of fifty black carbineers from the *Basuto Horse*, Alfred Henderson was part of Lieutenant Colonel Anthony Durnford's mounted No. 2 Column. The son of a prominent family in Pietermaritzburg, Alfred was educated in England, Germany, and his native South Africa. He was among the few colonials who were truly multilingual, speaking English and German, as well as various local dialects fluently. This was crucial with the indigenous Africans who supplemented the British invasion force. Many of the European officers and NCOs within the Natal Native Contingent (NNC) only spoke their national tongue, be it English, German, Dutch, or French. Very few could speak to the warriors under their charge without an interpreter, and those not of Anglo origins struggled to even speak with their British officers!

Earlier that morning, the mounted troops pursued what Durnford thought was a renegade band of warriors threatening to get between the camp and Lord Chelmsford's forces at Mangeni. A few miles from camp, they realised their folly. Instead of a few disorganised mobs, they came upon several thousand warriors from the main Zulu *impi*. As the small force of horsemen rode frantically back towards Isandlwana, Henderson noted the redcoats were spread in a long, thin line, facing an even larger horde of enemy warriors attacking from the north. The camp's commander, Lieutenant Colonel Pulleine, likely had no inkling of the emerging threat coming from his right.

From the beginning, things seemed to go wrong for No. 2 Column. Not only did they run into a large force they could not hope to contend with, but Durnford had earlier split off two of their troops to circle north. Granted, it was these men who found the Zulu *impi* and compelled them to launch their attack prematurely; however, no one riding with Durnford knew where they were. Adding to the ongoing disaster, the small rocket battery that accompanied them was overrun almost immediately and its commander, Major Francis Russell, killed. What baffled Alfred Henderson was that instead of taking his men and anchoring the right flank of the firing line, Durnford ordered his troopers to dismount in a donga well away from the camp. While the sloping ground offered excellent protection and could have held indefinitely against a frontal assault, it also left a sizeable gap of nearly a thousand yards between their position and the extreme right of the infantry.

Henderson was stunned. He thought to himself, *'You could march a division between us!'*

Not surprisingly, this was exactly what the Zulus would do later in the battle, as fresh regiments entered the fray.

As he assessed their precarious situation, the young officer took a deep breath and exhaled audibly. He fumbled for his water bottle, dismayed to find it empty. He ran his parched tongue over his sun-chapped lips.

What also rattled his nerves, nearly as much as the overwhelming Zulu onslaught, was the reaction of his column commander, Lieutenant Colonel Durnford. Henderson had been sent by Durnford, along with another officer and few troopers, back into the camp to find their ammunition wagon. However, neither the colonel nor anyone else in the column even knew where the wagon was! Their search quickly proved futile. With bands of Zulus now in the camp, the scratch detail had scrounged together whatever lose cartridges they could find and attempted to keep the onslaught at bay. The Zulus were swarming from multiple directions, and threatened to overrun Durnford's position. Henderson had little choice but to try to save as many lives as he could.

'Had I known the colonel would lose his head, I would have asked for another assignment', he thought to himself. He tried to unjumble all the events crammed into his mind. Whether a fair assessment or simply his emotions getting the best of him, he could not say. All he knew was Durnford was dead, and the 'Horns of the Beast' had completely enveloped the camp at Isandlwana.

Henderson was among the fortunate few to escape along the road leading back to Rorke's Drift. He had watched over his shoulder as thousands of warriors from the 'Right Horn' cut off any hope of escape for those who attempted to follow. Anyone else wishing to survive would have to find another way to the uMzinyathi before the Zulus cut them to pieces.

The sound of rifle fire, coupled with the sonic din of Zulu war cries, hung like a pall on the wind. The redcoats from the 24th Regiment were fighting for their lives. The lieutenant's heart pounded in his chest. He knew it would not be long before their furious volleys of musketry ceased altogether.

All Alfred had left were about a hundred mounted Africans from various troops and a handful of European carbineers. There was one officer with him, a German lieutenant from one of the other companies named Gert Adendorff. He was one of the first to sound the alarm that Isandlwana was under attack. Unfortunately, his grasp of the English language was very poor, and he'd struggled to make himself understood to the British officers. As such, he looked to Alfred to lead them to safety.

"Sizokwenza ukugijima eya emfuleni!" Henderson shouted to his horsemen, letting them know they would ride to the river. He knew of a drift that should be passable about ten miles away. He translated this into English for the handful of whites with him. When he noticed Adendorff's confused expression, he quickly reiterated in German before turning his horse and following the broken ground that would eventually lead them down the uMzinyathi River.

There were numerous other fugitives fleeing the murderous slaughter at Isandlwana. All were mounted. No man on foot could have hoped to outrun the fleet-footed Zulus. The remnants of one 24th company had tried to fight their way out. Exhausted and depleted of ammunition, they were surrounded and cut to pieces just before the Manzimnyama Stream, three miles from the battle. Instead of following most of the fugitives along the southern slope of a mountain called Mpethe, Henderson led his men to the north, skirting between the pursuing regiments of Zulu warriors in the direction of Rorke's Drift. Upon reaching the Manzimnyama, the band of survivors halted. The young lieutenant took stock of the situation once more. It appeared, for the moment, the 'Left Horn' was busy with the much greater number of fugitives to the south.

"Our horses are nearly blown, sir," a white carbineer spoke up.

"We'll take a few minutes to rest and water our mounts," Henderson responded. He leapt from his horse, thirstily filling his water bottle. "I need a volunteer to ride up to Rorke's Drift and warn the garrison."

"I go," Adendorff spoke up, just able to understand his fellow officer. "I warn soldiers."

"I'll go with him," a British carbineer said, not wishing to stay on the enemy side of the river any longer than necessary.

Henderson acknowledged the men and sent them on their way. He scanned the hills to the east where the sound of rifle fire was becoming sporadic and frantic. "I hope Spalding's lads can dig in and make a viable defence," he said quietly. "Not a chance in hell for them to make a run for it."

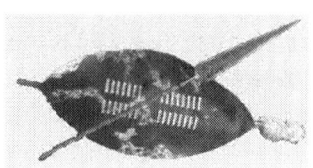

Rage consumed Prince Dabulamanzi. The regiments of the Undi Corps were the most senior and within the *amabutho*. Command should therefore have fallen to one of the king's closest kinsmen. The prince was Cetshwayo's favoured, not to mention most loyal, brother. Dabulamanzi was naturally furious when the king gave command of the corps to their distant cousin, Prince Zibhebhu. Many of the senior *izinduna*, particularly from the king's own uThulwana Regiment, shared Dabulamanzi's sense of resentment, viewing Zibhebhu as beneath a brother of the king.

And in what Dabulamanzi viewed as a personal slight, the army's commanding *inkosi*, Ntshingwayo, had kept these elite regiments in reserve during the attack on Isandlwana. From a strategic perspective, it made sense to maintain a robust reserve force should any phase of the assault falter. The regiments tasked with unleashing the 'Horns of the Beast' were all young men. Many were in their early twenties and fighting their first battle. What's more, the firepower wielded by the British was ferocious, able to tear warriors to shreds from several hundred paces. The *inkosi* knew, should the attack flounder, he would need the old warriors, distinguished by their white shields, to rally the army and win the day. This did little to assuage the sense of umbrage from the most senior regiments of the *amabutho*.

Under normal circumstances, the reserves sat with their backs to the battle, lest they be overcome by bloodlust and eager for glory. However, unfortunate circumstances led to the entire *impi* being spotted by a troop of Basuto cavalry commanded by British officers. First firing a series of volleys from their carbines before riding back to warn the camp, they compelled the *amabutho* to rise and launch its attack a day earlier than Ntshingwayo intended. It was nothing short of miraculous that the *inkosi* managed to maintain any sense of control at all. The Zulu commander-in-chief nearly had to physically restrain the senior *amakhosi* of the Undi Corps from leading their regiments into the fray. He had dispatched the youngest of these to support the 'Left Horn' while the other three followed an extremely wide arc to the west, acting as a reserve to the 'Right Horn', as it made the long trek around the backside of Isandlwana.

By the time they reached the place where the wagon track leading to Rorke's Drift intersected with the Manzimnyama Stream, the old warriors had already run nearly fifteen miles. Prince Zibhebhu was not with the main corps, having elected to accompany his own iNdluyengwe Regiment in its support of the 'Left Horn'. Despite his fury, Dabulamanzi was quick to recognise an opportunity. Who else would the remaining regiments look to for guidance, if not the king's favoured brother? This was made clear when several *izinduna* from the uThulwana approached the prince. These grey-haired warriors were in their early fifties, yet still as fit as any man half their age. Being the king's own *ibutho*, who served beside him for over thirty years including the civil war against the pretender, Mbuyazi, they loathed the thought of being robbed of their chance at glory against the invaders in red jackets.

One of the men said as much to Dabulamanzi. "What happens now, *inkosi*? Will we return to Ulundi with our spears un-bloodied? Do we allow these youths, many who were not even born when we won the throne for Cetshwayo, to insult us as old women when they parade before the king?"

Dabulamanzi beamed, his anger waning as he seized his chance. "To insult the uThulwana is to insult the king," he stressed. "And to deny the uThulwana their share in the spoils is to deny the king! Ntshingwayo may have disrespected you, but I will not. Will you follow me across the river and claim that share of glory which is rightfully yours?"

Every warrior in the Undi Corps was well aware of Cetshwayo's expressed order; under no circumstance was the *impi* to cross the uMzinyathi into British Natal. Yet how could the king deny his own regiment, especially after it had been so grievously slighted by the commander-in-chief, Ntshingwayo? Dabulamanzi knew their collective blood was up. It would take very little prodding to compel the entire corps to cross the river in search of plunder. And he knew exactly where he would lead them.

"Do not fear any rebukes from my brother, the king," he emphasised. "For he will sing our praises when we return to Ulundi with our spears bloodied, and the mountain of spoils laid before him!"

"You speak of kwaJimu," an *induna* said, with a wicked grin.

"Their numbers are few and rich is the treasure they guard," the prince continued. "And do not fear the river, sons of Zulu! It will no more stand in our way than the pitiful number of white men in red jackets at kwaJimu!"

The assembled *izinduna* gave a loud cry of *'Usutu!'* This was echoed by the closest warriors in earshot. Raising his prized musket high, Dabulamanzi gave a subsequent shout, and the host of warriors began the 10-mile run towards the river. Despite the distance already trekked, as well as being denied their breakfast by the untimely arrival of the enemy horsemen that morning, over 3,000 warriors from the Undi Corps followed the prince with a renewed sense of energy and purpose.

They hoped to bloody their spears in the guts of the fugitives; however, it appeared that any who tried to take the road to Rorke's Drift had already been killed by the regiments of the 'Right Horn'. So far, Dabulamanzi had seen no sign of Prince Zibhebhu and the remaining regiment of the Undi Corps, the iNdluyengwe. If they wished to join them in sacking the border settlements and slaughtering the garrison at Rorke's Drift, so be it. But under no circumstances would Dabulamanzi cede control of the Undi Corps back to his rival kinsman. Just a few miles from the river, at a small stream, Dabulamanzi dismounted and gave his horse a few minutes to quench its thirst. He stood in the ankle-deep waters and splashed handfuls upon his face. He heart was pounding and he was almost giddy with excitement. Certainly, he was flagrantly defying his brother and king. Yet he knew Cetshwayo would forgive him, perhaps even sing his praises, after he won glory for the uThulwana and the rest of the Undi Corps.

"Come, let us go fight at kwaJimu!" a warrior from the uThulwana shouted, his spear held high, as he caught up to his prince.

This particular *induna's* name was Mandlenkosi. At fifty-two years of age, he was among those old enough to have sons serving in the *amabutho*. His eldest, Kwanele, was a member of the uNokhenke, deployed on the right wing of the 'Chest' during the attack on Isandlwana. Early in the fighting, Mandlenkosi recognised the shields of his son's regiment as they charged headlong towards the enemy firing line. They were subsequently pinned down by British soldiers near the northern spur of the mountain. About half their number then joined the regiments of the 'Right Horn', making the long trek around the backside of Isandlwana. The remainder continued with their attack on the hard-pressed enemy line. Mandlenkosi had no idea which element his son was with, and from his position with the reserves, individual warriors were lost in the mass of humanity and clouds of black powder smoke.

As a father, he was concerned for his son's welfare, especially considering the murderous firepower wielded by the white men in red jackets. Even from a great distance, watching from the high ridges overlooking the battlefield, one could gage the fearsome toll being inflicted. By the same token, the old warrior was filled with a similar sense of jealousy and anger that afflicted most of the regiment. What a shame it would be, should the young warriors return to Ulundi with their spears bloodied, while those of the king's own uThulwana remained clean!

With their warriors chanting for battle and glory, Mandlenkosi had sought out Dabulamanzi. He was found pulling himself into the saddle of his magnificent horse. In truth, the prince loved many things European; their firearms, their horses, and even their clothes. Often he could be spotted from a distance, due to the slouch hat, jacket, and trousers he was fond of wearing. During the campaign, however, he understood that such attire might be viewed in poor taste and instead donned more traditional Zulu garb. He still insisted on riding his favourite horse, that he might better lead his men.

"Inkosi!" The prince turned to see the *induna* rushing over to him. "Does this mean we are launching a full-scale invasion of Natal?"

Dabulamanzi smiled and shook his head. "No, at least not today. Perhaps after we've savaged their lands, chastised those who assist the invaders, and slept with the white men's wives and sisters in Maritzburg, the king will commit the rest of the amabutho to punishing the British in their own lands."

It was all bravado, and both the prince and *induna* knew it. Despite his grand posturing, Dabulamanzi was concerned about just how far he could push the Undi Corps. The grey-haired warriors prided themselves on being as fit as their counterparts in the younger regiments. Yet by the time they reached the uMzinyathi River, they would have trekked twenty-five miles. To top it all, the lack of breakfast caused their stomachs to protest mightily.

The prince gazed upon the faces of his chanting warriors. He hoped that bloodlust and the desire for plunder would subdue their hunger pangs for the time being. With a loud cry of *'Usutu!'* he kicked his horse into a gallop, with 3,000 warriors following in his wake.

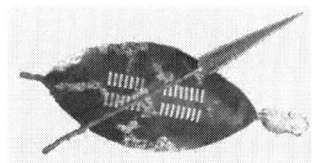

His vision clouded with fury, Prince Zibhebhu plunged his spear into the guts of an already injured redcoat; one of the Imperial Mounted Infantry, who had lost his horse in the ensuing fray. The badly injured man cried out, clutching at his guts as blood spilled onto his hands. Without pity, Zibhebhu stabbed him repeatedly. Then, with a swooping slash, he split the soldier's stomach open. He did not bother to strip the slain man of his jacket. He knew there would be others whose clothing he could claim for the purification rituals following the battle.

Giving an unholy scream of wrath, the *inkosi* raised his bloody spear and continued in pursuit of the fleeing British and their cowardly Natal allies. He and his warriors sprinted onward, bounding over the sloping, extremely rocky landscape as the ground channelled their quarry towards a passable drift, ten miles south of kwaJimu. Some of the white men and their black allies chose to fight back, preferring to die facing their enemy, rather than be stabbed in the back. Wherever red-jacketed soldiers could band together they made a valiant stand, with numerous warriors gutted by their protruding bayonets. It was all a brutal melee, as most of these men were out of ammunition. The Zulus, in return, showered them with throwing assegai, spitting many a soldier like a wild boar before charging home and disembowelling the lot of them. The black Africans, many still wearing the red headbands that identified them as friends of the invaders, shouted profane epithets towards the

Zulus in their native tongue, even as they were eviscerated and torn to pieces. It was an unholy slaughter, and Zibhebhu relished the cries of the dying and even the wicked stench of death.

A couple of hours later, they reached the cliffs overlooking what was known as Sothondose's Drift. Other elements of the 'Left Horn' had reached the river before them and slain any who failed to reach the far side of the uMzinyathi. Bodies, both European and African, littered the ground and the broken rocks below. It was here that Dabulamanzi and the rest of the Undi Corps met their wayward commanding *inkosi*.

With every white and traitorous black on the Zulu side of the uMzinyathi now dead, Dabulamanzi, Zibhebhu, and several of the senior *amakhosi* gathered along a ridge, overlooking the swollen river. The sound of rifle fire still reverberated in the distance behind them, though the volume and intensity had lessened considerably.

"It's not enough just to gut a few fleeing cowards, is it, dear cousin?" Dabulamanzi asked. Zibhebhu continued to stare across the river, listening to the mutterings of his warriors who were even more anxious than the rest of the corps.

As many warriors within the main *impi* were of similar age to Zibhebhu's iNdluyengwe Regiment, they felt an even greater sense of urgency to prove their manhood in battle. While the 'Left Horn' fell upon the mounted troops as they fled from the donga back into the main camp, the iNdluyengwe pursued the mass of fugitives already fleeing from the ongoing slaughter at Isandlwana. Any white soldier or African warrior not bearing a shield of the *amabutho* was cut down with unholy savagery.

And because Zibhebhu's regiment was the youngest of the Undi Corps, they had always felt out of place next to their much older peers, who constantly mocked them as 'unbloodied boys'. Many openly asked why they were assigned to the Undi Corps in the first place. Some of the *izinduna* suspected it was so Zibhebhu could assume overall command of the corps, instead of the king's erratic and unpredictable brother.

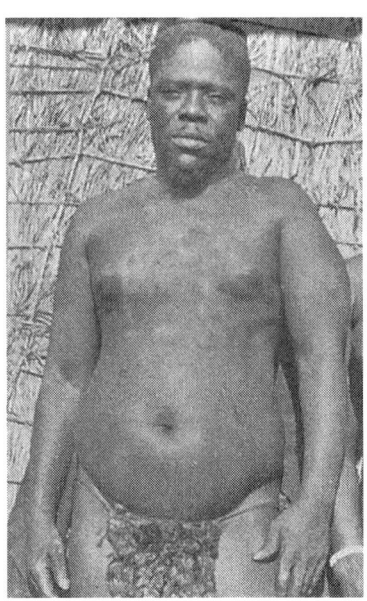
Prince Zibhebhu kaMaphitha

It was late afternoon, and the eclipse of the sun, which had dominated much of the afternoon, had since lapsed. Zibhebhu and his warriors rested, with some making their way down to the river to quench their thirsts and cool their sweaty bodies. Zibhebhu then decided to address his kinsman, who sat astride his horse, staring at him impatiently.

"The pursuit is over," he explained to the king's brother. "We have discharged our duty to the king."

"Yes, well done," Dabulamanzi said, trying in vain to mask the disappointment in his voice. Even during the pursuit, his men had missed out on all the fighting!

His gaze narrowed as he surveyed the river below. The waters were flowing fast, and he knew it would be a gargantuan undertaking to get his men across. Firstly, the Zulus were terrible swimmers. Cetshwayo had even stated, 'The river spirits are a greater king than I'. This was compounded by the king's order that his warriors were not to cross into British territory. But, the prince was determined. Natal was undefended and ripe for despoiling.

"We must find a place to cross," Dabulamanzi said plainly. He stared at his kinsman, daring the *inkosi* to rebuke him.

Instead, Zibhebhu simply nodded. He knew the blood of the Undi Corps was up, perhaps most of all within his own regiment. Chasing down and slaying a handful of fugitives had only stoked the fires of fury. Watching a number of survivors, who'd managed to ford the uMzinyathi, ride away further incensed them. Even Zibhebhu, whose rage had since subsided, was riled when he saw a white officer in a blue jacket reach the far bank. Despite having lost his horse, the man sat on a rock and calmly removed his boots to pour out the sand and river water before continuing on foot. The *inkosi* wished to spill the man's guts, yet the river stood impassable, mocking him and his warriors.

"What of the king's orders?" he asked half-heartedly, his gaze still fixed on the Natal bank.

"You let me worry about my brother."

Zibhebhu nodded, feeling the weight of responsibility lifted from his shoulders. As far as he was concerned, he had discharged his duty to the king and nation. If Dabulamanzi wished to lead his corps on a raid into Natal, there was nothing he could do to stop him short of plunging a spear into Dabulamanzi's guts.

"My duty is done," he said at last. "Let the glory…and responsibility for whatever happens in Natal be on your head."

Chapter IV: The First Alarm

Rorke's Drift
22 January 1879
2.30 p.m.

Colour Sergeant Frank Bourne
Senior Non-Commissioned Officer, B Company, 2/24th

By mid-afternoon, the soldiers at Rorke's Drift were becoming anxious for any news regarding their mates at Isandlwana. The cannon fire had ceased; it was around this time that Major Stewart Smith ordered the guns limbered, that he might redeploy or try to save them from falling into the hands of the Zulus. Rolling volleys of musketry from the six infantry companies of the 24th guarding the camp continued sporadically.

"Something's wrong," Second Corporal Atwood said quietly. He sat atop the railing of the stairs leading into the small attic in the storehouse.

"Oh, I don't know about that," Sergeant Joseph Windridge replied, joining the corporal. "Sounds like the lads are giving the Zulus a damn good thrashing."

Windridge had come to the storehouse to see about acquiring a patch kit for his section's tent, when he saw the Service Corps NCO looking despondent. The two men were in their mid-thirties, making them substantially older than most of the garrison at Rorke's Drift. As such, they had formed a friendship over the past few weeks.

"Perhaps," Atwood conceded. "And if that's the case, then I suppose we'll all be raising a toast of the finest whiskey to Her Majesty and Lord Chelmsford…beg your pardon, sergeant."

Frances felt awkward at the mention of Joseph Windridge's crippling vice. By his own admission, his want for the bottle was worse than William Allan's. A former quartermaster sergeant, and previously colour sergeant of 2nd Battalion's C Company, Windridge was, at one time, considered a potential successor to the battalion's sergeant major. He managed to confine his drunkenness to when he was not on duty, but in recent years it became an unbearable burden to both he and his family. After his latest stint in hospital for overindulging, Windridge requested a voluntary reduction of two ranks to sergeant, so that he might sort himself out. Though greatly disappointed, the sergeant major relented and recommended Lieutenant Colonel Degacher reduce Joseph back to sergeant, allowing him to command a section of riflemen in B Company. Though Windridge had previously served with C Company, both Degacher and the sergeant major thought it might cause a bit of awkwardness to place him back in the company where he previously served as their colour sergeant.

"Nothing to apologise for," he said, consoling Atwood. "I know my vices well, and what it's done to me, my wife, and even my children. Of course, Quartermaster Sergeant Leitch was all-too-happy to accept promotion into my former billet. It may have cost me in terms of pounds and shillings, but returning to the ranks saved my sanity, and possibly my life. Besides, the lads in B Company are a good lot. Even Lance Sergeant Williams, who likely thinks I 'stole' his promotion."

"Riders approaching!"

The call of a sentry distracted them. They were puzzled when they saw no signs of horsemen coming from the road that led northeast to the drift.

"Over there," Atwood said, pointing south.

"Who the bloody hell is that?" Windridge asked, squinting and using his hand to shade is eyes from the sun. His face was suddenly ashen, as he too was filled with the same sense of dread as Francis Atwood.

Lieutenant Bromhead and Commissary Dunne were enjoying a late lunch in the shade of Bromhead's tent, when they were alerted by the same call from the southern sentries.

"That's odd," Dunne remarked.

"What is?"

"Riders coming up from the south," the commissary answered. "Why did they not come via the ponts?"

"No idea," Bromhead remarked dismissively. With his hearing impediment, it was difficult for him to ascertain the origins of most noises. For all he knew, the sentries' reports could have come from the northeast rather than the south. He took a bite of tinned beef and suddenly paused mid-chew. "There's another drift, ten miles to the south. But why in God's name would anyone use it?"

"Especially with the river swollen from the recent rains," Dunne added. "It'd be a bloody nightmare."

"And from what I recall, there's no road," Gunny remarked. "It would take a madman to try and cross there."

"Or one under extreme duress."

The sound of sloshing footsteps came towards them. The commissary peaked around the open tent flap and saw Private William Jones escorting a pair of rather dishevelled soldiers from the Imperial Mounted Infantry. They were completely soaked, hair matted, and both had lost their helmets.

"Beg your pardon, Mister Bromhead, but these men come with an urgent despatch from the column," Jones reported.

"Good heavens, man," Bromhead said, as the two battered soldiers stepped into his tent. "What reason could you have to swim down from the column? Couldn't you have crossed at the ponts?"

"From Captain Gardner, sir," one of the men reported, handing Bromhead a hastily scribbled note. Alan Gardner was a cavalry officer from the 14th Hussars, serving as one of the column staff officers. Bromhead was well acquainted with him, yet it was baffling that a note would come directly from Gardner, rather than Lord Chelmsford, Colonel Glyn, or even Lieutenant Colonel Degacher.

Gunny's eyes grew wide in disbelief as he scanned the despatch before handing it to Dunne. It read:

Camp at Isandlwana taken by the enemy. Colonels Durnford and Pulleine dead, Lord Chelmsford cut off at Mangeni. Suspect Zulu impi will next attack Rorke's Drift. Hold position, if practical.

A. Gardner, Capt.

"We're lucky to be alive, sir," the other soldier added. "Can't say as much for the rest of the camp."

Like Henderson and his troopers, they had gotten away before the Zulu 'horns' sealed off any chance of escape. There was little doubt in their minds that the camp had fallen and everyone within would soon be dead. The two soldiers shuddered as a rifle volley echoed faintly in the distance.

"This cannot be," the commissary said, shaking his head; even though he recognised Captain Gardner's signature. "Pulleine and Durnford's commands gone, just like that?"

The first soldier extended his hand, asking for the message back. "Your pardon, sir, but we need inform Major Spalding and the lads at Helpmekaar. Can't say for certain, but we believe that is where any survivors will be headed."

Bromhead said nothing and handed the note back.

Their duty done, the two soldiers quickly backed out of the tent, anxious to ride away lest the officers order them to remain. They nearly stumbled into Assistant Commissary James Dalton. One of the men nervously blurted out, "The camp at Isandlwana has fallen. You'll want to bugger off as soon as you can."

Dalton showed little surprise at this news or at the unkempt state of the two men. Nothing was said as the IMI soldiers mounted and rode away towards Helpmekaar. James entered Bromhead's tent and was rather put out to see his immediate supervisor, Walter Dunne, as well as B Company's officer commanding sitting in a state of numbing shock. Dunne relayed the message to Dalton who, after a brief pause, clapped his hands together, breaking the men out of their stupor.

"Come on, Mister Bromhead," he said with emphasis. "No sense sitting around here on our arses."

The no-nonsense determination on the face of the old soldier gave Gunny the confidence needed to steel himself to his duty. Now was not the time to dwell on the ramifications of the disaster at Isandlwana. It was time to ready his men for battle.

As the two IMI soldiers rode with all speed towards Helpmekaar, similarly distressing news reached the men guarding the ponts.

"Over there!" Private Fagan called out, pointing to a pair of riders galloping towards the drift.

"They're certainly in a bit of a hurry," Lance Sergeant Williams said, before shouting over his shoulder, *"Mister Chard, sir!"*

This broke the lieutenant out of his daydreaming. He looked towards the NCO, who was pointing at the riders across the river. He set down his pen and paper and quickly walked towards the pont. Sergeant Milne and his civilian assistant were already working the ropes and pullies, sending the flat-bottomed barge lurching across the swollen river.

"Do you recognise either of them?" Chard asked Williams.

"The carbineer, no," the lance sergeant replied. "But I think the other fellow is one of the colonial officers from the NNC, sir."

The officer was Lieutenant Adendorff. His face was flushed and sweaty. From a distance, Chard could not tell if his florid complexion was brought on by exhaustion or from the burning sun on his fair Germanic skin. The two men dismounted and guided their horses onto the pont. Several of Williams' redcoats grabbed hold of the ropes to assist Sergeant Milne. Before the pont had beached itself, Adendorff leapt over the small ramp and splashed the last couple feet onto the bank.

"Please, I must speak to officer at once," he said quickly, in his heavily accented broken English.

"I'm an officer," Chard explained. "You come from the camp?"

"Yes, yes," Adendorff said, nodding his head. "Please...terrible disaster. The camp taken by Zulus."

"Say again?" Chard asked in disbelief.

"The camp...*taken*." The German officer was clearly distraught.

Lance Sergeant Williams and his soldiers were staring at him with much scepticism. From their guard post at the drift, they were oblivious to the continuous sounds of musketry and cannon fire in the distance. Nor had they any knowledge of the fugitives who arrived from another drift to the south. However, in that moment, Fred Hitch's eyes grew wide. He had come down to the river to clean and refresh himself, just as the riders were spotted by his mates. He then quietly recalled the lone rider who had spoken with Thomas Cole before riding away towards Helpmekaar. At the time, he'd thought the fellow was either a deserter or completely mad.

"How the bloody hell could the camp be taken?" Williams asked. "You said so yourself, sir. Lord Chelmsford was chasing down the *impi* only this morning. Between our 1st Battalion and Colonel Durnford's lot guarding the camp, there is no bleeding way the Zulus could have overrun them."

"Durnford dead!" Adendorff said. His expression was one of both fear and frustration; his mind racing as he struggled to make his words clear in English.

"It's true, sir," the carbineer, an Englishman, added, as he led both men's horses off the boat. "We buggered out just before the Zulus surrounded the camp. We joined up with Lieutenant Henderson and what's left of a few troops of native horsemen. He's the one who sent us ahead to warn you." The trooper shook his head in dismay. "Lord Chelmsford was off chasing shadows, while twenty-five thousand black savages came in the back door and swarmed Isandlwana. Durnford, Pulleine, all of 1st Battalion are gone, sir. For all we know, they could have come up behind his lordship and chopped the rest of the column to pieces."

His assertion was a falsehood, though only a mild one. In truth, Pulleine was not yet dead. At that moment, he and the battered companies of 1st Battalion were still holding against the relentless onslaught, albeit the situation was becoming graver by the moment. For both survivors, the result was a foregone conclusion. The camp could not hold for much longer. As commanding officer, honour would compel Pulleine to remain on the field until the very last. If so much as a single private remained fighting, so would he.

Lieutenant Chard and Lance Sergeant Williams struggled with the gravity of the men's message. Meanwhile, a thoroughly drenched Fred Hitch, plus the six riflemen of Williams' detail were now gazing at the river, wondering how well the Zulus could swim. A couple started making hasty range estimations in their minds and checking their rifle sights.

"Sergeant Milne!" Chard called out. "Moor the ponts midstream. If the Zulus are headed this way, I don't want to give them the gift of an easy crossing."

"Sir."

He then called over his shoulder. "*Dobson!* Wake yourself up, lad! Pack the wagon and prepare for immediate departure."

The young soldier rolled out from under the wagon rubbing his eyes. He knew something dire must have occurred, given his master's distressed state. He asked no questions and began to gather any lose tools and equipment, while tearing down his officer's tent. As Chard contemplated what to do next, a runner sprinted down from the path that led back to the mission station.

"Mister Chard, sir," the young private said, coming to attention. "Compliments of Mister Bromhead. He requests you return to the depot at once. There's been a terrible disaster."

"You'd best come with me," Chard said to Adendorff. He then addressed the carbineer. "Ride like hell until you reach Helpmekaar. Let them know what's happened."

"Yes, sir." The trooper's expression was one of profound relief as he mounted his horse and rode at the gallop, following the road which wound its way towards the rolling hills to the west. His horse was nearing total exhaustion, yet once he was out of sight from the doomed mission station, he would feel safe.

"Look sharp, sergeant," Chard said to Williams. "Give us fair warning if you see anything."

"If we do, sir, you'll know it." The lance sergeant patted the stock of his rifle.

The two officers quickly mounted their horses and rode the short distance back to the depot.

As his horse galloped into the main camp, Chard's mind was racing as he struggled to compose his thoughts. He was unnerved at the realisation that being in command was now a substantive, and in many ways terrifying, reality. While a highly skilled engineer and mathematician with a knack for designing fortifications, he had little actual leadership experience and had never fought a single action during his decade-long military career. By a perverse twist of fate, he was now officer commanding of the only British soldiers along the Natal border. His paltry force would soon face the same horrific onslaught which destroyed the garrison at Isandlwana. It still didn't seem real to him that Durnford and Pulleine were both slain and their commands wiped out.

'If a thousand men could not stand, what chance have I with a hundred?' he thought to himself. He shook his head, dismissing such unbecoming and ultimately useless thoughts from his mind.

He dismounted near Lieutenant Bromhead's tent, and the men were soon joined by Colour Sergeant Bourne. At Bromhead's recommendation, the highly experienced retired soldier, Commissary Dalton, was also present.

"There's been a terrible disaster, Mister Chard," Bromhead began. Chard raised a hand and nodded to Adendorff.

"So I heard." He took a deep breath, assessing the situation, fighting to control his feelings of extreme apprehension. "We must evacuate at once. We'll load the sick and wounded onto the wagons. It'll be a tight fit, but they'll have to manage. Unfortunately, it will mean abandoning our ammunition and stores to the Zulus. Have the men throw as many cartridge packets as they can carry into their packs. Helpmekaar is fifteen miles from here, but if we leave now, we should make it. And God willing, we will find Major Spalding with those two companies from your 1st Battalion."

While Bromhead and Dunne sombrely concurred, Bourne remained impassive. It was Commissary Dalton, however, who disagreed.

"We can't outrun them," he said plainly. "The Zulus know about the road to Helpmekaar. If they find this place abandoned, you can bet your last shilling they will pursue us. Even if you had an hour head start, without your wagons full of wounded, they would run you down. Our men can march fifteen to twenty miles in a day. The Zulus can *run* the same distance and fight a battle at the end of it."

"What do you propose we do then?" Chard asked. "Rorke's Drift is not exactly a fortress."

"You're an engineer, sir," he replied, nodding towards the storehouse. "Make it into one."

"Mealie bags and biscuit boxes…" Chard's eyes lit up.

"The storehouse is overflowing," Dalton continued. "And those sacks are extremely heavy; nearly two hundred pounds each. There's more than enough to build a wall around this entire station. You said the camp at Isandlwana was not fortified in any way. If we can build even a shoulder-high barricade around us, it just might be enough to keep the Zulus from closing in and using their numbers against us."

"The ground to the north is about a six-foot drop," Colour Sergeant Bourne noted. "It is steep and rocky, and makes for a natural barrier. If we pile the mealie sacks on top of it, no one will get in that way."

"See to it," Bromhead ordered. "And organise a detail to defend the hospital. We don't have time to move the patients, and I'd rather we not let the Zulus have the building as a stronghold."

"Sir!" Bourne rushed away, shouting for his section leaders in his ever booming voice that contrasted sharply with his youthful face.

"Alright," Chard said, his confidence growing. The idea of running now sounded as absurd as it did improper. He took a stick and drew into the dirt, sketching a rough outline of each of the station's buildings. His skills as an engineer would come in useful after all!

"We'll anchor the wall off the stone kraal to the east, following the rocky slope to the front of the hospital as Colour Sergeant Bourne suggested. The south wall will simply link the commissariat store to the hospital. We don't have any sort of terrain advantage here, so we'll utilise the wagons."

"Should we tip them over?" Bromhead asked.

"I wouldn't," Dalton replied. "Stack biscuit boxes underneath, that way the Zulus cannot crawl under them. Build a mealie bag wall on top, and you'll have an excellent firing platform. The approach is much narrower than to the north. I would say one section of twenty riflemen could make a good showing."

"Let's get this done before those darkies show up," Bromhead said, standing and donning his helmet. He gave a grim smile of acknowledgement to Dalton.

Though the assistant commissary was a civilian volunteer, Bromhead was aware of his experience in warfare, which continued even after his retirement from the ranks. Less than two years earlier, Dalton had taken part in a minor siege during the Xhosa War, where his small garrison at Ibeka was threatened. His quiet, yet very resourceful command presence inspired both calm and confidence in Bromhead. He suspected it was a trait which Dalton had used many times during his years in the Army to sort out skittish and inexperienced officers.

As he made his way to the storehouse, Bromhead called out, *"Private Hitch!"*

"Sir!" the young soldier replied. His boots squished and he was soaked from head to foot as he came to attention. In any other circumstances, Bromhead would have found his appearance comical. He knew Fred Hitch was one of Sergeant Gallagher's sharp-shooters, renowned for his keen eyesight and terrifying accuracy with the Martini-Henry. "Get your arse up on the roof, and let us know when you see those bastards coming!"

"Yes, sir."

"Here, Fred, you'll want these," Sergeant Gallagher said, handing the private his personal field glasses.

Bromhead sought out Stevenson, the NNC captain in command of the excess warriors left behind. With time not on their side, and given the sheer weight of all the mealie bags, they needed back-breaking labour more than anything.

"I heard rumours from a fleeing carbineer," Stevenson said, as he briskly walked over to Bromhead. "Please tell me they aren't true."

"I wish I could say that, old boy," Gunny replied, his expression grim. "Right now, I need every one of your men to form a labour gang and build us a wall, if you'd be so kind."

"Yes, of course." The NNC officer was in a state of disbelief, trying to wrap his mind around what had transpired at Isandlwana.

He shouted a few orders to some of his auxiliaries in their native tongue, while relaying to his three European corporals.

Bromhead had little regard for this group of levies, nor did he trust Stevenson and his NCOs. But for the moment, it seemed they were willing to do their part in building the defences. At Dalton's recommendation, the perimeter would encompass both buildings. Between the redcoats of B Company and Stevenson's NNC warriors, they had several hundred fighting men ready to face the Zulus.

"Keep your riflemen on the perimeter, with the NNC in reserve ready to plug any gaps in the defences," the assistant commissary stated. "We'll make the Zulus pay a heavy toll in blood if they wish to overrun us."

It was a monstrous undertaking. Yet when faced with certain annihilation, each man's strength and determination magnified considerably. While Sergeant Smith and Corporal Allan oversaw the building of the north wall, Sergeant Gallagher and his men began muscling the company's pair of wagons towards what would become the south rampart. Lieutenant Chard ordered Corporals Lyons and Saxty to strike B Company's tents, so they could not to be used as concealment by the Zulus.

What could not be helped was the cover offered by Shiyane Mountain, which loomed over the station like a great beast. Most likely, the Zulus would place marksmen along its slopes as well as the rocky shelf that jutted out, overlooking the station from about 300 yards away.

"We'll have to supress any bastards who get up there," Lyons noted, as he and his fellow corporal oversaw the small detail pulling down the company tents.

"From that distance, I doubt the Zulus could hit a damned thing," Saxty reasoned. "Their muskets are shit from what I hear."

"They'll hit something if they manage to place a thousand shit muskets along that ledge," Lyons countered.

Saxty nodded at the slowly growing ramparts. "I'd be more worried about the bastards simply walking in and gutting us," he reasoned.

The stone shelf that sloped down just north of the buildings was an ideal place to begin building the mealie wall. The ground further north was full of bushes and tall grass, which had grown thick from the recent summer rains. There was also concern over the unfinished wall north of the hospital. Beyond the wall and brush thickets was the wagon track which led to the river crossing. Further on was a fenced orchard of fruit trees. The six-foot cliff face, topped by four feet of mealie sacks, made for a formidable obstacle. However, the Zulus would have plenty of cover and concealment, negating the effective range of the Martini-Henry should they attack from the north.

The southern approach was far more open and exposed; the small cookhouse, a lone brick oven, and a short ditch bank were all that could be utilised as cover. These were all very close to where the wagons and defensive barricades were being erected; meaning the enemy would face withering fire from at least 600 yards.

"Too much damned cover for the enemy to the north and not enough time to clear away the brush," Chard grumbled.

He, Dalton, and Bromhead briskly walked the perimeter.

"Yes, but they will have to scale ten feet of steep rock and mealie bags," Dalton noted. He looked to the south. "There is no natural high ground for us to the south; however, the terrain is open and the Zulus will be far more exposed. The corridor between buildings is much narrower; they cannot maximise their numbers effectively."

"You seem very confident, Mr Dalton," Chard noted.

The commissary's expression remained passive. "No, sir, I am absolutely terrified."

"Just don't let them hear you say that," Chard remarked, nodding at the young redcoats who feverishly carried large mealie sacks from the storehouse to the defences.

The men of B Company knew of Dalton's fierce reputation as a soldier. Given he was the same age as many of their fathers, he had taken on a type of paternal role to the younger enlisted men.

"Not to worry, Mister Chard," the commissary answered, his tone and expression unchanged. "As long as I don't shit myself, I can be absolutely petrified and the lads won't be any wiser."

"A talent shared by all senior non-comms, I'm certain," Bromhead remarked.

The corner of Dalton's mouth turned upward in a half smile for a split-second. "Your colour sergeant may be called 'The Kid', but he's already mastered the art. Keep him close, Mister Bromhead. Before this is over, you will need him as much as the men in the ranks do."

Chapter V: Prepare for Battle

Near Sothondose's Drift
22 January 1879
3.00 p.m.

Contemporary depiction of Zulus crossing the uMzinyathi River

Crossing the formidable river was far more terrifying to a Zulu warrior than any spear, rifle, or bayonet. An enemy combatant could be dealt with; the river was like the hand of the divines. Yet, where the strength of the Zulus lay was in their collective courageousness and resolve.

Mandlenkosi watched as the iNdluyengwe were the first to brave the deceptive currents of the uMzinyathi. Linking arms at the elbow, their *izinduna* started a war chant, prompting the warriors to march in step as they plunged into the river. It was not particularly deep, reaching chest high on most of the warriors, yet their feet slipped on the smooth rocks beneath the surface. The pull of the current was threatening to drag the entire mass of men downriver. Still they persisted, step by step, their chants growing louder as they found strength in their unity. Should they master the river, surely they would be rewarded with much in the way of plunder and spoils.

Many tried to take their minds off their ordeal, closing their eyes and drawing power from their chanting. It was a short distance of less than twenty yards, but it felt like many miles to the surging mass of fighting men.

"We have conquered the river spirits!" warriors shouted, as they leapt onto the far bank. "Now to wash our spears at kwaJimu!"

Seeing the younger warriors filled the older regiments with determination. Dabulamanzi only had marginal control over the Undi Corps, and it was feared that the iNdluyengwe would sack Rorke's Drift without waiting for the rest of the *amabutho*.

"With me, my warriors!" Mandlenkosi bellowed, raising his spear. He stalwartly took several steps forward, right up to the edge of the large flat rock which dropped sharply into the river. The rest of the uThulwana soon followed. They would not allow the king's own *ibutho* to be bested by a younger regiment.

Besides the personal danger of being swept away and drowned, one of the greatest challenges was keeping shields and weapons out of the water, particularly firearms. Nearly one in every four warriors of the Undi Corps possessed a musket. Though mostly archaic flintlocks, pitted with rust and half-devoured by termites, they were a symbol of pride and status. And if they were to be of any use against the white soldiers, they knew they had to keep the flints and powder dry. Most carried their weapons over their shoulders, which made it more difficult to link arms with their companions. The pouches containing their powder and bullets were either slung over the neck or clutched between teeth.

Mandlenkosi did not own a firearm, though he had heard stories about the fearsome weapons wielded by the redcoats that required neither powder bag nor ramrod. Their effective range was several times that of any Zulu musket, and the old warrior hoped to claim one of these magnificent weapons for himself.

A short way downriver, Dabulamanzi and some of the mounted *izinduna* swam their horses to the other side. While seemingly an easier task than trying to wade across, it was rather harrowing for the prince. There was no one for him to cling to should he be swept from his mount. He was also concerned about his rifle; a percussion musket that did not require a flint, like those used during the American Civil War fifteen years earlier. However, the water proved shallower than at Sothondose's Drift, and the prince and the mounted *izinduna* had an easier time of it. Only once did his horse slip on the rocks, bucking and nearly throwing him off.

Once on the Natal bank, Dabulamanzi gave a broad, toothy grin of triumph and determination. Despite the awkward and hazardous nature of crossing the uMzinyathi, his regiments were making their way over with surprising speed. He galloped his horse up the steep embankment to where companies from the iNdluyengwe waited. He was surprised to see a large number of their men were missing.

"Where is Prince Zibhebhu?" he asked, looking around in confusion.

"He has gone, *inkosi*," a warrior answered. "Many of our warriors have sought easy plunder within the local homesteads."

"So be it." Dabulamanzi was relieved that he would not have to concern himself with potential interference from his rival kinsman.

While Zibhebhu sought to loot the homes of some defenceless farmers, the king's brother would destroy the last bastion of Queen Victoria's redcoats on the border of Zululand.

As *izinduna* took control of their companies, each regiment formed into long lines and sat to catch their breath, as well as take snuff. The snuff consumed by the Zulus was referred to as cannabis, yet its effects were far different than the usual calming high. The secret blend concocted by diviners caused the heart to race, skin to become flushed, and a man's senses to turn to rage. So powerful were the effects, only small numbers of warriors dared take it prior to going into battle.

"Over there, *inkosi*," Mandlenkosi said, pointing west with his spear.

All turned to see a column of smoke rising in the distance, the flicker of fire just visible.

"Zibhebhu has claimed his first quarry," Dabulamanzi muttered. He then addressed the growing number of warriors assembling on the plain just above the river. "Sons of Zulu! We come to drive the scourge of the betrayers from the lands of our ancestors forever! We make for kwaJimu; a place once home to friends of the king. Now, it is a place of desecration from where the White Queen makes war upon our people! Come, my friends, let us fight at kwaJimu!"

With the Zulus crossing just a few miles away, it became a race against time for the defenders of Rorke's Drift. One of the most critical tasks was selecting men to defend the hospital. There was no interior hallway and, in many cases, one had to step outside to go into an adjoining room. The rooms themselves were very cramped, especially with the thirty or so patients sprawled out on their crude pallet beds. In some rooms, there was only enough space for a single defender to be posted.

While Lieutenants Chard and Bromhead, along with Commissary Dalton, established the main perimeter, Colour Sergeant Bourne set about finding men to defend the hospital.

"We need soldiers with iron nerves and unbreakable courage if we're to hold this position," he explained to his section leaders.

Since he had no NCOs to spare, a certain level of experience and maturity was also needed. In most cases, the defenders would either be working in pairs or alone.

"I'll give you Harry Hook," Sergeant Gallagher volunteered. "He's pragmatic and can adapt to any situation. He also does not need an officer or NCO to constantly watch over his shoulder."

"And he's already assisting at the hospital," Bourne noted. He then said to Sergeant Smith, "I need William Jones from you."

"I'll give you both Joneses," Smith offered.

William Jones was thirty-nine years of age and one of the most experienced soldiers in B Company. Though he never admitted it publicly, Bourne often mimicked Jones' ever-calm demeanour. During the Xhosa War, he had once watched a flung assegai tear a gash in the thigh of his trousers. The old private neither flinched nor acknowledged just how close he came to dying. Except to say, as he shouldered his weapon to fire, "Bit rude of them to tear me trousers like that."

His mate, Robert Jones, was young enough to be William's son, and the two had become inseparable over the last three years. Most often, they referred to each other by their service number rather than their given names. The colour sergeant rightly reckoned they would fight well together.

Two other men with the same last name, yet unrelated, John and Joseph Williams, were also selected. John Williams was a mate of Hook's, and the two had served together during the Xhosa War.

Needing at least one more, Sergeant Gallagher recommended the young private, Thomas Cole, who first received word of the disaster at Isandlwana from a survivor of the ill-fated rocket battery.

"Half a dozen able-bodied men and whatever sick and wounded that can carry a rifle," Windridge added. "Not much of a defence, is it, colour sergeant?"

"It will have to do," Bourne replied curtly. He ordered the section leaders to send the men to him.

"I don't need to tell any of you how crucial this position is." Bourne briefed the soldiers as soon as they assembled. "I've ordered the storehouse to find a couple of pickaxes for you to chop loopholes in the walls. It will be safer than using the windows and leaving yourselves exposed to Zulu gunfire. And if need be, knock holes in the interior walls, so you can coordinate with each other and shift positions as necessary. Take an extra box of ammunition and enough rifles for our walking wounded."

He paused for a moment, noting the steely-eyed determination in the faces of his men. The colour sergeant knew he had chosen well. "The Zulus will be thick; remember your fire discipline. We may not be able to get aid or ammunition resupply to you, so pick your targets and make every round count."

"They won't get through us, colour sergeant," Joseph Williams said reassuringly.

"Colour sergeant!" an accented voice called out.

He turned to see Ferdinand Schiess from the NNC. The Swiss corporal had been convalescing with a badly injured foot since the attack on Sihayo's kraal ten days before. He limped over, using a makeshift crutch to keep the weight off his bandaged foot.

"Corporal," Bourne acknowledged. "You can take up position in the hospital with the other walking wounded."

"Beg your pardon, but it's claustrophobic as fuck in there," Schiess replied bluntly. "With your permission, I'd rather take my chances on the firing line."

"Can you even stand and fire your weapon?" Bourne asked.

"Place me there," Schiess said, pointing to a section of the growing wall, just off the northeast corner or the hospital. "If my foot doesn't hold, then I'll have a seat on the veranda and shoot the bastards from there."

"I like your style, corporal," the colour sergeant said appreciatively. The two men shared a knowing grin. "If you can hobble your arse over to the storehouse to pick up a weapon and ammunition, you can fight anywhere you like." He then turned to the hospital defenders. "Alright lads, get to it, at the double!"

Schiess limped his way over to the storehouse and the hospital detachment went about establishing their firing positions. Colour Sergeant Frank Bourne then took a moment to compose his thoughts.

Since his unexpected promotion the year prior, he had battled internally with the overwhelming nature of his responsibilities. Foremost was the matter of his age. The rank of colour sergeant was one of the highest an enlisted soldier could attain. Answerable only to the company commander, he was responsible for the training, good order, and discipline of nearly a hundred soldiers. This required a magnitude of experience, strong command presence, and a stern disciplinarian. It was he the sergeants came to for guidance and mentoring. And the officer commanding relied on him greatly for advice, particularly regarding the doling out of rewards and punishment. As such, most colour sergeants were long-service veterans, usually in their mid-thirties. Many were also big men, whose size and booming voices inspired confidence or terror, as needed. Frank Bourne was not a big man. Standing just 5'6", he was, by his own account, 'painfully thin'. Because of the experience the job required, colour sergeants were often of similar age or older than their officers commanding. In the case of B Company, 2/24th, however, Colour Sergeant Bourne was nearly a decade younger than Lieutenant Bromhead.

Months of chasing down and fighting the Xhosa in the bush the previous year had forced Frank to learn his duties and accept the responsibilities very quickly. It was one thing for the men to respect his rank; it was another to *earn* that respect. The grave injuring of Captain Godwin-Austen, Lieutenant Bromhead's unexpected elevation to officer commanding, and the loss of Lieutenant Godwin-Austen to G Company placed far more responsibility on Colour Sergeant Bourne than ever before. By the time of the war with the Zulus, he was as hardened and experienced as any colour sergeant twice his age. His moniker of 'The Kid' was one he now accepted with pride, rather than self-conscious resentment.

As he forced the cacophony of memories from the past year out of his mind, Bourne noticed Thomas Cole standing near the corner of the hospital. His head was bowed and his hand resting on the corner.

"Private Cole," he said. "Why are you not inside prepping your firing position with your mates?"

"Sorry, colour sergeant. I just needed a moment is all." What Cole could not bring himself to say was that he was terrified of confined spaces.

"To think we were all brassed up about being left behind," the private remarked. "Who would have thought we'd be the ones facing certain death?" He looked at his colour sergeant and slowly shook his head. "Why is it us, eh? Why us?"

"Because we're here, lad," Bourne replied with equal measures of calm and firmness. "And nobody else…just us. Now go on, you've had your moment."

Cole gave a grim smile, took a deep breath, and stepped around the building, into a doorway along the southern face of the building. This led into the Witts' bedroom and another that might have been a living room. While the feverish Sergeant Maxfield slumbered fitfully, the Joneses and a couple of patients were establishing their fighting positions.

"Tommy, you're on the far end with Hookie," William Jones said, nodding towards a door. He noticed Cole sweating. "Are you alright, mate?"

"Fine," the young private lied, nodding quickly. "Just a bit cramped in there is all."

"Well, someone's got to protect the southwest approach," Jones reasoned. "Joe and John Williams have the room next to you and Hookie. Me and 716 are taking these two rooms. Waters and Beckett are covering the veranda. So, get cosy and make some new friends."

Cole gritted his teeth and stepped back outside. He followed the southern face of the hospital until he found the corner room where his friend was cutting a loophole into the wall. A lone warrior with an injured leg from the NNC lay on a pallet in the far corner.

"Oi, Tommy," Hook said with a good natured smile. "I thought I was going to have to hold the corner by myself."

Along with the hospital, defensive preparations were made at the storehouse. This was viewed as less vulnerable, partly because there were no doors along the southern face that the enemy could breach. It also had an attic, which offered excellent firing positions for the handful of soldiers posted there. Among these was Second Corporal Atwood who, in addition to his basic allotment, threw an extra ten cartridge packets into his haversack, which he hoisted over his shoulder before making his way up the outside steps into the attic.

"Whatever you do, corporal, do *not* let them set fire to the roof!" Lieutenant Bromhead stressed.

"Well I don't much like the idea of burning to death, sir, so I'll do my best not to let the bastards smoke me out," Atwood replied, as he forced open the stuck door to the attic.

Had there been more time, Gunny Bromhead would have ordered the thatch pulled down from the roofs. However, time was something they simply did not have. He wasn't even sure if they'd have the ramparts completed before the enemy arrived. And even then, how long would they really hold against thousands of Zulus, fresh off destroying an entire battalion at Isandlwana?

Satisfied the defensive preparations were progressing well, Lieutenant Chard mounted his horse and rode back to the drift. Though so much had happened, it had in fact been less than thirty minutes since he first met with Lieutenant Adendorff and the English carbineer. Driver Robson had finished loading their tents and baggage into the wagon and limbered up the mules. As the ranking NCO present, Sergeant Milne had taken control of the small detachment of redcoats. He, Lance Sergeant Williams, and their six riflemen were dispersed along the riverbank, having hefted fallen logs and brush to conceal themselves. Even Mr Daniels, the civilian volunteer, lurked behind a log, his Swinburne-Henry carbine by his side.

"Mister Chard, sir," Milne said, standing and coming to attention. "We're set here. The ponts aren't going anywhere. Any

Zulus who get within a hundred yards of the far bank will get their guts shot out, courtesy of Misters Martini and Henry."

Chard gave a nod of appreciation to the soldiers for their ingenuity and determination, but he knew any attempts to hold the drift were futile. The Zulu muskets might be archaic and extremely inaccurate, yet if enough of them massed on the far bank, no nine men hiding behind rotting logs and scrub brush could stand for long. Besides, there was no guarantee that the Zulus would even cross at the drift. He said as much to Sergeant Milne, before ordering him and his men to return to the mission station.

"Right away, sir," the NCO acknowledged. He then called over his shoulder, "Come on, lads!"

Rather than disappointed, Frederick Milne was relieved at not having to defend the river crossing against ten thousand Zulus with less than a section of riflemen. When Chard first left that morning to meet with Lieutenant Bromhead, both Milne and Lance Sergeant Williams assumed that, in the absence of orders, their mission was to hold the ponts. Both knew that any such attempt was nothing short of madness. So it was with a sigh of relief that they withdrew from the river.

"At least now we can die fighting beside our mates," one private said, with a macabre sense of relief.

As he watched Sergeant Milne and the small detachment from B Company race up the embankment for the short trek back to the mission station, John Chard let out a sigh. It was with bitter irony that he recalled one of his chief missions from Lord Chelmsford; the establishment of a stone fort overlooking the ponts, which was to be manned by Captain Rainforth's G Company, 1/24th. Chard had intended to start on the morrow, after his sappers returned from Isandlwana. By the time Captain Walter Jones and the rest of No. 5 Field Company arrived, he hoped to have the ground cleared and scraped with the foundations for the outer wall established.

Since his assignment to Jones' company, John had been little more than an excess subaltern with little to no responsibilities. The arrangement had suited him well. Having a corporal, his batman, and a handful of sappers under his charge to fix some ponts and lay the groundwork for a company-sized fort was the perfect assignment. Over the past few hours, everything had changed. The Zulus had destroyed the camp at Isandlwana, and Corporal Gamble and the sappers were likely dead. Captain Rainforth was still somewhere between Rorke's Drift and Helpmekaar, with Major Spalding chasing them down, completely oblivious to the current crisis. Lieutenant John Chard, whose brother officers referred to as, 'a most unremarkable fellow', was now solely responsible for over a hundred soldiers and the defence of the last British bastion along the uMzinyathi. And rather than a proper stone fortress, his garrison had a few feet of mealie bags and biscuit boxes standing between them and certain annihilation.

The barricades were being erected when Surgeon Reynolds, Reverend Witt, and Padre Smith returned from their trek to the top of Shiyane. They had witnessed a few of the survivors crossing the uMzinyathi, including the two IMI soldiers who first warned Lieutenant Bromhead of the disaster. All the while, small numbers of bedraggled survivors galloped past the station. A few stopped to encourage the garrison to flee. One even said to Colour Sergeant Bourne, "Not a fighting chance for you, young feller."

With each rider who came through the station, soldiers ceased in their labours, wanting to ask questions. The most common being, 'Is it true?'

Colour Sergeant Bourne was angered to hear one of the riders reply, 'You'll all be murdered.' It further irked him that, with each passing fugitive, the barricades ceased being built momentarily.

"Alright!" he finally shouted. "Nobody told you to stop working!"

This was all the motivation the men needed.

Reverend Witt rushed over to his house, filled with dread at seeing his home being turned into a mini fortress. A trooper from the Natal Mounted Police named Harry Lugg sat on the veranda. Having fallen from his horse and injuring his knee the previous week, he had been convalescing at the hospital.

"Afternoon, reverend," the trooper said with a nod. "Fine day for a battle, isn't it?"

Witt was speechless and downright appalled when he walked into the small parlour of his house to see the wallpaper being ripped down, and soldiers chopping holes in the walls from which to fire their weapons. Pieces of furniture were scattered about haphazardly.

"In God's holy name, what are you doing?" Witt asked in exasperation.

Two of the soldiers in the parlour looked back at him quizzically.

A private named John Waters answered, "Our apologies, reverend. But, either we cause a bit of a mess or we leave this place to the Zulus." He smiled reassuringly. "Don't worry. I promise to personally help you mend any furniture that might get tossed around, once this is over. Tommy Cole was a paper-hanger back home. I'm certain he can help you pretty up the walls. Harry Hook is in the back. I'm sure he won't let the lads make too much of a mess."

Witt knew Hook from his time helping with the patients. As Hook was also a lay preacher, the two sometimes read from the Bible together. Witt nodded in acknowledgment and walked into his bedroom. Sergeant Robert Maxfield, the most gravely ill of those suffering from typhoid, lay on the reverend's bed, soaked in sweat, his breathing laboured as he slept fitfully. Witt had come to fetch the old Enfield muzzle-loader he sometimes used for hunting. As he grabbed the rifle from a corner near his wardrobe, he paused at Maxfield's side.

"Not much we can do for him, I'm afraid," Private Robert Jones said. He and his mate, William Jones, sat near the open window where Robert had his weapon resting against the ledge.

"Go with God, son," Witt whispered to Maxfield. He laid a hand on the stricken man's shoulder.

"Will you say a prayer for the rest of us, reverend?" William Jones asked. He was sitting on a wooden chest, his back resting against the wall. He'd gouged a loophole in the outer wall.

"Of course," Witt replied. "I will pray for all of your souls this day."

"Much obliged. If I do end up meeting the Lord of Hosts this day, I will be most grateful that you put in a good word for me." He sounded as if he made the statement in jest, but the soldier's expression was one of utter seriousness. William Jones had spent more than half his life wearing the uniform of Her Majesty's redcoats, and he lacked the delusions of invulnerability that were common among the younger soldiers. He was among the first to accept the brutal reality that the garrison at Isandlwana had been destroyed and, probably, he too would soon meet his end on the blade of a Zulu spear.

Privates (716) Robert Jones and (593) William Jones

His mind still reeling, Reverend Witt stepped back onto the veranda of his home. An even greater sense of dread crept up his spine. He sought out his visiting friend, August Hammar, who had been sharing his tent. His fellow countryman was equally unnerved by the news, as well as by the sight of British soldiers and African auxiliaries feverishly attempting to build a wall on the north side of the station. The Swedish man had found his own rifle and was debating whether to join in the defence or ride for safety.

"Intent on defending your home, old friend," August said, noting Witt's firearm.

The reverend shook his head. "I was." His next words betrayed the slow fraying of his nerves. "Elin… August, she doesn't know. What if the Zulus attack Msinga? Dear God, *my family!*"

From his observation point atop Shiyane, the reverend had seen the hosts of Zulus headed towards the river. They numbered in the thousands. If they crossed, there was little the tiny garrison at Rorke's Drift could do to stop them. He was suddenly filled with regret for dragging Elin and their children to this far-flung corner of the world. Otto had fully supported the British invasion, hoping Lord Chelmsford would punish Cetshwayo, who had expelled Witt and his fellow missionaries from the Zulu Kingdom. Would his family now pay the price for his callous desire for war against those he tried, and failed, to convert to Christianity?

"Mister Bromhead!" Witt called out, having found 'Gunny' inspecting Sergeant Gallagher's fighting positions along the south wall.

"Reverend Witt," the officer said. He noted the Swede's pale expression. "Are you alright, man?"

Otto shook his head. "My most profuse apologies, but I cannot stay here. I know I swore to fight beside you to defend my home, but my wife and children are at Msinga."

"Of course," Bromhead concurred. "Buildings can be rebuilt. There is no replacing one's family. Get them to safety, Mister Witt."

"Thank you." The reverend slung his rifle and rushed back to where August Hammar was saddling their horses.

As he took a moment to watch the two men make ready for their hasty departure, Bromhead recalled a rather morbid conversation he'd had about six months before with Lieutenant Teignmouth Melvill, the adjutant of 1st Battalion. Gunny told his friend, who was married and the father of two young sons, not to be so anxious to die for Queen and Country. Melvill had joking said the next time they got into a scrap, he'd point out Bromhead to the enemy and say, *'Shoot him, he's unmarried!'*

Gunny chuckled softly, the memory etched in sadness. He had to assume that Melvill was most likely dead. His heart went out to his friend's widow, Sarah, and their children, as well as Otto Witt, whose family faced a very real danger. As he quietly accepted the likelihood that he would meet his own end that day, Gonville Bromhead was glad he had neither wife nor children to mourn him.

Walking over to the storehouse, he was mildly surprised to see the other resident pastor, Reverend George Smith, assisting Commissary Dunne with the opening of ammunition boxes.

"Still with us, padre?" Gunny asked. "You know you have no obligation to remain. This day's work will be violent and dirty."

"I would be telling a falsehood if I said I did not consider departing with the good Reverend Witt," Smith replied. "But, it would seem my native groomsman has run off with my horse. And it would not be proper to ask you or Mister Chard for yours. Besides, where else should a man of God be, if not where his children need him most?"

His tone was surprisingly calm. But then, Reverend Smith was no stranger to the dangers of campaign. He understood the seriousness of their predicament. Bromhead asked him about this, and he shrugged.

"It was not my intent to meet the Lord this day. But, should the Zulus send me to him, the least I can do is maintain my poise and dignity. And don't worry; I may not be a fighting man, but I intend to make myself useful this day."

He held up a pair of cartridge packets before adding them to a stack he had set aside. Bromhead gave an affirmative nod and then called over his sergeants and corporals. The hour was growing late, and he knew the Zulus could arrive at any moment.

"The casualty collection point will be the storehouse veranda," 'Gunny' said, pointing to the large porch. "Section leaders will control your own volleys. Sergeant Smith, you will take the north wall from the cattle kraal to where the ramparts intersect the main road. Sergeant Windridge, your sector will be the remainder of the north wall to the hospital. Sergeant Gallagher, you are in command of the south rampart. Corporal Allan will take the eastern ramparts down to the storehouse."

"Very good, sir," the burley corporal replied.

"Designated marksmen are authorised to engage at 800 yards," Bromhead continued. "The main firing line will open up at 500. I know we didn't have time to establish range markers, so you'll have to make your own estimations and let your men know when to adjust their sights. We need to make every round count, and I don't want us wasting bullets shooting over their damned heads!"

"There is a lot of obscuration to the north, sir," Sergeant Windridge observed. "A pity we don't have time to clear the brush and knock down that bloody wall."

"Ah, Mister Bromhead." John Chard joined the men, having just finished checking the defences near the storehouse. "There's a rather large stockpile of rum and spirits in the storehouse that needs guarding." He looked to Joseph Windridge, who happened to be standing closest to him. "Sergeant, you can do the honours. If any man, British or Zulu, attempts to pilfer so much as a nip, you are authorised to shoot him."

Windridge looked to Bromhead, attempting to mask his feelings of horror. His officer commanding subtly shook his head, reassuring him that he would speak to Lieutenant Chard in private. It seemed utterly cruel that Windridge would be placed in such a position. He was the worst possible choice to guard the depot's supply of rum. This had not been done with malice. Chard simply did not know the men of B Company and he had no knowledge of Windridge's struggle with alcoholism.

As soon as the section leaders were dismissed, Bromhead pulled Chard off to the side. He did not wish to cause his sergeant any embarrassment, so he stressed that Windridge was indispensable as a section leader. He recommended another be given the task, such as Lance Sergeant Williams. Chard emphasised that he did not care who did it, just as long as it was a reliable NCO who would not allow the men to sneak a drink during the battle. With much relief, Sergeant Windridge was directed to return to his section.

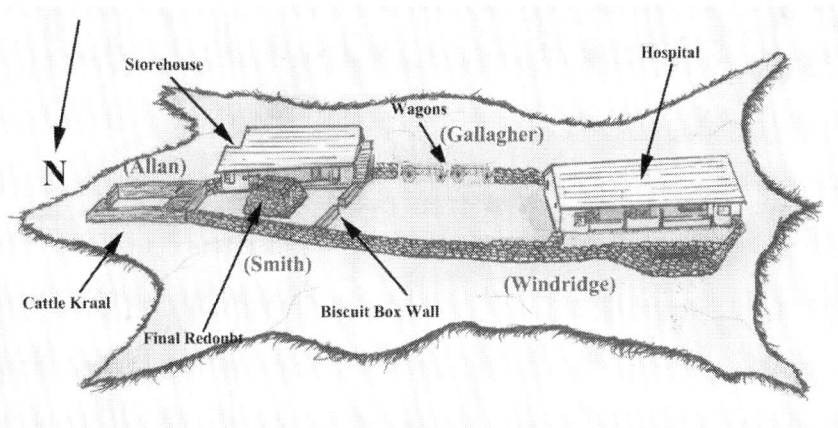

Layout of Rorke's Drift
4.00 p.m.

Chapter VI: Nothing Remains but to Fight

Rorke's Drift
22 January 1879
4.00 p.m.

Acting Assistant Commissary James Langley Dalton
Army Commissariat Department

Progress continued on the barricades, due in no small part to the several hundred NNC warriors from Stevenson's contingent. Their numbers alone provided several times the raw muscle needed for hauling the extremely heavy mealie bags across the compound. Because they were declared 'excess' by Lord Chelmsford prior to the invasion, there had been no requisition of firearms made for them. As such, all they had were their shields, spears, and knobkerrie clubs. Due to this, and the known skittishness of the Natal natives when facing Zulus, Dalton recommended Chard place them in reserve, behind the firing line. This was sound tactical advice. Should the Zulus breach the perimeter, there would be plenty of shields and spears to plug the gap.

"And with nowhere to run, they'll have no choice but to fight," Bromhead observed.

They watched the perimeter slowly form, with each mealie bag being carried by four men and laid along the north wall. In contrast to the work ethics of their men, Stevenson and his three European corporals simply sat on biscuit boxes and watched the local Africans and British redcoats do all the labour.

"Aren't they going to help?" one sweaty private asked with great irritation.

"Lazy shits will probably run off as soon the Zulus turn up," another added.

"They're not your concern," Corporal Allan said, chastising the men. Contrary to his colonial counterparts, he was setting the example for his soldiers. He toiled under the strain of carrying a heavy mealie sack with Sergeant Windridge and two other soldiers. Windridge was a powerfully built man, who Allan said could probably carry a pair of sacks by himself.

The south rampart was already finished. It was barely a third the length of the north wall, with the two wagons placed near the centre. With biscuit boxes stacked beneath, a single line of mealie sacks was laid across the wagon beds, providing firing positions for the soldiers behind them.

While the last few yards of the north wall were being built, soldiers took up their rifles and their section leaders directed them to their individual places along the defences. The line of redcoats was painfully thin, with approximately six feet between each soldier along the north wall. The southern ramparts, where Sergeant Gallagher's section stood ready, was much narrower. However, with only twenty rifles and the smattering from the hospital and storehouse, there was little confidence in how long they could stand. And there was still a noticeable gap along the northwest rampart, nearest the hospital veranda. Here the wall was only a couple feet high, with a large board stood upright, as if to plug the gap. There were no riflemen posted there, leaving a blind spot in the defences. Only a few of the patients and defenders of the hospital could see anything coming from the northwest.

Trooper Harry Lugg let out a sigh and leaned against the mealie wall. He was one of a few carbineers and local volunteers fighting beside their brother redcoats. "Nothing remains but to fight," he muttered.

It was now 4.00, and an eerie silence fell upon the makeshift stronghold. The only sound came from the grunting soldiers and warriors as they feverishly worked to finish the last of the defence works. All suddenly stood still. Hooves beating into the earth echoed from the northeast.

From his position atop the storehouse roof, Fred Hitch spotted roughly a hundred horses galloping towards the garrison. *"Cavalry approaching!"*

"That will be Lieutenant Henderson's lot," Bromhead surmised. "I was wondering if they'd turn up, or had been given the chop."

Chard allowed a smile to permeate his taught face as Lieutenant Alfred Henderson, a civilian meat contractor named Bob Hall, an iziGqoza chieftain, and about a hundred troopers rode towards the camp. Henderson's day had already been long and harrowing. It had only been that morning that they rode out with Lieutenant Colonel Durnford's column, but it felt like a lifetime ago.

As he rode up to the barricades, Henderson recognised John Chard, whom he had met earlier that day. He recalled the engineer officer's conversation with Lieutenant Colonel Durnford regarding the Zulus he spotted to the north of Isandlwana. In hindsight, Henderson knew, rather than some band of renegades or fugitives, these had been elements of the Zulu *impi's* 'Right Horn'. Had Durnford, or indeed anyone, realised this, they could have possibly launched a counterattack and disrupted the entire Zulu battle plan. Of course, given their futile attempts at halting the 'Left Horn', an assault on the warriors Chard had spotted could have just as likely ended in disaster.

"Well, fancy this," Henderson said, his eyes bloodshot and his voice gravelly with fatigue. "I'm glad to see Her Majesty still has soldiers on this side of the river."

"You are certainly a most welcome sight," Chard replied.

"I'm surprised to see Stevenson and his lot haven't hoofed it," the cavalry officer commented rather bluntly.

"We're hoping they finish the barricades first," Bromhead remarked. While the intent was for the NNC to form a mobile defence force within the perimeter, neither of the imperial officers had any faith in their courage or willingness to fight. "And what about your lot? Care to join us for this next dance with the Zulus?"

"My men are spent, as are our horses. We've been battling against them since around 11.00 this morning. We already fought against one 'horn' of the *impi*, and only a handful of us survived. Luckily, we managed to shoot our way out just before Colonel Durnford bought it."

"Well, can you help us or not?" Chard asked impatiently.

"We can, if you have any ammunition for our carbines. The way I hear it, those Martini-Henry rifle cartridges won't seat properly in our carbines. At least that's what the quartermasters told us. Don't know if I believe it or not, but I'd rather not risk having my weapon blow up in my face."

"Sorry, no," Bromhead replied, shaking his head. "All we have is our own company reserves."

"Well, bugger it."

"Can you at least provide a screen-line on the southern flank of the mountain?" Chard asked. "I've had to withdraw my picquets. Last we knew, the Zulus were approaching from upriver, likely using the mountain to mask their movements."

It was frustrating that, colonial officer or not, Henderson was still the same rank as he and Bromhead, and not under his jurisdiction. Therefore, Chard could not order the officer to reinforce the garrison. Alfred, however, took pity on the small band of imperial soldiers. The least he could do was offer what support he was able, before death came for this last bastion of British soldiers along the Natal-Zulu border.

"We can," he said. "But I'll tell you right now, once the Zulus come popping in we won't be able to hold for long. Our lads are down to their last three or four cartridges, and some have nothing at all. But we'll give ample warning and see if we can't send a few more of those bastards to hell before they come to gut the lot of you."

As the band of troopers rode east towards the southern slope of Shiyane, the two senior officers conducted a quick walk of the perimeter. Storekeeper Byrne and Commissary Dunne were staging the company's reserve stockpile of ammunition near the storehouse veranda with the help of Padre Smith. A handful of soldiers, including Second Corporal Atwood, had taken up positions in each of the rooms and the attic. Atwood's corner room gave him views of both the southern and eastern approaches.

Unlike the other colonials, who rode off as soon as they warned the garrison, Lieutenant Adendorff positioned himself in the small attic of the storehouse, along with a couple of injured troopers and carbineers from the hospital. His own ammunition almost gone, he acquired one of the few remaining Martini-Henry rifles from Storekeeper Byrne and several packets of ammunition.

"Comfortable, Mister Adendorff?" Bromhead asked.

"I make do," the German officer said. He pulled a tin of bully beef and some biscuits from his satchel and proceeded to have what he thought might very well be his last meal.

Bromhead left the attic and made his way down the outside steps. As he strolled over to the veranda, his thoughts were interrupted by the arrival of Surgeon Reynolds and his orderlies. They were dragging in the table that Reverend Witt used as an altar during church services. It had sat outside under a tarp since the army acquired the chapel for use as a storehouse.

"Beg your pardon, gentlemen," the doctor said, "But there is absolutely no way I can perform surgery on the wounded from inside the hospital. There isn't enough room for the lads defending it, let alone an operating table."

"With the mealie bags and biscuit boxes cleared out, we have room for you inside," Storekeeper Byrne stated.

"Kindly inform your men that this is where the casualty collection point will be," Chard instructed Bromhead.

"Already been done," Gunny replied. He then shrugged as Chard raised an eyebrow. "The hospital veranda is completely exposed, so this was the only practical place."

Chard nodded in concurrence and Bromhead left to speak with his section leaders once more. Despite the noticeable gap near the hospital veranda, the officer commanding for B Company was pleased with how the defences had come together. Though like most of his men, he found his gaze constantly drawn towards the south and east.

"Surgeon Reynolds is establishing his operating table just inside the storehouse," Bromhead explained.

"Keep your heads low, especially when evacuating the wounded," Colour Sergeant Bourne stated. "I expect they'll be occupying that ridge along Shiyane with riflemen. Corporal Allan, you'll be in the best position to suppress those bastards."

"They'll regret getting into a shooting contest with my lads."

"It's a shit situation, I won't lie," Lieutenant Bromhead added, with a rare dose of profanity. "But we will make do. The southern approach looks relatively clear, and I suspect that is where they will hit us first."

"After a few volleys, they'll think twice about attacking us from there," Sergeant Gallagher said, his good-natured grin never leaving his face. "I've promised a bottle of port to whichever one of my sharp-shooters scores the longest kill."

Bromhead gave an appreciative grin. The level of maturity and level-headed demeanour from the Irish sergeant contrasted sharply with his boyish face. Should he survive the day, Gunny was convinced Henry Gallagher had the making of a future colour sergeant, or perhaps even sergeant major someday.

"If there are no other questions, return to your sections."

Bromhead then returned to the storehouse veranda, where he joined Lieutenant Chard and Commissary Dalton. This was the most practical position for them to observe the defences, without exposing themselves to enemy marksmen.

While the officers discussed any last-minute issues they might have forgotten about, Colour Sergeant Bourne took one last walk around the perimeter. His rifle held at port arms, he spoke to his men in a calm, firm tone. There was nothing he said that they didn't already know, yet somehow hearing his steady voice telling them to *'listen to your section leaders'*, and *'mark your targets before your fire'*, helped soothe their collectively frayed nerves. The wait alone was insufferable.

The unsettling silence was soon shattered by the echoing of several dozen carbines firing in the distance, just beyond the southern slope of Shiyane. The shooting continued for the better part of a minute before all was silent once more.

"The cavalry is returning, sir!" Private Hitch shouted down from the storehouse roof.

The mass of NNC levies were starting to mull about, wide-eyed and panicky. Both Captain Stevenson and his European corporals were saddling their horses, which made the indigenous warriors even more restless. The imperial soldiers along the ramparts found their attention drawn over their shoulders into the compound, as the warriors fretted nervously.

"Just piss off and be done with it already," a private muttered angrily.

Within moments the Basuto horsemen galloped past the station, fear gripping them as they leaned into their saddles.

The civilian contractor, Bob Hall, shouted towards the garrison, *"Here they come, black as hell and thick as grass!"*

Alfred Henderson reined in his horse and paused for a moment. He and Chard locked gazes. The volunteer lieutenant grimaced and gave a nod of respect to his fellow officer. Like the redcoats of the 24th at Isandlwana, these men would fight and die unashamed, with their faces to the enemy. While sorry to see them go, Chard could scarcely blame them. They had been under no obligation to defend the mission station. Even if they had wanted to, without ammunition there was little they could offer except more corpses to add to the day's toll.

As the last of the cavalry rode away, the mass of NNC warriors started chattering fervently. Those carrying mealie bags dropped them; many threw down their weapons. Much to the chagrin of every redcoat at Rorke's Drift, neither Stevenson nor any of his NCOs said so much as a single word when their men scrambled over the ramparts and fled from the station. Instead, they were mounting their horses and readying to ride away. The men closest to the squabble did not take kindly to the desertion.

"Where the bleeding hell are they going?" one private scoffed.

"Sodding cowards," another spat.

"Captain Stevenson!" Chard implored, rushing over to the NNC officer. "Where are you going? Can't you see we need you?"

Stevenson said nothing, refusing to even look at the engineer officer. He kicked his horse into a gallop and rode away without so much as a glance.

Chard's expression divulged his feelings of betrayal. Bromhead, conversely, was indifferent. The actions of Stevenson and his NNC warriors were of no surprise to him. The men in the ranks reacted with scorn and a few shouted profanities.

It was Fred Hitch, however, whose indignation led him to take action as he watched the four men riding away. His rage getting the best of him, he jerked open the breach of his rifle and quickly chambered a round.

"Fuck this," he snarled. He checked the sites on his weapon and leaned against the edge of the rooftop.

He wished to kill the cowardly Stevenson, but with all the men dressed alike and the horses kicking up clouds of dust, he could not differentiate between them. He quickly estimated the range at just over one hundred yards; an easy shot for him, as the riders were galloping directly away rather than laterally. He took a slow breath and squeezed the trigger.

The loud crack of his rifle startled the men of the garrison. There were a few grins of satisfaction as one of the fleeing riders was struck in the back of the head, the bullet exiting out his forehead in a horrific spray of blood, brain, and splintered bone.

"Served you right, you sodding cowards!" one soldier shouted.

Stevenson's horse reared up as he quickly halted. He watched in horror as Corporal Anderson tumbled forward off his startled horse. Though clearly dead, his body convulsed violently in the grotesque throes of death. Several more parting shots were fired from men on the ramparts as the remaining deserters sprinted away.

"Cease fire, damn you!" Colour Sergeant Bourne shouted.

"Goddamn it, Hitch!" Sergeant Gallagher bellowed. He watched Hitch extract the spent cartridge from his weapon. "What do you think you're doing?"

"Saving Her Majesty a needless trial for desertion," the young private countered.

"Well save it for the Zulus," Lieutenant Bromhead called up. "We have a finite number of bullets. And besides, those cowardly bastards aren't worth it."

Under normal circumstances, Private Frederick Hitch would have been dragged down from the roof, shackled, placed under immediate arrest, and tried for murder. Yet no one who remained at Rorke's Drift gave a damn about the slain deserter. Colour Sergeant Bourne found it rather fitting.

Expressionless, he turned to Bromhead. "You know, sir, I'm half-tempted to put Hitch in for a medal."

Gunny gave an amused snort, shaking his head slightly.

Despite the string of desertions, every redcoat at Rorke's Drift demonstrated an outward sense of calm as they stood defiantly with their mates. The acts of cowardice only further steeled their resolve. Even the youngest and least experienced soldiers, some of whom had only been in the army a few months, were determined to die beside their friends.

For Lieutenant Chard, however, the tactical situation had taken a dire turn. His riflemen were simply spread too thin. One hundred and fifty men, about thirty of whom were hospital patients, covered a perimeter designed for twice that number. His eyes betraying his consternation, he looked to Bromhead.

"Nothing remains but to fight," Bromhead noted, echoing Harry Lugg's earlier assessment.

The partial eclipse of the sun, largely unnoticed due to the diligent work efforts of the garrison, was now beginning to pass. None knew that at that moment, ten miles away at Isandlwana, the last remnants of Captain Reginald Younghusband's C Company, 1/24th were executing their final bloody charge into oblivion.

Sergeant Henry Gallagher
Section Leader, B Company, 2/24th

The salvoes of gunfire forewarned Mandlenkosi and his fellow warriors of the uThulwana. Despite their best efforts to catch up to the iNdluyengwe, the younger regiment had a twenty-minute head start on the rest of the corps.

"They attack the whites and seek to rob us of glory!" a warrior lamented, as the lead companies of the uThulwana broke into a faster stride.

"Stay in formation!" Mandlenkosi shouted. "The king's own will not forget their discipline this day!"

There was a further barrage of shots echoing from near the southern spur of the Shiyane Mountain. They were fast and erratic; far more desperate than the controlled volleys they'd heard unleashed by the redcoats at Isandlwana. By the time the follow-on regiments of the Undi Corps reached the spot where Henderson's cavalry fired their parting shots, the iNdluyengwe were already gone. The bodies of half-a-dozen warriors lay sprawled in the tall grass, another ten lay badly wounded. One poor fellow clutched his ruptured stomach with one hand, reaching for the torn pile of guts that lay by his side with the other.

The *induna* raised his spear and shouted for his men to halt. The leaders of the other regiments did the same, and the bulk of the Undi Corps came to a halt. Some of the *izinduna* were mounted. They rode up and down the ranks, exhorting them to fight bravely but without reckless abandon. They knew, should the iNdluyengwe merely roll right over the garrison at kwaJimu, there was little they could do to stop them. Mandlenkosi secretly hoped their lead regiment would flounder against the small garrison of white soldiers, paying the price for their impetuousness.

"See anything, Brickie?" Corporal Lyons called up to Fred Hitch.

"Nothing yet," Fred replied, shaking his head. He scanned the horizon, most of his attention fixed on the southern slopes of Shiyane Mountain. From the little intelligence they gathered, it was the enemy's most probable avenue of approach. Given the speed with which the mounted troopers fled, they expected to see the black mass of Zulus crest the hill at any moment.

"Come on, you bastards," Fred said quietly. "Let's get this over with."

In the south end of the hospital, Privates Henry Hook and Thomas Cole occupied one of the smaller rooms. The only other man with them was an NNC warrior whose leg was heavily bandaged.

In the room facing west were John Williams, Joseph Williams, and another private named William Horrigan. Just off the veranda were John Waters, William Beckett, and a gunner from N Battery, Arthur Howard. He'd come down with a severe case of dysentery the week before. Though the worst of his symptoms passed the day prior, he had been scarcely able to eat or drink. His body depleted, he could barely walk. However, he had compelled Colour Sergeant Bourne into issuing him a rifle, and he lay on his pallet, gazing through a loophole, waiting for the enemy to come.

The southwest room occupied by Hook and Cole had a window and a door that led to the outside, though the soldiers barricaded this. Cole had cut a loophole in the wall, just large enough for him to shove the barrel of his rifle through and still able to look down the sights. It greatly constricted his field of view, making him feel even more claustrophobic. Hook had elected to use the window, which he leaned against.

"You know you're leaving yourself exposed to Zulu gunfire there," Cole cautioned.

"It's a risk I'll accept, since I can see much better than you," Harry replied. He chuckled. "And if they get close enough that their musketry starts bringing me some grief, I'll just shove you away from your loophole."

The two men shared a laugh.

Hook took a moment to take a deep breath through his nose. The air was dry and dusty despite the lushness of the green grasses that covered the landscape.

"So, the baking oven and ditch bank are only about twenty yards from here, agreed?" Hook asked.

"More or less," Cole concurred. "If the Zulus get that close, they'll be in our faces with their nasty stabbing sticks in a moment or two."

"Alright. Now how about that old fruit tree off to the left?"

"I'd say...two hundred yards."

"More like two hundred and fifty," Hook corrected.

"Well, you're the one with the sharp-shooter's badge," Cole said, nodding towards the cross rifles patch on Henry's left cuff. "Who would have thought it? Harry Hook, the non-drinking, soft-spoken gentleman who cooks breakfast for the sick and is a lay preacher, is also one of the best-trained killers in the company."

"I signed on to be a soldier in Her Majesty's Armed Forces," Harry reasoned. "I am ready to do my duty, whatever it may be. Now, how about that broken thicket, just to the right of the tree?"

"Four hundred yards," Thomas guessed, suspecting his friend would be correcting him once more.

"Close," Hook concurred. "Alright, those will be our range markers. Anything beyond that, and we're just wasting bullets." He slid the rear sight on his rifle back to the number *4* line. "We'll index four hundred yards. Once they reach the fruit tree, we'll drop it to three. Anything closer, and we'll just slide our sights all the way down." He leaned out the window and called over to the next room. "Oi, Johnno! Don't forget to adjust your sights, mate!"

"No, Harry, I think I'll just shoot over their fucking heads," John Williams retorted.

In the western room, John confessed his concern for their mate, Thomas Cole. "Blimey, I'm surprised the colour sergeant put Cole over here. He's claustrophobic as shit."

"Is he really?" Joseph Williams asked.

"He always sleeps with his head sticking out of his section's tent, even when it's pissing down rain. Hell, half the time he sleeps outside."

"I hope he'll be alright," Horrigan muttered. "It's going to get loud and smoky in these cramped little rooms. And he's got even less space than we do."

As the three privates worried about the fortitude of their mate, Colour Sergeant Bourne continued to walk the perimeter. He carried his rifle at port arms, pacing slowly and deliberately as he gave his men a few last minutes words of instruction.

"Look to your front. Listen to your section leaders. Adjust your sights, and mark your targets before you fire."

Sergeants and corporals echoed his command. The rest of the garrison stood silent in rapt anticipation of the coming battle. The perimeter was not very large. Just thirty-five yards separated the two buildings. However, with the NNC and carbineers having fled, many of the defenders felt they were stretched precariously thin.

Lieutenant Chard was also troubled by this. Between B Company, the NNC, and Henderson's mounted troops, he had thought he would have as many as 400 men defending the mission station. But with the mass desertions, he now had less than 150; many of whom were sick or wounded. He was particularly concerned about the cattle kraal, where he had intended to place a good portion of the Natal warriors. "Corporal Allan!" he shouted.

Allan was the NCO who first escorted him to his little camp at the drift and was one of the few names Chard could recall off the top of his head.

"Sir?" the corporal asked. He walked briskly over to the officer.

"Take seven men and reinforce the eastern defences," Chard ordered. "We don't want to leave the front door open to the Zulus."

As Allan shouted for seven privates from his section to follow him, Chard was joined by Assistant Commissary Dalton who shared his concern about the defences.

"Beg your pardon, Mister Chard, but with Stevenson's lot having hoofed it, we ought to establish a secondary defensive position, should the outer wall become untenable."

"What do you have in mind, Mister Dalton?"

Dalton turned to Storekeeper Byrne and Commissary Dunne. "There are still many biscuit boxes in the storehouse. We should form a detail to drag out as many as possible."

"Splendid idea," Byrne remarked with a trace of sarcasm. He then asked with a twisted grin, "Are we to have afternoon tea before the darkies arrive? Perhaps we can ask them to join us."

As rattled as his nerves were at the gravity of their situation, Chard could not help but break into an appreciative smile.

"Tempting," he said. "But I fear there is no time. Mister Dalton, where do you recommend we form this inner defence?"

"If we stack a line of boxes from the northwest corner of the storehouse to the north wall, that will bisect the camp and give us a second line of defences to fall back to."

Chard privately cursed himself for not having thought of this. He remained stoic and said to 'Gunny' Bromhead, "See to it, if you would be so kind."

Bromhead recognised the wisdom of Dalton's recommendation and called out to Sergeant Smith to take twenty men and build the inner rampart with all possible speed. He then said to Chard, "If the hospital did not make for such a strong defensive point, I would say pull everyone back now."

Chard shared this assessment. Both officers understood that if they handed it over to the Zulus, their adversaries would cover the high roof in marksmen, who by sheer force of numbers could obliterate their garrison with enfilade musketry.

As Sergeant Smith's section heaved the heavy biscuit boxes into a long row, approximately chest high, he thought it might be prudent to order the patients evacuated from the hospital to this tiny inner defence. The arrival of the Zulus told him he was out of time.

Chapter VII: Is that all?

Rorke's Drift, South Ramparts
4.20 p.m.

Private Henry "Harry" Hook
B Company, 2/24th Regiment

"There you are, you devils," Fred Hitch said. He scanned through Sergeant Gallagher's field glasses and noted a few small groups of skirmishers in the far distance, coming around the southern spur of the mountain.

They kept low, bounding from one piece of cover to the next; brush stands, trees, small rises in the ground. But then he saw a lone *induna* astride his horse on the rising spur. The man raised his musket high and shouted an order the young soldier could not understand. Waves of Zulu warriors immediately swarmed around the backside of the mountain, the lead elements sprinting laterally to Hitch's right as the enemy regiment formed into battle lines. From his position on the roof he could clearly see the defined lines between each company. Following subsequent shouts from their officers, they began a rhythmic jog towards the mission station.

Hitch found himself admiring the Zulus' drill and discipline, for it was worthy of any regiment in the British Empire. "Should parade this lot at Horse Guards for the Queen," he whispered. He then shouted down to Lieutenant Bromhead, *"Here they come, sir!"*

"How many?" his officer commanding asked.

"Oh, bugger me," the private swore quietly. "Does he expect them to halt so I can get a sodding head count?" He did a quick assessment, estimating how many warriors were in each rank, multiplied by the number of company lines he could count. He then spotted a multitude of warriors in the distance, and realised these men were simply the first wave of a much larger force.
"Four…maybe six thousand."

"Is that all?" Bromhead asked. "I'd say we can manage that lot very well for a few seconds."

Down below, the men on the south rampart were reporting that they could see the first wave of skirmishers about a thousand yards away. This was followed by a loud shout of *'Fix bayonets!'* from Colour Sergeant Bourne. For most of the rankers, these were 22-inch triangular spikes, while corporals and above wielded what looked like a short sword. These were meant to denote their status as non-commissioned officers, though many an NCO had noted rather bitterly that the sword bayonet was less sturdy that the triangular spike, and therefore more prone to breaking.

While his mates attached the bayonets onto the ends of their weapons with a series of audible clicks, Fred Hitch chambered a round into his Martini-Henry and aimed at the lone *induna* on the spur of Shiyane. It was difficult to say just how far away the man was; Fred indexed his sights to 800 yards and took a slow breath as he aimed. At such a range, even an able marksman like Hitch would be hard-pressed to strike his target. His rifle gave a loud crack as it fired. The private was disappointed to see his shot struck well in front of his intended target.

As he opened the breach of his rifle and rummaged in his ready pouch for another round, he took a deep breath. He watched the horde of Zulus continue to surge over and around the hill. Though he had fought in a few engagements during the Xhosa War, Fred Hitch had never even seen a Zulu before. These powerful men wielding cowhide shields and spears may have resembled his former adversaries in appearance, but there was something decidedly different about the Zulus. These were not marauding bands of barbarians but highly skilled and disciplined fighters worthy of the young soldier's respect.

With a profound sense of admiration, Fred reloaded his weapon, checked his sites, and fired once more.

About a mile from the mission station, Reverend Otto Witt looked back over his shoulder as he heard the first shots fired by Fred Hitch. The ground seemed to tremble under the marching feet of thousands of Zulu warriors, chanting and banging their weapons on their shields.

"Go with God, my friends," he whispered, making a sign of the cross towards the place that had been his home.

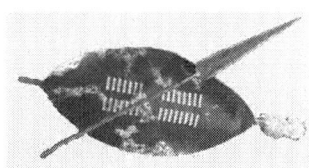

Dabulamanzi sneered contemptuously at the lone crack of a rifle shot coming from the station. A clod of dirt kicked up about fifty feet from where he sat astride his horse. Neither the prince nor any of the *izinduna* expected to meet any real resistance at the station. It appeared the British had built some sort of defence works, but these were no more than shoulder high. With the southern approach consisting of mostly flat, open ground, he reckoned his warriors would swarm over those in a matter of minutes.

"*Sukela!*" he shouted.

His warriors responded with a booming, '*Uzulu!*'

The lead elements broke into a quick jog, chanting a war cadence which kept them in step and slowly raised their collective fury.

There was a subsequent rifle shot from the defences, and a warrior screamed as he was struck in the hip. The impact of the bullet sent him sprawling onto his side. The heavy slug tore clean through, shattering the hip bone and leaving a horrific exit wound that spewed forth blood, bone fragments, and torn muscle. They were still roughly 800 yards from the defences and startled to see they were now in range of the redcoats' firearms. Maintaining their chants, they kept low, attempting to utilise whatever cover they could find. The *izinduna* occasionally barked out orders to keep the formations intact. Even against such a paltry enemy force, there was no glory to be had by losing their composure and becoming a mob of ill-disciplined barbarians.

As additional shots rang out from B Company's designated marksmen, the Battle of Rorke's Drift commenced.

"Such splendid discipline!" John Williams said with a strange sense of both admiration and dread.

The black-skinned warriors may have worn animal skins and carried spears, but they were no rampaging mob. Those appearing to be company officers shouted to their warriors, ordering them to bound forward to each new piece of cover or concealment. John could now differentiate the loose band of skirmishers bearing muskets. They advanced roughly fifty yards ahead of their mates. Knowing the enemy was almost in range, the private glanced over to Joseph Williams, who was leaning into his rifle, checking his sights. Private Horrigan lay prone on his pallet bunk, unmoving.

Sergeant Gallagher's sharp-shooters had commenced firing; their shots controlled and measured. Conscious of their own ammunition limits, the hospital defenders elected to wait until the Zulus were in range of the main firing line.

Outside, they heard Sergeant Gallagher shouting, *"South rampart, at five hundred yards..."* There was a pause as all soldiers checked their sights and aimed at the mass of Zulus who had quickened their pace. *"Present...fire!"*

The men in the hospital followed his command as well, and a crashing volley erupted from the south wall. The Zulus immediately went to ground, with several of their number flying backwards as their bodies were smashed by the shattering impact of large calibre bullets.

"Did you see that fucking bastard fly?" Horrigan asked. He jacked open the breach of his weapon. "Looked like an oversized bat for a moment."

"Did you get one?" John Williams asked, as they caught their breath and waited for the Zulus to show themselves again.

"Nah, I think it was your mate next door what done him. I overheard Gunner Howard saying it's a pity we couldn't stuff one of his 7-pounder cannon in here!"

With shouts from their officers, the Zulu lead regiment rose again. Each company sprinted a few yards before dropping onto their stomachs, relying on the tall grasses to conceal them. A second volley from Sergeant Gallagher's men tore into them. Now the Zulu marksmen were returning fire. A single round slapped the outer wall of the hospital. At least three times beyond the effective range of the Zulus' archaic muskets, their shots had only minor impact.

From his position at the window, Henry Hook spotted one enemy skirmisher lurking behind an anthill approximately 300 yards away. He adjusted his sights and fired. As he saw no discernible impact, he surmised his round had sailed over the man's head. The Zulu shot back just as Harry fired once more. This time his bullet slapped the earth ten feet in front of the mound.

"Damn it all," he cursed himself. He jacked open the smoking breach of his rifle and chambered another round. "Hold still, would you?"

He relaxed his breathing, trying to slow his pounding heart rate. He focused his sights just to the right side of the mound. The Zulu was left-handed, and Hook knew that's where he would show himself. A few seconds later, he saw the barrel of the musket then the man's face. Harry immediately fired. The cloud of smoke prevented him from seeing where his bullet struck.

John Williams called out from the next room, "Nice one, Harry! You took his bloody head off!"

Along the south wall, Sergeant Gallagher continued to give fire commands in his calm, steady voice. *"At three hundred yards! Present...fire!"*

"Watch your ranges, adjust your sights!" Corporal Lyons added, noting that several of their section's shots went high.

The Zulus had grown impatient as companies converged on their skirmishers. An *induna* chastised his men, who then surged forward with a loud cry of *'Usutu!'* There were no subsequent battle cries, which seemed strange. Those in the lead ranks stooped low, their gazes on the ground in front of them. Shields held high protectively, they rushed forward.

Lieutenant Chard stood close by, his pistol in hand. Enemy skirmishers were returning fire, despite the distance rendering their muskets all but useless. The occasional round slapped into the mealie wall or wagons, but most landed far short of the defences. He noticed Commissary Dalton had acquired a rifle and stuffed his pockets with ammunition packets. The old soldier took his cues from Gallagher, adjusting his sights and firing with the rest of the line.

"*At two hundred yards! Independent...fire at will!*"

Fire discipline was always paramount, lest overanxious soldiers expend their entire allotment of cartridges in just a few minutes. But now, an unstoppable wave of Zulu warriors surged towards the defences. Henry Gallagher knew his men needed to unleash a wall of musketry as fast as they could reload and fire, if they were to have any chance of holding. For every fifty yards the Zulus ran, the wall of redcoats smashed them with another salvo. The closer they came to the ramparts, the more accurate the soldiers' fire became. Both Chard and Gallagher could now hear the screams of stricken warriors as they were shot down. Yet, on they came without so much as slowing their pace. There were perhaps thirty men along the back rampart including the lads from the hospital and storehouse. Chard was suddenly fearful that this force of Zulus, who numbered at least a thousand, would easily surge like a great tidal wave and smash over the wall.

The *amabutho* were now compressing their files as they approached the narrow ditch bank near the cook oven. Few seemed to have any inclination to try and break down the doors of the hospital, and there were no outer doors on the south side of the storehouse for them to breach.

Just as Sergeant Gallagher thought they would soon be in a bayonet fight, a voice came from inside the storehouse.

"*Action right! Action right!*"

It was Second Corporal Atwood, who'd taken up position in the south side of the attic. He could see better than his mates, several of whom now switched to secondary loopholes along the western wall of the storehouse, which looked towards the Zulu flank. A crashing volley from these defenders smashed into the enemy right, as the men in the hospital fired into the Zulu left. A subsequent volley from Sergeant Gallagher's men at point-blank range shattered the enemy onslaught. The lead companies flattened themselves in the grass, while those behind began surging towards the British right.

"*Stay down, you bastards!*" Commissary Dalton shouted. He leapt onto one of the wagons and fired his rifle. He then threw his hat at the Zulus before jumping down and making his way towards the north side of the hospital.

"That's where they'll hit us next," he hastily explained to Lieutenant Chard. He tore open another packet of cartridges and sprinted to the hospital veranda.

The close-range onslaught of British firepower had stopped the advance in its tracks. Numerous warriors lay dead or badly maimed, and their companions were no longer in a hurry to rush into the barrage of redcoat musketry. The range at where they had started to land killing shots and the speed with which they could reload was unnerving. While every Zulu was impeccably brave, they were not suicidal.

Warriors flattened themselves in the tall grass. Many sought cover in the ditch or behind the cookhouse. Skirmishers began to return fire, and this closer range drove many of the redcoats to drop down behind their makeshift wall. However, the warriors behind them had lost their desire to charge into the hell-storm of death, the terrible effects of which were all around them. Nearly two score had fallen; the cries of the wounded causing a chill to run up the collective spines of both sides. Guts were splayed open, arms and legs shattered, throats ripped away, and heads smashed in.

The young men of the iNdluyengwe had taken a serious punishing in the first few moments of battle. Their horror was now compounded by frustration. Though they could count no more than thirty redcoats behind the wall, its confined space made it difficult for the Zulus to mass their numbers effectively. The *ibutho* had over a thousand men who could readily overwhelm the wall, but it was equally apparent that the lead companies would be torn to pieces before the rest could get over the ramparts. And in that moment, with many of their friends already slain or badly injured, none of the *izinduna* could compel their men to lead such a suicidal charge.

The marksmen in the first two companies were now engaged in a duel with the defenders. Shots continued to ring out. The rest crawled away and with a shouted order from one of the *induna*, they made their way to the left, keeping to the low ground on the west side of the hospital. The Zulus reformed near the lone water closet about ten yards west of the hospital's north side, keeping just south of the rocky slope the British had built their defence works on.

"Reform!" an *induna* shouted. It was maddening. With Zibhebhu having abandoned the field, the regiment was essentially leaderless. The company commander could only hope the other *izinduna* followed his lead. Hunkering to the low ground out of reach of the hospital defenders, he spotted a narrow gap between the veranda and the north wall. With an evil sneer, he signalled for his warriors to follow him.

"*Usutu!*"

"They're rolling right up on us!" Fred Hitch shouted the warning to Sergeant Windridge and his mates along the north wall.

"On me!" Windridge called to his men. *"Fire at will! Fire at will!"*

A handful of rifles came to bear, firing into the swarming Zulus at close range.

"Damn it all, this is the fucking blind spot," James Dalton growled, as he joined the young men. He sensed the danger as soon as he saw the Zulus moving away from the south wall. He'd rushed over to warn Sergeant Windridge's section, but it was too late.

"Bayonets ready!" Windridge shouted.

A wall of spikes was levelled into the faces of the Zulus. The enemy warriors gave a loud shout of defiance. Before the redcoats could reload, a hand-to-hand melee broke out within the ten-yard space where the wall angled from the hospital to meet the north rampart.

Though their wall was maybe four feet high, and in some spots not complete, it still gave the line of infantrymen just enough protection to prevent the Zulus from closing with their short stabbing spears. The sheer weight of the mealie bags meant the wall could not easily be toppled over. And the Martini-Henry rifle with bayonet fixed extended nearly six feet, giving the British soldiers a vast reach advantage over the short Zulu stabbing spears. Most of their skirmishers engaged on the south rampart, and it appeared none of the enemy in the immediate vicinity had firearms.

Fred Hitch made a quick mental note of this, reckoning a couple dozen enemy muskets could blast Joseph Windridge's entire section to shreds at such close range. He set his ammunition pouch on top the barricade and fired his weapon into the chest of one charging Zulu, bursting the man's heart and killing him instantly. As the young soldier jacked open the breach, an enraged warrior threw down his spear and shield and grabbed onto both the barrel and bayonet of Hitch's weapon hoping to disarm him. For his part, Fred kept a vice-like grip on the buttstock of his rifle. As the Zulu continued trying to wrench the weapon free, Hitch managed to chamber another round. Without even attempting to shoulder the rifle, he fired into the Zulu's stomach. The rupturing of intestines and bowels created a terrible stench, causing the private to gag. Fred took a deep breath and steadied his nerves. The stricken man lay sobbing and thrashing in a growing pool of his own blood and bodily fluids.

Though he had no intention of 'keeping score', his recollections told him this was the third man he'd killed this day. The first was the deserter, and now he'd slain or mortally wounded a pair of Zulus. *'At least I've done my bit should those bastards do me in,'* he thought.

One of Surgeon Reynolds' orderlies on the firing line almost had his weapon yanked away by a maddened Zulu, only to be saved by Commissary Dalton shooting the man in the face. Several more of their warriors fell to bayonet and rifle fire. With none able to strike a killing blow against the hated redcoats, the assault faltered. The Zulus were driven back towards the concealment offered by the tall grass and brush to the immediate west.

His nerves frayed, Hitch let out a maniacal laugh and shouted over his shoulder to his officer commanding, *"Looks like we held them for a few seconds, sir!"*

'Gunny' Bromhead had watched the short, yet harrowing skirmish near the hospital. The northwest corner near the veranda was a terrible blind spot, and the Zulus were quickly attempting to exploit it. The men inside the structure could only bring one or two weapons to bear; and even then, the defilade and rock wall protected the enemy until they were within just a few yards. Had they more time, the defenders would have built up the ramparts, cleared the brush, and knocked down that cursed rock wall. However, time proved to be a fickle mistress.

The officer commanding of B Company knew he had to adapt to the situation at hand.

"That's our weak point." He left his sword leaning up against the side of the storehouse and now carried a Martini-Henry. He called over his shoulder, *"Colour Sergeant Bourne, give me twenty men, now!"*

"Sir!"

The company's senior NCO directed each section to send its five best bayonet fighters to their commander. Within moments, the score of soldiers formed two ranks to the left of Bromhead. Bourne and the best bayonet fighters were in front, the lieutenant and the rest acting as designated marksmen.

"I apologise right now to any man I render deaf this day." 'Gunny' smiled morbidly. His own hearing already severely handicapped, he knew the ears of the men in the front rank would take a severe punishing from their friends firing over their shoulders.

They waited for the next assault, at what some of the men on the line were already referring to as 'the bloody angle', Commissary Dalton ran over, his weapon at port arms, and took up a position next to the officer.

"Mister Dalton," Bromhead acknowledged. "Good to have you with us."

"Thank you, sir. It's good to be here."

The score of riflemen stood unflinching, even as bullets from Zulu muskets kicked up gouts of dirt from the courtyard and slapped the hospital walls. The initial assault appeared to have subsided.

Bromhead took a deep breath. "They'll be back," he whispered.

Chapter VIII: With Rifle and Bayonet

Rorke's Drift, South Ramparts
4.30 p.m.

Fighting along the north wall

With the first assault successfully repelled, the men along the south rampart took a moment to catch their breath. Mealie spilled from numerous holes in the large sacks, and the south wall of the hospital was riddled with gouges from enemy marksmen. And yet, it did not appear anyone had been hit. Whether divine intervention or poor marksmanship on the part of the Zulus, the men of Sergeant Gallagher's section were grateful to be alive. The respite was short-lived, however. An even larger wave of Zulus was now advancing around the southern slope of Shiyane.

"Oh my God," Private James Dunbar uttered under his breath.

The *izinduna* in the distance were shouting orders to their men.

"Must be their reserves," his mate, Private George Edwards suggested. In essence, he was correct. The entire force attacking them had formed the Zulu reserves at Isandlwana. The truth, however, was these three regiments, including the king's own uThulwana, had travelled a greater distance and crossed the river after the much younger warriors of the iNdluyengwe.

A mounted *induna* was riding along the front rank of his men. He was pointing west with his assegai, around the hospital. Clearly, he did not wish for his men to rush across the open plain, where scores of dead and badly wounded warriors lay strewn about.

"Designated marksmen," Sergeant Gallagher called out. "At six hundred yards…fire at will!"

The six sharp-shooters, including Privates Dunbar and Edwards, adjusted their sights. The first couple shots rang out as the two young soldiers tracked the mounted *induna*. Edwards, who had raised horses in England, told his friend, "I'll shove my bayonet up your arse if you kill his horse."

Fighting to control their breathing while a spattering of shots echoed from their comrades, they waited until the *induna* halted his mount to give more orders to his men. Both men fired simultaneously. Neither would ever know who struck the killing blow. Even at six hundred yards, one could see the spray of pink mist when the stricken Zulu commander tumbled from his horse. The warriors nearest him ducked low, several kneeling down to check their fallen leader as the terrified horse sprinted away.

"They're moving around to the west, sir!" Sergeant Gallagher called out.

Lieutenant Chard rushed over and scanned the enemy regiments with his field glasses. He gave a quick nod and ran back to the defences near the front of the hospital.

"Get ready, Mister Bromhead," he said, as he passed his fellow officer.

"The front of the hospital is the weak point, sir," Bourne stated.

"And if we see it, you can bet the Zulus do," Dalton added.

Within the hospital, Harry Hook and the other defenders continued to fire at the Zulus manoeuvring around their flank in the distance. Their adversaries were keeping their distance. Crouching low, they raced to the lower ground to the west.

"Can't see a bloody one now," Thomas Cole griped. He rested the butt stock of his rifle on the crude straw mattress where he lay.

"Looks like they've gone to ground," Hook remarked, able to see better from his higher position at the window. He then shook his head. "Damn it all, the veranda! It's a sodding blind spot, and we're boxed in here." Hook stood and leaned out the window, shouting to one of the other rooms, "Johnno, shift towards the front of the hospital!"

"We see them!" John Williams called back.

Hook then called out to the Joneses in the rooms behind him to shift towards the veranda. Unfortunately, with no interior doors leading towards the north side of the building, there was little they could do. Meanwhile, one of his companions was close to breaking.

Thomas Cole had hoped that by keeping his gaze fixed out the loop hole in the wall, he might overcome his rampant claustrophobia. Even with the barrel of his rifle protruding through the gouge in the outer wall, there was a fair amount of blow-back, causing gouts of smoke to waft into the room every time he opened the breach to reload. The lone window in the room was cracked open, and it seemed the smoke from every rifle on the hospital's south wall was being sucked into the tiny room. This made the enclosed space feel even smaller, and Thomas felt as if he were choking. The sound of the Zulu chants coming from northwest of the stronghold added to his anxiety. His face was dripping with sweat. He grabbed at the high collar on his tunic as he struggled to breathe. As rifle fire erupted from the north wall, Thomas panicked. He had to get outside, lest he suffocate to death in that tiny cell.

Surging to his feet, Cole flung open the door, startling Harry who was not quick enough to stop him. Cole sprinted past the south rooms where the Joneses were firing at the Zulus swarming the narrow angle between the hospital front and the barricades.

"Tommy, what are you doing?!" Robert Jones shouted, as his friend rushed past their room and scrambled over the south rampart.

"I...I can't stay in there," Cole stammered.

"Damn it, man, don't be a fool!" William Jones pleaded. *"Tommy!"*

Cole continued around the hospital, finding himself near the Zulus in desperate hand-to-hand combat with Sergeant Windridge's section. Finding his courage once more, Cole gave a loud roar and charged into the fray.

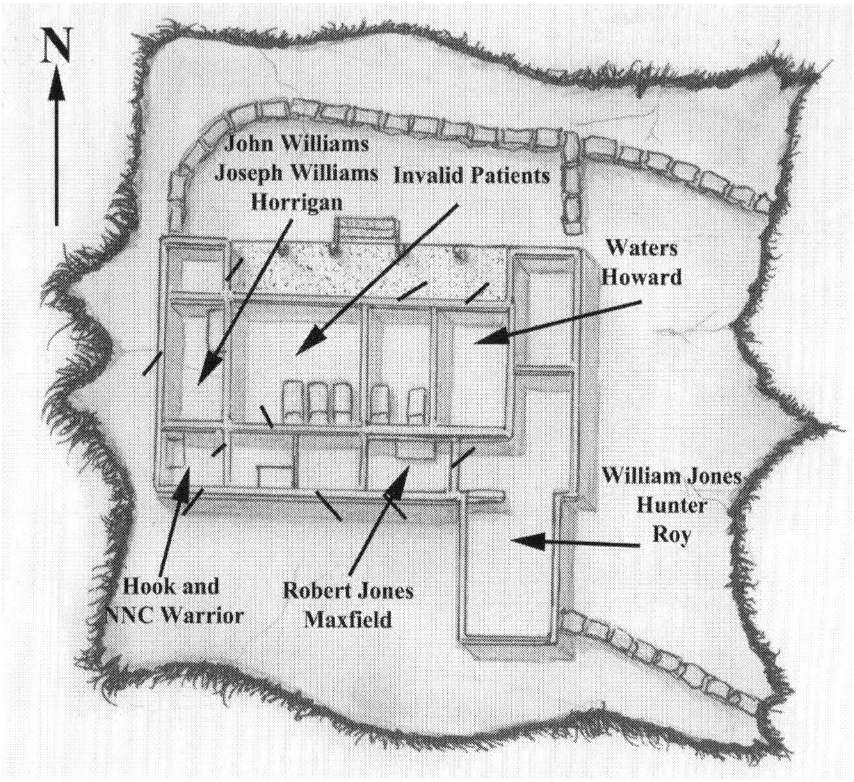

The hospital defences at the start of the battle

With the Zulus now flooding the low road, far garden, and thick brush to the north, it was confirmed that the northern defences were spread too thin. Dalton noticed this immediately and called out to Lieutenant Chard; who was reloading his pistol, having fired all six rounds at the enemy warriors threatening to breach the northwest defences.

"Mister Chard!" the assistant commissary shouted, rushing over. "The lads cannot hold the northwest ramparts. We must withdraw and anchor our barricades off the northeast corner of the hospital."

Though he was no tactician, Chard could see Dalton was right. Sergeant Windridge's men were spread thin and being assailed from both the front and right flank. He needed to pull them back soon, before they were overwhelmed. But, he also needed to secure the breach long enough to rebuild a short rampart to link the northeast corner of the hospital to the main wall.

"Thank you, Mister Dalton," he said.

The commissary took his position back with the flying platoon. Chard shouted to 'Gunny', *"Now, Mister Bromhead!"*

"Follow me!" came the reply.

As the twenty-three men sprinted beside their officer commanding, Chard shouted for Windridge to withdraw back into the centre compound.

As the last of Windridge's section rushed past them, Bromhead halted his men. *"Front rank...fire!"* A dozen Martini-Henrys unleashed a close-range fusillade into the Zulus who were scrambling over the crumbling barricades.

"Second rank...fire!" He then gave Colour Sergeant Bourne a hard slap on the shoulder.

"Charge!" the senior NCO roared.

With a fierce cry of rage, presenting a bristling mass of bayonets towards their enemies, the dozen men in the front rank stormed with fury into the fight. The Zulus, who had struggled mightily to close the distance with their foes, suddenly balked at this terrifying wall of death. They tumbled back over the ramparts, only to be chastised by their leaders into reforming and attacking again. This delay would prove costly, for they lost the initiative, as well as the ramparts.

While Bourne and the men in the front rank kept them at bay with their bayonets, Bromhead and those in the second rank reloaded and fired over the shoulders of their companions. The Zulus' superior numbers meant nothing in such a confined space. With the rampart of mealie sacks preventing them from closing the last few feet, their stabbing spears were rendered all but useless.

The survivors scampered away, leaving twenty of their fellow warriors strewn about in bloody heaps, either shot at point-blank range or skewered upon bayonets. The iNdluyengwe's first attack on Rorke's Drift had failed.

As the lead companies of the uThulwana scurried along the low ground, swinging wide and to the left of the iNdluyengwe, Mandlenkosi was surprised to see dozens of these younger warriors retreating from the narrow space between the enemy's hospital and the north wall.

"Keep low and make for those trees!" the *induna* ordered his men, pointing his spear to a large grove of fruit trees north of the complex.

He kept his white shield over his head, using his spear to part the tall grass in front of him. The sound of British rifle fire continued unabated. Mandlenkosi heard a sickening slap, followed by a loud scream. One of his warriors was struck through the upper arm. The bone shattered, splintered shards jutting through his torn flesh. The stricken man fell onto his side, his face contorted in horrifying agony. He gasped for air, but found he could not breathe. The pain in his arm so intense he wasn't even aware that the heavy bullet had smashed between his ribs and punctured a lung. Death would eventually come from suffocation.

Mandlenkosi bit the inside of his cheek. He rushed onward, refusing to look back. Every man in his company was a lifelong friend, not just a fellow warrior of the king. The uThulwana had been a regiment for more than thirty years, and many of these men had known each other since boyhood. As subsequent shrieks of pain came from more of his men, the old *induna* began to understand the ferocity of their foe. Reaching the first thick fruit tree, he signalled for his men to find cover. They were a couple hundred paces from the ramparts, yet the recoats' shots were felling men with terrifying accuracy.

"Skirmishers forward!" he shouted, waving for every man in possession of a musket to follow him. Lying on their stomachs, they began to crawl through the trees and grass, hoping to get close enough to punish the British for the toll they were inflicting.

As he rode along the southern spur of Shiyane Mountain, Prince Dabulamanzi was beside himself. The attack of the iNdluyengwe was now in disarray. He could see dozens of badly wounded men trying to crawl or drag themselves away from the scene of death. The rest of the Undi Corps appeared to be stalled in their attempts to breach the defences from the north and east.

"How are they still standing?" he asked his assembled *amakhosi*. The disbelief in his voice was evident. "How is it that a hundred men are able to keep the *Inhlabamasoka* at bay?"

The term he used referred to Cetshwayo's 'chosen men', those elite regiments of the *amabutho* who had never tasted defeat in battle, and were revered throughout all of Southern Africa.

"They hide behind a wall of grain sacks," an *induna* reported. "And their bayonets are fearsome."

"Then our own firearms will have to break them," the prince remarked. He dispatched runners to bring as many of their riflemen onto the slopes of the mountain as possible. There was a long rocky ledge that jutted from the side of Shiyane, looking down upon the compound from roughly 300 paces. Dabulamanzi summoned a further ten men from his personal entourage. Each was a skilled shot, many trained by the now-traitorous John Dunn.

The prince dismounted his horse, and hefted his percussion rifle. Though his was one of the finer pieces, he regretted that they were unable to loot some of those fearsome Martini-Henrys from the British dead at Isandlwana. Even if they had managed to return to Isandlwana to gather up sufficient arms, which few knew how to use, it would have been dark by the time they crossed the uMzinyathi. There was also the very real possibility that the warriors who'd conducted the assault on Isandlwana would have attacked the older regiments from the reserve for trying to steal away their prizes!

Heeding the prince's call, scores of warriors dashed up to the rocky shelf and western slope of the mountain. Dabulamanzi knelt and rested the butt of his rifle on the ground. He squinted to see better, trying to count the number of defenders inside the makeshift stronghold. The two buildings obstructed much of his view. He could only make out the south rampart, distinguished by the pair of wagons in the centre, and about half of the north wall. The men on the far rampart had their backs exposed, but the prince dismissed attempting to engage them, doubtful their musket shots could even reach that far.

"This is good ground, *inkosi*," one escort said, kneeling next to his prince. "A fine place to observe the battle."

"That may be, but it is well beyond the range of our muskets." As most of their weapons were thirty to fifty years old and in a terrible state of disrepair, Dabulamanzi knew they were only effective at perhaps fifty paces. He could only hope the sheer volume of gunfire would be enough to break the British defences.

"Aim into the compound," he ordered. "I'll not risk shooting our own men in the back!"

The prince raised his musket to his shoulder, gazing down the rusted sights. Though they wore red, the British were difficult to see. Their once white helmets had been dyed brown from the moment they arrived in South Africa, and their scarlet uniforms were faded from months in the sun. From a distance, one would think they were looking at small mounds of clay and dirt. Furthermore, the men along the ramparts were keeping low, just their heads and the uppermost quarter of their chests exposed as they fired. Finding a soldier he could focus on, he raised his rifle so it was aiming well over the man's head, took a deep breath, and squeezed the trigger. The loud crack of his musket was followed by dozens more from the growing number of Zulu marksmen.

Dabulamanzi had hoped to see a puff of dirt so he would know where his shot landed. With thick clouds of black powder smoke immediately enveloping them, it was impossible to see anything. The prince reiterated his order for his men to aim higher, fearing many of their rounds were falling short, among the companies of iNdluyengwe warriors still lurking in the tall grasses near the British cookhouse.

He removed his powder horn from his satchel and poured a measure down the barrel. He placed a round ball into the muzzle, removed the ramrod, and hammered the bullet home. He half-cocked the hammer, removed the spent percussion cap, and replaced it with a fresh one. The prince had spent many hours training and practicing with his favourite weapon, and could fire approximately three rounds per minute, if he rushed himself. Now was not the time for rushing. He had approximately a hundred percussion caps and bullets within his saddlebag and just enough powder to fire the lot. If any were to strike their intended targets, he needed to be able to see where they were landing. And besides, he had the entire battle to coordinate! It was readily becoming apparent that the British garrison at Rorke's Drift, despite being hopelessly outnumbered, were not going to lay down without a fight. Zibhebhu was nowhere to be found and Dabulamanzi was the king's brother. He was, by default, in command of the entire action.

"No shoulder-high wall of grain sacks will deprive me of my victory," he growled. He shouldered his musket and fired again.

Twelve miles to the west, Major Henry Spalding sat astride his horse, taking in the sights as he leisurely rode towards the small depot at Helpmekaar another three miles on. To call Helpmekaar a 'depot' was being rather generous. Consisting of just three iron sheds and a pair of makeshift huts sitting atop a grassy hill, it was little more than a waypoint where supplies could be temporarily stored along the way to the various border crossings. In addition to supporting the No. 3 Column, fifteen miles away at Rorke's Drift, Helpmekaar was a staging ground for supplies headed for Colonel Pearson's No. 1 Column. Their crossing point at Thukela Drift was about ninety miles to the south, and that for Colonel Wood's No. 4 Column was roughly sixty miles to the north. Its strategic location made Helpmekaar the perfect place to stage rations, ammunition, and other supplies that could readily be sent to any one of the three columns in an emergency.

Though the sun beat down on him this afternoon, the rutted and rough dirt road was still soggy in places. His horse's hooves splashed through the occasional puddle, and he wondered to himself how anyone expected wagons to use such a torn-up wreck of a path without their wheels falling off!

Spalding halted for a moment to check his watch and take a drink from his water bottle. The once cool liquid had warmed in the sun and tasted like bath water. The major choked down a few gulps, supressing the urge to gag. It was now 4.45, and he was debating making his horse gallop the rest of the way. He'd taken his time and enjoyed the leisurely pace, glad as he was to be away from Rorke's Drift for a time. 'Gunny' Bromhead meant well, but his constant talking in such a loud voice, due to his partial deafness, was excruciating after a while. And that newly arrived engineer officer, John Chard, was about as boring a fellow as Henry Spalding had ever met. The only man at the depot whose company he actually enjoyed was Commissary Dalton.

Despite the contented reprieve he felt from being away from the depot, he knew if he delayed too long, he risked having to camp under the stars at Helpmekaar rather than in his tent at Rorke's Drift. While he was certainly not opposed to sleeping under the night sky, he knew how volatile the weather was in Southern Africa, and in January the blistering heat of day could turn to a cold torrential downpour in very short order.

As he pocketed his watch, Spalding saw a column of redcoats cresting a hill about a mile distant. "No need to go all the way to Helpmekaar after all," he said with a relieved sigh.

He pulled out his field glasses and scanned the column. He counted about 180 soldiers, marching four abreast, a pair of officers mounted on horses at their head. Sure enough, it was the two companies of infantry that he'd set out to find. He recognised one of the men as Brevet Major Russell Upcher, officer commanding of D Company, 1/24th. He assumed the other man was Captain Thomas Rainforth of G Company. Spalding kicked his horse into a gallop and rode forth to meet his errant reinforcements.

"Afternoon, Russell," he said, reining in his horse.

The two officers did the same. Their perplexed expressions puzzled Spalding.

"Henry," Upcher replied. "What are you doing out here?"

"What do you mean 'what am I doing out here'? I came looking for my lost reinforcements. You were supposed to be at Rorke's Drift days ago."

"The road from Greytown is an absolute nightmare," Upcher explained hastily. "We only arrived at Helpmekaar yesterday and planned on waiting a day for our supply wagons to catch up. I was actually going to ride to Rorke's Drift myself to let you know, when we heard the news."

"What news?" Spalding asked, his irritation now evident. "What are you going on about?"

"By God," his fellow major said, his expression one of horror. "You don't know?"

There was an uncomfortable pause. Russell Upcher was not sure how to tell Spalding about the disaster.

Captain Rainforth broke the silence. "The camp at Isandlwana has been destroyed."

"The devil, you say!" Spalding stammered. "When you say 'destroyed'..."

"I mean the camp was overrun and the garrison wiped out."

The blunt statement almost knocked the major from his horse. He looked to Upcher who nodded in confirmation.

"A few survivors have reached Helpmekaar. I assume you never saw them because they crossed about ten miles south of Rorke's Drift."

Major Upcher went on to explain to Spalding what he knew. Lord Chelmsford had left early that morning with half the column, thinking he was heading out to meet the Zulu *impi* to the east. Instead, the entire enemy army came in from the north and swarmed the camp. Though nothing had been confirmed, the officers were fairly certain both Lieutenant Colonel Pulleine and Lieutenant Colonel Durnford were dead.

"Dear God, I only saw Colonel Durnford depart this morning," Spalding said under his breath.

"If what those ragged lads from the rocket battery told me is true, Durnford is most likely dead, and his command wiped out," Upcher continued.

"Rocket battery?" Spalding asked.

"It was actually a bombardier and three soldiers from our C Company," Rainforth explained. He struggled to keep his voice from cracking. C Company's commander, Captain Reginald Younghusband, had been a close friend for nearly fifteen years. "The riflemen were attached to them. According to their account, they were overrun early in the fighting and the battery's officer commanding killed. They held in a donga for a while. When

Durnford ordered the retreat, they became cut off from the rest of No. 2 Column. According to the bombardier, thousands of Zulus were converging on the camp from multiple directions."

Another pause followed; Rainforth struggled to keep his emotions in check. Another dear friend of his, Captain William Mostyn, commanded the battalion's F Company. He, too, had been delayed by the terrible road conditions. Last they heard, he had reached Isandlwana just a few days ago. Spalding removed his hat for a moment.

Upcher's voice was hard. "Believe me, Henry, no one is more upset at our delay than us. That was *our* battalion that his lordship left to guard the camp. It is our friends who lie dead on the slopes of that accursed mountain."

"And now we must get to Rorke's Drift before it, too, is overrun," Rainforth added. He asked quizzically, "You've not left 'Gunny' Bromhead in command, have you?"

"Actually, no," Spalding replied, turning his horse around.

Major Upcher signalled for the column to continue to march as Henry told them about Lieutenant Chard, who happened to have three years seniority on Bromhead.

"Well, that's lovely, isn't it?" Rainforth said, his voice dripping with sarcasm. "A bloody engineer who's been in country all of a fortnight, with no combat experience, is now in command of a tiny garrison that, for all we know, may be facing down the entire Zulu army."

"Durnford was an engineer as well," Spalding recalled.

Russell Upcher did not even try to hide his disdain. A seasoned veteran of fifteen years with the Colours, he'd commanded a British force at the Battle of Quintana the previous February during the Xhosa War. It was his heroic actions and tactical savvy that earned him his brevet to major. He shook his head at the thought of an inexperienced engineer commanding what few British soldiers remained on the Natal border. It filled him with dread and loathing.

"Damn sappers will be the death of us all."

"Bugger me, who left the damn door open?" Corporal Alfred Saxty yelped, as a pair of enemy musket balls slapped the base of the mealie sack wall near his position along the eastern defences. The assistant leader of Sergeant Joseph Windridge's section, he and six privates were detached to defend the stone kraal just east of the courtyard, which they had linked to the northeast side of the storehouse with biscuit boxes and mealie sacks.

"Get your fucking heads down!" Sergeant Smith shouted to the men, hunkering low as he ran to Saxty's position. Peering just over the wall, he scanned the far slopes of Shiyane with his field glasses.

Near the crest, there was a long plateau of flat rock, jutting out from the hillside. One could easily spot the scores of Zulus with muskets firing away. Many were kneeling, others lay flat on their stomachs. Less visible were those occupying the lower slope, particularly the numerous caves beneath the rocky ledge. However, he was able to discern the puffs of smoke each time these warriors fired their old muskets.

"Keep low, lads," the sergeant said. "Index four hundred yards and concentrate on the hillside. Aim for the smoke."

"That's bloody well all we can see is smoke," one private grumbled, as the enemy marksmen became obscured by the thick clouds emitted from their weapons.

"Controlled shots," Smith added. "Don't be popping off at random shit!" He then said to Saxty, "I'll get some more men over to help you. If we don't stuff those bastards on the hill, they could make life difficult for us."

The corporal nodded and set the slide on his rear sight to the number *4* line. He pulled the rifle tight into his shoulder, his eye fixed on the front sight post. A gentle gust created a break in the smoke; a Zulu feverishly worked the ramrod on his musket.

"Got you, you bastard!"

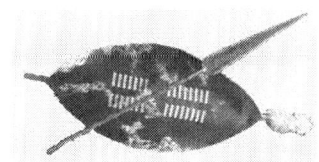

Lurking beneath the rocky ledge along Shiyane in one of the deep caves was John Chard's African driver, Sanele. He'd found a large cave, partially obscured by a bush, that overlooked the depot. It went back a few feet before turning sharply and paralleling the plateau just above his head for about a dozen yards before coming out at another cave entrance.

Sanele was no coward, but as a wagon driver he had not been provided any sort of weapons by the British. He had a small bundle of throwing assegais which he primarily used for hunting but no shield or firearms. He understood just enough English to discern that a terrible disaster had occurred a few miles across the river, and a massive force of Zulus was coming for them. Sanele felt there was little the small force of men in red jackets could do, and he did not reckon he could outrun the approaching warriors. He also knew, given his attire of a corduroy jacket and brown trousers, he would be identified as a British servant and immediately killed. Even more pressing was his concern for his son, who'd ran for the hills in the west as soon as the Natal warriors deserted. Terror gripping him, he knew his best chance of survival lay in hiding in one of the many caves that overlooked the mission station.

Caves beneath rocky shelf along the slope of Shiyane Mountain

Soon the sound of rifle fire echoed from below, accompanied by the chants and war cries of the first wave of attacking enemy warriors. Sanele hunkered low, occasionally peering through the cracks between the rocks that made up the cave wall. Within minutes he could see the Zulu regiment retiring away from the British south rampart. Many bodies lay scattered about, though it was difficult to tell if they were dead, wounded, or simply skirmishers seeking cover.

The bang of a musket firing over his head, amplified by the echoing off the cave walls, startled him. His heart leapt into his throat as more shots rang out. He was suddenly aware of movement just outside the cave. The hillside was swarming with Zulus. Sanele suddenly felt very foolish for choosing this as his hiding place. He heard the frantic voices of several warriors as they clambered into the cave. There were at least three of them, and Sanele reckoned there were more at the far end, where the tunnel came out again. The crack of their muskets pounded his ear drums. He struggled against the urge to cough as his lungs sucked in the acrid smoke. He could further see the shadows of warriors just outside where he lurked. He lay on his stomach, peering through a wide break between two support boulders of the cliff. His view was obscured by an enemy warrior kneeling behind a small bush. The man was ramming a fresh musket ball down the barrel of his rifle when suddenly the back of his neck exploded in a spray of blood and gore. The exiting bullet smacked into the rock wall, just above where Sanele lay. The wagon driver jolted and watched the lifeless body of the Zulu marksman fall onto its side and twitch a few times as death claimed him.

Curling himself into a ball, Sanele feared his friends below were as great a threat to him as the Zulus who now had him trapped inside the cave. It seemed his son had been wise in heading west!

Chapter IX: The Tragedy of Isandlwana

Along the trail to Mangeni, east of Isandlwana
22 January 1879
5.00 p.m.

Lieutenant General Sir Frederic Thesiger, Lord Chelmsford
General Officer Commanding (GOC)

"I don't understand," Lord Chelmsford moaned. He struggled to come to grips with the brutal calamity that had befallen the garrison at Isandlwana. "I left a thousand men to guard the camp!"

In the early hours well before sunrise, the GOC led over half of No. 3 Column, to include most of the 24th Regiment's 2nd Battalion, four of the column's six cannon, plus most of the mounted troops and NNC warriors, in what he hoped would be a decisive engagement with the main Zulu *impi*. Intelligence reports from the 3rd NNC Regiment encamped overnight near Mangeni Falls led Chelmsford to believe he was headed for a decisive clash with Cetshwayo's forces. Instead, it turned out the main *impi* was never at Mangeni Falls. The scores of campfires spotted throughout the night by the NNC had been a ruse by a much smaller Zulu force, likely belonging to a local chieftain, to make their numbers appear much larger than they were. This was likely to intimidate the British auxiliaries, so they would not attack their lands.

The column had arrived at Mangeni piecemeal. Troops of carbineers, mounted redcoats from the Imperial Mounted Infantry (IMI), and numerous bands of NNC warriors engaged in a series of skirmishes all along the valley and across several of the surrounding hills. By the time the regulars from 2/24th arrived on the field around midmorning, it was becoming plain that the *impi* was nowhere to be found. Though his men had killed around sixty Zulus with just a handful of losses suffered by the NNC, the GOC became convinced the *impi* was still at the king's royal kraal at Ulundi more than forty miles to the east. Instead, Ntshingwayo had led his massive army of 25,000 warriors to the north, running twenty miles over mountaintops and extremely rough terrain before descending on Isandlwana.

The whole debacle at Mangeni may have seemed like a ruse to draw Chelmsford away from the camp, but unbeknownst to him and the rest of the British column, Ntshingwayo had no idea they were even there. Given the surrender of several local chieftains near the Natal border, there had been much confusion and suspicion from many of the *amakhosi*, who doubted the loyalty of the very warriors Chelmsford would battle against that day. In the end, it was the most unfortunate of circumstances and false intelligence that led half of No. 3 Column away from the camp. That the Zulus were as blind to their enemy's movements as he was, may have in fact saved his lordship's life. With his assault force scattered along the route of march, they would have been a prime target for the Zulus. The two main adversaries, who wished to meet in a single decisive engagement, simply missed each other in the night.

His lordship had received a couple of extremely vague reports from Isandlwana earlier that morning regarding a force of Zulus approaching the camp. Given the lack of detail from Lieutenant Colonel Pulleine's despatches, Chelmsford had paid it little mind. He reckoned whatever bands of enemy warriors happened to be roaming the region, Pulleine and the lads from 1/24th would sort them out.

Convinced the Zulu *impi* was still at Ulundi. Chelmsford decided to make Mangeni Falls the next major camp along their axis of advance. The GOC sent Major Stuart Smith of the Royal Artillery back to Isandlwana with orders for Pulleine to break camp at once, and have the rest of the column meet him at Mangeni. Hours later, when no confirmation had been communicated back to him, Chelmsford took it upon himself to ride back with much of the staff to see what the issue was. Little did he know, Major Smith and almost his entire entourage were dead.

It was when they came across a battalion from the NNC detailed to provide a labour force for the camp, that his lordship knew something was terribly amiss. The news he received from Commandant George 'Maori' Browne of the NNC was so devastating and unbelievable, he at first berated Browne for telling him such a *'dreadful falsehood'*. Only when he could personally see the burning tents in the distance did Chelmsford come to grips with the brutal reality.

Having expressed his grief about the men he left to guard the camp, he quickly turned to Major Gosset, one of his aides-de-camp (ADC).

"Ride back to Mangeni," he ordered. "The entire column is to return to Isandlwana at once."

"Right away, my lord," Gosset replied, throwing up a quick salute before riding away.

The accompanying staff officers were talking amongst themselves as they scanned the camp in the distance with their field glasses, trying to ascertain what, exactly, had happened to Pulleine and his garrison. 'Maori' Browne was quite distressed, as Henry Pulleine was a close friend of his. The two had managed to reunite a few days earlier when Pulleine assumed command of 1st Battalion of the 24th.

The only officer not engaged in the frantic speculation was Colonel Richard Glyn. Previously the commanding officer of $1/24^{th}$, before being brevetted to full colonel and given command of the entire No. 3 Column, his heart sank as a feeling of dread came over him. In truth, he was column commander in name only. Lord Chelmsford had taken personal charge, thereby usurping Glyn of any actual control over his soldiers. Henry Pulleine had previously served as one of his battalion majors, prior to being dispatched to command his own locally-raised units during the last Cape Frontier

War. Richard was proud to see Pulleine assume command of their beloved battalion; the officers were like brothers to them.

As he sat in horrified silence, the names of all the officers from the battalion staff, as well as the five companies who garrisoned the camp, ran through his mind. He recalled during an inspection of Captain George Wardell's H Company all the young faces in the ranks; nearly a third were new men who'd been in the Army less than two years. Was every one of them now dead? Such thoughts were inconceivable. Yet, even without his field glasses, Colonel Glyn could clearly see the columns of smoke coming from the burning tents.

"My brothers," he whispered. "What happened?"

Along the slopes of Isandlwana, the sounds of gunfire and savage fighting had ceased, leaving an unnerving silence clinging to the land. A cloud of acrid smoke still hung over the landscape of horror. In a divine sign that the fighting was at last over, an eclipse of the sun that had cast an unholy shadow upon the battlefield throughout the afternoon finally passed. The broken rays of sunlight danced off the wafts of black powder smoke, accented by the flames and smoke from the burning tents, creating an ethereal pall over the scene of death.

The carnage was horrific. Red-jacketed British soldiers and European settler volunteers lay in pools of their own blood and entrails. Each and every one had been stabbed multiple times and then disembowelled. Black Africans from across the border in Natal who fought as auxiliaries for the invaders were treated no better. In many cases, their corpses had been treated with profound disrespect, as enraged Zulus mutilated them out of sheer malice. Civilian wagon drivers and other volunteers, along with carbineers and irregular members of the various Natal militias, were butchered beside their regular army counterparts. This had truly been a battle without quarter.

For the Zulus, the price in blood and abject suffering was severe. The ground was littered with the broken bodies of brave warriors who were subjected to the merciless hell-storm of British rifle fire. The dead lay twisted in gruesome positions: the backs of heads blown out, hearts and lungs shredded, limbs shattered, and guts torn through the gaping exit wounds caused by the large calibre Martini-Henry rifles. And for many of the far more numerous wounded, the dead were the fortunate ones. Even the bravest of warriors fought in vain to hold back their cries of agony from splintered arm and leg bones protruding through the skin. Others clutched at their mutilated guts. Some were missing arms or legs, with hideous stumps of shredded flesh all that remained as their life's blood gushed onto the trampled grass.

"A bloody, yet glorious day, *inkosi*," an older warrior said to his commander-in-chief. They stood atop the Nyoni ridge, overlooking the battlefield.

The Zulu *inkosi*, Ntshingwayo, stoically gazed upon the carnage of the devastated encampment down below. As one of King Cetshwayo's most trusted generals, and the man who had orchestrated the attack, he could expect much praise from his sovereign. He watched the survivors of his regiments, the *amabutho*, disembowel and loot the British dead. Despite the magnitude of their victory, he did not feel like the triumphant conqueror. At seventy years of age, having served in countless campaigns for the Zulu royal house, he understood the cost in suffering that came with every triumph. But never in all his years had he seen loss of life on such a dreadful scale. Watching so many of the sons of Zulu fall during each surge of the attack, it was a major credit to the relentless courage of his regiments that they managed to overwhelm their enemies in red jackets.

His sorrow at the sight of so many dead and maimed warriors also came with a distinct measure of relief. The phases of the moon had portended a day of ill-omen, plus he knew he needed to conduct a thorough reconnaissance of the enemy camp. It was only because the entire *impi* was discovered by a wayward band of British-led African carbineers that Ntshingwayo was compelled to launch his attack a day early. Blind to his adversary's strength and disposition, and with the omens promising disaster, his huge force of 25,000 warriors unleashed the 'Horns of the Beast'.

With thousands of warriors in each element, they attempted to surround the enemy camp, laid out along the eastern slope of Isandlwana. Much that could have gone wrong did, as the *amabutho* were soon scattered into a vast frontage extending for miles in either direction with no way to directly coordinate the dispersed elements. Many overzealous warriors in the 'Chest', conducting the main assault, had sprinted ahead in a rare lapse of discipline. It was only when volleys of British musketry cut swaths through their ranks that they went to ground and waited for reinforcements. The Left and Right Horns had to act on their own initiative, following Ntshingwayo's overall intent. The 'Left Horn', in particular, withstood a severe punishing from the enemy's mounted troops who had occupied a protective donga.

"Bravery and discipline carried the day," the *inkosi* said, with a slow nod of approval.

There were many tense moments when Ntshingwayo thought the attack would fail. For a time, the warriors in the 'Chest' simply could not move out of their defilades without being torn to shreds by their adversaries' terrifyingly accurate and relentless firepower. And despite outnumbering their foes 20-to-1, the Zulus' own firearms were archaic muskets in disrepair and terribly inaccurate. It was only when the 'Left Horn' managed to drive in the force of British and Natal cavalry on the southern flank that the battle finally began to turn in the Zulus' favour. The wayward regiments of the 'Right Horn' finally completed their long trek around Isandlwana by this time, thereby closing the trap. Still the redcoats refused to break, and as they formed into close-order squares, bayonets protruding, they made the *amabutho* bleed for every inch of ground.

"The battle is won, *inkosi!*" an excited messenger said, having sprinted his way from the heart of the British camp. The young man's spear was covered in blood; his excitement and feelings of triumph pushing any thoughts of sorrow at the loss of so many of his friends into the deep recesses of his mind for the time being.

Ntshingwayo acknowledged him and signalled for the other *amakhosi* to follow him down the hill. Regiments were scattered for miles, and the Zulu commanding general knew he needed to consolidate and account for his forces as soon as possible. He recalled the king expressly forbidding his armies from crossing the uMzinyathi River into British territory. Yet even the most disciplined of the *amabutho* were not immune to being overcome by bloodlust. Ntshingwayo was rightfully concerned that bands of wayward warriors in pursuit of the few survivors who'd escaped the slaughter, might continue the chase into Natal. Most Zulus were terrible swimmers, and the river served as a natural barrier between the two kingdoms. However, any barrier could be breached with sufficient numbers and relentless determination.

"Send runners to the Chest and Horns," he ordered his assembled *amakhosi*. "The *amabutho* is to muster at the enemy camp, that we might carry away our fallen brothers and begin the journey home."

Within the camp, the *induna*, Mehlokazulu, walked sombrely back along the path his regiment, the iNgobamakhosi, had taken as part of the 'Left Horn'. His spear was slick with blood, and he wore an unbuttoned tunic taken from a British officer he had slain. He knew the man was an *induna* like him, for he had carried a sword and pistol rather than a rifle. Both were claimed as prizes by two of his warriors, while Mehlokazulu stripped the corpse of its tunic. It was tradition that those who killed should wear a piece of clothing taken from their adversaries as part of the spiritually cleansing rituals that would follow any major battle.

"That jacket is a fine trophy," said a fellow *induna*, who then donned a captured blue patrol cap.

"A reminder of a worthy foe," Mehlokazulu concurred. He scanned the appalling landscape once more and shook his head. "Not that I could ever forget this day."

The starkest reminder of all would come when he sought accountability of his warriors. As one of the king's personal favourites, a member of a distinguished house, as well as a valiant and selfless warrior, Mehlokazulu had been given command over three companies prior to the *impi's* departure from Ulundi. This meant he had three hundred men to account for. When he called out to his warriors and assembled them near the base of a smaller hill where the enemy mounted troops had made their final stand, less than half heeded his call. He knew there were still others who were looting the camp for weapons and treasure, yet having so many of his men missing was unnerving.

As he inspected his warriors, most of whom were battered and exhausted, Mehlokazulu's thoughts returned to the seemingly endless horrors his companies in the front ranks of the iNgobamakhosi had endured. More than anything, he wished to find the bodies of every one of his fallen men, to kneel beside them, and say goodbye as their spirits made their way to the afterlife. But it was not to be. The day was growing late, and Ntshingwayo had ordered the *amabutho* to retire to their bivouac behind Mabaso Hill. This meant covering nine miles, while encumbered by thousands of wounded. There was little they could do for the dead at the moment.

For Mehlokazulu, the images of the dead burned into his mind would forever haunt him. The redcoats had been a worthy foe, one he admired rather than hated. Though the battle ended in victory for his people, Isandlwana would forever cast a shadow upon both Zulu and British alike.

Chapter X: Alright, Sir, We'll do it

Mangeni Falls, twenty-five miles east of Rorke's Drift
22 January 1879
5.00 p.m.

Lieutenant Colonel Henry Degacher
Commanding Officer, 2/24th Regiment

At Mangeni Falls, the only forces reasonably concentrated were the six companies of redcoats from Lieutenant Colonel Henry Degacher's 2nd Battalion of the 24th, along with the four guns from N Battery. Mounted troops and NNC warriors were still scattered about the surrounding hills. The sporadic fighting had ended hours before, and with the GOC riding back to see what the delay was with the rest of the column, Degacher was designating where his companies would encamp that night.

"It would be nice if our tents arrived before nightfall," one of his commanders, Captain Mainwaring, remarked.

"Thankfully, the skies are still clear," Degacher replied, his arms folded across his chest as he gazed at the large gorge that extended away from the falls. "Magnificent view, isn't it?"

"That it is, sir."

The grumbling in his stomach reminded Henry that he had not eaten since breakfast. For the men in the ranks, their hunger was compounded by exhaustion. Having been roused at 2.30 that morning, they had gotten very little sleep the night before. And while most of the officers had horses, the enlisted soldiers walked the fifteen miles from Isandlwana to Mangeni, and then fought a series of skirmishes throughout much of the day.

"All companies have marked out their camps, sir," the sergeant major reported. "They've designated picquets and sentry duties. Now all we need to do is wait for supper and our tents to arrive…not to mention ammunition."

"Thank you, sergeant major," the colonel acknowledged. "Do we know how many cartridges the men still have?"

"Yes, sir. I've compiled resupply requests from each company to give to Quartermaster Bloomfield. Though we didn't face the hordes of the Zulu *impi* like most of the lads hoped, they still went through about a third of their allotment."

Degacher nodded. "Let us hope that rations and bullets arrive soon, then. We may have missed them here, but the Zulu army is out there somewhere."

Like most of his fellow officers, his gaze was constantly drawn to the east towards the royal kraal at Ulundi. It would not be long before they discovered that the *impi* was not in the east, but to the west, behind them.

One of Chelmsford's ADCs, Captain Parr, was with the officers of the 24th when someone called out, *"Rider approaching!"*

Some nearby soldiers of the 24th heard the call. Many forgot the pain in their stomachs for a moment.

"Hallo!" a private said, as he pointed towards the trail of dust behind the fast-galloping rider. "There's a man in a hurry. He ought to have a fresh horse behind every hill at the rate he's riding. Here, can you see who it is?"

"By Jove, it's Major Gosset," a sentry replied, gazing through his sergeant's field glasses. "Why is he coming back in such a rush? I hope nothing has gone wrong."

A bevy of curious onlookers who spotted the major galloping with all speed gathered around as the major made his way to Lieutenant Colonel Degacher.

Gosset's face was flushed, his horse slobbering and panting from the extreme exertion. "Colonel, sir," he said, saluting.

"Major," the colonel replied. "You seem to be in a great hurry."

"The general's orders are to march back to Isandlwana at once." Gosset's expression betrayed the strain he was under. "There's been a terrible disaster; the Zulus have gotten into our camp."

"The Zulus?" Degacher asked in disbelief. "You're not joking, are you? Because if you are, it is in poor taste."

"I wish I was," Gosset replied grimly. "Commandant Lonsdale met Chelmsford about five miles from the camp. He'd seen the enemy among the tents. His lordship is waiting for you with the mounted men."

Degacher's face turned pale. "Find the bugler," the colonel ordered Captain Parr. "Sound officers' call and get the column on its feet."

Though his mind was filled with a bevy of questions, the captain kept them to himself and simply saluted before rushing to find the nearest bandsman with a bugle.

"You have got to be kidding me," Charlie Harford grumbled, when he heard the frantic and uneven calls from a bugle in the distance. As he sat on a rock, emptying all manner of pebbles and dirt from his filthy boots, he saw Major Dartnell of the Natal Mounted Police riding towards him from where the 2/24th was assembling. It was Dartnell who had led the expedition to Mangeni Falls the previous day. Neither he nor Harford had slept in two days, and all Charlie wanted was to crawl underneath the nearest shrubbery and sleep for about twenty hours.

"Come along, Mister Harford. Gather your men with all haste; we're headed back to Isandlwana."

"Your pardon, sir, but why?"

"I'm not sure, exactly," Dartnell said. "Though from what I overheard from the 24th officers, there's been a terrible disaster."

"The only disaster is that the rest of the column has not arrived with our supper and baggage," Harford muttered. He knew of Chelmsford's intent to bring the rest of the army to Mangeni. In fact, he had sent Commandant Browne's entire battalion of NNC warriors to assist. And with Rupert Lonsdale accompanying his lordship, that left Acting-Captain Charlie Harford in command of the rest of the

Natal Native Contingent. This would prove fortuitous when it came to rallying his wayward companies, as Harford was one of the only white men at Mangeni who spoke fluent Zulu.

"Hlangani amaqhawe!" he shouted, pulling his boots on, ordering his nearest fighters to begin recalling their mates.

Dartnell rode off to find his own troopers from the NMP and volunteer carbineers.

Because many elements of No. 3 Column were scattered far and wide among the hills and dales near Mangeni Falls, it took some time to relay Chelmsford's orders to the entire force. Unlike most of the column, Harford had been in a rather savage scrap with a sizeable force of Zulus defending the nearby caves.

"Come on, old girl," he said, rubbing the muzzle of his tired horse. "Let's go find our friends."

With a groan, he pulled himself into the saddle and assessed his surroundings. He shouted his orders in Zulu once more. As these were echoed by his men, the scattered companies of the NNC quickly made their way to the site of the main camp. One thing troubling Harford was that their numbers were noticeably fewer. While they had sustained some casualties during the day's fighting, they were not severe. Charlie gritted his teeth with the knowledge that some of his warriors had started to desert. Worse still, there was nothing he could do about it for the time being. He turned his horse about and rode towards the call of the bugles. Near the nek of a mountain called Mdutshane just north of Mangeni Falls, he came across Major Wilsone Black from 2/24th. The two already shared a number harrowing adventures during the campaign and had gotten to know each other quite well.

"What is happening, major?" Harford asked. "I heard the call to assemble but nothing else."

"The camp has been attacked." Black replied in his heavy Scottish accent. He shook his head. "I haven't heard the details yet, but if Chelmsford is ordering us to make for Isandlwana, something very serious has occurred." He gave a grin etched with nervousness and added, "Just keep your damned dark fellows out of the way."

"Well, they did take a beating today," Harford said with a strained look of his own. "No doubt they'll happily let the 24th take the lead back to camp."

When Black returned to his battalion, Degacher relayed to him his subsequent conversation with Major Gosset regarding the magnitude of the disaster. As best as anyone could tell, the camp had been completely overrun.

"I would like to think some of the lads managed to fight their way back to Rorke's Drift," the colonel added.

"A fighting retreat, over ten miles?" Black asked himself quietly. Like his commanding officer, he knew that such a feat was likely impossible, especially if Pulleine's lads had in fact faced the entire Zulu *impi*. His face taught, he simply said, "I'm sorry, sir."

Though he did his best to put on a stoic front, Wilsone knew Henry Degacher was completely devastated. Earlier that day, he had sent his adjutant, Lieutenant Henry Dyer, back to Isandlwana to help with the breaking down of 2nd Battalion's camp. To make matters worse, Degacher's own brother, William, was an officer with 1st Battalion. If the camp had indeed fallen, there was little chance either man had survived. Furthermore, 2nd Battalion's G Company under Lieutenant Charlie Pope had been left behind, ostensibly to give them a day of rest after having just completed a 24-hour picquet detail. Wilsone steeled his resolve. Now was not the time for sorrows, especially when most of the facts were still unknown. And yet, as a way of acknowledgement, he quietly hoped Charlie Pope and his men had died well.

As for the men in the ranks, the call to assemble and return to Isandlwana was, at first, met with much grumbling. After all, they had been up since 2.30 that morning, marched fifteen miles in the dark, and engaged in a series of skirmishes all afternoon. They were hot, tired, and had not eaten since they sat down for a humble breakfast of hard biscuits and tinned bully beef around 11.00. The NNC and carbineers under Major Dartnell were in an even worse state, having spent all night encamped on the ridge overlooking Mangeni, facing what they thought was the Zulu *impi*. And none had eaten since breakfast the previous morning. The minds of every man in No. 3 Column were muddled by exhaustion and ravenous hunger.

Irritation soon turned to alarm, however, as word of the reason for their hasty return spread throughout the ranks. Captain Mainwaring of A Company, 2/24th felt the need to address his men directly and bluntly.

"We were humbugged, lads," he said, pulling a quote from the Duke of Wellington prior to the Battle of Waterloo. "But I can only give you the facts as I know them. The Zulus have the camp, though we know nothing about the fate of our friends left behind to guard it." Mainwaring was a friend of Charlie Pope, and he had a high opinion of the battalion's young adjutant, Lieutenant Dyer. Though he feared the worst, he did not lend any speculation to his words. The enemy had sacked Isandlwana, and it was enough to change the demeanour of his men from grudging annoyance to fierce determination.

Despite the sense of urgency stressed by Major Gosset, it still took the better part of an hour to assemble their force and make ready to begin the long march back the way they'd come that morning. A detail from the NNC was left at Mangeni to see to the wounded warriors who they refused to leave behind.

"That's the last we'll see of them," Major Dartnell grumbled. "If the Zulus don't get them, they'll bugger off and head home."

"The iziGqoza will return," Captain Harford replied, referring to the Zulu cousins who had been violently expelled by Cetshwayo during his rise to power. Thus far, they were the only warriors within the NNC to prove their stalwart mettle in battle.

As soon as the battalion was assembled, Henry Degacher ordered 2/24th to move out. A handful of mounted infantry and carbineers screened their march, while the four guns from N Battery followed behind the column of redcoats. With shouted orders from Charlie Harford, the NNC slinked behind the main force. It was another two hours before they reached the GOC. Chelmsford was beside himself with frustration at their delay.

"In God's name, what kept you?" he asked with impatience. "You should have been here hours ago."

"Your pardon, my lord," Degacher replied, "But we had to first consolidate the column, which was scattered across the hills."

"Took some time to assemble my guns as well," Lieutenant Colonel Harness of the artillery spoke up.

Chelmsford gave a curt nod before riding over to the assembled companies from 2/24th. He could see the fatigue and hunger in their faces, but also the hint of anger at the Zulus. Never one to give grand speeches, the GOC felt compelled to at least say something to his battered soldiers.

"Men," he said. "Whilst we were skirmishing in front, the enemy has taken the camp. There are ten thousand Zulus behind us and twenty thousand to our front. We must win back the camp tonight and cut our way back to Rorke's Drift in the morning. No man must retire, no order to retreat given. There is only one way home for us."

Though he did not expect an ovation, Chelmsford was somewhat unsettled by the abject silence of his men. He hadn't said anything they didn't already know, and during the two-hour trek from Mangeni, many had time to speculate that they would have to make their way clear back to Rorke's Drift. After all, if the Zulus had sacked the camp, then there was little chance of them finding food. This paled in comparison, however, to the abject dread each man felt regarding the fate of their friends. And none dared speak aloud the fear they all shared, that the Zulus had attacked Rorke's Drift as well. If the depot had fallen, the column would be in a dire state come morning.

"Alright, sir," a corporal finally spoke up, breaking the awkward silence. "We'll do it."

"As if we have any fucking choice," a despondent private muttered a little too loudly.

Normally, such words would have been met with a sharp rebuke and the possibility of being brought up on charges for gross insubordination. Yet even Chelmsford's military secretary, Lieutenant Colonel Crealock, who under most circumstances would have voraciously demanded the man be court-martialled, was silent.

Chelmsford simply turned to Colonel Glyn. "Have the men refill their canteens, then be ready to march." By his presence, Chelmsford had usurped all authority from the man who was technically the commanding officer of No. 3 Column; however, in front of the men, the GOC gave the appearance that it was still Glyn's force. It was also a way of bringing the colonel out of his shattered stupor. Ever since 'Maori' Browne informed them of the calamity, the man who spent over twenty years with the 24th had been in a state of shock.

"Colonel Harness," Glyn said, finding his voice. "Your guns will occupy the centre of the formation, keeping to the wagon track.

Colonel Degacher, the 24th will form into columns of four on either side."

"Sir," both officers replied before turning their horses about to address their men.

As soldiers filled their canteens and artillery crewmen watered their horses, Glyn sought out Commandant Lonsdale of the 3rd NNC, ordering his two battalions to form up on either flank of the 24th. As Lonsdale was still in a muddled state, due to a recent head injury, he deferred much of the actual command to acting-Captain Charlie Harford. The Imperial Mounted Infantry and Natal Mounted Police were to the right of 2/3rd NNC, while the carbineers and other mounted elements rode to the left of 1/3rd NNC.

The column made its way in silence as the falling sun glared into their faces. Even the warriors of the NNC could sense something terrible had happened, though few spoke English and their officers mostly failed to tell them what transpired. There was no singing or chanting from them, just the cadence of their weapons against their shields as they trotted along next to the quickly marching columns of imperial soldiers.

Chapter XI: A Doctor's Bravery

Rorke's Drift, north side of the hospital
5.30 p.m.

Surgeon James Henry Reynolds
Battalion Doctor, 1/24th Regiment

While Lieutenant Colonel Degacher and Major Gosset were marching their men back to link up with Lord Chelmsford, the garrison at Rorke's Drift, particularly Lieutenant Gonville Bromhead, were surprised to still be alive. It was with macabre humour that he told Private Hitch they could manage the Zulus for just a few moments. He did not think that over an hour later he would still be among the living. The initial charge on the south rampart had been checked, and the Zulus' first attempt to breach the northwest angle had failed.

The officer commanding of B Company had personally killed or badly wounded at least five Zulu warriors during the fierce bayonet fighting near the hospital veranda. Once the attack was repelled, he recalled his detachment and ordered them to take cover near the hospital. Soldiers knelt and caught their breath, but for 'Gunny' Bromhead, there would be no reprieve. Though Lieutenant Chard was in overall command, the soldiers in B Company were still Bromhead's responsibility.

"Keep this section near the hospital, colour sergeant," he directed.

Between his own gasps for breath, Frank Bourne gave an affirmative, 'Sir!'

Bromhead crept low and made his way along the south wall, checking on Sergeant Gallagher's section. The Irish NCO was keeping low near the wagons. As Henry loosed another shot at the enemy skirmishers on the hillside, the lieutenant was startled to see what looked like a small flash coming from the breach of Gallagher's weapon.

"Everything alright, sergeant?"

"As well as can be expected, sir," Gallagher replied bluntly. "Those bastards on the hill aren't exactly the best of shots. Still, they are enough of a nuisance that they're keeping us pinned down. Plus, we're having to expend a lot of cartridges stuffing them. At this range, and with all the bloody smoke, it's difficult to tell how many of them we've hit."

A scream came from the hill just then, and the two soldiers watched as a Zulu marksman pitched headfirst off the rocky plateau.

"I'd say you're giving it to them far better than they are to you," Bromhead surmised.

"That we are, sir." The sergeant chambered another round, checked his sites, and fired once more at the hillside.

"Damn it, man, what's wrong with your rifle?" Bromhead asked, noting the flash again coming from the breach.

"One of the seams along the breach has come apart," Gallagher replied.

"Shouldn't you find a replacement?"

"There aren't any left. All the spare rifles in the storehouse were given to the walking wounded. Not to worry, sir. My weapon isn't likely to blow up in my face. Might just leave a bit of a mark is all." He rubbed his cheek where a red welt was forming.

At the far end of the line, the secondary wall of biscuit boxes bisected the compound from the edge of the storehouse to the north wall. Given the number of men in the hospital, Bromhead hoped they would not have to collapse the perimeter and pull everyone back behind this inner rampart. To do so would mean abandoning over thirty patients, as well as the men assigned to protect them.

"Ah, Mister Bromhead," Lieutenant Chard said, making his way across the veranda where Surgeon Reynolds was bandaging the wounds of a few of the minor wounded.

"Just checking on my men," 'Gunny' replied. "I take it you've come from the kraal."

Chard nodded. "Yes. I had Sergeant Smith place a few more men there, as your corporal…"

"Saxty," Bromhead replied, when Chard could not remember the man's name.

"Yes, Corporal Saxty has been pretty hard pressed by enemy muskets. But I think for the moment our southern defences are sound. It's the north wall that worries me now, particularly near the hospital veranda."

"I agree," Bromhead concurred. "Colour Sergeant Bourne and the flying platoon are ready to plug any gaps in the lines. But I feel we are spread too thin. We also did not have time to properly build up the defensive wall in front of the veranda."

Chard contemplated the situation for a moment, then shook his head. The thought of abandoning the defences on the north side of the hospital troubled him, yet he knew it would soon prove untenable. Zulu marksmen were converging behind the five-foot wall just below the short cliff. Scarcely ten yards separated the stone wall and the rampart. He made mention of this to Bromhead.

"At that range, even their marksmen can't miss," 'Gunny' said begrudgingly.

"Alright," Chard replied, making his decision. "We'll hold for now, but get ready to pull our men back from the veranda. The hospital defenders will have to hold the northern flank off the veranda on their own."

Bromhead said nothing but gave a grim nod of understanding. Chard took a deep breath, trying in his mind to keep a few steps in front of his Zulu adversaries. With each passing moment, this was becoming ever more difficult. He also knew that Colour Sergeant Bourne and their bayonet fighters would be called into the fray to plug the gaps soon enough.

"Return to the flying platoon, Mister Bromhead."

For Mandlenkosi and, indeed, every warrior of the uThulwana who hunkered in the brush, it was clear the defences along the north side of the hospital were the weak point. Further on, the gently sloping ground abruptly dropped off, forming a six-foot cliff. Normally, this would not be an obstacle for a fit Zulu warrior; however, this entire face was topped by a four-foot wall of mealie sacks. And the rampart was itself lined with British soldiers. His men were becoming anxious, but the *induna* knew there was little they could do, except continue to unleash a steady barrage of musketry into the defence works.

"*Usutu!*" a voice shouted from off to their left.

Mandlenkosi watched in dismay as a force of about 500 warriors from another regiment rose out of the brush and charged towards the rampart.

Though it shamed Mandlenkosi, he was relieved that this brazen assault drew some of the redcoats' fire away from his men. Salvos of musketry tore into the charging warriors, the impact knocking many off their feet as their bodies were smashed. A cloud of pink mist came off each stricken fighter as they were shot down; the rifle bullets tearing through them mercilessly. They had been within 200 paces when they rose up and charged; a distance the fleet-footed warriors could cover in less than a minute. However, within that minute, a desperate British soldier could fire ten to twelve rounds from his breach-loading rifle.

Nearly a hundred warriors had fallen by the time the rest reached the ramparts. At least twenty were dead, and an equal number would likely never rise again. Those who tried to scale the short cliff found themselves in an impossible situation. One simply could not effectively wield a shield and climb at the same time. A few brave souls discarded their shields and tried to scale the ramparts, carrying just their spears and knobkerries.

The first man gave a loud war cry to fuel his rage, clutching at the mealie sacks as he dug his feet into the rock face. As the tried to propel himself to the top a bayonet splintered his sternum, plunging into the warrior's heart. His mouth agape, he tried to scream, though not a sound would pass his lips. Blood gushed from the terrible wound. His heart spasmed and pounded violently as it was ruptured. The bayonet became stuck and the rifle was nearly wrenched from the soldier's hands. He managed to keep hold and pulled it free. The valiant warrior's eyes went dark. He was just able to sense his body striking the ground before his soul departed.

The slain man's companions fared little better. Their spears and clubs could not compete with the height and reach afforded to the imperial soldiers. Bayonets pierced faces and eyes, plunged into throats and hearts, while fired bullets smashed those still trying to reach the ramparts.

A subsequent force of several companies attempted to storm up the slope towards the centre of the compound. Many of these men were shot down before their companions could engage in close combat with the British. It was all for naught. Though the line of soldiers seemed precariously thin, from somewhere within the compound a large force rushed into the fray, driving the assailants back once more. There was no order to be had during each retreat, for the Zulus knew their shields were useless against the heavy slugs fired by the Martini-Henry rifle. And yet many a brave warrior scrambled away backwards, keeping his face towards his foe, lest his spirit bear the shame of being shot in the back.

"Brave fools," Mandlenkosi lamented. During all his years within the *amabutho*, he had never seen the need to possess a firearm of his own. He was among the very few *izinduna* of the uThulwana devoid of a musket, and he now realised his folly. Relentless musketry would win the day for the Undi Corps, not reckless charges against a fortified position bristling with bayonet-wielding redcoats.

The sun was starting to fall in the west, and Mandlenkosi noticed one of his skirmishers lying still in the grass. The man was on his stomach, and it looked like he had his rifle shouldered, ready to fire. Mandlenkosi parted the tall grass and saw the top of the warrior's head was caved in, where a bullet had smashed into his skull. His face twisting in anger, the induna took the man's firearm and ammunition bag. Rising to one knee, he shouldered the weapon and fired. It had been many years since he'd shot a musket and the kick startled him.

The grass and brush around him whipped and snapped from the defenders' return fire. At perhaps 200 paces from the ramparts, Mandlenkosi knew he was well within the effective range of the soldiers' rifles. He also knew that his newly-acquired musket was virtually ineffective at this range. His skirmishers were steadfastly continuing to shoot back, yet they were easily getting the worst of the exchange. Several of his warriors had crawled forward to claim the muskets of those who were either killed or injured to the point that they could no longer fight.

"With me!" the *induna* shouted, waving his men forward. He slung the bag of bullets and powder and began to crawl towards the depot. He was determined that the king's regiment would take kwaJimu, or he would leave his corpse as a sacrifice to the Zulu Kingdom.

"Heavens!" shouted Surgeon Reynolds. He saw the growing number of flashes from Zulu rifles closing the distance on the mission station. "I'd say they are no more than a cricket pitch or two away."

The fire was becoming steadily worse near the hospital veranda. Lieutenant Chard quickly ordered some men to drag biscuit boxes over to plug the gap between the north wall and the northeast corner of the hospital. Lieutenant Bromhead and Colour Sergeant Bourne's flying platoon was doing splendid work, driving back enemy assaults at bayonet point; however, they were starting to tire, and the engineer officer knew they could not be everywhere at once. Chard sprinted across the yard. Errant musket balls slapped into the earth around him. He found Sergeant George Smith near the left end of the line.

"Sergeant, withdraw your men from the front of the hospital," the lieutenant ordered.

"Sir," Smith replied with a quick nod before shouting for his soldiers to retire. In truth, he was relieved. The Zulu musketry from the stone wall, coupled with continuous assaults, was making the situation increasingly dangerous.

As his men scrambled over the hastily erected new barricade, Smith ordered six men to hold the corner while the rest reinforced the north wall. Sections had become intermixed as soldiers were tasked out to various parts of the perimeter. In addition to his own men, Smith also had Privates Fred Hitch and Thomas Cole from Sergeant Gallagher's section. Cole was supposed to be in the hospital, but his claustrophobia prevented his return. Hitch was told by his section leader to remain near the north wall, as that seemed to be where he was doing his best work.

Despite the ferocity of enemy assaults, there were only a small number of wounded evacuated to the storehouse veranda where Surgeon Reynolds set up a casualty collection point. Ever at his side was his Jack Russell terrier, Dick. As he scanned the defences, seeking out any men who may have fallen, he thought he saw frantic hands waving from inside the hospital.

"Ammunition," he said under his breath. He called to Commissary Dunne, "We need to get ammunition to the hospital, before they are overrun!"

Dunne did not seem to hear him, as he fired his own weapon through a loophole and began to reload. Reynolds gritted his teeth, and seeing an open box that had about two-thirds of its ten-round packets still inside, he rushed out as a hail of Zulu bullets whizzed by his head.

"Stay here, Dick!" he shouted to his dog, who was yapping at the snaps of close-flying musket fire.

The doctor grabbed one of the rope handles on the heavy box. Leaning over as it dragged across the ground, he ran as fast as he was able across the open ground towards the hospital. Bullets continued to kick up clods of dirt and dust nearby. When he was about halfway across the yard, a pair of musket balls smashed into the side of his helmet, tearing it from his head. He fell to his knees, fervently running his hand over his scalp to make certain he hadn't been hit. Taking a quick breath, sweat now running into his eyes, he rushed the rest of the way over to the now-desperate defenders of the hospital.

"Ammunition!" Reynolds shouted, banging on the open high window.

"You're a bloody saint, doctor," Williams Jones said. He leaned over and started taking packets of cartridges from the surgeon.

"What about the others?" Reynolds asked, as an enemy bullet smashed into the glass of the open window.

"716 is in the next room with me," Jones replied. "But I can't get to Hookie and Williams from here. The Zulus have taken the veranda, which means Waters and Howard are likely done for. The only way to reach anyone else is from the south doors."

"Start knocking a hole in the bloody wall," Reynolds directed. He then ran across the yard once more, drawing even more fire from enemy marksmen in the bushes to the north of the depot. As soon as he reached the veranda, he felt a hand on his shoulder.

"Reverend," he said, seeing it was Padre Smith.

"A brave deed, doctor, but one I would advise you not to try again."

"The men in the hospital needed ammunition," Reynolds explained.

"Yes, and the entire garrison may need its surgeon soon enough," Smith countered. He tied a large apron around his neck, and began stuffing cartridge packets into the pouch. "You take care of the wounded. I will see to the ammunition."

Reynolds gave the padre a smile and hoped the holy man had not just signed his own death warrant. He turned to see several men had been struck by spent bullets during the last few minutes. The doctor let out a sigh and set about his duties. As he and one of his orderlies helped a wounded soldier into the storehouse, he remembered the words of his counterpart from 2nd Battalion, Surgeon-Major Peter Shepherd. It was a mantra that he repeated over and over as he began to treat the injured.

'Wash, stop bleeding, and fix parts in natural position without delay. Repeat.'

Surgeon Reynolds tending to the wounded

Chapter XII: Loss of the Ramparts

Rorke's Drift
6.00 p.m.

Contemporary image of the fighting near the hospital veranda

Along the south wall, the battle had devolved into an exchange of gunfire between the Zulus on the hillside—as well as those using the brush stands for cover—and the defenders hunkered down behind the barricades. Corporal William Allan had been joined by his close friend, Corporal John Lyons, who brought several additional riflemen with him.

"Compliments of Sergeant Gallagher," John said. "Thought you might need a hand stuffing these bastards."

"Much obliged, Jack," Allan replied, even as a musket shot smacked the nearby kraal wall, sending stone splinters flying.

They were soon joined by Lieutenant Chard, who was continuously making his way through different parts of the defences to see how they were holding. His helmet was gone, and he had a streak of dried blood matting the hair on the left side of his head. He wielded his pistol, and as he knelt between the two corporals, he fired a shot in the direction of the hillside.

"You might want something with a bit more reach than that, sir," Corporal Allan mused with a chuckle, even as an enemy musket shot smacked the barricade near his head, causing him to wince as a handful of mealie grains dusted his face.

"Yes, silly of me, isn't it?" the officer concurred with a grin.

"If you stick around, sir, these bastards might get a lucky shot in," Corporal Lyons remarked. "Then you'll have yourself a rifle."

Chard chuckled macabrely at this, gave the corporal a friendly slap on the shoulder, and continued to make his rounds.

Despite the difficulty of scaling the short cliff and wall of mealie sacks, the Zulus were now concentrating the brunt of their assault along the north wall. Skirmishers within the brush and along the stone wall continued to fire relentlessly into the compound. All the while, subsequent waves of attackers tried to storm the ramparts.

While Lieutenant Bromhead and Colour Sergeant Bourne led their section of bayonet fighters to counterattack wherever there was a breach in the defences, Lieutenant Chard and Commissary Dalton directed the battle along the wall near the hospital. Chard may have been the officer commanding, yet it was clear he was relying heavily on the experience of the old soldier. The engineer officer wielded his pistol, and as the latest wave of Zulus battled with the redcoats, Chard leaned between two of his soldiers and fired several shots into the mob of warriors. He stepped back to reload as Dalton plunged his bayonet into the side of a warrior who threatened one of their men.

"Glad to have you with us, Mister Dalton," Chard said, echoing Bromhead's earlier sentiments.

"No place I'd rather be, sir," the commissary said, his teeth gritted in fierce determination.

Dalton paced behind the line, directing fire of the hard-pressed riflemen. As he raised his weapon to shoot down one of the enemy marksmen in the brush, he spotted another rising up just a few feet from the wall.

"Pot that fellow!" he shouted to a nearby private.

Both he and the soldier fired their weapons simultaneously, each striking down their intended targets.

A towering figure, James Dalton stood half a head taller than most of the men on the line, and his appearance was both inspiring and menacing. His height would get the best of him this day, however. Having shot the skirmisher in the brush, he opened the chamber of his rifle, wafts of smoke pouring out as he extracted the spent cartridge. He fumbled for another round in his pockets as three more enemy marksmen stood up from the brush and fired in his direction. One musket ball hit, striking him just above the right shoulder. The assistant commissary let out a cry of pain through clenched teeth as he fell to one knee. Using his rifle to prop himself back up, he looked down at the wound, which was bleeding profusely. He was suddenly dizzy, and the arm refused to function properly. His eyes wide, forehead sweating, he took a deep breath in through his nose and let it out slowly, forcing the pain from his mind.

"Mister Chard," he said calmly, holding his rifle up to him with his left hand. "You might want to take this. I think you can make better use of it than me. If you'd be a good man and fetch the cartridges in my pockets; my right arm seems to be of no use now."

Chard holstered his pistol and gratefully accepted the rifle from Dalton. He grabbed what few cartridges the commissary had before telling him he'd best go see Surgeon Reynolds. Though the wound was bleeding, Dalton's composed demeanour masked just how serious his injury was. His face was ashen behind his thick beard as he breathed deeply, trying to keep from fainting as he walked almost casually to the storehouse veranda.

All along the north wall, the battle raged. An NNC corporal named Carl Scammell, who'd been struck in an earlier barrage of musketry, had returned to the ramparts after having his shoulder hastily bandaged by Surgeon Reynolds. The wound was not causing him any discomfort now, and he felt he could still fight. Finding a place not far from the storehouse, he leaned against the ramparts and searched for targets. As the sun glowed red in the west, he could see hundreds of warriors teeming amongst the brush and in the far orchard. The current assault had been successfully repelled, and the Zulus were retreating. Scammell grinned as he aimed his weapon at a warrior not fifty feet from him. He never saw if he struck his intended victim. The murderous kick of the rifle tore open the wound in his shoulder; the pain blinding him.

"Idiot!" he shouted to himself. "Could have at least tried shooting the bastard left-handed…"

As he gasped for air, trying to clear his vision, he leaned against the ramparts, cursing his folly. He collapsed down to one knee, feeling a steady flow of blood seeping from the fresh tear in his flesh. He saw Lieutenant Chard just a few feet away, firing what few rounds he had managed to retrieve from Commissary Dalton. Despite his terrible discomfort, the corporal flashed a quick smile of appreciation. It spoke volumes to Chard's tenacity and courage that he would take up the rifle and fight alongside even the lowliest privates in the garrison.

Scammell knew his fight was over, for blood loss was making him feel faint. He then remembered he had nearly a full ready pouch of cartridges. He pulled himself up, and keeping low behind the defences, staggered over to his officer commanding.

"Here you are, sir," he said, pulling off his ammunition pouch with his good hand. "I can't very well make use of these."

Chard thanked the man and slung the pouch over his shoulder before returning to the line. Scammell's mouth was suddenly parched, and he felt dizzy. He collapsed back against the inner biscuit box barricades, his vision blurring.

"Damn it all," he swore before shouting, *"Water! Can someone please give me some water?"*

Just a few yards away, Storekeeper Byrne and Commissary Dunne were breaking open yet another wooden box of bullets, while Padre Smith stuffed as many packets as he could carry into his apron before returning to the line.

"Water!"

Byrne heard the shout. Taking pity on the stricken corporal, he helped Reverend Smith load another batch of cartridge packets into his apron and then fetched his personal water bottle. He sprinted across the compound and knelt next to the badly injured soldier. He unscrewed the cap on his bottle and held it to the injured corporal's lips.

"Here you go," he said consolingly. "No sense dying all parched." He gave a brief smile as Scammell gulped down the contents of the bottle.

"Much obliged, sir," Scammell said with a forced smile.

The storekeeper returned the smile and started to screw the cap back on his bottle. Just then, a concentrated volley of Zulu musketry erupted from the brush. Byrne felt his spine stiffen. He sensed the trickle of what felt like water running down his face. As his vision faded and he collapsed face-first into the dirt, he was never aware of the musket ball that smashed into his brain, ending his life.

John Chard fired off another round, then stepped back and surveyed the chaos around him. Between the enemy skirmishers lurking in the trench to the south, the marksmen on the hill, and now the growing number of riflemen in the brush to the north, Rorke's Drift was under continuous fire from all sides. Thankfully, the murderous and accurate barrage from Sergeant Gallagher's section and the men in the hospital and storehouse had halted any further attempts by the Zulus to attack the south ramparts. Yet the concentration of enemy assaults to the north and near the hospital, combined with the close-range salvoes of musketry was of grave concern to the officer commanding. The loss of Commissary Dalton was particularly unsettling. His calm demeanour and decades of experience had been a godsend to both Chard and the defenders of Rorke's Drift.

As wounded were dragged or hobbled away from the fighting, they left gaping holes in the already stretched lines, which Chard feared the Zulus would exploit, should they prove able to mass their numbers. Lieutenant Bromhead and Colour Sergeant Bourne's flying platoon was engaged in a fearful struggle near one such opening near the hospital veranda. Though few of these men had been injured, they had been engaged in numerous fierce melee bouts for the past couple hours and were completely spent.

Having driven back the latest assault, Bromhead ordered his detachment to withdraw towards the centre of hospital's eastern wall. All were filthy from the clouds of acrid smoke emitted from their weapons and soaked in sweat. Most bore numerous cuts and scrapes from enemy assegais. One private's eye was swollen shut where he'd taken a glancing blow from a Zulu knobkerrie club. All knelt, lest they present an easy target to the growing number of Zulu marksmen in the brush. Sweat streamed down their faces, and they were gasping for breath.

Meanwhile, the sun was falling in the west. Chard raced over to check on his flying platoon and quickly looked at his watch. It was 6.00, and would be dark within the hour.

"If they hit us again there, I don't think we can hold them," Bromhead confessed quietly to him.

"Make ready to abandon the north and south ramparts," he ordered. "We'll make our stand from the inner perimeter."

"What of the hospital?"

"There's little we can do now," Colour Sergeant Bourne spoke up. "But at least we can provide supporting fire from the biscuit box wall, which should take some pressure off them."

"Over here, sir!" Sergeant Smith shouted from the northwest corner of the storehouse. He and ten privates were in a fearsome struggle against a swarm of Zulus attempting to scramble over the barricade inside the biscuit box wall.

"Damn it all," Chard swore, bounding over to assist the sergeant.

"You three, with me!" Bromhead ordered, pointing to Fred Hitch and two of his mates. "Colour Sergeant, get everyone else behind the inner defences."

"Sir!"

While Bourne and Sergeants Gallagher, Windridge, and Smith ordered their men to abandon the north and south walls, Lieutenants Chard and Bromhead charged into the fray near the northwest corner of the inner perimeter. The inner biscuit box wall formed a right-angle here, and it was also where the ground was the least steep and rocky.

Fred Hitch summoned what remained of his strength and gave a hoarse cry of rage as he practically leapt into the swarm of riflemen and warriors. The point of his bayonet clipped one Zulu along the crown just above his headband, sending him sprawling backwards down the short drop. Hitch then brought his rifle butt up in a hard swing, smashing a warrior engaged with another British soldier in the face. The young redcoat's mind was clouded, his thoughts consumed by fury and the conflicting desires to stay alive or just die and end it all.

Nearby, Sergeant Windridge was struck down by a blow from a Zulu shield, driving him to his knees. As the warrior raised his spear to finish him, he stumbled on the uneven ground and fell onto his stomach along the rampart. Before he could recover, 'Gunny' Bromhead plunged his bayonet into the side of the man's neck. Blood spurted from the punctured artery, soaking the already filthy spiked blade. Two other Zulus were bayonetted in similarly gory fashion by the accompanying privates before the remainder withdrew back into the concealment offered by the tall grass and brush.

Private Hitch shouldered his weapon and aimed at the small of the back of one fleeing warrior. He grimaced and tried to squeeze the trigger. The weapon refused to fire. He cursed himself, realising he'd failed to reload. He jerked open the breach, only to find the spent cartridge stuck halfway.

"*Now?* You're doing this to me now?!"

Fred quickly drew out what looked like a musket ramrod from the end of his rifle, nearly burning his fingers as he accidentally touched the scorching barrel. The rod was an extraction tool, used for clearing such jams that happened all-too-frequently when the barrels became hot and the breach clogged with burnt black powder residue. This was further compounded by the poor manufacturing of the cartridges, which were a flimsy foil rather than solid brass. These often crimped in the soldiers' ammunition pouches, leading them to become stuck in the breach when loading or extracting. As Hitch violently smashed the ramrod down the barrel, he could see others along the firing line with similar issues. At any time, approximately three in every ten soldiers were stepping back to clear jammed or broken casings from their rifles. With all the advantages afforded by the Martini-Henry rifle, it was still far from a perfect weapon.

"There we are." Hitch chambered another round and quickly shouldered his rifle once more. Though it had taken him less than a minute to clear and reload his rifle, his quarry was long gone.

"Damn it all," he muttered, quickly dropping behind the wall as several enemy muskets fired in his direction from the nearest stands of brush. He took a moment to slowly work the breach lever of his rifle, to see if he was going to have further difficulties. The cartridge moved back and forth rather stiffly. Fred feared he would face another jam when the flash of heat expanded the casing when fired.

"I don't suppose the Zulus will offer to give us a few minutes to clean the shit out of our rifles, sir?" he asked Lieutenant Bromhead, who hunkered behind the wall near him.

His officer commanding appeared not to hear him; doubtless his already impaired hearing had taken a pounding from the constant assaults of rifle fire. Fred's own ears were ringing, and he wondered if it would ever go away.

A musket ball then slapped the top of the barricade, tearing open the sack and spraying mealie kernels into the soldier's face. Hitch let loose a few words of profanity and brought his rifle up once more. The Zulus in the brush were getting harder to see, yet there were plenty of muzzle flashes for him to shoot back at. Despite the fear that he might be shot at any moment, Fred took a moment to control his breathing and carefully aimed at the low bush where the enemy marksman lay. With a loud crack and waft of smoke his rifle erupted. He could not see if he struck his intended target, but he confidently thought no one behind that bush would be threatening him again. He was further relieved when he worked the lever of his rifle and the spent case flew out of the breach.

As Fred Hitch fought his one-man battle against the Zulu marksmen lurking beyond the northern ramparts, scores of riflemen from the north and south walls quickly heeded the frantic bugle calls to retire behind the inner defences.

"Come on, come on," Henry Gallagher said repeatedly, slapping each of his men on the shoulder as they rushed past him. He scanned the wall, making certain none of his soldiers had fallen during the hasty retreat, before following them around the storehouse and over the biscuit box wall.

"There, *inkosi*!" a Zulu rifleman atop the rocky plateau shouted, pointing towards the southern defences. "The red soldiers are fleeing!"

Even through the persistent haze of smoke with the falling sunlight dancing off it, Dabulamanzi could see the British defenders abandoning the main ramparts. His riflemen along the hillside fired a rapid barrage in hopes of cutting some of these fleeing cowards down. But, as had been the case most of the afternoon, their shots landed far short or sailed off into oblivion. Two hundred muskets must have unleashed in those few moments, yet the prince did not see a single redcoat fall. He doubted anyone along the slopes of Shiyane struck a single enemy soldier that day.

"How many shots have we wasted?" he lamented. "And how many of our brothers did we accidentally shoot in the back?"

He summoned one of his men to send word to every company within the vicinity of the hospital; they were to press the attack, slaughter the defenders, and establish a stronghold there.

The past couple of hours had been alarming. Such a paltry number of imperial soldiers withstanding the relentless onslaughts of the Zulu Kingdom's best regiments was inconceivable. And while victory was still an absolute certainty in Dabulamanzi's mind, it became more tainted by the minute as the king's warriors fell. Cetshwayo would be unforgiving if too many men from his personal regiment were slain with nothing to show for it.

"We have nothing left to shoot at, *inkosi*," a skirmisher bickered. Their collective cheers at seeing the soldiers flee turned to dismay. From their position on the hill, the inner compound was completely shielded by the large storehouse.

"Fire on the stone kraal," the prince said, pointing to the stone works east of the storehouse.

The soldiers behind these walls caused the Zulu marksmen much grief, and it was time to put a stop to it. More importantly though, was Dabulamanzi's intent to capture the hospital. If he could place marksmen on the roof, they would pour enfilade fire into the British inner compound at a range that was far more compatible with their muskets. He could also use it as a staging point for the final assault.

For John Chard's wagon driver, Sanele, his thoughts of finding safety away from the camp had turned to abject terror. The cave he hid in was very low, scarcely three feet in height, though it extended a ways back into the hill. His small size allowed him to skulk behind a rock outcropping in the back, which was too small for the average man. Knowing the merciless nature of the Zulus in battle, Sanele understood, should they find him he would be killed without a second thought. He was filled with terror as a pair of warriors crouched in the mouth of the cave, firing their muskets at the British defenders below. The return fire from the redcoats was proving to be as much of a threat to the man as the possibility of being seen by their adversaries. One errant shot smacked the ceiling of the low cave, ricocheting into the darkness and nearly striking the wagon driver.

As he struggled to control his panicked breathing he heard an audible 'slap' and was sprayed by what felt like a splash of water. He closed his eyes for a few moments, opening them as he heard a cry coming from one of the Zulus. He could see the warrior on his left clutching the twitching body of his friend. The man had been struck beneath the chin by a Martini-Henry slug, ripping away part of his throat and bursting out the back of his head. Sanele quietly wiped his fingers over his face, the blood and splinters of bone nearly causing him to wretch.

Despite the loss of the outer walls, which now left the hospital exposed, the inner ramparts proved to be far more manageable than Lieutenant Chard could have hoped. The biscuit box wall was well within the protective cover offered by the storehouse from enemy fire to the south. Thus were the Zulu marksmen along the slopes of Shiyane rendered all but useless. The stone kraal was the only place on the defences still threatened by their ceaseless barrage. In contrast to the 'thin red line' from the past two hours of battle along the lengthy perimeter, the British were now concentrated behind the inner defences. The enemy's vastly superior numbers were negated. They could not bring any more fighters to bear than the British at any given moment. And while their marksmen to the north were still very much a threat, the imperial infantrymen could concentrate more counter-fire against them.

The Zulus, thinking their adversaries were beaten, surged over the north wall, intent on overtaking the hospital. As they did so, Colour Sergeant Bourne took control of the riflemen along the row of biscuit boxes.

"*Volley...fire!*"

With less than thirty yards separating the Zulu assailants from the wall, the imperial soldiers scarcely needed to aim their weapons. At least a dozen warriors were torn to pieces by the eruption of musketry from the inner wall.

"Fire at will! Fire at will!" the colour sergeant shouted. Shouldering his rifle, he shot a Zulu just thirty feet away. The man was knocked onto his back and lay clutching at his badly injured side.

Sergeant Gallagher's section, having withdrawn from the south wall, formed a second rank behind those kneeling over the biscuit boxes. Withering swaths of musketry slew or maimed the mass of enemy warriors who brazenly dared to storm the compound. A bloody mist hung in the air as waves of Zulus were ripped apart by the relentless volleys. No less than fifty warriors fell within the span of a minute. Their surviving companions tumbled back over the ramparts. Many of the fallen were struck numerous times. Those not fortunate enough to be killed instantly lay in growing pools of their own blood. Guts were torn from their bodies, skulls spit apart, arms and legs shattered in a hideous wreckage of human suffering.

Provided their ammunition lasted, the redcoats behind the inner walls were confident they could hold indefinitely. And to that effect, Padre Smith continued to make his way around the defences, handing out the much-needed cartridge packets. Due to their sheer weight, the reverend could only resupply a few soldiers at a time. Every soldier at Rorke's Drift had long since expended his allotment of seventy rounds. Commissary Dunne and his aides were dragging ammunition boxes to the veranda and breaking them open as fast as they were able. Yet no matter how fast the commissaries and Padre Smith worked, they could not seem to get cartridges to the battered line fast enough. As soon as the reverend delivered his the last of his packets, soldiers on the far end of the line were screaming for ammunition.

Meanwhile, a salvo of Zulu musketry tore into the outside steps leading to the attic as Second Corporal Atwood scrambled down. His face was blotched with the stains of black powder smoke, streaked with beads of sweat.

"Corporal, what do you need?" Dunne asked, as he unscrewed the lid on another box. Piles of lids and empty boxes lay scattered about.

"Ammunition," Atwood said bluntly.

"Of course, you do." The commissary waved over his shoulder. "Don't stand on ceremony, man. Grab a box and go!"

Atwood gave a nod of affirmation and sped into the storehouse. He grabbed the nearest box by one of the rope handles and drug it across the ground. At eighty pounds each, they were heavy and awkward to handle, especially for one man. Francis Atwood found his strength in desperation. He stepped backwards up the outer stairs, the large box banging against each step as he heaved it upward. The handrail splintered when a Zulu musket ball smashed into it, giving the corporal an added surge of energy. With a shout of fury, he practically flew the rest of the way up to the attic. Tumbling through the door, he fell onto his face. Bullets slapped the outer wall.

"Here we go, lads!" he shouted breathlessly.

There were a handful of soldiers in the attic with him, including the NNC officer, Lieutenant Adendorff. One of the privates, out of ammunition for the last ten minutes, clambered over.

"Bugger all, we don't have a tool for loosening the screw!" he bickered.

Atwood gave him a perplexed look, grabbing the rifle he'd left near his firing loophole. He smashed the butt of it against the edge of the lid. The wood splintered, and the screw bent as it gave way.

"It's a lot quicker this way," he said with a touch of satisfaction.

His soldiers eagerly pried out the tightly packed and much-needed cartridge packets.

Despite the vexing ordeal he'd just undergone and the continuous dance-of-death the garrison was engaged in, the corporal maintained his outward composure. Taking four packets of ten rounds for himself, he crawled back to his firing position.

Adendorff was the senior man present, but as he could scarcely speak a word of English, it was the Service Corps NCO who maintained control over the small band defending the storehouse. Adendorff was content to occupy his own position in a corner and take random shots at the Zulus.

As they shoved ammunition into their pouches, Atwood explained to the remaining soldiers their greatest threat was that the enemy would set fire to the roof. "We must prevent it at any cost," he stressed.

Outside the storehouse, Lieutenant Chard took a moment to visit Surgeon Reynolds' casualty collection point. His was profoundly surprised their losses were not significantly higher. Three were confirmed dead, while seven or so bore various injuries mostly brought on by Zulu muskets. He knew the enemy's losses were horrific by comparison, though he did not allow himself any sense of reprieve or arrogance. The situation was still extremely grave. Fatigue was wearing down his soldiers. And there was the matter of ammunition, which they were expending at an alarming rate. As terrible as the Zulu casualties were, the more they suffered the greater their fury to finish off this small band of impetuous redcoats.
    Chard sat for a moment on the edge of the veranda, tore open a couple of ammunition packets, and dumped the contents into the pouch he'd been given by Corporal Scammell. He then took a moment to assess the defences from where he sat. The firing line seemed to be holding well enough. The cattle kraal was still taking fire, yet the men hunkered behind its stone walls continued to return fire at a punishing rate. His attention was now drawn to the hospital. He cursed himself for not ordering its evacuation sooner. Roughly thirty of his men were trapped inside and completely cut off.

Chapter XIII: Fight for the Hospital

Rorke's Drift, the Hospital
5.30 p.m.

Private Hook fighting to keep the Zulus at bay

"Well, that's it boys, this is the blind spot," Harry Hook grumbled. He heard Robert Jones shouting that the enemy was massing for another assault.

With no one along the north wall, the Zulus could use it for their own protection while they rallied for another surge against the northwest corner of the veranda. Indeed, the entire western flank of the station was now one massive blind spot, as Private Hook grudgingly noted. Since there were no officers or NCOs among the defenders, it fell to the initiative of individual soldiers within to decide their next course of action. Everyone concluded that their position would soon be untenable. Should they be unable to hold, they would need to find a way to evacuate both themselves and their charges from the building and cross the open compound. Little did any of them know that this was now an abandoned 'no-man's-land' for both sides.

For Harry Hook, the battle took on a surreal tone. The setting sun gleamed in the windows along the western wall. Its rays danced off the clouds of acrid smoke that permeated each room and burned the eyes of attacker and defender alike. Every man shouted to his mates, their hearing deadened by the constant echoing from firing their rifles in such a confined space. There was also the total loss of perception regarding the larger battle. Neither Hook nor those in the rooms closest to him knew the north and south walls had been abandoned. The small band of men protecting the wounded was now completely cut off.

Following Dabulamanzi's orders, the Zulu attacks were becoming ever more furious. Musket shots fired from close range slapped constantly into the outer walls. Throwing assegais were flung through the windows by desperate warriors, anxious to exact retribution against the soldiers. As one short spear embedded itself in the wall behind him. Harry was glad he had taken over Thomas Cole's abandoned loophole, rather than continuing to fire from the window.

Since Cole's claustrophobia had gotten the best of him, Private Hook felt very much alone. The only other man in the crammed space with Harry was the iziGqoza warrior, whose heavily bandaged leg kept him from standing or even crawling.

"Please, take my bandage off!" the man pleaded in heavily accented English. "Let me come!"

Even if Hook had wanted to oblige, there was little he could do but continue to fire his weapon at any shadows which manifested themselves. One Zulu brazenly tried to scramble in through the window, bringing a terrified shout from the iziGqoza man. With astonishing speed, Hook slid his rifle back through the loophole. In one swift motion, he plunged his bayonet into the man's heart, just beneath the armpit.

As he knelt and tried to catch his breath, he fell into a deep coughing fit. He realised the room was filled with a smoke that did not come from his Martini-Henry rifle.

"Hey, Harry!" a voice called from the room to his right. "Bastards have set fire to the roof!"

"Bugger it," Hook replied quietly in a raw show of profanity.

The Zulus' attempt to burn the thatch came as no surprise. If anything, it astonished him they had not attempted this sooner. A chill ran up Harry's spine despite the incessant heat and the sweat dripping down his face.

"I'll not die by burning to death," he said under his breath. He called out to all who could hear, *"That's it boys, we're leaving!"*

Hook then kicked in the small bedroom door to his left. The door leading to the outside was being pounded on by an enraged mass of Zulus. Their numbers had greatly increased, for Dabulamanzi had ordered them to concentrate their efforts to overwhelm the hospital.

Leaning his rifle against the wall, Harry grabbed the iziGqoza warrior beneath the arms and began to drag him away. The outer door splintered, and several Zulus swarmed towards him. Hook fell over backwards, grabbing his rifle and piercing the side of an enemy warrior who lurched backwards, crying out in pain. The other Zulus were screaming abusive epithets at the injured iziGqoza; the hatred between kinsmen surfacing with unbridled ferocity. Harry grimaced as he watched the poor man brutally slain by a pair of stabbing spears. The warrior he'd injured clutched at his bleeding side as he smashed the iziGqoza's brains in with his knobkerrie club.

In the westernmost room, John and Joseph Williams were making a defiant stand along with an injured patient, Private William Horrigan.

"We're running out of bleeding ammunition!" Horrigan said, his voice breaking in panic.

"I've got five rounds left," John Williams muttered, still maintaining his composure. He then heard Hook's voice from somewhere in the maze of rooms.

"Start knocking a hole in that damned wall," Joseph said. "I'll hold these bastards off."

Private Joseph Williams was one of the best shots in B Company, as attested to by the crossed rifle patch on his left cuff. He had won numerous marksmanship badges and several regimental shooting prizes during his four years in the army. And now, he was utilising his skill with deadly precision. Fond of the expression, *'Whatever I see, I hit'*, it did, indeed, seem as if every time he squeezed the trigger another Zulu warrior fell. Were they not in such a fearful struggle against insurmountable odds, his mates would have been content to watch him ply his trade. At least ten had been slain already by his steady hand, mostly shot through the heart, lungs, or stomach. One man who'd been hunkering low had his face smashed in and the back of his skull burst apart by a well-placed shot.

Joseph's terrifying precision with his weapon filled his companions with awe. For the Zulus, it came with overwhelming hatred and sorrow. To the British, the slaughtered were little more than barbarous black-skinned savages in loin cloths. To the Zulus, every man who lay dead or dying was a lifelong friend and brother. Being among the oldest regiments in the *amabutho*, there were many fathers, and even a few grandfathers, among them. With rage boiling over, a host of Zulus surged forward, intent on avenging their friends.

John Williams and William Horrigan grabbed the pickaxes they'd previously used to chop loopholes for their rifles and began hacking away at one of the inner walls. They had to step over three patients, all in various states of feverish delirium and unable to move, let alone defend themselves.

"We don't need much room, just enough to drag everyone through," John said.

The two soldiers hacked at the wall to create a hole just large enough for a man to crawl through.

Joseph's weapon fired twice more in rapid succession as the Zulus reached the outer door. "Hurry up, damn it! I can't hold them!" he shouted. His cool-headed demeanour now reaching its breaking point.

"We're though!" Horrigan called back, as the soft brick smashed away. He scrambled over and helped John drag the first patient to the breach. How they were going to get thirty sick and injured men through the various rooms in the hospital, all while being assailed by enraged Zulus, with the roof burning over their heads, he could not begin to fathom. Yet he refused to buckle and was fiercely determined to see his duty done, or die trying.

"Oh, fuck!" Joseph cried out as the upper hinges of the outside door were torn away.

The attacking Zulus quickly smashed and kicked away the rest of the broken door and debris used as a crude barricade. Knowing he could not possibly make it through the small 'rabbit hole' in time, Joseph fired his rifle into the chest of the nearest warrior. His weapon jammed as he attempted to extract the spent cartridge.

Shoving the dying Zulu into his mates, he attempted to force his way past his attackers via the outside door.

The subsequent piercing screams caused the hair to stand up on the back of John Williams' neck. He looked back just in time to watch his friend being butchered by half a dozen spears; the Zulus exacting their revenge against the man who had inflicted so much suffering on their mates. With much shame, John knew he could not possibly save the poor souls still trapped in the room. He scrambled through the hole just as the enemy surged into the room, slaying all who remained within. Fighting back tears, Private Williams hoped their fevers rendered them incoherent, and that they did not suffer.

In the next room, Harry Hook shoved a couple of pallets against the door he'd come through. He was the only able-bodied soldier in this room. The rest were sick and injured patients including one whose back was against a wall, his bayonet plunging through the guts of a mortally wounded Zulu. The door leading to another room was suddenly kicked open. Hook made ready to fire when he recognised John Williams through the growing cloud of thick smoke.

"Damn it all, Harry! They've dragged Joseph Williams out and killed him!"

Hook grimaced. He motioned to the pickaxe his friend still wielded. "Start knocking a hole in that wall," he said, pointing to the eastern inner wall behind him. "We've got to find the Joneses, provided they're still alive in this shit. The only way out is east to towards the inner compound. You start hacking, I'll hold the Zulus off."

John cringed as Hook made the same assessment Joseph Williams had only moments earlier. He and the wounded patient began smashing away with their pickaxes. Their hearing dulled by the incessant rifle fire and din of battle, they were unaware of the ongoing struggle in the next room. Robert and William Jones had been driven back from the Witts' living room, and were now trying to keep the Zulus away from another group of patients.

All the while, the smoke within the hospital grew thicker. Mercifully, the incessant summer rains had left the roof thatch completely soaked. It therefore slowly smouldered rather than bursting into flames. Hook reckoned, had the battle taken place during the dry winter months, the entire hospital would have already been consumed with fire, killing them all within minutes. The flames and smoke continued to grow, and both he and his companions knew that time was running out.

As the Zulus hammered away on the barricaded door, firing the occasional musket shot through, Hook leaned against the nearest corner and fired into what he knew to be a mass of warriors just on the other side. He reloaded and fired his rifle several times in rapid succession. He surmised that Zulus were falling with each shot, yet they continued relentlessly in their assault. In a macabre sign of the effectiveness of Hook's close-range shooting, blood began pooling under the door, sticking to the soles of his shoes. The door was soon smashed open, and Harry plunged his bayonet into the neck of one assailant. He screamed in fury, keeping the enemy at bay with the fearful spike on the end of his rifle, streaked with glistening blood.

As he chambered another round, one bold warrior grabbed the barrel of his rifle and attempted to wrench it away, the heat burning his hands. The doorway was narrow. Several dead and maimed Zulus created a macabre obstacle for their fellow warriors. As he struggled to keep a grip on his weapon, Harry's foot slipped on several spent cartridges. He fell backwards, inadvertently squeezing the trigger on his rifle. The Martini-Henry erupted with a loud boom, the heavy slug catching the Zulu in the chest, ripping through his heart and leaving a gaping exit hole in his back. Hook fell onto his backside, his face and chest sprayed with blood.

The Zulu attack halted briefly. They struggled over their fallen comrades, all the while trying to avoid the fearsome bayonet of the maddened redcoat who quickly scrambled to his feet. One warrior managed to tumble into the room; a young lad probably in his teens. Far too young to be a member of the *amabutho*, he was most likely a mat carrier for his father or one of his elder brothers. Becoming caught up in the excitement of the battle, he had joined the fray. But rather than trying to aid in the struggle, he sought plunder and was carrying away Hook's greatcoat and blanket.

"Oi, that's my rug and top coat!" the enraged soldier shouted. Hook caught the young lad in the thigh with his bayonet, sending him sprawling onto his stomach. Feelings of unholy rage surged through Harry, brought on by the butchery of the invalid patients and now the insulting indignity of having his possessions stolen out from under him. Rather than killing the boy outright, he proceeded to smash him about the face and body with the heavy butt stock of his rifle. Bones broke and blood spurted onto Hook's shoes. After a few moments, he stopped and caught his breath. Seeing the mortally stricken Zulu blink his eyes, the soldier gritted his teeth and chambered another cartridge into his rifle. He placed the barrel over the boy's temple and fired; blood and bone sprayed him once more. It was a brutal act. Should he survive, he knew it would forever haunt him. He wasn't certain whether God would forgive him for his wanton barbarism.

"Come on, Harry!" The pleading voice of John Williams brought Hook back to his senses.

The young private had reached the next room where the Joneses were fighting for their lives, as well as those of their charges. William Jones was bleeding from the face, where he'd caught the thrust of an enemy spear. His jacket was torn in several places, and he clutched at his side where he'd been struck in the ribs by a knobkerrie club.

The Zulus struggling through the bodies and debris began flinging their throwing assegais in Hook's direction as he made for the breach. One caught him along the scalp, parting his hair and leaving a fearful gash in its wake. His blood pumped so hard he did not even know he'd been injured. At first, he mistook the blood streaming down his face as sweat brought on by furious exertion.

Harry slid his battered rifle through the hole before crawling through, half-expecting to take a Zulu spear to the buttocks. He emerged and saw the room was crammed with patients who had either crawled or been dragged through by John Williams and the Joneses.

"Where's Bill?" Harry asked. He did not see Bill Horrigan among the defenders.

John bit his lower lip and shook his head.

In the gloom of smoke and failing sunlight, Harry then spotted their mate. He lay crumpled in the far corner, his chest soaked in blood. His throat was torn away and his mouth was agape, his tongue protruding past his lower lip.

"And where the fuck are we?" Williams asked. In the ongoing confusion, the young private had no idea where, exactly, they were in the confusing maze of rooms.

"We're close to the east wall," Robert Jones explained. He was a fearful sight. His face was covered in blood, his right cheek blistering from a burn. His left sleeve was torn and bloody, courtesy of a stray Zulu musket shot.

"Beckett and Waters are missing," William Jones added, shaking his head in frustration. He looked to Hook, who seemed the most in control in the ongoing chaos. "There's a window in the next room that leads to the courtyard. We'll get everyone out that way and hopefully have a little help carrying them to Surgeon Reynolds."

Robert Jones took up Horrigan's pickaxe. He and John Williams began the task of breaking through the inner walls once more. They were suddenly aware of loud crackling above their heads as flames licked the rafters. The inner thatch was not nearly as soaked as the top layer. The fire took hold, and the flames began to spread at an alarming rate.

"Time to go," Harry Hook said, his composure returning. He and William Jones fired their weapons into any Zulus attempting to breach either the outside door or windows.

The attacks had lessened slightly. The warriors had no more desire to burn to death than their red-jacketed adversaries. The butt stock of Hook's rifle was splintered from the fearful beating he'd given the poor Zulu mat carrier, and it tore into his shoulder as he fired.

"We're through!" John Williams shouted excitedly.

A queue of anxious men formed at the hole, those able to move under their own power crawling into the easternmost room. Williams and the Joneses dragged those who were completely invalid. All the while, Harry Hook fought his one-man war against the continuous assaults from Zulu warriors. The last of the patients remaining was Private John Connolly. Injured in a wagon accident during the arduous trek through Natal, he had dislocated his left knee. It was heavily bandaged.

"Hookie, give me a hand here!" William Jones shouted, trying to drag the injured soldier to the breach.

Connolly was a big, muscular man. With his leg splinted and bandaged, he was very awkward to move.

"Go on, Jonesy, I've got him!"

Hook, a strong man in his own right, reached underneath the injured soldier's armpits and clasped his hands over his chest.

"Don't let them kill me, Harry!" Connolly pleaded. He then saw a Zulu warrior climbing through the window.

His knees scraping over chunks of broken plaster and spent cartridges. Hook was pulling the stricken soldier through the breach when Connolly's splint caught on the wall, and he could not budge further.

"Damn it, Harry, get me through!"

Knowing what had to be done, Hook took a deep breath and rose to his feet, still clutching the soldier beneath the arms. "Hold on, this is going to hurt."

Driving his heels into the floor, Harry gave a violent pull. With a loud snap, the splint broke. Connolly cried out as his knee was dislocated once more. The force of Hook's vicious yanking likely saved his life. He flew the rest of the way through the gap as Zulus on their stomachs thrust their spears through. They were met by a well-placed rifle shot from William Jones.

"Sorry about that, old boy," Hook said.

Connolly lay across his lap panting, gritting his teeth in pain. "Not at all," he said with forced nonchalance. "Just be a good man and don't break anything else on me."

"Oh, bugger all," Robert Jones swore, as he looked out the high window. "The bleeding compound has fallen!"

Hook and Williams rushed over to see the courtyard completely deserted, aside from the bodies of dozens of slain and injured Zulus. Across the way, they could clearly see a line of their mates hunkered behind the inner wall of biscuit boxes.

"Blimey, when did they set that up?" Williams asked.

"Doesn't matter," Hook said. The room was filling with smoke and he coughed violently. The heat from the flames was becoming unbearable. "The Zulus can gut me if they wish, but I'll not burn to death in here."

Despite his reinjured leg, Private Connolly had hauled himself over to a stack of mealie bags, which he now heaved towards one of the high windows. Considering their colossal weight and his physical limitations, this was a testament to his immense strength. Using his arms and one good leg, he pulled himself on top of the stack and tumbled gracelessly out the window. He gave a loud yelp as he landed on his injured leg. None of his companions had seen him jump, and he was completely alone. He tried to crawl away as the bullets of their fellow soldiers along the biscuit box wall whistled over his head.

"Oh, bugger this," he muttered under his breath. His companions were keeping up an intense barrage of covering fire for the men in the hospital, but many of the shots flew dangerously close to him. With darkness quickly falling, he felt the risk increasing with every inch he crawled. He decided then to hide behind a fallen section of the ramparts and take his chances waiting out the fighting. If the inner defences fell to the Zulus, it would not matter where he ended up.

Within the burning hospital, John Williams began the laborious task of assisting the sick and injured out the other window. At the same time, Harry Hook and the Joneses continued to fight a furious battle against the Zulus who'd breached the hospital. With the flames now completely engulfing the thatch and rafters, the remaining enemy warriors on the outside abandoned their attack on the hospital. They still used the building as cover, however, hoping to attack the inner redoubt. Their musketry and return fire from the line of riflemen presented a dangerous predicament for both the patients and their defenders. With the growing flames threatening to swallow them up, they had little choice but take their chances.

The first man through the window was a trooper from the Natal Mounted Police named Sydney Hunter. Injured during the attack on Sihayo's kraal two weeks before, he had hoped to return to his company within the next few days. Instead, he escaped from the burning hospital, only to land hard on the ground just a few feet away from a band of Zulus lurking behind an abandoned section of the north wall.

"Uzulu!" one of the warriors shouted, lunging forward and stabbing the injured man in the side.

Hunter gave a cry of agony as the Zulu was torn to pieces by numerous rifle shots from the redoubt.

"Fuck!" John Williams swore. Guilt consumed him as he helplessly watched the trooper slowly bleed to death.

Across the compound, Sergeant Henry Gallagher's section was manning the biscuit box wall. He shouted orders at his men to provide suppressive fire to the northeast corner of the hospital.

Patients surged from the window, either of their own volition or assisted by Private Williams. Those that were able crawled towards the perceived safety of the redoubt.

Meanwhile, Hook and the Joneses continued their furious battle against those Zulus who stalwartly remained in the hospital. The ceilings had fallen in behind them, and the warriors who'd breached the defences were trapped with flames encroaching behind them and British bayonets and rifles in front.

Two soldiers missing for the past half hour were Privates William Beckett and Jon Waters. Both were wounded patients, fighting from a corner room in the northeast area of the building. As the Zulus swarmed the hospital, they were compelled to withdraw. Cut off and unable to link up with their mates, they burst into a tiny cloakroom where Otto Witt hung his greatcoats and pastoral vestments.

"What in the bleeding hell do we do now?" Beckett hissed.

The smoke grew thicker, and the trampling feet of the Zulus echoed just outside. What's more, both men were out of ammunition. In their weakened state, they knew they could not survive for long with only their bayonets.

"Nothing we can do except wait until dark and hope the damn roof doesn't come down on our heads," Waters whispered back.

Though the sun was quickly falling in the west, there was still enough light for the enemy to see by, should the trapped soldiers attempt to make a run for it. The heat of the roof fire was becoming ever more intense, as was their collective sense of panic.

Beckett was not fond of enclosed spaces. Unable to stand it any longer, he burst forth from the closet and rushed towards the open door leading onto the veranda. He crashed into a startled Zulu who quickly regained his footing and stabbed the unfortunate soldier in the ribs. Beckett gave a loud cry of pain and stumbled away, collapsing in a thick stand of tall grass in a low-lying ditch. He clutched at the bleeding wound, trying to slow his breathing and cope with the pain. Several ribs were broken, and he feared his lung was punctured.

"I don't want to die," he whimpered softly, fighting against the pain. Though he could see very little, he sensed the trampling feet of Zulu warriors all around him. One man kicked him hard in his injured ribs, as he tripped over the stricken private. The concealment of the grassy ditch and the failing sunlight were the only reason Private Beckett had not been gutted by a rampaging Zulu. Trapped in the ditch with darkness closing in and the sound of his enemies surrounded him. The soldier closed his eyes and waited for death to come.

A few minutes later, with the heat and smoke threatening to utterly consume him, Private John Waters also made a run for the door. Fortune smiled upon him. The Zulus lurking behind the ramparts simply did not notice him. It was a further stroke of luck that he was not hit by a stray bullet from the intense volume of fire coming from his mates within the redoubt. Heat exhaustion and the fatigue brought on by his previous injuries made the young soldier delirious.

He stumbled through the encroaching darkness, his addled mind unable to discern which direction he should run. Having gone around the southern end of the hospital, somehow without being cut down by any number of rampaging Zulus, he spotted the cookhouse a few yards away. Thinking it was his only means of salvation, he toppled forward, pitching head first into the smoky shack. There were several slain or horribly injured Zulus nearby. They'd attempted to ignite sticks bound with clumps of grass with the still smouldering ashes from Harry Hook's tea brewing of that morning. His exhaustion overwhelming him, Waters nodded off; his last conscious thought was a question to the divines, asking whether or not he would awaken.

"Is that the last of them?" Harry Hook asked. The smoke was billowing into the eastern rooms of the hospital, the heat threatening to sear them to their tunics.

"I think so," John Williams replied.

Neither man could be certain.

Suddenly, Hook's eyes grew wide in horrified realisation. "God help me." He then called out despondently towards the Witts' bedroom, "Maxfield!"

"Oh, bugger it!" Robert Jones swore, recalling the young NCO with terrible fever. Surgeon Reynolds had given him Witt's bed, and during the hasty evacuation and running battle against the Zulus, they'd simply forgotten about him. Filled with remorse, Jones rushed after Harry.

Burning embers were falling from the thatch ceiling in Otto Witt's bedroom. Robert Maxfield lay sprawled atop the blankets on the bed, his eyes shut and breath coming in gasps, yet still very much alive.

"Come on, young Robert, we need to get you out of here," Harry said, grabbing the sergeant by the arms.

Far from docile in his delirium, Maxfield lashed out at his old friend. "No!" he shouted, his eyes still shut. "The 24th does not run! Hold fast, Mister Pope, we'll hold the line!"

As strong as he was, Hook found he could not drag the violently delirious man by himself. "Jonesy, give me a hand!"

Robert Jones grabbed the sergeant by the sleeves of his checkered shirt as several Zulus swarmed into the room. The terrified men were attempting to escape the inferno, yet now they sought to sate their bloodlust at the sight of British soldiers.

"God…damn it!" Hook shouted, grabbing his rifle and attacking the men with renewed fury. The force of his charge plunged his bayonet between the ribs of one assailant, causing the weapon to become stuck. Harry grabbed the dying man's assegai and thrust if furiously at the warrior's companions. One of the Zulus smashed Harry across the mouth with his fist, sending him sprawling backwards, his vision blurring. As Robert Jones struggled to drag the feverish Sergeant Maxfield to safety, the remaining two Zulus plunged their assegais into the invalid man's chest and stomach.

"Fuck!" Jones screamed in terror and dismay. The Zulus were incensed and repeatedly stabbing the twitching corpse of Robert Maxfield, completely ignoring the two living soldiers. Jones took this brief respite to grab Harry Hook by the sleeve and lead him away from the slaughter. No sooner had they reached the eastern room, the ceiling behind them collapsed; the Zulus within shrieking in wretched horror as they burned to death.

"Come on, Harry, it's just us now," Robert said, as they reached the far side of the room and saw the others had departed. The side of Jones' face was charred where a series of painful blisters formed along his cheek.

From the window, they could see many of the patients crawling on their bellies. John Williams and William Jones took turns dragging those who were unable to move. They'd drag each man a few feet, then scramble back to grab another, who likely had no idea where he was or that they were in the midst of a fearsome battle. The bodies of fallen Zulus created an additional obstacle, and the fear was that many of these men were still alive and could pose a threat. But the enemy wounded seemed to have lost the will to fight; they watched listlessly as the white soldiers crawled past them.

Across the yard, the section of soldiers covering their escape fired with such intensity that many of their rifles became fouled by the build-up of spent powder. At any time, at least one in every five soldiers needed to use his ramrod tool to clear broken or jammed cases from the breach.

While Robert Jones pitched himself head-first out the high window, Harry Hook made one last sweep of what rooms he could see in the billowing clouds of smoke. He was filled with a deep sense of anguish at having failed to save several of the patients during their fighting retreat, especially poor Robert Maxfield. Fierce now was his determination that no other British soldiers would be left abandoned. He hunkered close to the floor to avoid the thick clouds of smoke that threatened to swallow him up. Satisfied there was no one left among the living inside the doomed structure, he crawled back towards the window and salvation.

He suddenly paused, seeing several bottles on a low table that he had not noticed in the confusion earlier. One was clearly marked *'brandy'*. Surgeon Reynolds used it to help ease the pain of the more seriously injured, particularly when chloroform proved scarce. His mind bewildered, Harry grabbed the bottle and smashed the neck against the table. He took a long drink, awakened by the burning sensation as it ran down his throat. Letting out a loud cough, he tossed the bottle aside.

"No, still doesn't do anything for me." He then picked up the bloody assegai he'd taken from the stricken Zulu, took a deep breath, climbed through the smoke and out the window.

The Defence of Rorke's Drift, by Alphonse de Neuville

Chapter XIV: Give it to them!

Rorke's Drift, eastern ramparts, near the storehouse
7.15 p.m.

Corporal William Allan

Though the Zulus along the hillside were at times difficult to spot, they were completely exposed, with little but tall grass and small brush stands between them and the trained marksmen of B Company. Conversely, the redcoats kept low behind their barricade of mealie bags, biscuit boxes, and the stone wall of the cattle kraal. And while the distance between the battling forces was well beyond the reach of the archaic Zulu muskets, it was well within the range of the Martini-Henry rifle.

"They're falling fast over there," Corporal John Lyons observed, watching another Zulu marksman tumble down the slope of the hill. He extracted the spent cartridge from his weapon, giving a grin of satisfaction as his friend, Corporal William Allan, fired once more. An enemy warrior flew backwards with a noticeable puff of blood from his chest. "Nice one, Allan, that got him!"

"Yes, we're giving it to them alright," Allan replied, almost nonchalantly. His section had been tasked with holding the eastern defences and cattle kraal, and was grateful when Sergeant Gallagher dispatched his corporal and a handful of riflemen to support his suppression of the Zulu marksmen on the hill.

Lyons gritted his teeth in frustration as yet another spent case became stuck in the breach of his rifle. He'd set the extraction ramrod on the mealie bag pile, knowing that as he continued to fire, the heat and fouling from burnt powder build up would cause more frequent malfunctions. Musket balls continued to slap the barricades and kick up gouts of dirt within the kraal. It seemed by random chance if they landed anywhere near the defenders. However, the corporal's luck was about to run out. For as he turned his back towards the hill, leaned against the stone wall, and slammed the ramrod home to extract the casing, he felt a blinding pain as a musket ball smashed into his neck, sending him flying into the mealie bag barricades.

For the first time since launching the attack against kwaJimu, Prince Dabulamanzi allowed himself a smile of satisfaction. A gentle, yet steady breeze had kept the billowing clouds of smoke at bay, and he was able to gauge where they struck as they smacked into the stone wall of the kraal. Then a foolish redcoat stood up with his back to him, making himself the perfect target. The prince sat and rested his rifle across his raised knee, gazing down the sight as he steadied himself. He elevated the weapon to just above his target's head and fired. There was a noticeable pause, and then the soldier spasmed as the round struck home.

"Time to send the rest of you to your ancestors," Dabulamanzi said, his voice cold like steel. He took his powder horn and reached into his pouch for another bullet. He had, perhaps, six or seven rounds remaining. Determined to make every one count, he slowly poured the powder, trying to use the exact same measure as before. Smoke wisped from the barrel of his rifle. It was hot to the touch. Though he'd tried to coordinate the attacks on the station as much as he was able, there was little he could now do except try to use his musket to beneficial effect. He was incensed that the hospital had caught fire, utterly ruining his plans for taking the inner compound. Whether it was his overzealous warriors who set the blaze, or the British defenders, he would never know.

Bringing his rifle up to his shoulder once more, the prince sneered. He saw another red-jacketed soldier quickly rush over to aid his stricken friend. Dabulamanzi carefully took aim and fired.

"Jack!" William Allan shouted, grabbing his friend by the tunic as he watched him tumble into the mealie wall. Before Lyons could answer, Allan felt a hard blow against his arm and he fell to one knee, loosing the grip on his fellow corporal.

John Lyons lay against the barricade, scarcely able to move as blood trickled down his neck. Surprisingly, he could still speak. "Give it to them, Allan," he stammered, his body trembling in shock. "I am dying."

"All right, Jack." Though Allan nodded his head, his eyes were lost and distant. His mind had not yet grasped that he, too, was hit.

Lyons struggled to look up for a moment. Despite the terrible and paralyzing pain, he took pity on his friend whose right sleeve was covered in blood.

"Allan, you are shot."

"Yes, I am," William replied. His voice was strangely blank, likely due to shock. He staggered briefly as he stood and looked down at his stricken mate. "Goodbye, Jack."

Zulu marksmen had come down from the hillside and were teeming along higher ground much closer to the kraal. The remaining soldiers on that section of the wall scattered as enemy fire became more intense and accurate.

Corporal Lyons lay on his back, gritting his teeth as tears of agony streamed down his face. His vision nauseatingly shifted between blurred, countered by moments of clarity. He noticed Lieutenant Chard scrambling along the wall, a rifle clutched in his left hand as he hunkered behind the mealie wall.

The officer commanding had seen the soldiers scatter and sought to ascertain the situation for himself. Allan staggered past him as Chard made his way over to Corporal Lyons, still sprawled on his back. Thinking the poor man was dead, he started to withdraw.

"Sir!" Lyons pleaded with the last of his strength. "You're not going to leave me here like a dog?!"

Chard stopped and looked back, his face filled with pity for the fallen soldier. Setting his rifle against the barricade, he grabbed Lyons by both ankles and with a surge of strength dragged him away from the outer rampart. Then grasping the corporal's wrist, Chard pulled him upright and heaved him onto his back. There was no time to see where Lyons had been wounded. The risk of moving a man with a terrible neck injury was great. But if he did not, the poor corporal would surely perish where he lay. With musket shots striking the mealie bags and kicking up clods of dirt at his feet, Chard carried the stricken NCO to the storehouse veranda. Surgeon Reynolds was applying a bandage to the shoulder of another wounded soldier, while his orderlies sorted the most seriously injured. As Corporal John Lyons was laid on his back, the agony of his fearful wound crippling him, Reynolds' Jack Russell terrier, Dick, came over, gave a short yap, and licked the tormented soldier's fingers.

John gave a pained smile, recalling a similar dog he'd had as a boy. He wished to give the Jack Russell a pat on the head, but the pain was overwhelming and he could not move his arms. Dick sensed this and rubbed his face against Lyons' outstretched hand. During the crucible of battle, with hell raining down around them, the presence of the doctor's pet gave the wounded the smallest measure of comfort.

Despite the vast corps that had most of Rorke's Drift enveloped, Mandlenkosi felt startlingly alone. Thousands of warriors lurked in the bush, trying to remain hidden from the imperial soldiers'

incessant musketry. The British compound was so small, with the terrain and various obstacles channelling any attacking forces into such a confined space, the Zulus simply could not mass their numbers effectively. Four thousand warriors invested kwaJimu, but no more than a few hundred could attack at any time. And each assault was met with a murderous barrage of rifle fire that left scores of men fallen, and the Zulus repelled in defeat.

With the hospital building burning after the defenders abandoned the outer walls, the Undi Corps was in no better position to overwhelm them than before. The now-empty courtyard was nothing more than a killing ground for any who tried to attack from that direction. However, it also meant that the *induna* and his skirmishers could get closer to the compound, as they were no longer subjected to enfilade fire from the north wall.

Leaving the cover of the fruit orchard, Mandlenkosi and several marksmen crawled towards the abandoned north wall. With the continuous din of musketry coming from the defences, he expected to feel the horrific impact of a British bullet at any moment. He tried to move quickly and quietly, strangely fearful that the redcoats would somehow hear him rustling through the grass and brush over the continuous loud crack of their rifles.

About fifty feet from where the ground sloped upward, Mandlenkosi found a battered scrub brush. It only stood knee high, but it would be enough to offer at least some concealment. Partially hidden in the surrounding trampled grass were a pair of warriors. One was clearly dead, half his head shot away; brains, blood, and shattered skull fragments lay in a sickening pile nearby.

Mandlenkosi thought the other man was dead as well, for there was a hideous exit wound in his back. Then he saw the man's torso slowly move up and down as he struggled for breath. His head was turned to the side, eyes wide, beads of sweat covering his face and scalp. The warrior was a member of the uThulwana, and Mandlenkosi knew him well. The man had led an adventurous, if also tumultuous, life. He had settled down some in his later years and recently became a grandfather. How he had longed to visit his son, who lived near the old mission station of Eshowe, and hold his granddaughter for the very first time!

His heart breaking for the old warrior, Mandlenkosi placed a hand on his shoulder. "I shall avenge you," he said quietly.

The man responded with a sputtering gasp; whatever words he hoped to say lost to oblivion.

The *induna* was satisfied that he was close enough to the enemy stronghold to use his rifle more effectively. He had six shots remaining, though he wasn't sure if he had sufficient powder. He'd misjudged how much was needed several times and nearly broken his shoulder with the subsequent fierce kick. He reckoned he was lucky he had not burst the barrel! He poured a small measure of powder down the barrel and rammed the musket ball home. The flint on the hammer was worn, and he hoped it would still spark. He wondered what he should do once he loosed his shot off. In the growing dark, the British could clearly see their muzzle flashes, and he was certain his would be met by murderous return fire. *'Shoot, then lie flat. Use your fallen friends as cover, if you must.'*

Finding his determination, he fired, filled with satisfaction as he watched the head of a red-jacketed soldier snap back. Several of the slain soldier's mates fired at Mandlenkosi. One shot smashed into his musket just above the hammer. It fell useless to the ground. Grabbing his assegai and shield, he signalled for a small band of warriors to follow him. They crept low along the cliff below the north wall, finding refuge below the right angle of the inner rampart. Other warriors saw this as the perfect place to launch an attack from, and they sprinted towards the *induna*, keeping low with their shields held high. A couple who were carrying muskets fired as they raced towards the wall. One of these men was shot down by a pair of Martini-Henry bullets, one striking him in the chest while the other shattered his thigh bone. Soon Mandlenkosi had about twenty warriors with him. A few more and he'd be able to storm the defences.

It was Private Thomas Cole, the poor claustrophobic, that was killed by the Zulu *induna's* bullet. The musket ball smashed clean through his forehead, ricocheting as it passed through the back of his helmet and flying sideways into the face of Private James Bushe who fell to his knees, hands over his bloodied nose.

"Son of a bitch!" Bushe's nose was clearly broken. The velocity of the bullet was slowed enough that this was the worst of his injuries. He saw Thomas Cole slump forward, collapsing against the mealie bag wall, lifeless eyes staring at the ground. James crawled over to him and placed a hand on his shoulder. "Oh, Tommy, I'm so sorry."

"Bushe, what the bleeding fuck are you doing?" Sergeant Smith shouted at him.

"It's Cole, sergeant. He's dead."

"Well, get to your sodding feet and pick up your rifle, unless you care to join him!"

The incoming fire from Zulu skirmishers to the north was getting decidedly worse, while that from the hillside slackened considerably.

Because many of their shots failed to even reach the barricades, the *izinduna* commanding the hillside skirmishers were tempted to order a complete cease-fire. Not only were their shots creating an even greater risk to their own warriors assaulting the barricades, but the return fire from the defences had been frighteningly accurate. At least thirty Zulu marksmen lay dead or dying along the Shiyane terrace. Concluding that his guns on the hillside were all but useless, Dabulamanzi had ordered nearly half of his marksmen down from the hill. It took them some time, creeping along in the enclosing darkness, but by the time they reached the tall grass and brush to the north of the station, they could concentrate their fire at a much closer range. The effects were now being felt by the British defenders.

Further exasperating the situation were the growing number of Zulus using the low ground up against the north wall for cover. John Chard was aware of this, yet he could not fathom how to dislodge these assailants. To engage them would require standing up from behind the protection offered by the inner defences, thus exposing oneself to enemy marksmen who were now dangerously close to the perimeter.

"Wait here, Mister Chard, I'll sort them out," a slightly accented voice said behind him. It was Ferdinand Schiess, the Swiss NNC corporal who'd been injured in the foot during a skirmish ten day previous. His foot was heavily bandaged, and he walked with a pronounced limp, yet his eyes were fierce and full of determination.

He'd spent much of the battle along the north wall, near the hospital. Despite having to rest the knee of his injured leg against the ramparts, he'd utilised both rifle and bayonet with terrifying effectiveness.

Before Chard could respond, Schiess practically leapt over the biscuit box wall, landing on his stomach within the abandoned courtyard. He crawled on his knees until he got to where he reckoned the enemy warriors were huddled. Pulling himself up onto his good leg, he brought his weapon to bear, only to feel the blast of a musket shot go off in his face, leaving him blinded for a moment and his ears ringing. It also blew the slouch hat from his head. Loosing a string of profanities in both English and Swiss-German, he pulled himself on top of the rampart and plunged his bayonet down into the neck and shoulder of his assailant. As the man screamed in terror and agony, Schiess wrenched the bloody spike free and shot a second warrior not ten feet away. A third rushed to their aid. Before he could raise his shield to protect himself, the enraged Swiss corporal stabbed him through the throat.

The remaining warriors started to flee from this furious demon, whose silhouette was highlighted by the glow of the inferno that now engulfed the hospital roof. Fighting against the renewed pain in his foot, Schiess chambered and fired another round. It struck a warrior in the back of the shoulder. This particular man was wearing a headdress with long feathers. He tumbled head-over-heels, staggered to his feet, and disappeared into the darkness before the corporal could shoot at him again.

Lieutenant Chard was filled with amazement at what he'd just witnessed. Despite his obvious handicap, Corporal Ferdinand Schiess fought with a savage fury unmatched by anyone, British or Zulu. During the previous fighting along the north wall, he'd bloodied his bayonet in the bodies of at least six enemy warriors. One could only guess how many he'd shot. Chard reckoned that Schiess alone was worth any ten imperial redcoats, and suddenly found himself wondering if the Swiss had a medal equivalent to the Victoria Cross.

"There we are, sir," Schiess said with a curt nod. He retook his place on the firing line. "All better now."

Chapter XV: As Bright as Day

Rorke's Drift
7.30 p.m.

From 'The Defence of Rorke's Drift', by Lady Butler (1880)

Gouts of flame shot from the collapsing roof of the hospital, creating a hellish glow on the landscape of horror that had once been a place of Godly worship. Along the compound, the survivors from the hospital were making their painstaking escape towards the line of biscuit boxes. Those patients still able to move under their own power crawled and pulled themselves along the rough ground, each fearing they had escaped the burning hell of the hospital only to be spitted by a Zulu spear out in the open.

John Williams and Henry Hook were each heaving delirious men whose fevers rendered them oblivious to the ongoing battle. Hook clutched his captured assegai between his teeth as he dragged his man to safety. Blood from his split scalp streamed down his face, partially blinding him. Robert and William Jones still wielded their Martini-Henry rifles, taking time to fire the occasional shot at skulking enemy marksmen attempting to shoot them.

"Private Jones!" Colour Sergeant Bourne shouted to the two soldiers. "Get those men to the wall, we'll cover you!" With subsequent orders to Sergeants Smith and Gallagher, groups of redcoats unleashed volleys along the abandoned ramparts.

"Come on, come on," John Chard whispered under his breath. He had no way of knowing just how many of their soldiers died in the hospital, yet he was determined not to lose any more. He directed Sergeant Smith to maintain their constant barrage of covering fire.

Along the storehouse veranda, Commissary Dunne continued breaking open ammunition boxes as fast as he was able. Reverend George Smith's apron was stuffed with packets of cartridges.

"Get these to the inner wall, if you'd be so kind, reverend," Dunne said, knowing Sergeants Gallagher and Smith's soldiers were expending bullets at an alarming rate.

Despite the ferocity of battle all around him, what troubled the pastor most was the coarse language being spewed forth by the soldiers behind the wall.

"Fucking twats, come on and die!"

"Come at me, so that I may skewer your cock on me sodding bayonet!"

"Filthy shits! Get ready to feel hell's embrace!"

The reverend knew their situation was desperate, and he could not necessarily blame the men for their feelings of rage and revulsion. Yet, the graver the situation became, the more their bursts of profanity troubled him.

"Will you stop cursing!" he chastised one particularly vulgar private. He slammed a pair of cartridge packets onto the biscuit box wall next to the man. "We may all die soon and have to account for our actions!"

"Piss on it, reverend," the soldier retorted. "The murders I've committed this day far outweigh any coarse words I may shout at these fucking black devils. If God wishes to condemn me for my swearing, so be it."

Another man added, "I'll quit swearing when the last of these sodding bastards is dead!"

Reverend Smith continued to berate each soldier, even as he hurriedly brought much-needed ammunition to them; for the language spouted by the enraged redcoats would have made even the madam of a London brothel blush.

"You're a good man, padre," one genial private said, as he struggled to extract a bent shell case from the smoking and filthy breach of his rifle, loosing a *'God damn it!'* in the process. "If you'd be so kind as to say a prayer for us sinners this day, I'll send as many of these black bastards to hell as I can before having to explain my actions to the Lord."

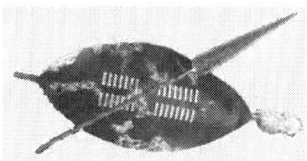

Mandlenkosi clutched at his injured shoulder, gritting his teeth. It had been a grazing shot, though enough to tear a deep gash in the flesh and send the *induna* tumbling. He crashed into a thicket, which may have saved his life, for it concealed him from the eyes of other British marksmen. His own musket had fallen from his grip when he was struck and lay somewhere in the darkness.

He lay on his non-injured side, catching his breath for a few moments. The man who'd driven them from the defilade near the wall was dressed different than the redcoats. Wearing a corduroy jacket and slouch hat, he was likely one of the European colonial troops. Yet to Mandlenkosi and his warriors, he was more of a wild demonic beast. From where the *induna* lurked, it appeared one of his marksmen had shot the man in the face, yet it had no effect on him. The speed with which he killed his assailant and two other warriors was unnerving. In the darkness, Mandlenkosi had not been able to see their faces well, and he wasn't sure which of his friends had fallen. Regardless, he knew he would be shedding tears for them later.

With the fall of night covering the compound below, Dabulamanzi came down from the rocky plateau and set about finding the British weak points. The battle had taken a surreal plunge into madness. The depot should have been overrun in the first few minutes, its garrison slain, and the Undi Corps on its way back to Ulundi, laden with spoils. The prince thought by this point he would have claimed one of those new British rifles as his own!

At the base of the hill leading to the abandoned south ramparts, he came upon numerous warriors still lurking near the shallow trench that ran parallel. He quietly placed a hand on the nearest man's shoulder. He did not move. It was only when he looked closer that the prince saw the gaping exit wound beneath the warrior's armpit where a bullet escaped after plunging through his neck and shoulder.

"*Amaqhawe wami, landela isikhulu senu,*" he said in a low voice. "My warriors, follow your prince!"

There were a few affirmative mutterings in the grass. Numerous fighters were glad to have someone to lead them again. Since the initial attack on the south wall had failed, many of the surviving warriors from the iNdluyengwe had been cut off from the rest of the Undi Corps. Even after the white soldiers retired behind their inner defences, the occasional shots still rang out from the storehouse and cattle kraal. Hearing the voice of Dabulamanzi reassured them, and those that were able, eagerly followed him. They kept low as they neared the burning hospital. A series of shots were fired from the inner rampart towards them. A pair of warriors cried out when they were struck in the back. He hated to simply leave them, but the prince knew the rest of the corps needed him. Besides, with the horrific injuries inflicted by the enemy's rifles, there was little he could do for them.

One unintended consequence of the Zulus setting fire to the hospital roof was that the tall flames lit the surrounding area, denying the *amabutho* the protection of darkness. Dabulamanzi cursed their misfortune. He and his band of warriors sprinted to the low stone wall where some of his skirmishers lurked. A few were continuing to shoot back at the defenders, though most simply laid low in the grass, uncertain what they should do next.

He swore he could hear cheering coming from the red-jacketed soldiers hiding behind their inner defences as the latest attack was repulsed. The prince shook his head, speculating, had they waited for nightfall, and captured rather than burned the hospital, they could have used the encompassing darkness to surround and smother the British. Instead, the roaring blaze lit the ground within a hundred paces of the depot, bringing incessant rifle fire onto any Zulus who showed themselves.

This relentless barrage of musketry coming from their adversaries troubled Dabulamanzi. He knew their enemies had a finite number of bullets, yet their fire had not slackened at all since the battle began. Conversely, many of his own marksmen had expended their bullets and powder; their muskets now rendered useless as little more than clubs.

"We never should have occupied the heights," he quietly chastised himself. Aside from the prince, and perhaps a couple of others who'd landed a well-placed shot or two, the endless bombardment of musketry from the slope of Shiyane had been completely wasted.

Continuing through the low brush, he came upon an injured *induna*. Dabulamanzi recognised the man as Mandlenkosi, a member of the uThulwana. His right shoulder was bleeding from a deep and hideous gash.

"I am ashamed, *inkosi*," the *induna* said, his eyes averted. "Many of our brothers lie butchered along the slope, while the red-jackets stand and mock us."

"They won't for much longer, I promise you." The prince's imploring words were as much for his own benefit as the *induna's*. It pained him to see an old, proud warrior from brother's regiment physically and mentally beaten like this.

What he needed was to coordinate all his regiments into a massed assault on all sides of the depot at once. As it was, only disparate bands of fighters, usually no more than a couple hundred, were launching attacks of their own volition whenever their *izinduna* could rally them. Driving the redcoats from the outer walls and destroying the hospital had made the Zulus' task more difficult rather than easier.

"We'll butcher every one of them, if some order might be restored," the prince said quietly. He directed Mandlenkosi to rally as many warriors from the uThulwana as he could near the tree grove and wait for his command. Dabulamanzi continued on his way, seeking out other *izinduna* and trying to find out exactly where the rest of his regiments were in this savage and bloody nightmare.

Within the compressed inner compound, Commissary Dunne was consciously aware of their cartridge expenditure. The ground nearest the storehouse veranda was littered with empty wooden boxes. As best as he could tell, the defenders had fired well over half their reserve stock of ammunition. He rushed over to Lieutenant Chard and made his concerns known.

"Mister Chard, if the men continue to fire at this rate, they'll run out of bullets before midnight."

The officer commanding conceded his point. He was doubtful that his men could continue to make a viable stand with nothing but their bayonets for protection.

"We should lessen our rate of fire, Mister Bromhead," he said to 'Gunny'.

Colour Sergeant Bourne spoke up against this notion. "Forgive me, sir. But I must recommend that we *not* slacken our fire. If we ease up now, the Zulus will know we are running short on cartridges. They will become emboldened and simply wait us out. There is no way for them to know our supply situation, and if we keep our fire hot and in their faces, they may lose hope. It is a gamble, I'll grant you. But one we stand a far better chance of winning than if we try to conserve bullets with several thousand warriors still out there."

Chard looked to Bromhead who paused for a moment before nodding in concurrence with his colour sergeant.

"Very well. It seems we take a grave risk either way, whether we continue to burn through our ammunition or not. Let us hope the Zulus break before our ammunition runs out."

Bromhead then added, "Walk the line, colour sergeant, and reemphasise that the men take their time, mark their targets, and only shoot at what they can hit."

"Sir!"

Bromhead returned to the wall where he and a group of seven soldiers, including Private Fred Hitch, held the northwest corner of the inner defences. The Zulus continued to surge forward only to be beaten back by the bristling wall of bayonets and relentless volleys. During each withdrawal many were shot down, illuminated by the light of the burning hospital. Rifle barrels became extremely hot from the constant firing, the heat and fouling of the breach continued to cause jams and other malfunctions.

"Well, I'd say we've manged rather well, for a few seconds, sir," Hitch said with a grin, as he stopped to catch his breath. He fumbled for his water bottle, distraught to find it near empty. "Damn it all," he muttered through parched lips, recalling that their water cart was over by the hospital.

Despite being deterred, the Zulus were far from finished. As the group of redcoats stared over the ramparts into the darkness below, a salvo of enemy musketry erupted from less than thirty yards away. Four of the seven men with Lieutenant Bromhead were hit. Private Edward Nicholas' forehead was smashed in by a large musket ball, which then burst out the back and through his helmet. Blood and brains splattered those nearest him, and the fatally stricken soldier stood there for a moment, eyes lost and confused. He then collapsed onto his back. There was a brief pause before he gave several violent twitches, and then he was still.

The cries of the wounded brought Bromhead out of his stupor, as did Hitch's shout of, *'Here they come again!'*

"Bastards have more guts than we have," the lieutenant mumbled, reloading his rifle and firing once more into this latest wave of enemy assailants.

Suddenly, Bromhead's rifle jammed. He feverishly fought to extract the spent casing. As he struggled to clear the weapon, a Zulu flung himself up onto the barricade, his spear poised to plunge into the officer's neck. Hitch, who had just fired his rifle, aimed it at the man anyway. The warrior tumbled back over the side, having fallen for the soldier's bluff. Hitch rushed over to Bromhead's side, beating back a pair of warriors who were trying to pull themselves up the short cliff. He spotted a lone marksman lurking about twenty feet away. Shouldering his rifle, he then remembered that he'd not had time to reload. He stood frozen, unable to move in the split second it took for the Zulu to fire.

Hitch felt the impact of the musket ball before he even heard the shot. The bullet tore through his right shoulder, splintering his scapula, and exited out the back. The young soldier was knocked to the ground, gasping for breath as the wind was taken from him and his helmet went flying.

Lieutenant Bromhead had just cleared and reloaded his rifle. He quickly shot down the Zulu who felled Hitch. "I got him for you, son," the officer said, as he knelt next to his badly injured soldier.

"Damn it all, sir, I can't move my arm," Fred grumbled, pulling himself to his feet. The arm and shoulder were numb, and he could not tell how badly he was hurt. "How the fuck am I going to continue to fight with one sodding arm?"

"Here," 'Gunny' said, producing his pistol and handing it to the private. He pulled out a dozen loose rounds, which Hitch stuffed into his left pocket.

"Much obliged, sir." His right arm hanging bloody and useless at his side, the soldier gave a howl of rage as he returned to the wall.

Fred had only fired a pistol a few times in his life and never with his left hand, yet he managed to use it to advantageous effect. As another rush of Zulus surged forward, he fired all six rounds from the revolver, striking one man in the arm and toppling another with a shot to the thigh. No longer able to engage in close combat, he stepped away and allowed his mates to handle the bayonet fighting. Fierce as the brawling was, the Zulu warriors desperately tried to get inside the reach of the redcoats' fearsome bayonets. Most of the fighting ended in a stalemate, and the Zulus were forced to withdraw once fatigue and casualties inflicted by British sharp-shooters overcame them.

As this latest surged dissipated into the brush, Fred Hitch returned to the wall and began fumbling with the cylinder on the revolver as he attempted to reload. Several of his mates could see just how fearful his injuries were, the hideous entrance and exit wounds oozing blood. None dared say a word to him.

One soldier, Private George Deacon, did mention, "Bugger all, Brickie, they're going to have to rip your head off to stop you!"

"Just a flesh wound," Hitch said dismissively. He then glanced down at the hole in his shoulder. He became light-headed for a moment, as the dull ache in his shattered scapula intensified. "Damn it all, would those filthy bastards attack?"

A loud cheer erupted from the biscuit box wall when the first survivors from the hospital were pulled over the defences. The worst of the sick and injured were carried to Surgeon Reynolds' casualty collection point near the storehouse veranda.

"I'm alright," Gunner Howard protested, when an orderly tried to help him to the doctor. He was one of the only walking wounded who still carried a rifle; many of the rest had been lost or discarded during the escape from the inferno. "Was just shitting my guts out for the past couple weeks is all. Now, does anyone have any extra cartridges they don't mind parting with?" The artillery crewmen found a place along the inner rampart taking solace in that, should he die this night, at least he would not burn to death.

Harry Hook was the last man over the wall. Having heaved his charge onto the biscuit boxes, where two privates pulled him the rest of the way over, he did a quick visual search of the abandoned compound for anyone they might have missed. Aside from poor Trooper Hunter, whose bloody corpse lay illuminated in the light of the hospital flames, the only bodies within the yard appeared to be Zulus. Unbeknownst to him, Private Connolly still lay hidden behind a crumbled section of the south wall and a pile of Zulu bodies. Satisfied that he'd done his duty, Hook clambered over the short wall and dropped onto his backside, exhaustion finally taking hold.

"Nice souvenir you've got there, Harry," one soldier said, noting the bloody assegai.

"Damn it, man, you look like hell," another remarked. "Did you stab yourself in the head or what?"

"He's right you know," John Williams said, as he helped his friend away from the wall.

The two dropped down near the western edge of the storehouse. Hook held a bloody rag up to his scalp. He did not think wound was serious, though it hurt like the devil and refused to quit bleeding.

"You should go see Surgeon Reynolds and get that stitched," John Williams muttered quietly, noting his friend's discomfort.

"Do you not hear the groans of the seriously wounded?" Harry chastised. "I'll not waste the good doctor's time with this little scratch when there are men dying."

"Well, let's at least get that thing tied to your head," John remarked, tearing off a strip of his undershirt. He balled up the rag, and pressed it over the gash before tying it into place with the long strip. "Can't have you missing your shots if blood gets in your eyes."

"Right, I suppose I should find me another rifle," Hook replied with an appreciative grin. "Hope the quartermaster doesn't make me pay for the one I lost in the hospital!"

Finding a new weapon proved to be fairly easy. There were numerous discarded rifles taken from the dead and wounded stacked against the storehouse. Taking his time, while trying to catch his breath after their harrowing ordeal, Hook found one rifle that appeared to be in reasonable condition. He took some cartridge packets from an open box before re-joining his section along the biscuit box wall.

"Private Hook, glad to see you still among the living," Sergeant Gallagher acknowledged.

"I've never felt so alive in my entire life, sergeant," the soldier replied.

He hunkered down next to John Williams, and they resumed their scanning of the ramparts nearest the burning hospital. The compound was strewn with bodies. These were mostly enemy warriors, though they did see a few of the unfortunate patients who failed to make the trek to the inner defences. John Williams' gaze kept falling on the unfortunate Trooper Hunter. He'd shoved him out the window during their initial escape, only to watch him get cut to pieces by waiting Zulus.

"How many times have they come since nightfall?" he asked Sergeant Gallagher, trying to take his mind off the poor fellow whose death he blamed himself for.

"I lost count about an hour ago," his section leader replied, shaking his head. "Gutsy bastards, you have to hand it to them."

"Bright as day, that is," Private Williams said appreciatively. He looked over the sights of his rifle, scanning for any signs of movement.

"Just don't look directly at the fire, lads," Colour Sergeant Bourne stated as he walked down the line. "You'll end up blinding yourselves." This seemed like a needless order to give, but the company's senior NCO knew that morbid curiosity would get the best of some of his soldiers. It was difficult not to stare in wonder at the sight of the burning structure.

Williams' thoughts were soon interrupted by the loud cry of *'Uzulu!'* from the encroaching darkness. Scores of warriors rose from the north and south ramparts. With no access via the southern face of the storehouse and the cattle kraal creating a nearly impassable hazard, the only approaches left to the Zulus were the north wall and the open compound between the hospital and storehouse.

"I think they're braver than us, by God," Harry Hook said, leaning into his rifle and firing once more.

Chapter XVI: Retaking the Camp

Isandlwana
7.30 p.m.

Mahlabamkhosi Hill, immediately south of Isandlwana
Later known as 'Black's Hill'

The last glows of the setting sun illuminated the hills to the west, while the low ground on which the No. 3 Column marched was slowly enveloped in darkness. Every man had his gaze turned towards the remnants of the camp, filled with the vain hope that they might find their friends still among the living. Was Isandlwana really taken or were the reports from Commandant Lonsdale simply the ravings brought on by his head injury?

Imperial redcoats from the 24th advanced in close order, bayonets fixed, their eyes scanning for any sign of enemy warriors. The NNC on their flanks were becoming skittish and had to be prodded constantly by their officers and NCOs. Carbineers and volunteer cavalry screened the far flanks of the column, while the Imperial Mounted Infantry acted as a vanguard. These men were led by Lieutenant Anthony Walsh; a regular army officer from the 13th Light Infantry, who'd volunteered for service in Southern Africa. It was he who the previous night had brought some much needed rations and blankets to the beleaguered NNC troops at Mangeni.

About two miles from the camp, they spotted a lone rider coming out of a donga to the southeast of Isandlwana. He waved to the men and quickly galloped his horse over to them. "Thank God, they did not get you as well!" the man said excitedly. He saluted the officer and introduced himself. "Trooper James Raymond, Newcastle Mounted Rifles, sir."

"Are you all that's left?" the lieutenant asked.

"Of those who did not escape, sir," the trooper replied. "We ended up with Durnford's mounted darkies and fought those savage niggers from a donga about a mile up that way." He waved over his shoulder towards the mountain. "Some of us got scattered when the colonel ordered the retreat. Saw a couple of lads from the rocket battery on stolen horses heading west. I thought the rest of you had gotten the chop, so I was waiting until dark to make my escape."

"So, the Zulus are still between here and the camp?" Walsh persisted.

"No idea, sir," Raymond confessed. "Once I got clear of the immediate danger, I went to ground."

"Alright," the officer replied. He felt a mixture of pity and loathing for the man. He had clearly been through a terrifying ordeal, yet he ran instead of falling back with his mates. Given the extreme improbability of there being any witnesses to his conduct, Lieutenant Walsh reckoned he could not order the man arrested and court-martialled for cowardice. Under the circumstances, simply being alive was not exactly a crime. Still, it irritated him that the trooper had no useful intelligence for them. Walsh dismissed him, ordering him to report to Lieutenant Jones who had a handful of men from the Newcastle Mounted Rifles on the left flank.

The column continued on about another quarter mile when a loan African wielding a spear and shield sprang up from the tall grass.

"Hostiles to the front!" a mounted infantryman shouted, leaping from his saddle and firing a shot at the man. In his haste, the private had not bothered to check his sights, and the bullet flew over his target's head. Twice more his weapon cracked before his sergeant rode over.

"Cease fire! Are you fucking blind?" the NCO roared. "That man is wearing a red scarf on his head. He's one of ours!"

"And who the hell taught you to shoot?" one of the soldier's friends called out to him.

The sergeant gave the man a hard cuff across the ear and told him to get back in formation. The terrified African man was on his knees, hands held high, pleading with the mounted redcoats. Several NNC warriors were calling out to the man, who they appeared to know. Trooper Symons, who spoke a little Zulu, rode over and listened to the man's story.

"What's he saying?" Lieutenant Walsh asked.

"Hard to say, sir, he's speaking so damn fast. Something about… he yearned for home and left the camp that morning. Found his way blocked, and so he was waiting for night."

"Another filthy coward," the lieutenant spat. "Get rid of him."

Symons told the warrior to leave and never return. Relieved, he picked up his shield and spear and began to run past the columns of soldiers. He waved at his friends from the NNC before heading south, away from the British and Zulu.

"Strange happenings in this land," the IMI sergeant said to Walsh, before they ordered their men to continue. The lieutenant was in a foul temper. Now he would have to explain to Lieutenant Colonel Russell why one of his men had fired on one of their own natives.

As the sun set, they continued their sombre journey and were about three miles from the mountain when suddenly a handful of fires sprung up from within the camp.

"What's happening there?" a mounted soldier asked.

"Perhaps the camp has been retaken?" one of his mates answered with his own question.

Lieutenant Walsh scanned the camp with his field glasses, yet could not make out any details aside from the fires. He rode back up the column and reported to Lord Chelmsford what they had seen.

"Thank you, lieutenant," the GOC acknowledged. His eyes were fixed on the road ahead, his expression unchanged.

"Will…will that be all, sir?" Walsh asked, confused at the lack of additional instructions.

"The Zulus were burning our tents earlier," Lieutenant Colonel Crealock explained. "Carry on, lieutenant, and keep us informed if anything substantive arises."

It would not be long before the column did find something of note. A little further on, hundreds of voices shouted *'Zulus!'* while pointing to the north, off to their right.

Chelmsford halted his horse and pulled out his field glasses. "So those are the warriors who vanquished my men," he said quietly. The Zulu *impi* he had so fervently sought a decisive engagement against was several miles away on the slopes of a mountain called Nqutu. The ground was covered in a great moving black mass that extended for miles. As a gentle breeze blew in from the north, Lord Chelmsford could hear the faint chants of their war songs as they marched away from the mountain. He had no way of knowing what was being said, yet their tone sounded both triumphant, as well as mournful.

Behind his battalion, Lieutenant Colonel Henry Degacher watched the spectacle of withdrawing enemy warriors in the distance. Their sheer numbers told him that, had they found them at Mangeni, his battalion would have been in serious trouble. If such a huge force caught them scattered on the march, as they had been all morning, they would have been chopped to pieces. Like most of the column's officers, Degacher had been dubious of the reports that the Zulus had gone all the way around to the north and across mountaintops to reach the camp. Seeing this mass of dark-skinned humanity, and what he guessed was at least 20,000 warriors, utterly perplexed him.

"Seems we've found his lordship's Zulus," Major Black said, trying to mask the disdain in his voice.

His commanding officer did not bother to hide his growing feelings of loathing. "The only reason we're still alive, Wilsone, is because the Zulus did not know we were fumbling around in the dark, fifteen miles away."

The strain in his voice was apparent and he refrained from saying anything further. Seeing the Zulu *impi* for himself filled him with feelings of dread for Henry Pulleine and the lads from 1st Battalion. Adding to this was the fear he felt for his brother, William, who'd been serving as Pulleine's acting-Major. Though they knew nothing of what transpired at the camp, in his heart, Henry Degacher knew his brother was dead.

As the British saw the withdrawing mass of Zulus, so too did the *impi* spot the column of redcoats returning to Isandlwana. Ntshingwayo stood atop Nqutu Mountain, squinting as he tried to make out the enemy force in the distance.

"It would seem we did not destroy their entire army, *inkosi*," one of his senior commanders, Vumandaba, said as he stood beside the old warrior. "Should we send word to the *amabutho* and have them ready for battle once more?"

Ntshingwayo shook his head slowly. Though elated at their great victory over the white soldiers at Isandlwana, he knew his army was in no condition to fight another battle. Being deprived of their breakfast, coupled with the miles they had run, and the hours-long ferocity of battle had sapped them of their strength. They were burdened by droves of wounded, many of whom were being dragged on makeshift litters. And while he could not ascertain the exact size of the British force, for they were several miles away, he sensed their numbers were even greater than the garrison they defeated earlier that day. They appeared to be fairly concentrated, not spread out like the defenders at Isandlwana. He relished the thought of even greater glory and spoils for his warriors, but Ntshingwayo knew the risk was far too great for his exhausted and depleted army.

It baffled the *inkosi* as to just where these enemy forces had been all day, and why they were returning now, as opposed to when the battle still raged. Not knowing this force of British soldiers was even out there had been a failure on his part, yet by the same token, he surmised that perhaps the white soldiers had not even know the *impi* was at Isandlwana.

In addition to the fearful losses suffered by the *amabutho*, the entire Undi Corps had disobeyed the king and conducted its own invasion across the uMzinyathi. It angered the *inkosi* that

Cetshwayo's own regiment, the uThulwana, was among those now missing. How could those who'd stood beside their king for decades, who helped him seize the throne of amaZulu from the pretender, so impetuously defy their sovereign? Had the Undi Corps followed orders and remained in reserve, perhaps Ntshingwayo would have allowed them to test their mettle against this force of imperial soldiers approaching from the east. He seethed at such a lost opportunity!

"We have won a great victory," the *inkosi* said solemnly. "The *amabutho* completed the mission set forth by their king. The remnants of our enemies flee for Natal. Our dead require burial, the wounded medicine and healing. And all of our spirits must be cleansed and purified before we return to Ulundi."

Much to the relief of his warriors, the *inkosi* ordered the impi to retire to the gorge behind Mabaso Hill, where they had previously encamped, and to remain there for three days while the wounded recovered and details were sent out to see to the dead. It was nine miles over rough ground, but at least the men of the *amabutho* knew they would finally be able to rest. The wounded were numerous, and their injuries horrific. Scores of men succumbed, even as their friends carried them along. Many more would perish from infection or blood loss in the coming days. Ntshingwayo reckoned that in three days, he would know which of his warriors could make the long journey back and which ones would never see home again.

Night had fallen. The last traces of the sun disappeared beyond the hills that led to Rorke's Drift. The column was now passing the conical koppie known as Amatutshane and approaching the Nyogane donga where Durnford's column made its stand against the Zulu 'Left Horn'. They were still about a mile from camp, and the handful of burning fires provided the only light in the enclosing darkness. The mounted men noticed their horses behaving strangely, walking about in odd patterns as if they were trying to avoid something.

Charlie Harford, riding alongside his 2/3rd NNC with the mounted redcoats of the IMI, took it upon himself to dismount and see what the matter was. He knelt and felt around, his hand coming upon flesh and what he could make out was a shield.

"What is it, Mister Harford?" Major Dartnell asked.

"Enemy dead, sir," the officer replied. "They're all over the place. Seems their companions were unable to give them a proper burial. Instead, they just laid them facedown and covered them with their shields."

"Which means some of our lads made a good stand from the donga," the major noted. He shook his head. "But that donga is at least a mile from the camp. What in God's name was Durnford thinking?"

The order to halt was soon passed along from the GOC, and the column made ready to launch its assault upon the camp. Though they had seen the Zulu *impi* in the distance, there was a very real possibility that a force had been left behind to ambush any wayward bands of imperial soldiers that dared return to Isandlwana.

"The 24th will lead the attack," Chelmsford explained to Henry Degacher.

While the commanding officer of 2/24th ordered his two majors to form their companies for battle, the GOC rode over to Lieutenant Colonel Harness and told him to unlimber his guns.

"Fire three salvos into the camp," he ordered.

"Beg your pardon, my lord," Harness replied, "What if our men did actually retake the camp, and it is their campfires that we see?"

"I am beyond wishful thinking, colonel," Chelmsford replied curtly. "The only people that may still be amongst the living at Isandlwana are the Zulus. We may have seen their main army in the distance, but that doesn't mean there aren't a few stragglers waiting for us."

Harness gritted his teeth and nodded. His men then set about unlimbering their guns and forming them into a firing line. This was no easy feat in the dark, and men tripped over rocks and ruts in the uneven ground. Powder charges and shells were brought forward, and within minutes the booming of their four guns shattered the silence in the night. The first shell sailed in a low arc, with one soldier pointing out that it looked like a meteor falling from the sky, before it burst over the nek of Isandlwana. Another shell struck the mountain itself, sending shards of rock falling to the earth, while the remaining two burst among the wreckage of the tents. The campfires were almost immediately extinguished.

"Seems there are some Zulus lurking about," Harford murmured.

"Well, they're smarter than our own natives. They wouldn't have the sense to put out their fires while being shelled," Major Dartnell added.

Meanwhile, Lieutenant Colonel Degacher rode in front of his assembled companies. They were approaching from the southern end of Isandlwana where 1st Battalion had encamped just south of the wagon track.

"Battalion will fix bayonets!" he ordered, before turning to the ever-reliable Major Black. "Wilsone, take four companies and assault the heights of the southern hill. Major Dunbar will take the rest and breach the south end of the camp."

"Sir," the Scottish officer said with a salute.

The hill, known as Mahlabamkhosi to the Zulus, lay south of Isandlwana and would be the perfect place for the enemy to spring an ambush.

Major Black dismounted his horse and drew his pistol. "Ready, boys?" he asked over his shoulder. Without waiting for a reply, he ordered the four company commanders to follow him. With nearly four hundred riflemen on his heels, Major Wilsone Black made his way quickly yet methodically up the hill.

In the encompassing darkness, soldiers kept just a few feet between each other lest they lose their mates in the night. There weren't many signs of struggle, as most of the fighting had taken place north of the hill. Only a handful of Zulu dead were found along the slope. As a precaution, these were bayonetted by the nervous redcoats. One warrior, clearly not quite dead, let out a loud groan. The man who stabbed him leapt back, startled to find anyone alive in this unholy place of death.

"Serves you right, you goddamned heathen," the soldier snarled quietly, once he regained his composure.

Advancing a few paces ahead of his men, the burly Scotsman, Major Black, held his pistol at the ready, maintaining a strong posture to inspire confidence in his soldiers despite the lingering terror that twisted his guts. As they reached the top of the hill, with no signs of the enemy, he called down, *"All clear, my lord!"*

This elicited a series of ovations from the rest of the column; their cheers contrasting with the stillness of night and the unseen spectacle of death surrounding them. Near the southern edge of Isandlwana, Lieutenant Colonel Degacher controlled the retaking of the camp.

"Major Dunbar, clear the camp with the rest of the battalion. Major Dartnell, Commandant Browne, advance in support."

As redcoats, European volunteers, and African auxiliaries made their way through the ruined remnants of 1/24th's camp, the scope of the wreckage and numerous bodies created an endless series of obstacles and tripping hazards. The horses of the mounted troops became increasingly skittish, often refusing to go any further as they came across piles of dead men, unseen by their riders in the darkness.

Lieutenant Nathanial Newham-Davis of the IMI dismounted and hunkered down next to a body he spotted lying in front of his horse. The face was turned towards him, eyes vacant and expressionless. "By God," he whispered quietly, making a 'sign of the cross'.

"What is it, sir?" one of his soldiers asked.

"It's Captain Bradstreet," the officer replied.

The commander of the Newcastle Mounted Rifles, whom he knew personally, had originally been tasked with accompanying Lord Chelmsford to Mangeni. Lieutenant Newham-Davis, who was not originally supposed to be with the expedition, had offered to go in his place. A chill ran up his spine. That could very well be him lying there as a disembowelled corpse.

Emerging from a donga, Lieutenant John Maxwell of the Natal Carbineers found himself amid several supply wagons. These were mostly empty; either they were among those Horace Smith-Dorrien had intended to send back to Rorke's Drift that morning, or they had been looted by the Zulus. Remnants of a campfire illuminated one of these wagons, upon which sat eight to ten enemy warriors. These men had discovered the 24th's stockpile of spirits and were completely inebriated. They were talking and laughing, without a care in the world. They knew the British column had returned, yet in their drunken state it became an amusing game of hide-and-seek.

As the officer carefully drew his carbine from its scabbard, he could not see any of his troopers, who were lost somewhere in the darkness. Maxwell fumbled for a cartridge in his pouch. He could only feel five or six remaining. And as close as he was to the Zulus, he knew that he could shoot one, maybe two, before they were upon him. He gulped a deep breath as he saw the flashing of red jackets in the firelight beyond the wagon.

"Contact right!" he shouted to the men, who abruptly turned his way. The lieutenant removed his hat and waved it frantically a few times, before pointing towards the wagon.

A 24th corporal waved for his men to follow him, and they quickly swarmed the wagon. A few startled cries in the night as the Zulus were bayonetted, and it was over. Maxwell let out a sigh of relief as the corporal walked over to him; blood trickling along the sword bayonet protruding from his weapon.

"You alright, sir?" the NCO asked.

"Yes, thank you. Seems not all the Zulus have buggered off after all."

The corporal hefted his rifle and gazed at the crimson streaks along the blade. "I hope we find a few more of the bastards. The regiment has some scores to settle."

Another scream in the night alerted the men, though this was followed by maniacal laughter from a pair of soldiers who'd found another victim for their bayonets. While the killing of enemy wounded, as well as any who attempted to surrender, blatantly defied the accepted conduct of war, not to mention common decency, neither Lord Chelmsford nor any of his officers felt inclined to stop their men from vengeance killing this night.

On the far right of the formation, Charlie Harford dismounted and was leading his horse through the trampled grassy plain that lead from the main camp at Isandlwana to the Nyoni Ridge to the north. He had no way of knowing exactly where Lieutenant Colonel Pulleine had established the firing line, nor from which direction the Zulus attacked. The high ridge that looked down upon Isandlwana and the surrounding plain made the most sense. If the Zulus had followed their standard protocol, they would have attempted to encircle the camp using the 'Horns of the Beast' tactic. Harford surmised that the donga to the east, where they'd found numerous enemy dead, was likely one of the 'Horns'. This meant that Nyoni Ridge was where the 'Chest' had launched its attack.

The ground here was strewn with boulders and felt extremely damp, despite the lack of rain from the past few days. Harford expected to feel the tall grasses brushing up against his knees, yet all was trampled flat. He then understood. The ground beneath his feet was not wet with rainwater but slick with the blood of hundreds of fallen warriors. The Zulus had hastily dragged away many of the bodies, yet he stumbled across a few, and even stepped in a pile of shredded entrails.

"They must have taken one hell of a beating," he said softly to himself. There were fewer actual bodies to be found in this section of the battlefield, as the Zulus had dragged away those who fell furthest from the camp. In the coming days, bands of warriors would return to Isandlwana to find their mates who were missing and most likely lying among the rows of slain redcoats and their African allies.

The acting-captain noticed his NNC warriors were clustering close together rather than maintaining their battle formation of two ranks.

"Kuyini lokhu?" Harford shouted at the men, demanding to know why they were huddled together. He wished he could remember a few choice profanities in isiZulu. Instead, he barked at the men to get back into formation. *"Singene kumiswa!"*

Were it not for the macabre and tragic spectacle all around them, it might have been amusing to watch his terrified warriors haphazardly try to maintain some semblance of formation. Even their *izinduna* were equally terrified that the Zulus would somehow leap out of the darkness and disembowel the lot of them. Taking a deep breath through his nose and blowing it out in frustration, Harford remounted his horse and rode up and down the line of his NNC companies. He berated his European NCOs with equal fervour, demanding to know why they could not keep control of their wayward fighters. It only added to his frustration that most of those who filled the ranks of his non-commissioned officers were of Dutch or Germanic stock. Their grasp of the English language was tenuous at best. And since almost none spoke Zulu, Harford could not even communicate with them this way.

"Bloody worthless mercenaries," he muttered, after swiftly shoving a cowering Dutch corporal with the heel of his boot.

It was nothing more than inherent prejudice and the perceived superiority of anyone with white skin which prevented the Natal Native Contingent from electing their own leaders and fighting in their traditional manner. Instead, the GOC had been convinced that only white Europeans were fit to lead. While the indigenous warriors would have to fight with mostly their own weaponry, they were compelled to organise themselves into European-style infantry companies. It was an absurd series of directives which only set up able officers like Charlie Harford for failure. But, the average warrior of the 3rd NNC was a far cry from the valorous fighters from the land of the Zulu. Aside from the iziGqoza, most of the Natal contingent were utterly terrified of the Zulus. Some had only joined the ranks for the pay, or because their local chieftains—who were hoping to gain favour with the British authorities—had compelled them to do so. None had any desire to die for Queen Victoria and the British Empire, and they wished for nothing more than the chance to slip away into the night. Indeed, many did just that, once they figured their white officers were no longer watching them.

"They're even more anxious than usual," the civilian magistrate, Henry Fynn, said as he joined Harford. "I keep hearing some of the amaChunu muttering the name, Gabangaye; the prince of their tribe and eldest son of Chief Pakade."

"He remained here while most of us left for Mangeni," Harford recalled. "He was a brave man. I suspect if it were daylight, we'd see his body lying amongst our lads."

As they slowly trekked closer to the ruined camp, the stench of death nearly made the young officer gag. Many of the dead had loosed their bowels as they were killed, and all of those slain by the Zulus had their guts splayed open.

"Smells like someone tried to cook a rotten sweet potato," a trooper from the Newcastle Mounted Rifles muttered, as he fought against the retching of his stomach.

In addition to the horrific smells were the unholy cries that filled the night. Aside from the occasional Zulu straggler there were no signs of human life left at Isandlwana; however, there were still plenty of badly injured animals the Zulus had attempted to slay but not quite finished the job. One trooper nearly burst into tears at the cry of dying mules, stating that they sounded like sobbing children. The howls from a pack of wild hyenas added to the cacophony of horror. As he dismounted his horse near where he thought his tent was, Charlie Harford speculated this night would drive them all mad.

"I wonder if I'll ever sleep well again after this," he said quietly.

The faint booming of Harness' cannon could be heard at Rorke's Drift. The nerve-frayed soldiers perked up at the first sounds of life coming from across the river.

"Seems his lordship is still in the fight," Sergeant Windridge thought aloud.

"I recall he'd taken most of the cannon with him," Lieutenant Chard mentioned to Bromhead. He then pulled his fellow officer aside and added, "It would seem the column has returned to Isandlwana. I just hope your lads from the 24th can make it back here in time. We're running out of ammunition, and the lads are completely spent."

"If we're close to breaking, then so are the Zulus," Bromhead countered. "And should we fire our last cartridge, we can still make a right many of them bleed on the ends of our bayonets before the end comes."

Though he had mastered the art of maintaining a stalwart demeanour in front of his men, Gonville Bromhead's nerves were completely shattered. He could not for the life of him see how he was going to make it through this night alive. Even if Lord Chelmsford and 2/24th had retaken the camp at Isandlwana, they were still ten miles away. It was unlikely they would attempt the journey in the dark. If they were able to see the glow of the burning hospital, as was likely, they might assume the garrison had been wiped out; negating any sense of urgency to return. And so the defenders of Rorke's Drift were still very much on their own. Still, 'Gunny' knew that to show fear or a loss of composure was unbecoming of an officer holding the Queen's Commission. If he was to die this night, then he would make certain it was in a manner worthy of the name 'Bromhead'.

Pacing along the line, his left arm holding numerous ammunition packets, was Private Fred Hitch. Having shot the last of Lieutenant Bromhead's pistol cartridges, he decided the best way to still be of some use was to help ferry ammunition to the firing line. The task was simply too much for the beleaguered Reverend Smith to manage on his own. He was joined by Private Hitch, as well as Corporal William Allan. Allan's injuries had bled profusely; leaving him in a weakened state after Surgeon Reynolds patched him up with a hastily applied compress and bandage. But like Hitch, he was determined to do as much as possible so long as he could stand.

Near the low wall along the south side of the storehouse, Hitch became dizzy and collapsed to his knees, the cartridge packets flying from his good arm. His friend, George Deacon rushed over to his side. Noting that Fred's wounds were bleeding afresh, he found a discarded blue jacket belonging to Commissary Dunne. Deacon ripped out the lining, which he fashioned into a bandaged that he wrapped around Hitch's terrible injuries.

"Even the immortal Fred Hitch has reached his limit," he said quietly, noting his friend's pale complexion as the blood drained from his face. Shaking his head, he asked, "When the end comes, do you want me to put you out?"

"No," Fred replied, shaking his head. "No, I don't think so, even though I may not have the strength to finish myself. The Zulus have nearly done me in, so I'll grant them the courtesy of putting me away when the time comes."

Despite his blurred vision and the terrible pain which extended from the wounds throughout his body, Hitch fumbled around in the dark and picked up a pair of ammunition packets, which he handed to his friend. "Here, you'll be wanting these."

Deacon gave a weak smile, clutched his friend reassuringly by the shoulder, and then returned to the line. Hitch took a few deep breaths and pulled himself to his feet once more. He wasn't even sure how long it had been since that Zulu shot him. It felt like hours, yet all concept of time had left him. Though he could scarcely stand, he was determined to continue to do what he could. He would use the ramparts and storehouse to prop himself up and store any cartridges he could scrounge into his left ammunition pouch. Whatever happened, he was resolved to die standing.

The Zulus were now shifting away from the light cast by the burning hospital roof. Soldiers continued to fire at shadows and silhouetted figures, as the enemy sought the cover of darkness east of the depot. To attack from the west meant only death. Companies from the *amabutho* were scattered about, with many warriors either in small bands or alone in some cases. Uncertainty now gripped them, as individual warriors felt very much alone. Was the rest of the Undi Corps even out there? Or had they abandoned the field and left them behind?

Even Prince Dabulamanzi could not say with any certainty where his regiments were. He privately confessed that it had not been a well-thought out plan of attack; the iNdluyengwe rushing into the fray without waiting for the rest of the corps. The remaining regiments had attacked of their own volition with little to no coordination. Dabulamanzi knew that a simple council-of-war could have alleviated much of the subsequent confusion. That said, there had been no scenario in his mind where the white soldiers could have possibly held out until after nightfall.

To the east of the cattle kraal, he found a pair of *izinduna* and several companies from the iNdlondo Regiment. They had spent most of the evening skirmishing to the north and east of kwaJimu. They were clearly exhausted; their stomachs ravenous with hunger. One warrior said as much as the prince joined them.

"I promise, you will all feast once we take their last ramparts," Dabulamanzi reassured them. Seeing the trace of doubt etched into the faces of the warriors closest to him, the prince sought to reassure and inspire them for that final push that would win the day. Standing tall, he addressed all who could hear him in the encompassing darkness.

"My uncle, the great Shaka, once said that the glory of victory is measured by the hardships the victors face. Many times did he seize victory, even as defeat threatened to snap its vile jaws around him. You are sons of Zulu! No amount of white men cowering behind their walls of grain sacks can withstand the might of the king's *Inhlabamasoka,* the chosen men! Come, my friends. Who will follow me into kwaJimu?"

With shouts of *'Usutu!'* from the *izinduna,* hundreds of warriors rose from the grass, echoing the sacred war cry of their king, and charged into the fray once more.

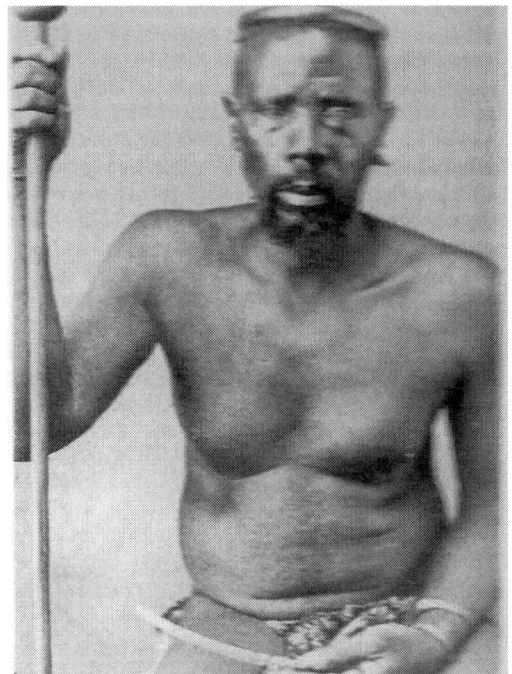

Zulu Induna

Chapter XVII: Night of Horror

Isandlwana
11.30 p.m.

Major Francis Clery
Staff Officer, No. 3 Column

With the threat of any prowling Zulus taken care of, Lieutenant Colonel Henry Degacher formed his battalion into a protective square near the ruined camp of 1st Battalion. He then sat with his back against a rock outcropping, his gaze fixed on the glowing embers of nearby tents, wagons, and various equipment. Major Dunbar kept the other officers and men away from their commander, who he knew wished to be left alone.

Lord Chelmsford ordered the entire column to form a defensive perimeter near the wagon track. The four companies from 2/24th under Major Black anchored the square from atop the hill south of Isandlwana with all other elements dressing off them.

"Post sentries and allow the men time to rest," Chelmsford ordered his assembled staff officers. "But be ready to depart before first light."

The GOC wished to spare his men the sight of seeing their slain friends, and so they would have just a few hours to rest before departing for Rorke's Drift. His stomach growled, and he knew his men were being tortured by want of food. He could only hope the Zulus had not sent regiments across the border into Natal. Given their lack of food, sleep, and the miles they had already trekked, his men would find the remaining journey back to Rorke's Drift a gruelling slog as it was. If the mission station had fallen, the depot looted, and Major Spalding's command wiped out, they would have an additional fifteen miles to reach the next nearest possible source of rations at Helpmekaar. Having completely lost the initiative, as well as nearly half the centre column and all their supplies, Chelmsford could do little except hope for the best.

Despite the GOC's order that no one be permitted to explore the camp for missing friends or personal belongings, small bands of soldiers and carbineers crept out into the darkness. For one thing, the want of food was overpowering at this point. The redcoats and artillerymen had long since consumed the humble rations they'd tossed into their haversacks that morning. The NNC had not eaten since the previous evening. The punishing exertion of having trekked nearly thirty miles in less than a day, plus fighting a running battle at Mangeni, compounded their hunger and extreme fatigue.

As he attempted to make himself as comfortable as possible, Henry Fynn noted a pungent stench far different than that of the dead and disembowelled. He heard a slow groaning coming from a wagon just twenty feet from where he laid his bedroll. The wagon had belonged to the veterinary surgeon, containing medicines and salves used for treating the column's horses and draught animals. Fynn crept towards the sound of moaning and found an older Zulu warrior lying up against the spoked wheel of the wagon. A pair of bottles lay broken open next to him. He clutched his stomach, yet was devoid of any injuries that Fynn could see.

"A poor choice of refreshment," the magistrate said to the man, speaking to him in his native tongue. He read the contents of one such bottle.

"For many years, I have heard of the spiritual waters consumed by the whites," the Zulu man replied, gritting his teeth in pain.

"Sorry, baba, but these are not 'spiritual waters'," Fynn replied consolingly. He stopped himself from speaking further. He knew the man was not long for this world, even if the patrols of furious redcoats had failed to find and gut him. Having drunk an entire bottle of ointment used for disinfecting animal wounds, as well as some other unknown substance, it was a wonder he was still alive. In a great show of compassion, Fynn decided to stay with the man, providing him some measure of comfort so he would not have to die alone.

Having placed his men in the square with designated guard shifts, Lieutenant John Maxwell sought to get some much-needed sleep. He fed and watered his horse; pouring water from his canteen into his slouch hat that the tired animal might sate its thirst. He then removed his saddle, which he lay on the ground to use as a pillow. His mind clouding over, he folded his hands on his stomach as he drifted off to sleep.

An hour later he was woken by a member of Chelmsford's staff. "Damn it all," he said quietly. "What is it?"

"Your pardon, but the GOC has asked for you personally," the unknown voice said in the darkness.

"I didn't even think he knew my name," the officer said, groggily pulling himself to his feet.

He was soon taken to Major Clery, who was carrying an oil lamp. There were several officers with him from the column staff, as well as Chelmsford's ADCs. Once Lieutenant Maxwell joined them, they began a slow walk of the outer picquets. The ground was rugged and broken. As he stumbled about, reckoning he would have difficulty even in broad daylight, Maxwell could not figure what any of this had to do with him. At the last sentry post, near a rather steep precipice, Lord Chelmsford stood waiting with Colonel Glyn, Lieutenant Colonel Crealock, and about a dozen escorts.

"My lord," Maxwell said.

The GOC's eyes bore into him. "You're a pretty fellow not to know where your sentries are," Chelmsford said, his voice cold.

"Beg your pardon, sir?" The lieutenant's expression betrayed his confusion.

"This section is supposed to be manned by the 2nd NNC," the GOC stressed.

"And how does that concern me, sir?" Maxwell asked.

Chelmsford raised an eyebrow, a scowl forming across his face. The officer quickly explained, "These aren't my sentries."

The GOC's expression softened, and he nodded in understanding. "I beg your pardon," he said by way of apology. "I was informed you were the officer on duty. I am sorry you were disturbed. Do you know where your staff officer and duty officer are?"

"I can find them for you, sir," Maxwell said with a tired nod.

"Be a good man and send them here."

The lieutenant gave a tired salute and stumbled back, hoping he could find his camp in the incessant blackness. Before, there was Major Clery's lamp to see by. Now there was nothing. He had gone perhaps a dozen paces when he tripped on an unseen rock and pitched headfirst down the slope. He instinctively extended his arms to catch himself, his hands and wrists landing in something soft and squishy. He let out a loud yelp which brought the major with his oil lamp. To his abject horror, Maxwell realised his hands were buried in the guts of a slain soldier. He frantically pulled back, scrambling away from the dead man whose body he had unwittingly defiled further.

"Good God, man, are you alright?" Clery asked.

"Better than this poor fellow," Maxwell replied hoarsely. He gazed in disgust at his hands and sleeves soaked in blood, body fluids, and bits of entrails. Moments before, he wanted nothing more than his saddle pillow and a few hours' sleep. With this added horror, John Maxwell knew there would be no rest for him this night.

Despite being unable to see more than a few feet in front of him, Charlie Harford inexplicably managed to find the ruins of his own tent in the wreckage of the camp. Commandant Rupert Lonsdale's tent was next to his own; however, his attempts at finding any of their personal belongings proved futile. There was nothing left except the fallen and torn swaths of canvas. As he crept along, Harford saw a pair of artillerymen lying between the two tents. Like the others, their guts were split open, and they were terribly mutilated.

He was soon joined by Major Clery who asked what he was doing away from the square. Harford explained that he was checking on his picquets. Both men knew this was only a half-truth. The major said nothing more but agreed to accompany him, providing some lamplight for the acting-captain to see by. Walking along the nek of the mountain, they came across a rolled-up tarp.

"Not that I'll get any sleep this night, but I could use a sit-down for a few minutes," Clery remarked.

Charlie agreed, and the men sat on the tarp. Both immediately leapt to their feet when they realised there was a body lying underneath. They turned and stared at the mass, not sure what to do.

The major swallowed hard and said, "I don't know if you have the stomach for curiosity, because I certainly don't."

Harford could only shake his head in dismay. Whether the body belonged to a British soldier, allied warrior, or fallen Zulu they would never know. How it came to be rolled up in a tarp was a bizarre mystery that would trouble them both. Neither could bring themselves to see who the poor soul was.

For Colonel Richard Glyn, the return to Isandlwana was soul-crushing. His entire career of service to the Queen and Empire had been with the 24th. Though he'd recently been brevetted to full colonel in command of the entire No. 3 Column, his substantive billet was still commanding officer of 1st Battalion. While there could be little doubt that Chelmsford mourned the loss of so many fine officers and men, these were not his soldiers; he had not spent twenty or more years bonding with the officers and their families. Nor did he know a thing about any of the enlisted rankers, except perhaps the names of Sergeant Major Gapp and a handful of the most senior NCOs. To Richard Glyn, the officers were his brothers and the enlisted men his sons.

With Francis Clery handling much of the column's placement and posting of sentries, Glyn was free to wander about the devastated camp alone. Chelmsford, like always, paid him no mind. He could not go far, for the darkness of night was all-consuming and the ground very rugged. Plus, he felt it heartless to trip or step on the bodies of his slain soldiers. By the faint light of some burning tents, he spotted a lone body lying on its side. It was difficult to say for certain, but he felt sure it was Lieutenant Colonel Henry Pulleine;

his former battalion major who'd assumed command of 1st Battalion just five days before.

"Oh Henry," Glyn mumbled sadly, shaking his head. "I'm so sorry."

In the flickering light of the fires, he saw another officer lying amongst half-a-dozen soldiers. All had their tunics removed, and were covered in blood from having been gutted by the Zulus. Though he did not have the stomach to investigate closer, given the officer's smooth, boyish face, Glyn was almost certain it was 24-year old Lieutenant George Hodson. Hodson was the lone subaltern in Captain Reginald Younghusband's C Company, 1/24th. Ever eager to prove his mettle and self-conscious about his inability to grow a proper 'manly' set of whiskers, the young lieutenant was one of the bravest officers Glyn could recall. Respected by the enlisted men, *mentioned in despatches* three times during the Xhosa War, he had a fine career ahead of him. That career, however, had ended in a sea of carnage on the slopes of a mountain in Southern Africa that no one back home in Britain had ever heard of.

"At least he died a proper soldier," Glyn said, trying to reassure himself. It was a futile gesture. In his heart, he knew there was nothing manly or glorious about the way his battalion had been destroyed. While it was noble that the officers had stood beside their men, willingly giving their lives, the colonel knew it had all been in vain. Were he given actual command, rather than usurped by the GOC, Richard would have never divided his forces. He would have kept his column intact, advancing methodically towards the Zulu capital in accordance to his lordship's intent. However, he had not been in command, nor could he take back what had happened. His greatest regret now, which would haunt him for the remainder of his days, was that he had not died with his men. His surviving battalion major, Charlie Bromhead, who was on leave in England and whose brother was now fighting for his life at Rorke's Drift, would doubtless feel equally shattered once the news reached him. Though his body still drew breath, Colonel Richard Glyn's soul died on the slopes of Isandlwana.

The knowledge that they lay among the bodies of the fallen in a hell-scape of horror, and the fear that the Zulus might return and finish off the column, haunted every man who struggled to rest that night. How they outwardly handled the situation varied considerably. Captain 'Offy' Shepstone was a nervous wreck, no doubt made worse by fears for his brother, George, who was as staff officer with Anthony Durnford's column. During a series of false alarms throughout the night, he could be heard saying goodbye to his fellow officers, stating 'we shall not see the sun rise again'. That such an assertion was made, while no actual threat materialised, was viewed as unbecoming by several redcoats and volunteers who overheard his shaken words.

In contrast, the indomitable Major Wilson Black diligently remained with the four companies from 2/24th atop Mahlabamkhosi Hill, his booming voice providing strength and calm reassurance to his men every time there was an alarm.

"Steady lads!" he shouted. "Don't be shooting blindly into the darkness. Cold steel is our motto!"

One of the carbineers who overheard the major's calls to his men would later note, "Major Black is the man for me...no going around saying goodbye about him."

Another trooper, near the ruins of the looted commissary stores, thought he saw a pair of young lads hanging from the butchers' hooks. To him, it appeared they had been hung from the hooks beneath their chins and disembowelled while they were still alive. Such was the birth of a myth which would echo down the generations as fact; that the ten to twelve-year old *'little drummer boys'* had been barbarously butchered by the inhuman savages. In truth, most of the drummers of the 24th were in their twenties. The youngest was sixteen; a grown man by the measure of the day. What the trooper saw that night was never known. He compared the sight to that of 'gutted sheep', and it may have been butchered livestock hanging from the hooks. The myth of the slaughtered drummer boys aside, the carnage and devastation left at Isandlwana was still an epic tragedy.

Just a few miles west of Rorke's Drift, Major Henry Spalding and the two companies from 1/24th continued to march in silence. Holding date-of-rank on Russell Upcher, Spalding assumed overall command of the detachment. After their initial conversation, little was said. They made the painstaking trek to the mission station in silence. Their pace had slowed considerably once the sun fell. The road was rutted and gouged so badly that soldiers kept tripping and oftentimes falling onto their faces, as they stumbled across unseen hazards. Most of the soldiers elected to walk on either side of the trail, though the trampled grass with the occasional brush stand proved little better.

It was also the night of the New Moon. With clouds blotting out most of the starlight, it was impossible to see more than a foot or two in front of one's face. Jittery young privates muttered their fears of Zulus springing up from the ground and slaying the lot of them. NCOs were quick to remind them that if they could not see in the dark, then neither could the Zulus.

He could not see his watch in the smothering darkness, but Spalding reckoned it was about an hour before midnight. They were still at least two or three miles from Rorke's Drift, which would likely take them at least a couple hours at the rate they were crawling along. It was maddening. As they cleared a small rise, he signalled for the column to halt.

"What *is* that?" Captain Rainforth whispered.

They all saw the unmistakable glow on the horizon.

"That is Rorke's Drift," Spalding replied with a sigh. "It would seem we are too late."

"Do you want us to continue the advance?"

"I wouldn't advise it," Upcher spoke up. "If the mission station is on fire it means the Zulus have crossed into Natal and likely wiped out the garrison. We have less than two hundred riflemen, and the enemy may number in the thousands. Even if they are bumbling around in the dark, they can still overwhelm us by sheer force." He stopped himself and looked to Spalding. "It's your call, Henry."

Spalding's stomach turned in knots. He found himself in an utterly hateful dilemma; one which he wasn't certain there was a right answer to. If they retired back to Helpmekaar and, in fact, there were members of the garrison still alive, depriving them of support would be nothing short of handing them a death sentence. On the other, it was impossible to tell if anyone was alive or not. And even if they were, it was quite probable that their two companies would run right into swarms of Zulus, who likely had the mission station surrounded. The horizon was red with fire, which burned into his mind. In all probability, his small command at Rorke's Drift was gone.

Fearing whichever decision he made would be the wrong one, Henry steeled himself to whatever fate his next words brought him to. "Turn the column around. We're heading back to Helpmekaar."

Atop Mahlabamkhosi, Major Wilsone Black pulled his greatcoat around his shoulders. A faint drizzle had begun, and the clouds blotted out even the faintest traces of starlight. He was joined by Commandant Browne and Captain Duncombe of the NNC, along with an African interpreter named Umvubie.

"Major, sir," 'Maori' said, as he knelt next to the officer. He could scarcely see two feet in front of his face. The only way he could tell it was Black was by the very faint glint off his pistol. Black was also wearing a wide-brimmed hat he much preferred over the issued Foreign Service helmet.

"Commandant," Wilsone acknowledged. He nodded towards what appeared to be a series of flashes to the west. "What do you make of that? Looks like fireflies."

Brown pulled out his field glasses. Through the drizzle and engulfing darkness, he could not make out any sort of detail. It was impossible to know how far away the flashes were or what they might be. He cocked his ear towards them, seeking to confirm what his instincts told him. And though he heard not a sound, except the soft patter of the occasional raindrop and the nervous breathing of the nearest soldiers, his heart sank.

"Those must be flashes of musketry," he surmised. He asked Captain Duncombe to confirm with Umvubie.

After a few moments, the captain replied, "Yes, it would appear the Zulus are attacking the camp at Rorke's Drift. And that glow…by God, the mission station burns!"

Maori gritted his teeth and turned to Major Black. "Sir, do you know if the camp was laagered?"

"Laagered with what, exactly?" Wilsone asked. "Gunny Bromhead's two wagons and a handful of biscuit boxes?" A fluent speaker of Gaelic, he began muttering under his breath for the greater part of a minute. Browne first thought he was praying, but the bitterness in his words told him otherwise. As a gentleman officer, it would be improper for Major Wilsone Black to use the coarse language of the enlisted soldiers; thus, whenever he needed to spew forth a string of profanities, he did so in Gaelic.

"Oh, fuck me," a private near Brown stammered. "The Zulus are in Natal!"

"So they are," Captain Duncombe concurred.

It was then they saw a series of glows where they guessed the riverbank was. No doubt these were the homesteads of various settlers and border policemen. "God help the women and children."

They could not be certain how many Zulus had crossed into Natal. Though they had seen the main *impi* retreating from Isandlwana, the British had no way of knowing just how large the Zulu army was. For all they knew, a second *impi* could be launching the very counterthrust that Lord Chelmsford had feared since the beginning of the campaign. Even more distressing for Major Black and Commandant Brown was the red glow that rose behind where many of the rifle flashes could be seen.

"I think that answers your question about whether the camp was laagered," Wilsone noted with bitter resignation. If the storehouse and hospital were burning, he knew Major Spalding's tiny command was not long for this world. 2nd Battalion had already lost Charlie Pope's G Company, and now it appeared that 'Gunny' Bromhead and the rest of B Company were doomed to oblivion. Wilsone could only hope they died well.

Chapter XVIII: The Final Redoubt

Rorke's Drift
Midnight

An injured Private Fred Hitch, carrying ammunition to the line
From 'The Defence of Rorke's Drift' by Lady Butler (1880)

Unbeknownst to Major Black or any of the survivors at Isandlwana, the burning of the hospital was proving to be a source of salvation for the battered garrison huddled behind the inner barricades at Rorke's Drift. Had they simply left the hospital intact, the Zulus could have used the cover of darkness to crawl right up to the inner biscuit box wall undetected. As it was, the glow of the still-burning thatched roof lit the ground within fifty yards of the compound.

Besides Lieutenants Chard, Bromhead, and Colour Sergeant Bourne, the only other person making any sort of movement behind the obstacles was Reverend Smith. His apron full of cartridge packets, he was making his way around the defences once more. Though he made no mention of it, he knew their reserve stockpile was fast running out. Commissary Dunne had broken open the last box of 800 rounds, handing a few extra packets to Smith's already full apron. As he walked around the perimeter, he tried to count how many men remained in the fight. Many of the invalid patients, as well as those who'd been wounded during the fight, still manned their posts. They were determined to die fighting rather than capitulating and begging the Zulus for mercy.

He returned to the storehouse, handing up his last two packets to Lieutenant Adendorff and Corporal Atwood in the attic. Reverend Smith then took a deep breath and closed his eyes. Though he had not ceased in his silent prayers during the last eight hours of battle, the lull in the fighting was discomforting. Despite his private chastisements, he was suddenly afraid. Tales of Zulu barbarism and cruelty haunted him, coupled with extreme exhaustion and the encompassing night.

"If I fall this night, let me die well." He prayed for what felt like the hundredth time. He further implored the Lord to forgive the soldiers for their blasphemous conduct. Even the most devout, such as Private Henry Hook, had their breaking points. Surely God understood this!

Just outside the storehouse lay a large pile of unused mealie sacks. Lieutenant Chard kept looking at them, thinking they might be put to some better use.

"Mister Bromhead, Colour Sergeant Bourne!" he called out. The officer and senior NCO walked briskly over and saw their officer commanding staring at the large pile.

"I need some men to form these sacks into one final redoubt next to the storehouse. We'll place some riflemen inside. They can then provide supporting fire over the heads of our troops on the line."

"We should place the worst of the wounded in there, as well," Bromhead spoke up.

"I'll sort it out," Commissary Walter Dunne said, as he joined the men. He waved his hand towards the empty ammunition boxes scattered about. "We're down to our last box and-a-half anyway, so not much else for me to do."

"Very good, Mister Dunne," Chard replied. "The outer rampart should be seven feet high with a firing step inside. As Mister Bromhead suggested, we'll place the worst of the wounded within."

Despite their terrible fatigue, a handful of soldiers came to assist Commissary Dunne in forming the large piles of mealie sacks into a single strongpoint. They worked with surprising speed and were glad to not have to carry the heavy mealie bags dozens of yards like earlier that afternoon. The circular redoubt was raised quickly with Dunne standing on top, shifting the upper layers of bags into place. A tall man, he stood out conspicuously, particularly with the still-burning hospital roof illuminating the ground. Numerous shots rang out from Zulu skirmishers, and even a few assegais were flung in his direction.

"Well, that's a bit rude of them," the commissary said, falling onto his face as a pair of musket balls whizzed high over the redoubt. Dunne called out to the men below, "Right you are lads! In you go!"

Three or four soldiers from each section were directed to man the final redoubt under Colour Sergeant Bourne's command. Though just a few feet above the heads of their mates, the position gave them an uncanny view of the surrounding area. Even in the enclosing darkness to the east, the men could make out the movement of shadows in the direction of the cattle kraal.

"Here they come!" a private shouted.

Colour Sergeant Bourne squinted his eyes and stared hard in the direction the soldier pointed. He spotted numerous shadows dancing about. "They're making for the cattle kraal, sir!" he called down to Lieutenant Chard.

The company's senior NCO checked his sights and tried to discern distinctive shapes within the dancing shadows. He could make out the outline of the kraal, and he decided to aim just above its ledge. His rifle cracked, followed by several more from the men in the redoubt. Soldiers below could discern a Zulu warrior flying backwards as he was knocked from the top of the kraal. Sergeant Windridge, whose section was covering the eastern approach, ordered his men to fire a pair of controlled volleys into the kraal.

"Aim just above the wall," he instructed.

"Bloody hell, sergeant, I can't even see the damned wall!" a private bickered.

"Then shoot in the same direction as everyone else!" Windridge snapped before issuing a command to his section. *"Volley...fire!"*

Twenty rifles thundered as one, their psychological impact even greater than any possible casualties inflicted. Most of their shots had flown high or struck within the kraal. Only two Zulus were hit. However, as Sergeant Windridge quickly ordered his men to reload and unleash another volley, it became apparent an attack from the east was no more feasible than any other direction. With shouts from their *izinduna*, the attack force scattered into the night.

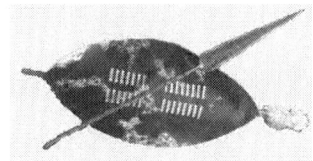

The eruption of scores of rifles shattered the stillness of the night. The small band of redcoats used the glow cast by the burning hospital and the elevation of the innermost redoubt to spot enemy warriors. Though the Zulus could get much closer than during the daytime, those approaching from the north and west had to cross at least thirty to forty yards of illuminated ground. And as the latest barrage of musketry demonstrated, it was no use trying to come from the east either. The cattle kraal acted as a natural barrier to slow the Zulu assault. Even in the darkness, the redcoats could see enough of its wall to use it as a marker for their volleys.

The British kept low behind their mealie bag and biscuit box ramparts, negating the effectiveness of Zulu muskets. For Dabulamanzi, it was utterly disheartening to watch helplessly as swaths of his warriors were shot to pieces by the incessant volleys of British rifle fire.

Leading this latest desperate charge from the east were two companies from his own iNdlondo Regiment. They had already suffered many dead and injured over the course of the day, and their combined strength numbered just over a hundred warriors. The intent was for those in the lead rank to reach the small rocky cliff face, and then offer up their shields as steps for their mates to leap onto the ramparts. It was not to be, however, as the compressed files of imperial soldiers loosed a terrible salvo of musketry, ripping apart the lead companies. Twenty men fell dead or shattered in the first few seconds, with the rest immediately dropping onto their stomachs.

The prince grimaced as this last attack foundered before it had even begun. There was very little return fire from the Zulu skirmishers. Most were simply out of ammunition. His own pouch had just two crude bullets remaining, plus he was out of percussion caps. Dabulamanzi did not even consider trying to find a useable weapon in the thick brush. He could see very little and did not have the stomach to see which of his skirmishers were dead or simply trying to stay hidden from the enemy.

British fire continued unabated. He saw several bands of warriors making an assault on the biscuit box wall. They fared no better than those attacking the north wall. Murderous enemy fire ripped to pieces those unable to find cover.

Prince Dabulamanzi came to the bitter conclusion that this battle could no longer be won. "They can keep Jim's house," he said to his nearest *izinduna*.

Under most circumstances, the leaders of the Zulu warriors would have chastised the king's brother as weak and cowardly. However, they, too, were completely demoralised. They had been running or fighting since earlier the previous morning. Ravenous from lack of food, they had run nearly thirty miles following the right and left horns of the main *impi*, then pursued the fleeing fugitives all the way to the uMzinyathi River. What transpired just a few hours before felt like a lifetime ago to the Zulu prince. Their complete failure to capture the depot, despite destroying what had once been Jim Rorke's house, filled them with shame. This indignity tore at Dabulamanzi's soul even more so than the deaths of so many of his brave warriors.

Without another word, he and the nearest *izinduna* began to slink away from killing fields surrounding Rorke's Drift. As the Zulus did not use bugles, the only way to sound the retreat to the rest of the corps was by shouted commands, yet no one wished to draw attention to themselves while the defenders were still firing at whatever they could see or hear. The other regiments would have to figure out for themselves that Jim Rorke's place could not be taken.

Pockets of fighting continued for the next couple hours as wayward bands of warriors attempted one last time to capture the ramparts. However, these were further met with horrendous volleys of British musketry. It was unfortunate for Prince Dabulamanzi that he had no way of knowing just how close the British were to breaking. Their ammunition was nearly gone, and the constant fighting had sapped them of their strength. If he could simply wait until dawn with his skirmishers continuing to draw fire from the defences, he could utilise the unified strength of his corps to overwhelm the garrison. As he stole away, he ceded control over the *amabutho* to any who wished to continue the fight.

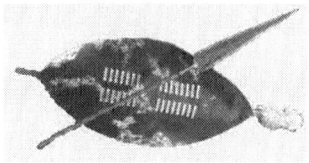

Not all the Zulus were defeated, however. To the west of the burning hospital, scores of warriors from the uThulwana readied themselves for another attack on in the inner stronghold. As the king's personal *ibutho*, the idea of returning to Ulundi in defeat was a worse prospect than even a brutal death by British bullet or bayonet. It was here that, despite his injuries, Mandlenkosi managed to rally roughly a hundred scattered fighters.

"We've been fools," he said candidly. "The burning of Jim's home has denied us the cover of night. Now we shall turn the fires against them." He then took a spear from one of his men. With his good arm he began to pull up long clumps of dried grass, which he then wrapped around the end of the spear.

"Take these and bring fire to their remaining building," he directed. "The red-jackets have nowhere else to run. Set fire to the thatch, and we'll incinerate them where they lie."

Several warriors followed the *induna's* example and began to wrap swaths of grass around their assegais. A pair of men boldly surged forth from the cover of darkness towards the scorching inferno that consumed what had once been Jim Rorke's home.

"Over there!" a private along the biscuit box wall shouted, pointing to the southern face of the hospital. At least six or seven warriors were visible near the wall. The ends of their spears were wrapped in dry grass they were now setting alight.

Shots rang out, and one of the warriors was struck several times while his friends dropped into the low trench behind the depot. Soldiers within the perimeter could clearly see the light from the torches; however, the Zulus were keeping low and out of reach.

Riflemen standing in the final redoubt could have reached them, except its placement within the inner compound meant the storehouse was in the way.

"Damn it all, they're going to burn the storehouse!" Chard moaned, mildly surprised the Zulus had not already attempted this.

There was an uncomfortable pause as the chain of burning lights continued to move laterally towards the loan remaining structure. A single shot rang out from the storehouse attic, then another. From his position, Second Corporal Francis Atwood could clearly discern this latest threat; the very one he'd been warning about all day. It was he and Lieutenant Adendorff who opened fire upon the Zulu torchbearers. Three were struck down in rapid succession before the NNC officer's rifle jammed. This allowed two enemy warriors to get dangerously close to the storehouse. Atwood maintained his composure, shooting one man through the chest, quickly reloading, and felling his last victim when just thirty feet from the building. Unlike regular torches, the clumps of grass tied to the ends of spears burned very quickly and within a minute or so were completely extinguished.

"We got that sorted out, sir!" Atwood called down from the attic window.

"Thank you, corporal," Chard acknowledged. "Keep a sharp watch on the hospital, and let us know if any others try to bring fire to bear."

"Right you are, sir." Atwood's voice was shaking, no doubt brought on by his terrible fear of burning to death.

Something that distressed Private Henry Hook perhaps even more than the possibility of the storehouse catching fire were the cries of the sick and wounded coming from the veranda, as well as the final redoubt.

"Water!" most of them pleaded. "Please, give us some water!"

"Poor bastards," John Williams said, lying his head against the biscuit box wall. He fought against the overwhelming exhaustion that consumed him. His very soul was consumed by the nightmare that he feared he would never wake from.

"And to think, we have a water cart just beyond the damned hospital," Hook added. He set his rifle against the barricade.

Hunkering low, he sprinted to the western edge of the storehouse, where a pile of metal buckets was stacked.

He was soon joined by Williams. Each man looked the other in the eye for a moment before finding their resolve.

"Where do you two think you're going?" William Jones asked, bemused at seeing his mates each carrying a pair of buckets.

"Our charge was to care for the hospital patients," Hook explained. "It doesn't do much good to save them from the Zulus only to have them succumb to thirst. I'll die before I allow them to suffer any more."

"Well, you're not going without us!" Robert Jones asserted. He and William each grabbed a single bucket, while also hefting their rifles. The four men then scrambled over the barricade, much to the alarm of Sergeant Gallagher who was checking on his soldiers near the far end of the wall.

"Private Hook!" he shouted.

"Keep us covered, sergeant!" Harry called back before his section leader could say another word.

"Damn impetuous," Gallagher grumbled, though he found himself smiling with pride at his soldiers' selfless bravery. He patted four soldiers on the shoulder at the north end of the rampart. "You men, lay suppressive fire near the water cart."

"Right you are, sergeant," one of the privates replied.

He and his companions began firing shots in the general direction north of the water cart that was illuminated by the hospital's flames.

Hook and Williams kept their heads low. Zulu skirmishers still prowled about the fruit orchard and stone wall, firing random shots in their direction. Robert and William Jones paused a couple of times, kneeling and dropping their buckets as they returned fire. Harry and John quickly fell behind one of the spoked wheels of the cart, suddenly fearful there might be Zulus hiding beneath it. There was one man lying beneath, yet he lay perfectly still. In the flickering light, it was difficult to tell if the man was dead or simply pretending to be. If he were still alive, Hook prayed he would not notice that his unexpected visitors were unarmed.

Knowing they had just moments to spare, they turned open the spigot. A torrential gush of water drenched the ground, while splashing into their buckets. Williams even took a moment to stick his head under the spigot; the cold downpour on his head felt like it was heaven sent. A few seconds later, the Joneses joined them. They kept watch while Hook filled their buckets.

"Come on, before the Zulus see us," Robert Jones said nervously.

"They'd have to be blind to miss us," Hook retorted, as he closed the spigot. A musket ball slammed into the side of the cart, causing all four men to flinch. Robert loosed a shot in the direction it came from. They grabbed the life-saving water and started back towards the inner defences.

The wire handles dug into Hook's hands, as he tried not to spill any of the precious liquid. He could not run nearly as fast as before, and was having to keep low behind the north wall while Zulus continued to shoot at them. His eyes were fixed on the ground. He stepped over and around several Zulu bodies that littered the yard. So fixated was his gaze, he nearly ran straight into the low biscuit box wall and had to abruptly stop himself short, lest he spill his cargo.

"Here we are, lads!" he said excitedly, hefting the buckets onto the rampart.

Williams and the Joneses were right behind him. Even as frustrated Zulu skirmishers continued to fire in their direction, all managed to clamber over the wall.

Hook then dropped down to one knee and slowly caught his breath. He was suddenly aware of his section leader kneeling next to him.

"I don't know if that was brave or foolish, Private Hook," he said sternly.

Harry thought he could see a trace of approval in the young sergeant's countenance.

"Had we been shot down, we'd be rightly named fools," he replied. "But I will let the poor suffering lads from the hospital judge us."

The four soldiers made their way the short distance to the hospital veranda. Harry noticed Lance Sergeant Thomas Williams lying on Reverend Witt's altar, which Surgeon Reynolds had commandeered as an operating table. Shot through the ribs during the same salvo that struck down Fred Hitch, he lay trembling. His entire body was soaked in sweat, as the doctor probed the terrible injury. Hook watched for a few moments as Reynolds extracted the musket ball. Upon further examination of the wound, Harry thought he saw the surgeon shake his head before directing his orderly to bandage the lance sergeant and carry him outside.

"We brought water, doctor," Harry said, catching Reynolds' attention.

The surgeon's eyes were bloodshot, his face sweating as he took a deep breath. His addled mind then realised what the soldier had just told him.

"If anyone cares more about these patients than I do, it's you, Private Hook." He allowed himself a brief smile. "Leave two buckets here. The rest can be used to provide water for the wounded."

The four soldiers did as they were told and then quickly returned to their places on the firing line. Surgeon Reynolds, Sergeant Gallagher, and indeed the entire garrison were awestruck by what they had just witnessed. To Private Henry Hook and his mates, they had simply fulfilled their duty to the patients of the hospital.

Around 2.00 in the morning, the firing from enemy skirmishers ceased altogether. No one within the Rorke's Drift garrison took this to mean the enemy was beaten. It was generally assumed that the Zulus had run out of bullets or were saving their shots in support of the next attack.

"Could be they are waiting for dawn to come," John Chard surmised. He joined Bromhead at the corner of the ramparts looking northeast towards the drift.

"It's a double-edged sword if they are," 'Gunny' remarked. "On the one hand, we'll be able to see them. But on the other, they'll be able to coordinate their attacks better."

"Nothing to do but wait, I suppose."

Bromhead concurred. "It's their move now. Sort of like playing chess, only we cannot see our opponent's pieces."

With a lull in the fighting, the officer commanding of B Company decided to go check on the wounded. As he made his way quietly over to the storehouse veranda, he noted the dried streaks of blood that clung to his bayonet. The acrid smell of scorched black powder and spent casings stung his nostrils. He sighed and stood the weapon against the veranda railing.

Since the first assault, he had been so consumed by the actual fighting that he wasn't able to spare a single thought to his fallen soldiers. What immediately caught his attention were the dead. Surprisingly few, yet the lieutenant knew there were others slain during the fighting in the hospital.

The first body he knelt next to was Storekeeper Louis Byrne, whose act of pity had cost him his life. He'd been shot through the head while bringing water to a wounded soldier on the line. Next to him was Private Edward Nicholas, who'd also taken a bullet through the brain. There were three others whose names Bromhead did not know. He could only assume they were hospital patients who were subsequently killed on the firing line. His gaze turned to the hospital, still a burning inferno. Flames licked through the windows of the outer stone walls. The engulfed thatch roof collapsed on itself.

"How many did we leave in there?" the officer asked despondently. He slowly rose and made his way over to where the wounded were being gathered within the inner redoubt.

A pair of soldiers were assisting poor Fred Hitch. His indomitable strength had finally failed him. The wrist on his useless right arm was belted to his waist; the crude bandages applied to his shoulder and back were saturated in sticky blood.

"Poor old Brickie," said Private Deacon, who'd hastened over to help his friend.

"Never mind, boys," Hitch managed to reply. "Better a bullet than an assegai."

There were other gravely wounded kept inside including Corporal Allan and Commissary Dalton; both of whom Bromhead noted had behaved heroically throughout the day.

Bromhead knelt next to the gravely injured commissary, whose eyes were half shut. "If we survive the night, every man here will owe his life to you," 'Gunny' confessed quietly.

"I no longer wear the uniform," Dalton replied through parched lips. "But I still have my duty to perform. Have to hand it to the boys, Mister Bromhead. Fresh-faced youths most may be, on this day they fought like lions."

"That they did, Mister Dalton. That they did."

Chapter XIX: The Sombre Return

Isandlwana
23 January 1879
Dawn

Commandant George Browne, saluting the body of his fallen friend, Lieutenant Colonel Henry Pulleine

It was hard to fathom that anyone from No. 3 Column got any sleep, lying among the mutilated bodies that had once been their friends. They could see little in the shroud of night, yet the stench of so many disembowelled corpses made many of them nauseous. Before the faintest glow of predawn illuminated the ground, Lord Chelmsford ordered the men roused and ready to depart. His intent was to spare his soldiers, and likely himself, from seeing the horror and devastation around them.

A bleary-eyed Henry Degacher found the GOC and the staff officers gathered around Major Clery's small oil lamp. Richard Glyn was conspicuous by his absence.

"2nd Battalion is ready to march, my lord."

"My lads are just finishing up saddling their mounts," Lieutenant Colonel Russell of the mounted troops added.

"Cavalry will screen our front and provide vedettes on the flanks," Chelmsford said, anxious to get his men away from this terrible place. "Artillery will take the centre of the column. Colonel Degacher's infantry will march in column-of-twos on either side. Commandant Browne will oversee the rear guard with his natives and a few mounted volunteers."

What was left unspoken, yet consuming everyone's thoughts, was whether the depot at Rorke's Drift had been destroyed. There was also a very grave concern as to enemy forces still in the region. Degacher's infantrymen were down to about thirty rounds apiece. The IMI and mounted volunteers had done far more of the actual fighting at Mangeni and had, perhaps, ten cartridges each. As much as he'd longed for a decisive battle against the Zulus, at that moment, all Chelmsford wanted was to get what remained of the centre column back to Rorke's Drift in one piece.

Hardly anyone in the column spoke. Soldiers quietly pulled on their boots and packs. Sergeants and corporals wordlessly conducted a quick inspection of their men before following their officers down the sombre track that would take them to the uMzinyathi.

Though the GOC intended to be well away from Isandlwana before light, the sun was just starting to break over the hills to the east as Commandant George Browne's rear guard made ready to depart. He sat astride his horse, his eyes taking in the surreal sight. The voice of Charlie Harford startled him.

"You want to see it too, don't you?" Harford was mounted, his face ashen and eyes bloodshot. Whether from tears or lack of sleep, Browne could not be sure.

The NNC commandant nodded and trotted his horse over to where his camp had once stood. There were a few other officers on horseback milling about, willing to take their chances of a berating from the GOC, should he come back to check on them. Though the camp was completely ransacked, Browne was able to find where his tent had been. Lying next to the shredded flap was his old Irish setter; an assegai pinning her body to the ground. His two spare horses lay slain nearby, still tied to their post. 'Maori' shook his head in disbelief. Horses were a great prize to the Zulus. The fact that they killed his mounts rather than stealing them away spoke volumes about the madness they succumbed to.

Not far from the horses he saw the bloodied bodies of two European officers from his NNC battalion. Their carbines were missing, yet there were piles of spent cartridges strewn about. Their guts were split open, and flies gathered around to feast on the entrails.

"They were two of my finest shots," Browne said quietly. "I reckon those black bastards paid a high price bringing them down."

The two rode onward to the left front of the camp, careful not to allow their horses to trod upon the bodies of the dead. Most of the slain redcoats had their jackets and helmets taken as part of some bizarre Zulu post-battle ritual. Every corpse, European and allied African alike, was disembowelled. It was plain to see where entire companies fell, for they were laid out in squares where they had made their final stands. The largest of these was Charlie Pope's G Company, 2/24th which had his own troops, as well as all the soldier-servants and other attached soldiers from the battalion who'd remained at Isandlwana.

What surprised Harford was how vast the battlefront was. There were many slain Zulus, as well as a few British troops, about a mile north of the camp facing the Nyoni Ridge. He surmised that was where the firing line had been before withdrawing back on the camp, where most of them were killed. From what he could see, it was readily apparent they had been spread precariously thin. Henry Pulleine likely had no idea what he was up against until it was too late. If the Zulu 'Chest' had come down from Nyoni Ridge, the right and left 'Horns' could manoeuvre around their flanks and behind them without ever being noticed.

"The Zulus did a terrible job of caring for their dead," Harford remarked. The ground leading to the nearest dongas was littered with enemy corpses. So thick had they fallen, that it would be impossible to take more than a couple steps in any direction without tripping over bodies.

A strange sight greeted the two officers as they reached a wagon where the remnants of C Company, 1/24th had executed their charge. Of course, neither man knew about their stand from atop a small ridge below the nek of the mountain before fixing bayonets and charging, once their ammunition was expended. It was what they saw just behind the wagon that perplexed them.

"That's Reginald Younghusband," Charlie noted, having met the officer commanding of C Company a few times.

The captain's forehead was partially caved in and the back blown away from a close-range musket shot. Like all the others, his uniform jacket was gone and his guts split open. His arms were folded across his chest, his eyes closed, and he lay atop a Zulu shield. There were eight additional shields laid out in neat rows on either side of his body.

"He must have made a hell of a stand for the Zulus to lay him out so reverently," Browne reckoned. "I'll wager those shields belonged to men he killed."

There were ten additional fallen soldiers nearby. They had been dragged over and laid in a single row near the head of their fallen captain. Harford then saw a lone soldier lying about twenty feet away, conspicuous in that he had not been dragged over with his mates, and he still wore his red jacket. Charlie dismounted and walked over to the man. An assegai protruded from just beneath his ribcage. His eyes were open and lifeless, fixed upon the heavens. His right arm was extended out from his side. When his eyes adjusted to the encroaching shadow of the mountain, Harford saw that the soldier was clutching the hand of a slain Zulu. The fallen warrior lay on his side, a broken bayonet stuck between his ribs. The officer gave a sad smile and a nod of appreciation. He assumed the two men had slain each other, and then reached out and clasped each other's hands as they lay dying in an eternal bond of mutual respect. Because the Zulus had left them undisturbed and not bothered to take the soldier's jacket, he knew that they, too, recognised this splendid display of comradeship and honour, in what was otherwise a horrific scene of merciless slaughter.

"Rest well, my brothers." Charlie removed his hat and bowed his head for a moment. Though he would never know the names of Arthur Wilkinson and Kwanele kaMandlenkosi, their faces were forever etched into his mind.

The call of a bugle snapped him out of his stupor.

"Come on, Mister Harford," Browne said. "Let's not keep his lordship waiting."

It was a mile from the wagon path to where they found the remains of Captain Younghusband and his men. They kept their horses at a slow trot, lest they step on the bodies of their mates.

Finding a relatively clear path, the NNC commandant kicked his horse into a gallop. Just north of the track, not far from where 1/24th had made their camp, 'Maori' reined his horse in sharply. Even in the pale light of the early morning dawn, he recognised the body of his old friend, Lieutenant Colonel Henry Pulleine.

"Damn it all."

The man who had led the defence of Isandlwana lay on his side, his lower arm extended slightly. His jacket and helmet were missing, and he was covered in blood where his guts had been split open. Browne could see a gaping hole just beneath the neck, where he was shot. His tongue protruded slightly past his lower lip, his eyes were scrunched shut, and his glasses askew on his face. 'Maori's' heart sank. There was nothing manly or glorious about how his friend had been slain. Henry Pulleine, Lieutenant Colonel and commanding officer of 1st Battalion, 24th Regiment, husband to Frances, and father of a young son, was dead, and that was it.

As he abruptly halted his own mount, Harford also recognised the body of Pulleine. Though he had only known him in passing, he was aware of his friendship with George Browne. He gave the commandant a moment to reflect before speaking up. "Come on, there's nothing you can do for him."

"Nothing," 'Maori' echoed, swallowing hard. It sickened him to know he could not even give his friend, or any of the fallen for that matter, a proper burial. Within days, Henry Pulleine and the other 1,300 British and allied slain would be set upon by wild dogs and other foul beasts. Swarms of flies were already feasting on the dead flesh. Browne let out a sigh of resignation, saluted his fallen friend, and spurred his horse onward.

Sadness consumed the men as they returned to their battalion. Near the wagon trail, Harford noted the sorrowful sight of a young African lad, probably a voorlooper. The boy was on his knees, knelt forward, his face buried in his hands. The hideous gash where an assegai was plunged into the back of his neck was clearly visible. The officer shook his head sadly.

"They spared no one, regardless of age."

Just south of 1st Battalion's camp were large numbers of bodies near what had once been Quartermaster Pullen's staging point for ammunition. These had mostly been European volunteers, with a few of the more stalwart African allies who'd stood beside them until the very last. The large wooden boxes of cartridges had been plundered, as had anything else of value. A civilian doctor who accompanied the column as a volunteer dismounted near the body of an engineer officer. He noticed a glint coming off a watch tucked halfway into the man's pocket. Not wishing for it to be looted by scavengers, he took the watch and promised to find the owner's next of kin.

The carbineers of the rear guard had not gone far when they saw an overturned wagon in a nearby donga. The draught animals were all still in their yokes, their throats cut. As they rode past, one of the oxen let out a loud groan and tried to stagger to its feet.

"Bugger me," a startled Trooper Symons said, taking a deep breath. Feeling pity for the poor creature, he dismounted and waved one of his mates over. With as much care as they could manage, they cut the leather straps and freed the animal from its yoke. The ox lurched from the wreckage of its fallen fellow beasts and lumbered away, following the path to Rorke's Drift.

"If it gets all the way to the drift, maybe we can have it for supper," the other trooper muttered.

They continued in silence for about three miles, where they reached a shallow stream called the Manzimyama. Harford overheard an argument between a dismounted trooper and Inspector Mansell of the Natal Mounted Police. It was Mansell who accompanied Lieutenant Coghill on his ill-fated 'mission' to fetch a chicken for Lord Chelmsford's supper, a few days prior.

"What do you think you're doing, man? Damn it all, have you no respect for the dead, that you would rob them?" the inspector shouted.

The trooper was removing the spurs from the boots of a slain carbineer. "My own spurs are missing. What, you think I should leave these as a prize for the goddamn Zulus?"

"Let it go, inspector," Harford said to Mansell gently. "The dead would rather their mates make use of equipment they no longer need, rather than the enemy seizing it as a trophy."

The inspector grumbled under his breath and trotted his horse away.

Harford sighed and rubbed his fist vigorously into his tired eyes. More than two full days had passed since he'd gotten any sleep, and like everyone else in the column, he was extremely hungry. He knew his NNC warriors were in an even sorrier state, to the point that even the volatile and unmercifully prejudiced Commandant Browne took pity on them.

At the stream, many troopers dismounted to water their horses and sate their own thirsts. Harford saw one officer vigorously trying to wash dried blood and gore from his hands and forearms. He overheard that the poor fellow had tripped during the night, his hands and arms accidentally burying themselves in the guts of a slain soldier.

"That's a good deal more comfortable," the man said, as soon as he'd washed the last of the distasteful remnants from his arms.

Harford decided to wash his face, hoping the cool water would help wake him up. He dunked his hat in the stream and dumped it over his head. The shock of the cold sent a jolt down his spine, serving its purpose of bringing him fully awake. He rubbed his hand over his sore neck before remounting his horse and continuing on their melancholy way.

Dabulamanzi and several hundred warriors from his iNdlondo Regiment crept away during the hour prior to dawn. With the glow of the burning building at kwaJimu behind them, he knew its name would forever mark their disgrace. At that moment, however, with hunger gnawing at his stomach, and fatigue threatening to devour him, he did not care about things like victory or glory. There was an even greater hazard to face, if they were to return to their homes.

Crippled by exhaustion, with many of their wounded fellows to assist, they stared into the waters of the uMzinyathi River. The moored pont was visible midstream. Even if they were able to run it, it would not be sufficient to get his men across in a timely fashion. He was further concerned that the glow from the fire at kwaJimu might bring enemy reinforcements to the drift.

"There's a passable crossing further down, *inkosi*," a runner said, having found the fording point used by the British cavalry less than two weeks before.

The river levels were extremely volatile along the uMzinyathi and known to change drastically with little warning. Mercifully for the Zulus, the level had fallen drastically during the night, making the crossing far less perilous than when they'd crossed at Sothondose's Drift the day before. Since abandoning kwaJimu, their numbers had grown as scattered bands of warriors from the Undi Corps converged on what they knew was the closest possible crossing point of the treacherous river.

The prince saw one injured warrior with a chunk of flesh torn from his thigh. It was bound with grass, and two of his companions struggled to help him along.

Dabulamanzi's heart went out to the poor man, who was clearly in much pain. "Come, my friend. I will help carry you across."

He dismounted his horse and knelt down, allowing the injured warrior to climb onto his back. Another even more gravely stricken fighter was helped onto the prince's mount. Though not quite as large as the hulking beast that was his brother, Cetshwayo, Dabulamanzi was still a very big man. He lifted his charge with ease. The warrior's two friends linked arms with their *inkosi* and helped each other cross back into Zululand.

Lord Chelmsford and his staff officers rode in silence. The sun warmed their backs, and despite the cloud cover from the previous night, it promised to be another blistering day. The exhausted redcoats from 2/24th marched with their rifles at port arms, anxiously scanning for any sign of the Zulus. They had seen the main *impi* from a distance, withdrawing from Isandlwana, but the sky had been red with fire in the direction of Rorke's Drift, telling them there was an enemy force still out there.

The GOC had to assume the worst; that Major Spalding's command, B Company of 2nd Battalion, and possibly D and G Companies from 1st Battalion were lost. If so, then it was likely the stores had been plundered or destroyed. His bedraggled force would have no choice but to attempt the journey of an additional fifteen miles to Helpmekaar. His infantry had already marched fifteen miles from Isandlwana to Mangeni then back again before nightfall. Now they were making the ten-mile trek to Rorke's Drift on empty stomachs and with no sleep.

"I wish the Zulus would turn up," Lieutenant Colonel Crealock grumbled. "A chance for retribution will wake the lads up."

"I've already ordered the column not to attack any stray bands of Zulus unless they threaten us," Chelmsford countered.

A brawl with the enemy would most certainly wake the men, but he knew they were in no state for a sustained action. Fatigue and hunger had not only sapped their strength, but also the ability of their officers and NCOs to think clearly. The last thing he wanted was to risk losing more men by allowing them to fall into another Zulu trap.

The GOC was startled by the sound of gunfire coming from the direction of the cavalry vedettes to the right. "Colonel Glyn" he said, addressing the column commander for the first time in more than a day. "Who is covering our flank?"

"Newcastle Mounted Rifles supported by two companies from Commandant Lonsdale's NNC."

The colonel's voice was gravelly and strained. He had said little since they first received word of the disaster. Richard Glyn's heart was completely shattered. Henry Pulleine, William Degacher, James Pullen, and Teignmouth Melvill were dear friends of his. The younger officers and the men in the ranks, he loved like his own sons. And though he only knew Anthony Durnford as an acquaintance, he still greatly respected the man. He could not help but wonder if Chelmsford would try to pin the blame for the disaster on him.

Had he been given actual command of his column, like Evelyn Wood to the north and Charles Pearson to the south, Glyn was certain his men would still be alive. Under no circumstance would he have divided his forces and chased after shadows. He would have continued with the plan, and slowly marched his column towards

Ulundi, keeping his firepower concentrated and allowing the Zulus to come to him. Lord Chelmsford may have been a decorated veteran with ample years of experience and numerous campaigns to his credit, but against the Zulus, he had allowed his arrogance to blind him. The result was a bout of gross negligence and utter incompetence. Richard Glyn knew he would never forgive the GOC for leaving his boys to die. Their deaths ruptured his very soul, and he felt like a shell of what he'd once been. His one regret now was that his men had died, and he had not.

They were alerted to the galloping hooves as Henry Fynn, the civilian magistrate Chelmsford had ordered to accompany the column, came riding towards them from the direction of the right flank vedettes.

"Ah, Mr Fynn," Chelmsford said casually. "No trouble from our mounted rifles, I hope."

"No trouble for us, my lord." Fynn's face was taught. He had been privy to a shooting by the Newcastle Mounted Rifles. Their officer commanding sent him back to explain what happened rather than facing the GOC himself.

"Our men better not be disobeying the general's orders," Crealock snapped, even though he himself had suggested taking the fight to any Zulus they found mere moments before.

"We came upon some huts that were previously deserted. I can vouch that the Zulus we came upon were armed. I even recognised their shields as belonging to the iNdluyengwe regiment of the *amabutho*."

"You know the Zulus too well," Crealock sneered.

Fynn shot him a contemptuous look. "My father was with the expedition that first encountered King Shaka and the Zulus. It was they who acquired the port at Natal for the British Empire in the first place. Or have you forgotten? I've spent a lifetime around them and know more about the Zulus than you ever will, *colonel*." Being a civilian magistrate, he cared nothing for Crealock's rank or position. However, he composed himself as he addressed the GOC. "Your pardon, my lord. As I was saying, we saw shields and weapons leaning against the huts. There was an *inyanga* burning medicines…"

"A what?" Crealock interrupted; fighting the urge to punch the insolent civilian in the face.

"A sodding witchdoctor!" Fynn's patience was waning, and he wanted nothing more than to abandon the ill-fated column and return to his post at Msinga. "He was cooking medicines over a fire. His presence incensed the NNC warriors. They blamed dark magic for our army's defeat. In their rage they slew him. Warriors emerged from the huts, and the mounted rifles were compelled to fire on them."

Chelmsford gave a short nod of understanding and waved for Fynn to leave him. He did not care if his vedettes murdered a few stray Zulus, so long as they did not allow themselves to run off and risk being drawn into an ambush. He was more irritated by the offensive bickering between Fynn and Crealock. The truth was, he needed both of them. Henry Fynn knew more about the Zulus than any man in the column that was still alive. And despite his waspish nature and generally being loathed by his peers, Lieutenant Colonel John Crealock was, at that moment, the GOC's most loyal and trusted staff officer. Even if his conduct was at times unbecoming of a gentleman holding the Queen's Commission, he always told Chelmsford what he needed to hear, no matter how unpleasant. His lordship knew that in the coming days, as he sought to deal with the pending political aftermath of this terrible disaster, he would need Crealock more than ever.

Two hours after departing the graveyard that was Isandlwana, the carbineers and NNC comprising the column's rear guard emerged from Manzimnyama and reached the Batshe Valley where they had destroyed the *inkosi*, Sihayo's kraal eleven days earlier.

"Captain Harford," a trooper said, nodding in the direction of their left front. "What do you make of that?"

About a thousand yards away, a black mass appeared on the open grassy fields.

"Looks like about ten acres of mealie that's been blackened by fire," Harford said, fumbling for his field glasses. His breath caught in his throat as he saw that the mass was not burned grain fields, but a host of Zulu warriors marching away from the uMzinyathi River. "Damn it all."

"What is it, man?" 'Maori' Browne asked upon hearing the commotion.

"Zulus, and a lot of them." Harford handed his glasses to the commandant.

"Does his lordship not see them?" he asked, perplexed.

"If he has, then why aren't Degacher's boys unleashing a few volleys into them? At the very least, Colonel Harness' guns could ruin their morning in a hurry."

Charlie Harford kicked his horse into a gallop and raced towards the head of the column about two miles up the road. He came upon Lieutenant Colonel Arthur Harness, who had ordered his four cannons to unlimber and await orders.

"Looks like blackened mealie stalks," the artillery officer said, echoing Harford's previous assessment.

"I'm riding ahead to warn Lord Chelmsford. If he hasn't seen them, then Degacher's battalion could very well be walking into a trap."

"Good man," Harness said. "And while you're at it, ask him if he wants me to 'reap' a few of these bastards."

It took acting-Captain Harford just a few more minutes of hard riding, with imperial redcoats and NNC warriors parting for him, to reach the head of the column. The riflemen from 2/24th were glancing nervously off to their right. The GOC appeared to be unconcerned.

"My lord!" Harford said, hastily saluting as he reined in his horse.

"Yes, what is it, Captain Harford?"

"Zulus, sir, lots of them. We spotted one…maybe two thousand scarcely a half-mile distant. And if we've seen them, surely they know we're here."

"Yes, I know." Chelmsford's tone was dismissive, almost condescending. "We noticed them long before you did. Some of our NNC vedettes came within three hundred yards of them. If they were looking for a fight, they would have attacked."

"Your pardon, my lord, but don't you think they might be leading us into an ambush?"

"Unlikely. The ground here is mostly open. If they wanted to ambush us, they would have done so back at Isandlwana. I suspect this is some ragged band of warriors who've likely been in a scrap of their own and have no fight left in them. I wouldn't be surprised if this was the same lot who attacked Rorke's Drift. A pity none of them seem inclined to tell us what remains of the mission station."

Harford was dumbfounded, but he said nothing more. He snapped off a salute, which the GOC did not seem to notice, and rode back down the column.

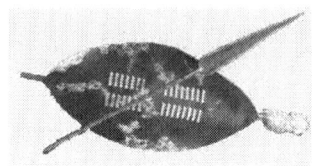

Lord Chelmsford's assessment was more correct than he realised. These were, in fact, some of the remnants from the Undi Corps. What he did not know was that they were withdrawing in shame following their defeat at Rorke's Drift. They were as surprised to see the white soldiers as the British were to see them. For all they knew, the entire enemy column was wiped out at Isandlwana. Where this force of men and cannon came from, they could not say.

It was obvious to them that this band of imperial troops was significantly larger than what the *impi* had destroyed. However, as Chelmsford had surmised, the Undi Corps' will to fight was completely shattered. Many of those making the long, sad journey back to Ulundi were terribly wounded. And like their British counterparts, they were deprived of both food and sleep. The fighting around Rorke's Drift had lasted nearly twelve hours. Hundreds of their friends were killed by the incessant volleys of British rifles and horrific stabs of the bayonet. Even the burning of the hospital and overrunning of the outer defences proved insufficient. Only a scant few had been able to claim an enemy kill, and none were able to retrieve a piece of their victims' clothing for the purification rituals. Aside from the brawl within the hospital, the Zulus had been unable to get close enough to mass their numbers and use their stabbing spears effectively.

For Prince Dabulamanzi, his embarrassment mirrored that of Lord Chelmsford. Both had disobeyed the expressed orders of their sovereigns and met with disaster as a result. Though he would attempt to deflect blame for the losses at Isandlwana, Chelmsford could not entirely avoid responsibility. The same could now be said for Prince Dabulamanzi. He had defiantly led 4,000 warriors across the uMzinyathi River, depriving Cetshwayo of the 'moral high ground' of fighting a purely defensive war in defence of his kingdom. Furthermore, nearly one in every three of his men were either dead or seriously wounded with nothing tangible to show for it. The old warriors of the Undi Corps were proud men. The shame that awaited them, especially from the younger regiments who reaped victory at Isandlwana, would be unbearable.

The bulk of Shiyane Mountain loomed ahead of the returning column. It shielded the mission station from view, though they could see a thick column of black smoke emerging from behind the northern slopes. This left little doubt in their minds that the garrison was destroyed, and the Zulus they passed were yet another victorious enemy army.

'What's become of our mates?' was the most asked question, especially from the soldiers of 2/24th. It was enough of a tragedy that Charlie Pope's G Company had been wiped out with all the soldier-servants, bandsmen, and detached troops the battalion had left at Isandlwana. Had 'Gunny' Bromhead and Frank Bourne shared the same fate?

"They're gone," Henry Degacher whispered mournfully. Though most of the officers and NCOs with field glasses were frantically scanning the remains of the station, the commanding officer of 2nd Battalion did not bother.

"Here, the ponts still look intact," the battalion's sergeant major said, scanning towards the drift.

Chelmsford halted the column and called all senior officers to him.

"I can see just one column of smoke, my lord," Degacher said. "Perhaps the entire depot was not burned?"

"That the pont is still intact is a positive sign," Lieutenant Colonel Russell added.

Chelmsford did not acknowledge either of these remarks. "Colonel Degacher, 2nd Battalion will cross at the pont," he ordered. "Ensure any soldiers still on the Zulu bank are able to provide covering fire for those crossing. But wait until you are supported by the cavalry before you advance on the mission station. Colonel Russell, take all mounted troops and natives downstream and cross as best you are able."

"Right away, my lord."

A sense of anxiousness came over the men. Though it appeared the depot was indeed destroyed, every soldier was anxious to see it for himself. While two companies formed firing lines along the bank, men from Captain Mainwaring's A Company heaved on the rope to guide the pont over to them.

"Index 400 yards," Degacher ordered his companies providing fire support. "Scan the ridgeline to our front, and sound the alert if you see anything suspicious. Company commanders, keep control of the line, and don't go blasting at shadows!"

His two captains gave tired nods. If there were still friendlies alive on the Natal side of the river, it would not do to fire upon them! They and their sergeants raised their field glasses, as riflemen set their sights to four hundred yards. The men fidgeted about, their legs aching and feet battered to the point that most were numb. As the wind blew into their faces from the west, they heard strange sounds coming from the direction of the depot.

"What the hell is that?" one private asked quietly.

"Sounds like bloody ghosts," another remarked.

"Men who will soon become ghosts, more like," a sergeant surmised.

This perplexed the soldiers. After all, the Zulus had gutted every redcoat and allied African warrior they cut down. Why would they leave any fallen British soldiers at Rorke's Drift alive? It was equally unthinkable that they would abandon their own wounded!

About three hundred yards downstream, Lieutenant Colonel Russell and the mounted troops found what seemed like a viable fording point. The professional soldiers of the IMI were collectively his best shots, and he ordered them to dismount and form a firing line to cover the rest of their forces as they crossed. The water was chest deep and deceptively swift; however, within thirty minutes the carbineers and Imperial Mounted Infantry made their way back onto the Natal bank. None were worse for wear, aside from sore bottoms from having been in the saddle for more than a day. Plus, all were now completely drenched.

"Looks like it's going to be another bastard of a sweltering day," Trooper Symons remarked. He filled his wide-brimmed hat with river water and doused his head.

He and the other carbineers left their mounts with designated horse holders and crept through the brush towards the mission station. Though the grass was tall and the bushes thick, they oriented on the column of smoke coming from the hospital. Troopers on the left flank signalled to the infantry as they advanced parallel to the ponts.

"Hold up," the colour sergeant of A Company said, crouching low. He waved Captain Mainwaring over and pointed to the centre of the compound. "Is that what I think it is?"

The officer held up his glasses, struggling to see through the brush. He grinned and gave a sigh of relief. "By God, it looks like Rorke's Drift still stands!"

Chapter XX: What are You Waiting for?

Rorke's Drift
23 January 1879

Zulu Warriors

Dawn came just after 5.00, and the pale glow cast its light on the fearful scene of destruction. The thatched roof of the hospital had fallen in and been completely consumed by the blaze. Fires still licked skywards from the thick rafters. A grisly stench came from within, emanating from the charred corpses of Zulu warriors and British soldiers who'd failed to escape the inferno. Harry Hook noted sadly that poor Sergeant Robert Maxfield was among them.

All had been relatively quiet for the past three hours. There were a few shouts of *'Usutu!'* coming from the darkness, as roving *izinduna* attempted to rally their men for one last assault. These, however, had lacked any sort of resolve or conviction and were not answered by their warriors. Fatigue at last took hold of the surviving members of the Rorke's Drift garrison. Many nodded off at various intervals. Soldiers would elbow their mates whenever they heard one of them starting to snore. Even the officers and NCOs struggled mightily. Their bodies protested the gruelling grind they'd been put through over the past twelve to fourteen hours. It was with bleary-eyed wonder they watched the sun begin to rise.

In a daze, Lieutenant John Chard wandered about the courtyard between the hospital and inner defensive wall. It was littered with scores of broken bodies. Shields, spears, muskets, smashed British helmets, and other pieces of broken kit lay strewn about. The early morning sunlight gleamed off the thousands of spent cartridge casings which covered most of the ground nearest the walls. Empty wooden ammunition boxes were discarded in large piles. Hundreds of torn paper packets whipped about with the slightest gusts of wind.

"You're not going to believe this, Mister Chard," Sergeant George Smith said. He and a private carried over an opened ammunition box missing about a third of its cartridge packets. "This was our last box. One more push and the Zulus would have done us in."

"Yes, but they didn't," Colour Sergeant Bourne said, walking up behind them. Like most of the others, his face was filthy and covered in both sweat and filth. His hands, still clutching his Martini-Henry rifle, were red and battered. His knuckles were scabbed from being grazed by Zulu spears or torn while punching assailants in the face. He nodded to Lieutenant Chard, who said nothing, but returned the gesture before continuing his walk.

Unlike many of the men he led, John Chard had never witnessed a battle before. The brutal carnage unnerved him. The Martini-Henry was powerful enough to take down an elephant, and its destruction on the human body was disturbingly horrific. Chard stared into the faces of countless slain Zulus. He noted one warrior whose head hand been split down the middle, as if by an axe. Another was missing the entire back of his head. The face looked like a rubber mask, its only blemish, the hole between the eyes. The eyes of many of the dead were open, and some had their now stiffened arms reaching towards the sky as if pleading to the heavens. Along the charred ruins of the hospital veranda, where the fighting was particularly fierce, the bodies of the slain formed a macabre carpet, piled two or three high.

Pacing along the south rampart, Chard found 'Gunny' Bromhead sitting by himself on a biscuit box, his eyes staring vacantly into oblivion.

"Mister Bromhead, I need you to form a detail and start collecting discarded weapons. We also need to pull down the thatch from the storehouse and clear away the Zulu bodies."

At first Bromhead did not move, and Chard wondered if he'd heard him. The ringing in his own ears was unsettling, and it would be no surprise if 'Gunny' couldn't hear a thing. The engineer officer opened his mouth to speak again when Bromhead abruptly stood. He did not look at his fellow officer, but called out to Colour Sergeant Bourne, repeating the directives he had been given.

"Apologies," he said afterwards, turning to face Chard. He slapped his hand against his right ear. "Just a bit rattled is all. Can't hardly hear a blasted thing."

Their banter was interrupted by a loud cry of *'Uzulu!'* coming from the direction of the cattle kraal. A lone warrior, his eyes wide with madness, fired a single shot from his musket. It slapped harmlessly against the side of the hospital. He then leapt over the barricades and sprinted towards the river.

"Get that son of a bitch!" someone shouted.

Several shots rang out, yet the nimble warrior soon disappeared into the brush.

"One has to admire his pluck," Bromhead said with tired admiration, and a laugh born out of frayed nerves. "To be honest, I'm almost glad he got away." Another voice nervously shouted from the south ramparts, *'Zulu!'*

As the door to the cookhouse was flung open, several rifles pointed to where a lone figure emerged. He wore a red tunic, but his face was covered in soot to the point that he was easy to mistake for the enemy. The terrified soldier fell flat onto his face.

"God damn it, I'm not a sodding Zulu!"

"Who the hell is that?" a curious soldier asked, lowering his rifle.

"It's Waters…you fucking arsehole!" the man replied, slowly rising to his feet.

"Good God, man, you look terrible!"

"Yes, well, I think I need a change of trousers now…"

While Private Waters and his friends exchanged expressions of relief, along with a slew of choice profanities, Henry Hook walked slowly along the southern rampart. He carried his rifle in his left hand, while pressing a rag against his forehead with his right. At the time of his injury, it felt like a mere scrape. It refused to quit bleeding, and each time it scabbed over during the night, it got torn afresh during the next frenzied brawl. To Harry, it hurt far worse than it should have. "Feels like they cut through my damned skull," he muttered coarsely.

He lowered the rag as he saw a lone redcoat among the slew of Zulu dead along the southern rampart. The man was on his knees, leaning against the wall of mealie bags. Hook assumed he was dozing and knelt next to the man, gently placing a hand on his shoulder.

"Hello," he said. "What are you still doing out here?"

The soldier's helmet covered his eyes. Harry tipped it back, hoping to wake him. He recognised the man. It was Private Thomas Cole. Tilting the helmet revealed the gaping hole between Cole's eyes. In a chilling display, a portion of his brains slid out from underneath his helmet. Hook said nothing. He replaced the helmet. And though not a Catholic, he made a 'sign of the cross' with his right hand and whispered a quick prayer for his friend.

He then stood and continued along the barricade until he came to the ruins of the hospital. His eyes fell on the mound about 400 yards from the south wall, where he had engaged a Zulu marksman early in the fighting. Curious, he climbed over the barricade.

"Where you off to, Hookie?" Sergeant Gallagher asked.

"Something I need to see, sergeant."

The NCO nodded. "Alright, just be careful. I suspect there are more than a few of those bastards lying about who aren't quite dead."

Harry kept his rifle close, bayonet protruding low in front as he tried to make certain he did not step too closely to any of the bodies he came across. Their numbers were thick, especially within the first hundred yards of the post. The flattened grass and dirt was black and sticky from torrents of spilled blood. Just behind the mound he saw the Zulu marksman. He was flat on his back, his battered musket at his side. Hook's bullet had struck the man above the left eye near his hairline. The shock of the blow had shattered his skull, leaving a scattering of brain, blood, bone fragments, and chunks of flesh with hair still attached in its wake.

He most certainly was not the only man Harry had killed, and he wasn't sure why he felt he needed to see this particular warrior. Perhaps it was simple curiosity, wondering if he scored a hit with his rifle against a partially shielded target at such a range. Or possibly, since he had no way of knowing which among the enemy in the compound had fallen to him, he needed confirmation so he could ask the divines for forgiveness. Although, if there was anything his soul felt it needed forgiveness for, it was bludgeoning the youth who'd tried to steal his greatcoat to death. In his addled and sleep-deprived state, he could not say for certain what his reasons were.

Letting out a sigh of acceptance, he turned to make his way back to the depot. He absently carried his rifle at his side rather than clutched close to his chest at port arms. He passed by a large Zulu with a fearful wound to his left thigh. A bullet had shattered the femur, leaving the limb a mangled and bloody mess. Hook paid him no mind.

Suddenly, the Zulu's hand reached up and grabbed his rifle by the buttstock. *"Ngizokubulala zonke!"* the man shouted, pulling himself onto his non-injured knee. His heart racing, Harry grabbed the barrel with both hands and tried to wrench the weapon free of the maddened warrior's grip. After a few seconds, he kicked the man hard in the face. The Zulu gave a loud grunt as he fell onto his horribly maimed leg. Gritting his teeth in agony, he forced himself up onto his knees once more.

His panic turning to rage, Harry, jacked open the breach of his weapon and chambered a round. As he raised it to his shoulder, he could swear the Zulu was smiling at him.

"Ukukwenza manje," the warrior said. He stared at Hook, his hands held out at his sides, as if asking the private to shoot him.

Without another thought, Harry squeezed the trigger. His rifle shattered the man's face from just a few feet away. He immediately turned and walked away, not bothering to wait for the wisps of smoke to clear.

"It's alright!" he shouted to the alarmed soldiers he saw rushing to the barricade. "Just found a live one who tried to take me weapon."

"Damn it all, Hookie, I told you to be careful!" Sergeant Gallagher snapped.

"Yes, sergeant," Hook said. He climbed back over the wall of mealie bags. The morning light had grown brighter. For the first time, Hook noticed the charred blisters on his section leader's face. From below his right eye all the way down his cheek was scorched.

"Bugger me, sergeant, what's happened to your face?"

"Breach block on my weapon started coming apart," Gallagher said, hefting his rifle. There was a noticeable gap in the seam along the left side of the breach block. "I'm lucky the damned thing didn't blow up in my face."

"Well, you are Irish." Harry gave a wink. His sergeant shook his head and patted him on the shoulder.

Near the corner of the biscuit box inner wall and the outer rampart of mealie sacks, Privates Thomas Lockhart and Michael Deane scanned the brush and stone kraal for any signs of movement. They were soon joined by their assistant section leader, Corporal John Key.

"See anything out there?" the NCO asked.

"Just a lot of bodies," Deane remarked. "I can't help but wonder how many of those poor devils are still alive and were abandoned by their mates."

"How is Sergeant Williams?" Lockhart asked, turning to face the corporal.

Key frowned and shook his head. "I went to check on him…" He paused for a moment and swallowed hard before continuing. "He died. I found him under a blanket by the storehouse with the other dead. Surgeon Reynolds thinks his shattered ribs must have punctured his lung, suffocating him to death."

"Damn it all," Lockhart swore. "You know we came through The Depot together. He practically carried my sorry arse through recruit training. Thought for certain he was destined to become another 'regimental high flyer' like The Kid. Guess there's nothing to be done about it now."

The private turned back towards the perimeter, taking a deep breath and fighting hard against his tears. His silent mourning was interrupted by the sight of a lone figure sprinting down the dirt road towards them. "What the bloody hell is that?"

"One of the Zulus coming back to say 'hello'?" Deane asked, as he raised his rifle up to his shoulder.

"Hold on," Corporal Key chastised, fumbling with his field glasses. "He's carrying a red rag in his hand. He might be one of the NNC from Isandlwana."

"Probably a filthy coward who left our boys to die," Deane spat.

Key placed a hand on his shoulder and ordered him to lower his weapon.

"*IziGqoza! IziGqoza!*" the man shouted, his hands raised in the air as he waved his red rag over his head.

His shouts alerted the officers and NCOs, who gathered near the rampart.

Chard shook his head as he tried to understand what else the terrified warrior was shouting. "I don't suppose any of you speak Zulu?" he asked the assembled soldiers.

"Mr Daniels does, sir," Sergeant Milne spoke up. "Or at least he knew enough to shout profanities at those damned lazy darkies every time they abandoned their post on the ponts."

"It'll have to do." Chard turned to Key. "Corporal, have him escorted to Mr Daniels."

The warrior was unarmed, his eyes wide and bloodshot. Daniels, the civilian ferryman, was wielding Major Spalding's sword, waving it about as he questioned the man. He nearly nicked him on the cheek several times, and Chard finally grabbed him by the arm. The warrior spoke quickly, waving and pointing wildly.

Daniels furrowed his brow, trying to understand him. "Damn it, man, slow down," he said, trying to remember an appropriate phrase in Zulu. After a few moments, he nodded and turned to Chard. "He says he was with James Lonsdale's iziGqoza detachment; says they fought the Zulus near a band of redcoats on the firing line. He keeps saying the officer in the red jacket wore metal wires on his face…I think he might mean spectacles."

"That could have been Charlie Pope," Bromhead conjectured. His old friend was one of the few officers in the regiment who wore glasses.

"Ask him how he escaped," Chard directed.

This was followed by a few more minutes of Daniels attempting to ask the right questions, interpreting what he was able from the man's speech. "He says they were driven back to the camp, and that he only ran when he knew all was lost. He watched the 'man with his arm pinned inside his jacket' fall."

"That would be Colonel Durnford," Bromhead remarked grimly.

Daniels nodded and continued. "He says he was only able to survive by throwing down his shield and taking the red rag from his head. Several of his companions did the same, but when the Zulus did not recognise them as their own, they were killed. He says the divines must have been watching over him."

Chard folded his arms across his chest and apprised the warrior with much scepticism. He turned to Bromhead and asked, "Do you believe a word of this?"

"You say he mentioned Lonsdale by name?" 'Gunny' inquired.

Daniels asked the man again. He spoke for a few moments, slapping his hand across his chest a few times. "He says the man he served under was kinsman to their regimental commandant."

Bromhead gave an affirmative nod to this revelation. He then explained to Chard, who had little knowledge of the column's organisation or officers, "James Lonsdale was Commandant Rupert Lonsdale's cousin. No Zulu would know this, nor would they care even if they did. I don't see any reason for him coming into our camp as a spy. It's not as if he could discover anything about our state that the enemy doesn't already know."

"Alright," Chard said. "Tell him I believe him."

The warrior let out a deep sigh of relief and spoke a few words of thanks, bowing his head slightly and holding his hands up near his face in a show of respect.

"He asks if he can have some food," Daniels translated. "He hasn't eaten in two days."

"Of course. And tell him not to run off. I have a little mission for him."

Chard walked over to the storehouse, searching for a scrap of paper and a pencil.

Bromhead followed, giving him a quizzical gaze. "Can I ask what you're doing, old boy?"

"May as well try to get word to the lads at Helpmekaar," Chard explained, as he began scribbling. "I figure this man may as well be of some use to us. And if he runs off…well, we haven't lost anything."

Once he finished scribbling his note, he told Mr Daniels to ask the warrior if he knew where Helpmekaar was. When he said he did, Chard gave him the message and told him to give it to the first British officer he came across.

The message was brief, but direct.

Zulu attack on Rorke's Drift repelled, but ammunition stores exhausted. Send assistance as soon as possible.

Lt. J.R.M. Chard

Having sent the NNC warrior on his way, Chard removed his jacket and ran his fingers through his hair. He dug out his pocket watch and saw that it was now exactly 7.00. The sun was already beating down on them in what promised to be another scorching day.

"Zulus!" a lookout on the storehouse rooftop suddenly shouted.

Chard and Bromhead turned their attention to where the frantic soldier on the roof was pointing.

"Oh my God," Bromhead breathed in dismay.

On the slopes of kwaSingqindi Hill emerged several Zulu warriors. They were approaching from various directions, mostly the south. As their numbers grew, Lieutenant Chard ordered the bugler to sound 'stand-to'.

"Move your backsides!" Colour Sergeant Bourne shouted. He fetched his rifle from against the side of the storehouse. "Sergeant Smith, take your lads and those from Corporal Allan's section and cover the north wall. Make sure none of those bastards sneak around behind us. The rest of you, on me!"

As dozens of haggard redcoats surged to the outer defensive walls, William Allan emerged from the storehouse. He was shirtless, his chest and shoulder heavily bandaged, and his arm in a sling. He carried the sword bayonet taken from his rifle in his good hand. His face was pale, yet there was a determined gleam in his eyes.

"Can you even stand, Bill?" Sergeant Smith asked him. "You've lost so much blood, you look like a sodding albino."

Allan scanned the hillside noting the growing force of Zulus. He knew they were finished. "I'm not going to hide in the storehouse waiting for one of these bastards to finish me. They can bloody well do it out here."

Along the remainder of the defences, Colour Sergeant Bourne checked with each section leader, ensuring their soldiers had a full allotment of ammunition. Every last man was filthy, shabby, eyes bloodshot, covered in cuts and bruises, and utterly exhausted. Scarcely half were wearing their red tunics. Many were in their shirtsleeves, and some were bare-chested with bandages wrapped around battered arms, shoulders, and torsos. As fearful as they appeared, with annihilation staring down on them, their spirits were unexpectedly high.

"At least they let us see one last sunrise," Private Patrick Tobin reasoned.

Lance Corporal William Bessel was cursing that his rifle's rear sight had been knocked off during the night. "Well bugger," he swore. "I guess I won't be making any 500-yard shots with this damned thing."

The encompassing darkness of night had hidden the fearful plight of the British from their Zulu assailants. But now, as the sun shone brightly on the devastated mission station, it had to be plain to the Zulus that their adversaries were spent. 'Gunny' Bromhead sat on a biscuit box, his borrowed Martini-Henry held loosely in his hands, the butt stock resting on the ground. His frayed nerves at their end, he broke into a fit of laughter.

"Well, what are you waiting for?" he shouted towards the hillside. "Come on, then!" Still grinning inanely, he muttered to Chard, "Rude of the bastards to keep us waiting like this."

While Lieutenant Bromhead taunted the Zulus from alongside the hill, Prince Zibhebhu sat and stared in disbelief. During the night, he had cursed himself for not accompanying Dabulamanzi in the sacking of *kwaJimu*. The red fires that could be seen for twenty miles told him of the mission station's destruction. As a supply depot for the redcoats, it likely had the greatest stores of plunder in both treasure and weapons. Having done little except pillage a few abandoned homesteads, he and the warriors accompanying him were reluctantly making the long trek back to Ulundi. It was only when he came across a dishevelled warrior from Prince Dabulamanzi's regiment that he heard disaster had struck the Undi Corps. In his state of disbelief, Zibhebhu decided to see it for himself.

Word must have reached other wayward bands of warriors, for scattered groups began converging soon after. The Zulu prince sat on the grass and watched in fascination as the white soldiers hurried to their makeshift defences. The entire ground within five hundred paces of the compound was black with the bodies of slain warriors.

"It would seem the king's favourite brother has failed," the *inkosi* muttered bitterly. Even from the hillside, he could discern some of the patterns on discarded shields that lay scattered amongst the bodies. "How could this happen? Even the king's own uThulwana regiment has been repulsed!"

A rather sombre *induna* then walked over and knelt next to the prince in the grass. "*Inkosi*, we have nearly five hundred warriors on this hill. Give us the order, and we will swat away these white soldiers like flies. Let us restore honour to the elder regiments of the *amabutho*."

Zibhebhu glanced to his left and right and assessed the state of the gathered warriors. They came from various regiments, mostly stragglers and renegades who elected to go for easy plunder rather than join the attack on the depot. It would be very difficult to coordinate a disciplined attack using men who were not used to fighting together. They were also very tired. They had run nearly twenty miles the previous day, from Mabaso to the uMzinyathi, conducted a harrowing crossing of the river, and spent the entire night raiding the Natal countryside. There had been little in the way of food to plunder, just a few head of cattle. Eventually, they would need to cross back into Zululand and make the long journey back to Ulundi. He had no idea where the main *impi* was or, for that matter, Dabulamanzi and the rest of the Undi Corps.

The warrior from the uDloko regiment made no mention of the king's brother. Was he among the slain, scattered about the landscape below? If so, he was indeed fortunate; for those who remained would now have to bear the ignominy of telling the king that, while his armies achieved their greatest triumph, his most senior regiments had disobeyed him and failed to overrun such a pitiful garrison of white soldiers.

Zibhebhu turned his attention back to the mission station and assessed the redcoats left defending her. They were few in number.

The prince could count them easily and saw they numbered less than a hundred. And while he could not understand the shouts that came from the lone figure within, the inflection made their intentions abundantly clear. The British clearly wanted the Zulus to attack.

Despite his trepidations, Zibhebhu was filled with desire to oblige his adversaries. "Assemble the *izinduna*..." his words were then cut off by signs of movement in the distance. His vision was far better than most of his companions, and through squinted eyes the prince saw what looked like a pair of horses with white riders approaching from the east. He then looked towards the rising sun and saw movements coming from the direction of the drift. He swore he could even see the distinctive red jackets of British soldiers approaching the station. His thoughts were confirmed when an *induna* noticed them as well.

"Redcoats," the man said in disbelief. "Where, by the divines, did they come from? I thought their army was completely destroyed."

No one from the Zulu *impi* had seen the British camp at Isandlwana prior to the battle, and since they never came across Lord Chelmsford's detachment at Mangeni, they did not know how large the British column was. For all any of them knew, the force left at the camp was the entire column rather than less than half of it. But as the approaching figures came into clearer view, it was plain to see that a large force had escaped the slaughter. Zibhebhu could discern that the number of redcoats and horsemen outnumbered his assortment of warriors on the slope of kwaSingqindi.

The prince said nothing, his head hung in regret. The Undi Corps was his responsibility, and he had allowed them to be led to humiliation and destruction. He waved with his spear for the gathered bands to withdraw. The sight of the approaching soldiers sapped whatever strength and desire and of them had left for battle. Without waiting for orders from their *izinduna*, they crept away, disappearing behind the hill and quickly making their journey south to a known crossing point.

As for Prince Zibhebhu, he remained for a few moments longer, standing alone on the side of the hill. Before departing, he raised his spear in salute. To the outside observer, one would not know if he was paying tribute to his fallen brothers or to the small band of redcoats who withstood their furious onslaughts against overwhelming odds. Perhaps it was both.

Chapter XXI: Dawn Riders

Rorke's Drift
23 January 1879

The Relief of Rorke's Drift, by Lieutenant Colonel John North Crealock

The relieved garrison watched the large band of Zulus disappear behind the hill. "Dirty twats don't want to play no more," a private said incredulously.

"Now what do you suppose has gotten into them?" Private John Williams asked as he leaned against the ruins of the south rampart.

Many of the mealie sacks were torn open by musket shots and assegai stabs. Streams of grain ran onto the soldier's feet.

"It's the damnedest thing," Robert Jones added. He was in a fearful state. His face, hands, and chest bore numerous gashes from assegai thrusts. The left shoulder of his tunic was ripped open and sticky with dried blood where a spent musket ball had grazed him. He looked to his friend, William Jones, who had slumped down with his back against the wall. "Well, 593, it looks like you'll be able to go home and find yourself a nice English lass after all."

For Lieutenants Chard and Bromhead, the sight of the Zulus departing was as perplexing as it was a relief. What stood out most to them was how disorganised their abrupt arrival and departure appeared. It was a far cry from the precision drill and discipline they had shown since first appearing on the horizon the previous afternoon. The two officers were joined by Colour Sergeant Bourne and James Dalton. The assistant commissary's arm was in a sling, and he was in a lot of pain. However, the old soldier's demeanour had lost none of its resolve. As the last warrior disappeared over the horizon, they got their answer as to why the Zulus departed as suddenly as they had arrived.

"Signallers on the roof, sir," Sergeant Windridge said, pointing to the men atop the storehouse, frantically waving their white rags.

"What the devil is it?" Chard asked incredulously. "Don't tell me there's more Zulus coming from the east."

"No, sir!" one of the men called down. "Horses…our horses!"

The man's companion stood tall and removed his red jacket, waving it at the unseen men coming from the direction of the ponts.

The riders approached cautiously, but then galloped their horses to the depot as scores of soldiers climbed onto the barricades and started shouting and cheering. Men removed their jackets and waved them in the air along with their helmets.

Walter Dunne first recognised the men. "Mister Chard, it's Colonel Russell from the Imperial Mounted Infantry."

Relieved to see that the mission station had held, Lieutenant Colonel John Russell, accompanied by Lieutenant Harry Walsh, reined in their horses near the storehouse. Dunne greeted the men and saluted Russell.

"Colonel, sir. By God it is good to see you!"

"And you, Commissary Dunne." Despite his relief, Russell's expression was still one of grave concern. "But I must know, did any groups of survivors from Isandlwana join you?"

"No."

The single word seemed to crush the colonel's spirits. Biting his knuckles, he leaned forward, using his horse's neck to try to mask his sobs of sorrow. It was a vain effort. Having witnessed the carnage of so many hundreds of his comrades, he had hoped that at least some had escaped.

Few in the garrison even knew about the drift ten miles to the south, where small bands of fugitives had made it across the uMzinyathi. These had made their way to Helpmekaar, thinking Rorke's Drift was a lost cause. Still, they were few in number; forty-eight out of over a thousand left to guard the camp at Isandlwana.

John Chard had spotted the officers approaching. His face was covered in soot. He took a moment to rinse himself in a muddy puddle.

"Here you go, sir," said the voice of Private Bushe. His face was covered in blood from his smashed nose. He handed Chard a relatively clean towel. "You need this more than I do. After all, officers don't care what us rankers look like."

Chard thanked the man and quickly wiped down his face. He was in his shirtsleeves, having removed his tunic and quite forgotten where he left it. As he walked towards the officers, there was a loud cheer from outside the camp. Companies from 2nd Battalion were surrounding the camp from a couple hundred yards away. All were gazing in astonishment at the haggard survivors.

There was another shout of ovation as Lord Chelmsford himself rode into the camp, accompanied by his staff officers. He stared at the battered soldiers, marvelling in disbelief that any were still alive. He dismounted and walked over to Bromhead.

"By God, sir, it is good to see you!" Bromhead came to attention and saluted.

Chelmsford returned the courtesy. "And you, Mister Bromhead. But where is Major Spalding? I would speak to him at once."

"Major Spalding is missing, sir," Gunny explained. "Well, not *missing*, exactly. He left for Helpmekaar yesterday morning with the intent of bringing up the two errant companies from 1st Battalion." He then nodded to Chard, who had quickly walked over to join the men. "It was Lieutenant Chard who assumed command of the station in his absence."

"Indeed." The GOC and engineer officer exchanged salutes as Chelmsford apprised him. The two had never met, and Chelmsford tried to recall where he'd heard Chard's name before. He gave a nod as he remembered. "You're the engineer officer from No. 5 Field Company I sent for."

"Yes, my lord. My sappers were ordered forward to the column yesterday morning. Colonel Pulleine explained that I was not needed and he sent me back." He paused for a moment, thinking about the young men who had been his soldiers. "I…I can only hope they died well, sir."

"That is about all any of us can hope for at this point, Mister Chard. But what about Captain Stevenson? He had several hundred NNC warriors here. Don't tell me they deserted their post."

"I'm afraid so, my lord. It is with much regret that I must tell you that Captain Stevenson and his NCOs abandoned their post along with all of their natives." What Chard made no mention of was Fred Hitch's killing of the deserting European corporal.

Hearing about Spalding's absence and Captain Stevenson's absconding filled the GOC with irritation and wonder. He was angry that the officer commanding had neglected to fight beside his men. If he had gone back for reinforcements, surely they should have arrived during the night at some point! His feelings of wonder came from the realisation that the defence of Rorke's Drift had been conducted by a single rifle company and a few 'walking wounded'. Between the three rifle companies and NNC detachment, there should have been six hundred men manning the ramparts. Instead, Rorke's Drift was held by scarcely a hundred.

"Mister Chard, if you would be so kind as to find us some breakfast, you can tell me everything."

The order was given to stand down, and soldiers from B Company once more began searching the ruins for missing friends. For Henry Hook, this meant returning to the wreckage of the hospital. The heat was still great and the thick roof beams continued to burn. Each step kicked up clouds of ash. He carefully sought out where the Witts' bedroom once stood. The fires from the falling thatch had been so intense that there was nothing but charred ruins inside. It was impossible to tell what had once been furniture or men.

Stepping over a still-smouldering hulk that might have been Witt's bed, Harry saw a swatch of blue and white checker cloth. He knelt down and recognised it as part of the shirt Robert Maxfield had worn. It was stuck to a charred lump that Hook could only assume was Maxfield's mortal remains. Protruding from the mass was what appeared to be an arm. The skin was mostly burned away, with only some burned strips of flesh still clinging to the lower arm bones and skeletal hand.

Hook closed his eyes, bowed his head, and placed his hand on the charred hand. "Be at peace, old friend."

All along the perimeter, companies from 2nd Battalion swept across the killing fields littered with Zulu corpses. Lieutenant Colonel Henry Degacher watched from astride his horse, taking in the fearful sights. He jolted slightly as he heard a scream coming from near the south wall. One of his soldiers was wrenching his bayonet from the back of a fallen Zulu.

"Just found me a live one is all," the private explained.

The man's sergeant was uncertain as to whether he should berate the man for killing the enemy wounded. He looked to Degacher, who nodded affirmatively. The number of Zulu wounded was surprisingly few; no doubt due to the destructive effectiveness of the Martini-Henry rifle. The grassy ground leading away from the station was flattened and covered in hundreds of drag marks, accented by wide swaths of drying blood. Degacher admired the Zulus' comradery. They had tried to drag away most of their wounded friends. Yet, neither he nor anyone else from No. 3 Column was feeling particularly charitable towards those left behind.

"It's no worse than what they did to our lads at Isandlwana," he said quietly to his sergeant major. They watched for a moment as another gravely wounded warrior was bayonetted by a vengeful redcoat.

"We're treating them with greater mercy than they did our boys," the battalion's senior NCO reckoned.

They soon made their way into the compound. Section leaders from various companies were gathering around the line of biscuit boxes which had served as the inner defensive wall.

"Bloody hell, you lot must be hungry," Sergeant Gallagher said to an NCO from C Company.

"Damned right we are. We haven't had a bite in two days."

"Well, we can sort that out," Commissary Dunne said, giving his first genuine smile since hearing about the disaster at Isandlwana the previous afternoon. He then made a great showing of breaking open one of the boxes. "Let's see, here we have dried biscuits. And in this next box is bully beef…oh, and if we go to another box we have even more tins of bully beef!"

"Meals fit for the Queen herself," Gallagher laughed.

Fortunately for all, food was something the garrison had in ample supply. Dunne and several soldiers broke open the boxes, handing out tins of biscuits and bully beef. Despite their famished state, the battalion's NCOs kept their men from swarming the commissariat, taking it upon themselves to collect and distribute rations for their soldiers.

"We have plenty of tea and sugar, but no cups or utensils, I'm afraid," Dunne remarked.

"That's alright, we'll make do," the sergeant major replied.

He knew that soldiers are nothing if not able to improvise. Devouring tins of bully beef, they scraped out the juices and then used them to boil water for their tea. Henry Hook had just emerged from the ruins of the hospital, when he overheard the collected soldiers discussing their tea.

"I know where to find an extra kettle and some cups," he said. Anxious for any sort of distraction, he walked briskly to the cookhouse where Private Waters had hidden from the Zulus during the night.

His heart nearly stopped when a figure leapt up from a nearby trench.

"Hey, Hookie!" shouted Gunner Howard, throwing off his greatcoat.

"Damn it all, man!" Hook swore at him. "You almost made me soil my trousers."

"You mean like I've been shitting mine for the past two weeks?" the artillery crewman retorted, referring to the bout of dysentery that landed him in the hospital in the first place. "Sorry old boy, didn't mean to scare you. I've been hiding beneath a pile of brush since our breakout from the hospital. I'm surprised none of those black devils found me."

"Yes, it is good to see you still among the living. Anyone else lurking in the brush?"

Howard shrugged and then started to look around him. His eyes grew wide as he spotted the slumped form of Private William

Beckett. His face was ashen, his blood-soaked hands clutching at his chest.

"Oh, bugger me," Howard said quietly. He then shouted to a group of soldiers from A Company crossing the thick brush nearby. "Here! We got a wounded man, needs attention!"

The soldiers rushed over and gathered around the critically injured man. Four of them gingerly picked him up underneath his shoulders and hips. Beckett cried out in renewed pain, whispering over and over that he did not want to die.

"Take him to Surgeon Reynolds," Harry Hook directed. "He's set up his surgical table in the storehouse."

Beckett was in terrible shape, and Hook feared that even the skilled hands of James Reynolds would not be able to save him. He watched for a moment as Arthur Howard followed the men back into the compound before continuing with his task. The inside of the cookhouse was a complete disaster; pots, tin plates, cups, and various implements were scattered everywhere. Hook stripped off his tunic before digging around, looking for his extra kettle and something to carry all the tin mugs in.

"Harry!" the voice of Sergeant Gallagher shouted.

Hook emerged from the shack to find his section leader walking briskly over to him.

"Come as you are, straight away. His lordship wants to speak with you."

"Oh, bugger me, not in trouble, am I?"

Gallagher laughed, though he said nothing more. The two soldiers made their way to the storehouse where Chelmsford sat atop a stack of biscuit boxes. They both came to attention and saluted.

"Private Hook, sir," Gallagher said, nodding his head towards Harry.

"My lord," the soldier added with a nod.

The GOC stared at him for a moment. Hook wondered if he was about to get a dressing down for his slovenly appearance. Given all that had transpired over the past two days, Chelmsford could have cared less if his soldiers walked around naked.

"I understand you were the last to leave the hospital," he said plainly.

Major Francis Cleary stood nearby, a pad and pencil in hand.

"Yes, my lord. Though I sadly regret that we were not able to save everyone."

"According to your officer commanding, many of the patients, who would have otherwise burned to death or been butchered by the Zulus, are alive because of you."

"We did what we had to, sir. Colour Sergeant Bourne tasked us with protecting the sick and injured, so that's what we did."

"Who else was with you?" Major Cleary asked.

"I want all their names and as much detail as you can provide," Chelmsford demanded.

Hook took a deep breath and composed his thoughts. He knew this was not the time for false modesty, and so he described everything he could recall, from the moment they opened fire on the first assault, to when he last left the burning structure. He stressed that he was not initially in the same room with the Joneses, but he knew they had behaved heroically and could name at least six men whose lives they saved. He gave much credit to young John Williams, who not once lost his head, even as the burning thatch and marauding Zulus threatened to slay them. Once he had finished, the GOC wordlessly dismissed him with a wave of his hand. Hook saluted and returned to his errand of finding a kettle and cups for tea.

His face completely non-expressive, Chelmsford turned to Lieutenant Bromhead, who was standing to his left with Chard and Lieutenant Colonel Degacher. "Mister Bromhead, if I don't see a Victoria Cross recommendation for each of those men, I shall relieve you of your command."

In truth, the officer commanding of B Company was already considering who to recommend for awards and commendations. He told Chelmsford as much. He and Colour Sergeant Bourne would give their written recommendations to Lieutenant Chard, who would then pass them up the chain-of-command. Though Chard was not a member of the 24th, and would eventually return to his own No. 5 Field Company, he had served as officer commanding during the Battle of Rorke's Drift. Therefore, all official reports and awards recommendations were his responsibility.

Outside the depot, 'Maori' Browne and Charlie Harford were joined by Henry Fynn. He was apprising the Zulu dead nearest the ramparts. The civilian magistrate pointed to the black rings woven into the hair of each man.

"These are all married men," he explained. He then noted the grey hair that adorned many of the heads. "I would assume there are more than a few grandfathers amongst the fallen. Not many men back in Blighty—even half their age—who could have run twenty miles and then fought a battle such as this."

"Look at that big fellow there," Browne said, pointing to a very large warrior. "I'd reckon he's seven feet tall, if he's an inch!"

The man's face had been shot away at close range, and he lay on his back; his feet were at the base of the ramparts, with the rest of his body lying backwards down the natural cliff face.

"I know these shield patterns," Fynn added. "These men were from the uThulwana *ibutho*."

Browne shrugged. Harford explained, "This was Cetshwayo's personal regiment; the *ibutho* he grew up with and served in."

"These are the same warriors who won him the crown more than twenty years ago," Fynn added.

"One dead nigger is the same as any other," Browne said dismissively.

Harford winced slightly, but did not bother replying. It puzzled him that someone who seemed to hate any indigenous people's not of European stock spent most of his military career leading them into battle.

The acting-captain rode his horse over to a group of carbineers, about a hundred yards away from the post. As Charlie approached, he saw that they were staring at the body of a slain European from the NNC. The man lay on his stomach, a large, hideous exit wound protruding from his forehead.

"That was no musket what done him in," Trooper Symons observed, pointing to the gaping hole. "One could fit a tea cup in there readily enough."

"I know this man," Harford said. "Or at least I know who he was. Name was Anderson, I believe. He was one of Stevenson's men. Strange, the Zulus didn't gut him like the others."

"Probably just missed him in the dark," Symons reasoned. "His men may have fled the approaching Zulus, but that was no excuse for deserting his post. I'd say our friends at the mission station did Her Majesty a favour by sparing the embarrassment of a trial for desertion."

Flies were already gathering to feast on the bloodied flesh and gore, which made one trooper's next remark all the more disturbing.

"Well, with that sorted, how about breakfast? I hear the lads of B Company are breaking open the biscuit boxes."

While Sergeant Gallagher's section oversaw the distribution of rations and brewing of tea for the column, the rest of B Company began to form fatigue details to sort out the wreckage of the battle's aftermath. They were soon joined by carbineers and fellow redcoats from 2nd Battalion. The men took a few minutes to satisfy their hunger before starting the labour of policing up the carnage. Ropes were tied around the less stable walls of the hospital, and they were heaved down in a series of loud crashes. Zulu shields, spears, clubs, and muskets were tossed into large piles. The most back-breaking work of all, though, would be clearing away the enemy dead.

As men tied a long rope around one of the broken walls of the hospital, Lieutenant Bromhead walked over to the veranda with an old friend from 2nd Battalion, Lieutenant Henry Mainwaring. He wanted to show him one Zulu warrior in particular whose courage he admired greatly.

"See that old boy with the plume headdress?" he asked, pointing to an *induna*. "I watched him lead three separate charges against the ramparts. We got him the third time."

As Bromhead walked back to the centre of the compound, Mainwaring stood and stared in awe at the sheer number of bodies, many stacked two and three deep.

"Mister Bromhead," he heard Lieutenant Chard's voice call out. "Come with me."

The engineer officer led him outside the compound, towards his wrecked sapper wagon. With the various details assigned, and far more senior officers now on hand to assume responsibility for the mission station, John Chard and Gonville Bromhead took a few minutes for a well-deserved respite.

There were several bodies strewn about. One was sprawled over the wooden seat of the wagon, having been gutted by a Martini-Henry shot, courtesy of the diligent Driver Robson, who sought to protect his charge even from a distance. The two officers heaved the slain man off the wagon. Chard pulled back a ripped tarp to reveal an amber bottle hidden beneath a pile of discarded tools.

"Would you look at that," he said with a grin. "Boer beer. I purchased this from some chap I met in Port Natal when I arrived in country. It's likely warm and tastes of horse urine. But I'd be honoured, 'Gunny', if you would join me in a drink."

"The honour is mine, John."

Chard opened the bottle and offered it first to Bromhead, who took a long drink, nearly choking at first.

"Ugh, tastes like it came straight from a horse's willy," he coughed. Chard laughed, though as he finished a pull off the bottle, his face twisted into an expression that seemed to confirm Bromhead's description.

"Here's to having survived after so much danger," he said. He handed the bottle back to his fellow officer.

They continued to drink through a variety of toasts.

"To the 24th," Chard said, taking a drink and handing the bottle back.

"To Her Majesty's Royal Engineers," Bromhead courteously replied.

"To Colour Sergeant Bourne; may they make him an officer for this!"

"To Harry Hook and the brave lads from the hospital."

"To William Allan; may he recover from his wounds and stay sober enough to receive the Victoria Cross!"

Bromhead chuckled at this last toast. It seemed Allan's reputation for love of drink preceded him. In fact, Chard had had several conversations with the corporal over the past few days. Allan was quite candid during many of their discussions while helping Chard establish his camp by the drift.

"To Her Majesty, the Queen. May she know well the valour of her soldiers, who fought and died in her name."

"To Her Majesty," Chard replied, finishing the last of the bottle.

Not surprisingly, they avoided the usual officers' toast, *'To a bloody war or a great plague'*.

They had known each other for just a few days and would only see each other in passing, if at all, once Chard returned to his own company. And yet, the crucible of battle had forged a bond of both friendship and mutual respect between them that would never be broken.

Chapter XXII: Overtures of Disaster

Pietermaritzburg, Natal
23 January 1879

News of Isandlwana reaches Pietermaritzburg
From *The Graphic*, 8 March 1879

After their tedious journey by steamship and the harrowing landing at Port Natal during a hellish rainstorm, Elisa Wilkinson was relieved to finally arrive at Fort Napier outside of Pietermaritzburg. She and her travelling companion, Eleanor Brown, had paid a Dutch trader to allow them and their baggage to ride in the back of his wagon. The Army made little to no provisions when it came to families wishing to join their soldier-husbands who were already overseas on Foreign Service. Unless they managed to catch the troop transport with the regiment itself, they were pretty much left to find their own way. Thankfully for Elisa, Eleanor was born into the army and had already travelled around the world before she married her husband, Colour Sergeant Thomas Brown, ten years prior.

"There it is, my dear," Eleanor said.

The stone ramparts of Fort Napier came into view along a high ridge overlooking Pietermaritzburg.

"Finally," Elisa said with a jolt, as the wagon hit yet another pot hole in the heavily rutted dirt road. "I thought we'd never arrive!"

"Had we been bound for India, we'd still be at sea," Eleanor mused, recalling as a young girl accompanying her father to one of the furthest flung corners of the Empire.

Having made an early start, they arrived during the late morning of 23 January. What baffled the two women was that the fort was all but abandoned. A handful of soldiers were all who remained.

They were halted outside the gate, while a private sought out the sergeant of the guard; a very young soldier whose smooth face had likely never required a shave.

"Can I help you, ladies?" he asked, noting their tired and dishevelled appearance. "What brings you to Fort Napier?"

"What brings us here is our husbands," Eleanor said with a trace of unintended snark. "My name is Eleanor Brown, wife of Colour Sergeant Thomas Brown of C Company, 1st Battalion of the 24th. Be a good man and tell us where we can find him…or anybody for that matter. This place looks like a ghost town."

The sergeant was taken aback by the last statement. "Blimey, you mean you haven't heard?"

"Heard what?" Elisa asked anxiously.

"About the war between the Crown and the Zulus. The whole regiment's gone off and invaded the Zulu Kingdom about a fortnight ago…well, except for us that is."

Elisa was crushed. Six months had passed since she saw her beloved Arthur. The last time she held her husband was the morning after their wedding, when he left their home in Stratford-upon-Avon for South Africa. It had taken several months for his pay stoppages to reach her, which gave her just enough funds to purchase transportation to the Cape. That Colour Sergeant Brown had asked his wife to accompany Elisa had been a godsend. The past month was quite the adventure for the young woman. During her near-nineteen years, she had scarcely left home, and she was not sure if she could have made it without Eleanor's help. But now, they had finally reached Fort Napier, only to find their husbands were gone and a war now raged between The Crown and an African tribe she'd never heard of. It was overwhelming.

"Excuse me, but can I get these bags unloaded and then be on my way?" the trader asked impatiently.

"Yes, of course," the sergeant said, his heart filled with pity for the distressed young woman who stood before him. "Private Harris,

Private Jones, take the good ladies' bags to the orderly room. And have a runner sent to find Mrs Edwards at the flats."

"You say we are at war?" Eleanor asked, composing herself.

Elisa bit her lower lip and looked like she would burst into tears if required to speak.

"I'm afraid so. We heard the lads destroyed an enemy stronghold and were advancing on the Zulu capital. Lucky bastards…beg your pardon." The sergeant's face was flushed with embarrassment at his profane outburst.

Eleanor simply smiled at him. "You told your man to find a Mrs Edwards. That wouldn't be Mary Edwards, would it?"

"Aye, it is. Best I can recall, she's the most senior spouse from C Company here; excluding yourself of course."

Eleanor nodded appreciatively. She knew that Captain Younghusband's wife, Evelyn, was with child and had remained in England. Lieutenant Hodson, the company's lone subaltern, was unmarried. As the wife of their colour sergeant, this left Eleanor Brown as the senior spouse for the company. She thanked the sergeant, who offered to escort them to the fort's headquarters building.

"Who is the senior officer here?" Eleanor asked as they reached the large brick building.

"That would be me," the young sergeant replied. "There's only twenty of us here now. Entire bleeding army—those not lucky enough to take part in the invasion—is scattered around the sodding Cape…beg your pardon. A few of us have been detached out on garrison duties, such as us here. I'm sure Mrs Edwards will help get you sorted. Most of the wives and children of the enlisted ranks live in a block of flats not far from the fort. And if you need anything, the name's Rogers."

"Nice young man," Eleanor said, as soon as Sergeant Rogers left to return to his duties.

Elisa was wiping her eyes, taking a few breaths to compose herself. "Aren't you worried at all? I mean, who *are* the Zulus?"

Eleanor turned to face her, raising an eyebrow. "Of course, I am, my dear. But this is the life we accepted when we married our husbands. We knew it would be fraught with risk. After all, Her Majesty does not pay them to simply look smart in their fancy uniforms."

Elisa said nothing as she removed her hat and fought against the trembling in her hands. It was true; even the ceremonial guardsmen outside Buckingham Palace were still combat soldiers first. And colonial wars throughout the Empire were nothing new. Most of the time, citizens back in Britain paid them little mind, unable to even find on a map most of those places with unpronounceable names where Her Majesty's soldiers were actively engaged. Still, this did not help her growing sense of trepidation and dread.

"A pity we've arrived just as a war has started," Eleanor continued. "It might be months before we see them again. As for the Zulus, I only know their king was a friend and trading partner of the Natal government. Strange that we are now at war with them."

"And what of our own safety?" Elisa persisted. "Might we be in danger? This place feels so desolate."

Eleanor looked around the austere building. There was an orderly clerk's desk in the centre of the room, with rickety wooden doors leading to a series of offices in the back. A faded Union Flag stood in the far corner, while a portrait of the Queen in a tarnished frame hung from the opposite wall.

"The Zulu Kingdom is at least a hundred miles from here," she reasoned, still gazing about the room. "Besides, if Thomas, Arthur, and the rest of the 24th are invading their lands, they probably have far greater concerns than giving us trouble all the way down here."

Elisa gave a nervous smile. She appreciated Eleanor's pragmatism, as it helped calm her immensely. She was very distraught that her long sought-after reunion with Arthur was dashed once again. "I think I need a drink."

"That makes two of us, my dear."

For Lieutenant Harry Davies, the past two days seemed a blur. A member of Lieutenant Colonel Durnford's No. 2 Column, he had led a troop of indigenous cavalry from Basuto Horse. Perhaps the only reason he was still alive was, during the fighting in the donga, he had implored Durnford that his men were almost out of ammunition. The colonel sent Harry and several of his men back to the camp to find their supply wagon. In what would prove to be a catastrophic oversight, no one knew where the wagon was. Davies, now accompanied by the column's transportation officer, William Cochrane, had scoured the nearest tents for whatever cartridges they could find.

Once the Zulus swarmed into the camp with the rest of Durnford's troops retreating from the donga, they knew all was lost. With enemy warriors nearly upon them, they were compelled to take to their horses and flee. At one point, they came upon a hospital wagon led by Surgeon-Major Peter Shepherd. Regrettably, neither Harry nor his troopers had enough rounds left to protect the wagon. It was subsequently overrun by encircling warriors from the Zulu 'Right Horn'. He had watched in dismay as the African driver and all the patients were butchered by enraged Zulus.

Pursued by their fleet-footed foes, Davies and Cochrane somehow managed to ford their way across the uMzinyathi River. The two later separated; Cochrane riding for Helpmekaar, while Davies rode south towards Pietermaritzburg to warn the government. He was joined by another man, Walter Stafford, who was equally relieved to just be alive. They rode hard through the night, and Davies feared his horse would die of exhaustion long before they reached Pietermaritzburg. Near Greytown, approximately seventy miles from the battlefield, they came upon No. 5 Engineer Company; the same unit which had dispatched Lieutenant John Chard and his sappers to Rorke's Drift a few days prior. Davies quickly explained the situation to Captain Jones. He obliged the two men with fresh horses and implored them to *'ride like hell'* and warn the city.

It was nearly nightfall on the evening of the 23rd when they rode into Pietermaritzburg. The indigenous people eyed them with concern, talking feverishly amongst themselves. Harry spoke a bit of Zulu and thought he heard some of the people muttering words about 'a great defeat' at the base of a far mountain.

"How the devil could they have heard about this already?" he asked Stafford, who could only shrug in reply.

"It would seem word-of-mouth spreads quicker in these parts than even the fastest messenger riders."

At Rorke's Drift, it was now midmorning and promising to be another blistering day. Though every man at the depot was on the brink of falling over from utter exhaustion, there was still much work to be done. Chard informed Chelmsford about the NNC warrior he'd dispatched to Helpmekaar, but the GOC was unconvinced that any message would reach Major Spalding.

"Colonel Russell," he said to his senior cavalry officer. "Ride at once to Helpmekaar. Find Major Spalding and tell him he is to return to Rorke's Drift with all haste."

"At once, my lord." Russell walked over to where his horse was tethered. He was joined by the civilian magistrate, Henry Fynn.

"Colonel Russell, would you like some company on the journey?"

"I'd be delighted, Mr Fynn."

In truth, Fynn was still very much irritated with Chelmsford, and especially Crealock. Any chance to get away from them, even for a few hours, was a welcome respite. In light of the disaster, he was especially worried about his magistracy. He feared what would happen, if the Zulus raided into Natal once more.

"Should the Zulus come again, Msinga is not exactly a fortress," he explained to Russell, while voicing his other concerns. The colonel nodded his head. He wasn't entirely sure why the GOC insisted on keeping Fynn with the column. His original purpose, to utilise his knowledge of the region and the Zulu language and people, was moot at this point. Still, he kept these thoughts to himself, as it would not be proper to question his commanding general's orders in front of a civilian.

"Once we return, I'll personally see to it that riders are sent to Msinga," he reassured the magistrate. "Though I imagine his lordship has the foresight to see to this."

He thought to say something more about the 'damn good thrashing' B Company had given the Zulus at Rorke's Drift, but his mind was consumed by the thrashing the Zulus had given the garrison at Isandlwana. Doubtless, the enemy paid a high price for wiping out Henry Pulleine and the rest of 1/24th; however, Russell knew he would never forget the sight of thousands of Zulu warriors covering the hills the evening before. There were so many of them! How difficult would it be for Cetshwayo to dispatch a few thousand to cross the uMzinyathi again, this time simply ignoring the British forces at Rorke's Drift and laying waste to the Natal side of the river?

Their horses were already extremely tired from the long night's ride. They rode at a modest canter, following the long path to the small supply depot at Helpmekaar, fifteen miles to the southwest. An hour later, they happened upon a group of officers riding up the road towards them. In addition to Major Spalding, Russell was filled with joy and relief when he saw Lieutenant Curling from N Battery, as well as Lieutenant Horace Smith-Dorrien, the No. 3 Column's assistant transportation officer.

"Colonel, sir," Spalding said, rendering a quick salute. "By God, it is good to see you still among the living."

"Same with you, my good man. His lordship sends his regards and ordered us to fetch you back to Rorke's Drift with all possible speed."

"Yes, we received the note from Lieutenant Chard. Upcher and Rainforth's companies are about a mile up the road. They should arrive at the depot by supper."

There was much tension in the major's words, and Russell could sense a great deal of frustration and embarrassment in Spalding's voice. No doubt Chelmsford would berate him for not coming to the aid of B Company, and would likely become incensed when he learned they were but a few miles from the drift when they turned around, thinking the depot was a total loss. It was unfair, of course, and Arthur Russell knew it. The darkness of the previous night had been all-consuming, to the point where it was impossible to see more than a foot or two in front of one's face. For all Spalding or anyone else in the column knew at the time, Rorke's Drift had been destroyed. To continue to walk blindly into the waiting spears of several thousand Zulus, with less than two hundred riflemen, would be reckless negligence. It was doubtful the GOC would see it that way.

Chapter XXIII: Bitter Aftermath

Rorke's Drift
23 January 1879
***

Like the other survivors of the massacre at Isandlwana, Lieutenant Horace Smith-Dorrien was still in a complete state of bewilderment. Throughout the battle, he and his immediate superior, Captain Edward Essex, had utilised a donkey cart to ferry ammunition to the beleaguered, and ultimately doomed, companies on the firing line. They became separated at one point and when the camp was overrun, and Horace was compelled to flee for his life. With the Zulus in pursuit, he and a few others fled down a rocky canyon leading to the uMzinyathi River. Swamped from his mount by the strong current, he had only managed to survive by holding onto the tail of a rider-less horse. Upon reaching the Natal bank, he stopped to empty the river water and sand from his boots, while a few dozen troopers from Basuto Horse laid down a barrage of covering fire for the desperate fugitives trying to escape the slaughter. Around nightfall, the young officer had reached Helpmekaar, where he, Essex, and less than fifty fellow survivors spent a sleepless night. He recalled seeing the burning horizon in the direction of Rorke's Drift and was utterly stunned to hear the garrison had held.

Horace was the youngest officer in the entire No. 3 Column, yet his experiences of the past two days had drastically aged his mind and soul. As the group of officers made the journey to Rorke's Drift, he could still see the faces of those brave soldiers at Isandlwana, battling valiantly against insurmountable odds. He particularly recalled a group of sharp-shooters from Captain Younghusband's C Company holding the high ground off the northern spur of the mountain. What struck him most about so many of the men on the firing line was how young they were. At just twenty years of age, Horace felt his own life had only just begun. Yet how many of those brave lads, some of whom were even younger than him, had their time in this world cut short by Zulu spears?

"Would you look at that?" he said softly, as the carnage surrounding the mission station came into view.

"Seems your boys gave those darkies a damn good thrashing, Henry," Major Upcher said appreciatively to Spalding.

Despite his relief, Spalding winced in reply.

"One would not recognise this place now," Smith-Dorrien added.

Only the morning prior, he had arrived with a message for Lieutenant Colonel Durnford while coordinating with the depot for the return of some of his empty supply wagons from Isandlwana. He had even acquired some pistol rounds from Lieutenant Bromhead, 'just in case'. He'd expended nearly all of them during his rather harrowing escape.

As he, Major Spalding, and the others returned, neither man recognised what was left of the mission station. The hospital was in ruins, while the defenders had managed to encompass the once-open depot with a shoulder high wall. An impressive feat in its own right! Their horses had to tread carefully, for the ground was littered everywhere with the broken bodies of Zulu warriors.

"There's my wagon," he noted with a derisive chuckle. The general-purpose wagon, which had carried his personal baggage and kit, sat approximately 200 yards from the perimeter. It was riddled with bullet holes and completely looted.

In addition to the hundreds of human bodies scattered everywhere were all the dead cattle and draught oxen. The volume of death and debris was so great, Horace wondered if it could ever be cleared away. Or, would Rorke's Drift remain permanently scarred? As he dismounted his horse near the smouldering ruins of the hospital, he heard cheering coming from some of the men near the inner redoubt.

"Hey, it's Flip!" one of the soldiers exclaimed.

Just then, Horace saw a spotted Dalmatian limping its way towards the men. The poor animal was exhausted and clearly hurt. There was a snapped piece of rope tied around his neck, and his left foreleg was covered in dried blood. The lieutenant smiled as he watched the men excitedly gather around the tired beast. They rubbed him behind the ears and neck. One of them went to find the dog's master, Lieutenant Colonel Degacher.

"Flip, old boy!" the colonel said excitedly.

Despite exhaustion and his injured leg, the animal practically leapt onto him. Degacher knelt and wrapped his arms around the dog. Flip rubbed his face appreciatively into his master's chest.

Surgeon Reynolds' Jack Russell, Dick, came running over. He crouched low, eyeing the wounded Dalmatian's shoulder. The reunion between the two provided a short, yet much needed happy respite for the officer. He was still coming to grips with the death of his brother, along with so many of his friends and fellow soldiers.

Horace allowed himself a brief smile. He then spotted Captain Parr, one of his lordships aides-de-camp.

"Ah, Mister Smith-Dorrien," the captain acknowledged. "I am glad to see you made it."

"Thank you, sir. Is there anything I can do to assist?"

"Not unless you want to grab a shovel or start dragging these filthy darkies away, before they stink up the place."

"No relief for any of us," Horace noted.

Indeed, there would be little reprieve for the survivors of No. 3 Column. Chelmsford had given Captain Parr the rather dubious honour of supervising the burial of the Zulu dead. He directed Rupert Lonsdale to have his NNC warriors begin digging the mass graves. Unfortunately, there were insufficient pickaxes and shovels, even with those from John Chard's engineer wagon. Driver Robson distributed what he had to the NNC warriors. They would simply have to make do. While twenty or so began the laborious task of digging a grave large enough for hundreds of bodies, there was arguing coming from the ranks of indigenous warriors.

"What in bleeding hell are they going on about?" 'Maori' Browne asked in irritation.

Charlie Harford cocked an ear towards the *induna* of the band of warriors. "They keep saying *'umnyama'*. It means 'darkness'. They believe the bodies of the dead are cursed. Unless proper purification rituals are observed, they will not touch them."

"Oh, piss on them!" Browne snapped, drawing his revolver. "I'll show them 'purification' with my pistol shoved halfway up his arse!"

"Take it easy, 'Maori'," Lonsdale said, interrupting his subordinate's tirade. "Captain Harford, have the men keep digging. I'll get the rest of this sorted."

"Something amiss, Commandant Lonsdale?" Captain Parr asked, having heard the commotion.

"These damned niggers won't touch any of the bodies," Browne spat. "And what the hell do they mean by 'purification'? Do they want us to wash the fucking corpses first?"

"Damn it, man, that's enough!" Rupert barked, his head throbbing from his previous injury and this latest aggravation. "Take two companies of iziGqoza and check the tree grove for any enemy wounded. Mister Harford, carry on with the grave digging."

"The natives take issue with having to bury the dead?" Parr asked when Browne was out of earshot.

"According to Harford, they think the bodies of the slain are cursed and must be purified before burial."

"Oh, hang it all," Parr retorted in exasperation.

Lonsdale held up his hands in resignation. "Captain, I understand your frustration. But we have fifteen hundred Natal natives with us. I'd rather not incite a mutiny."

Parr was less-than-pleased, but he understood Lonsdale's reluctance to try to force the issue. "Alright, I'll have Captain Church and Captain Logan's companies from 2nd Battalion see to it. But I advise you to sort out this lot once they've finished digging."

Redcoats and carbineers soon formed into work details, some collecting the Zulu weapons and tossing them into a large pit. Most undertook the strenuous task of dragging away the enemy dead. Every slain warrior bore fearful wounds wrought by the Martini-Henry rifle and bayonet. Arms and legs, destroyed by the large calibre bullets, hung by ruptured tendons and shredded flesh. Many were gutted by close range shots, and so an equally grisly task involved shovelling away the piles of guts and entrails.

"Come on, you black devil," one soldier griped, when a foot from the body he was dragging got caught on a stone. The private fell onto his backside, the Zulu's bloody torso in his lap. "Damn it all, you're causing me more trouble in death than when you were alive!"

As soldiers cleared away the bodies from the north wall near the hospital, they found a fellow redcoat lying beneath several Zulu corpses. It was Private John Scanlon, a member of A Company. A patient in hospital, dealing with chronic dysentery, he had died on the barricades, fighting the Zulus. It filled his mates with both pride and sorrow.

"It's your turn now, comrade," a fellow soldier from A Company said. "I'm sorry to put you away, mate, but at least you died well and had a soldier's death."

In addition to the Zulu bodies, there was the matter of sorting the British dead. Sixteen defenders were killed during the battle, if one included the NNC deserter, Corporal Anderson. It would soon be seventeen, as the badly stricken Private Beckett was slowly breathing his last. The GOC ordered them buried on the flat space behind the buildings near the foot of Shiyane. What was, perhaps, most surprising was that only four of the dead were from B Company; Lance Sergeant Thomas Williams, who had died of his injuries during the night, along with Privates Thomas Cole, John Fagan, and Joseph Williams.

Despite the sheer numbers of slain Zulus, plus the utter destruction wreaked upon the mission station, there was still plenty of labour to assist the survivors from B Company. In all, there were nearly 600 redcoats from Henry Degacher's 2/24th plus the No. 1 Squadron, Imperial Mounted Infantry. There were also more than a hundred volunteer and mounted police and fifty gunners and crewmen from N Battery. Regardless of their level of enervation, the men worked with great cheer, in no small measure out of relief that they were still alive. Having filled their bellies also helped renew their strength.

Some of the soldiers had to walk further afield to collect the enemy dead. About twenty redcoats accompanied 'Maori' Browne and his iziGqoza companies who, unlike the rest of the NNC, had no issue with handling their dead enemy kinsmen. Below a short rise, in a field of flattened mealie, they came across roughly twenty badly wounded Zulus.

"They must have used this as a casualty collection point," a private muttered, keeping his bayonet protruding towards the prostrate warriors. Most were drenched in sweat and breathing heavily, and all bore fearful wounds.

"What would you have us do?" another soldier asked Browne, seeing as how he was the only officer present.

"The only thing we can do." The commandant picked up a discarded assegai, and after staring into the eyes of a wounded Zulu for a moment, plunged the blade into the man's heart. The Zulu grimaced in pain for a few seconds, and then it was over.

"Use your bayonets. No sense in wasting ammunition."

There was only a trace of reluctance from the 24th soldiers. It felt unmanly and cruel to slay the enemy's wounded, but there was still the lingering rage from what happened to their mates at Isandlwana. For those who thought to gain a measure of satisfaction by helping to avenge their fallen brethren, there was only hollow numbness. One particularly young soldier had only arrived in Natal from the recruit depot a couple months prior to the war. He felt his stomach twist in knots as he plunged his bayonet beneath the ribs of one badly injured warrior. Dark crimson gushed onto the triangular spike. The Zulu convulsed violently in the few moments it took for his life to leave him. The redcoat stood open-mouthed, trying not to vomit. For the past few weeks, all he'd spoken of was the chance to kill an enemy warrior. As he wrenched is bayonet free and stared into the lifeless eyes of the first man he'd slain, he was struck by the vulgar and harsh reality of what it was like to kill another human being.

"Nothing like playing with your toy soldiers, is it?" an older private asked the young lad.

His face was pale and sweaty. "Nothing at all," he confessed, wiping his sleeve across his brow. "I hope it's different…killing them in battle, I mean."

"Not really," the older soldier remarked. "Except when they can fight back, one has to deal with the urge to shit oneself in terror."

In sharp contrast, the iziGqoza fell upon their badly mauled kinsmen with vengeful relish. Many plunged their spears repeatedly into the wounded, stabbing with malice and hate long after their victims had expired.

The screams of the wounded being killed sent a chill up the spines of most of the men back at the depot; however, none of the officers attempted to stop the slaughter. For his part, Lord Chelmsford sat in silence, drinking his tea, appearing unfazed by the shrieks and piteous cries of the dying. There would later be a trace of collective remorse. Captain Parr would attempt to downplay the event by saying there had only been a couple of wounded Zulus found, and that their killing was done by a few ill-disciplined NNC warriors. For those whose bayonets now dripped with blood, they would forever struggle with the internal conflict; bringing what they felt was a measure of justice to their murderously butchered friends, and remorse at having slaughtered those who could no longer defend themselves.

While the sombre task of dealing with the dead was being attended to, Sergeant Henry Gallagher led a patrol of ten men down to the drift. John Williams and Henry Hook—his head now heavily bandaged—accompanied him. All along the riverbank they found scores of discarded weapons and Zulu shields. Most of these were covered in blood.

"Makeshift stretchers for their wounded," Hook noted, as he knelt and picked up one of the shields. It was completely soaked in sticky dark crimson.

"I wonder how many of those poor bastards drowned trying to cross," Williams remarked. It was well known that Zulus were terrible swimmers. Any attempts to cross the swollen river would have been precarious, even for those not afflicted by terrible injuries.

"A feast for the crocodiles, no doubt," another private added.

Gallagher, Hook, and a few others slowly crept through the undergrowth nearest the ponts. Leaning against a tall shade tree they found three more Zulu bodies.

"Toss them in the river," the sergeant ordered.

"The crocs should be loving us for this," Harry said, echoing Williams' sentiments. He leaned his rifle against the tree and helped his companions drag the bodies into the current.

By late afternoon, the Zulu corpses in and around the depot were buried, as were the British dead. Chaplain Smith said a few words and read from Psalms as the last shovelfuls of dirt were tossed onto the soldiers' graves. Henry Degacher had men mark the new cemetery with an encompassing line of rocks, with the intent of eventually erecting a proper stone wall. The ramparts around the depot had been rebuilt and reinforced, and the large pile of enemy weapons continued to burn. The occasional crack of a discharging burning musket alarmed the men, leading to a quick condemnation of, *'Whichever damned idiot threw loaded muskets into the burn pile!'*

For Lord Chelmsford, there was the practical matter of deciding what was to be done with the remnants of No. 3 Column. There were also the northern and southern columns that would require his attention. In the span of just two days, the entire invasion had come unravelled. As such, he assembled what senior officers remained. The highest ranking was, of course, Brevet Colonel Richard Glyn. His demeanour on this day was sullen and quiet. Doubtless he was still in deep shock and mourning over the loss of nearly all his former battalion.

"Colonel Glyn," Chelmsford said, addressing him directly for the first time in more than a day. "No. 3 Column is to remain at Rorke's Drift and prepare for defence against a Zulu counterthrust. Colonel Durnford may have cost me most of 1st Battalion, as well as his entire column, but we cannot shirk in our duty of defending Natal against those murderous savages."

Glyn nodded, though his face twitched at the mention of Durnford's name. Chelmsford was already making a less-than-subtle attempt to begin placing blame for the disaster on Anthony Durnford while absolving himself.

The GOC then addressed the commanding officer of 2/24th. "Colonel Degacher, your battalion makes up the corps of our professional infantry. Upcher and Rainforth's companies from 1st Battalion will operationally fall under your charge for the time being."

"Very good, my lord."

The GOC then added, "Major Upcher, you will, for the time being, report to Colonel Degacher. As your battalion's senior remaining officer, you are now commanding officer of 1/24th."

"Understood, sir," Upcher replied.

Of the eight companies that originally made up the battalion, three remained; Upcher's, Rainforth's, and Captain Harrison's B

Company, which was on garrison duty near Pondoland. In time, the remaining companies would be reconstituted, as would Charlie Pope's G Company, 2/24th. However, he knew they would forever live in the shadow of the 'hill of the sphinx'.

As the GOC continued to brief the column officers, Lieutenant Colonel Henry Degacher was surprisingly better composed than most of his peers. He sat on a rickety camp chair while his dog, Flip, rested his head in his lap. The loyal animal's front quarter was bandaged from where he'd been stabbed by a Zulu assegai. In time, Henry would allow himself to mourn his brother, William, but not while there was work to be done.

Because his battalion was mostly intact, he understood that any further actions by the column would fall mostly be his responsibility. While they had lost all of Charlie Pope's G Company at Isandlwana, along with the soldier-servants and various detached troops, he still had seven full companies; nine if one counted the two from Helpmekaar. This gave him over 800 riflemen; a formidable force, provided he could acquire ammunition for them.

"Ammunition is in critical shortage, sir," he spoke up. "Most of my lads are down to half their basic load, and the carbineers are in even worse shape. Only B Company's riflemen have a full allotment of cartridges, and their reserves are almost completely exhausted. According to Lieutenant Bromhead, they have less than 800 spare cartridges remaining."

"There's also the matter of our tents and other equipment," Glyn's ADC, Major Clery, added. "The weather is likely to take a bad turn on us, and we have nothing with which to protect ourselves from the elements. Even B Company has nothing, since their tents were looted and destroyed during the battle."

Chelmsford was unmoved. "They're soldiers. They'll learn to make do." He turned to Colonel Glyn. "Send word to Captain Essex at Helpmekaar. Have whatever ammunition is available brought to Rorke's Drift with all possible speed. Meanwhile, post the picquets and have your men rest up. Tomorrow I leave for Pietermaritzburg. Your task is to build this place into a proper fortress and stop any further incursions from the Zulus."

Chelmsford then shot a quick glance to Degacher, who gave a subtle nod. Richard Glyn may have been the column commander, but the GOC was concerned by his distant and broken demeanour.

He suspected that much of the actual management of the column survivors would fall onto Henry Degacher's shoulders.

His greatest concern was re-establishing chains of supply, while restocking lost ammunition and stores. While there had been a veritable feast of biscuits and tinned beef to fill the stomachs of the ravenous survivors, the rations available at Rorke's Drift were certainly not unlimited. The cattle herds, used to provide 'food on the hoof', were also completely lost.

To complicate matters, both quartermasters of the 24th, James Pullen and Edward Bloomfield, were killed at Isandlwana, as were their quartermaster sergeants and commissaries. One of Degacher's battalion majors, William Dunbar, offered to assume the quartermaster duties. A venerable and physically imposing officer with twenty-four years under the Colours, Dunbar had nearly resigned his commission two weeks earlier, following a heated argument with Lieutenant Colonel Crealock. It was only after the personal intervention of the GOC, who had all but begged the major to reconsider, that Dunbar relented. Chelmsford gladly allowed him to assume duties as the column's acting quartermaster.

"I understand Storekeeper Byrne was killed," Degacher noted. "But you'll have Commissary Dunne to assist you. Assistant Commissary Dalton was badly wounded during the battle, I'm afraid."

"Such a pity," Dunbar stated. "I could use an old salt with his experience."

"And colonel," Chelmsford continued, addressing Glyn, while making the occasional eye contact with Degacher. "Inform Lieutenant Chard that he is to continue his task of laying out the foundation for a proper fort overlooking the drift."

"His detachment was wiped out at Isandlwana, sir," Major Clery noted.

"Surely even the thickest of our men can scrape the ground, if properly supervised," the GOC snapped in irritation. "Once Captain Jones and the rest of No. 5 Field Company arrive, I want the river crossing properly secured. Starting tomorrow, you will begin work on fortifying the depot with stone fortifications. Mister Chard can oversee that, as well. A few bouts of rain and those mealie sacks will begin to rot. And now, gentlemen, I will leave you to it."

Chapter XXIV: Blood of the Heroes

Rorke's Drift
23 January 1879

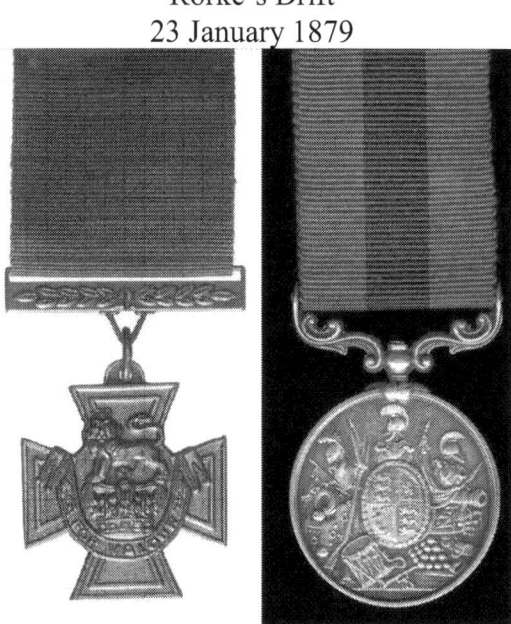

The Victoria Cross and Distinguished Conduct Medal

While the GOC and remaining senior officers of the column discussed the immediate defensive plans for Rorke's Drift, John Chard held one last meeting with 'Gunny' Bromhead and Colour Sergeant Bourne. He wished Dalton could have joined them, but the assistant commissary was terribly weakened by blood loss and was asleep in the makeshift ward Surgeon Reynolds had established in the storehouse.

"His lordship has given me one final task as officer commanding at Rorke's Drift," he explained, as he lit his pipe. "I know every man standing fought with valour and extreme courage. That said, Lord Chelmsford has directed me to provide a list of names and proposed citations for those who most distinguished themselves."

"Yes, he made it plain to me that he wants VC recommendations for all the men who defended the hospital," Bromhead remarked.

"They risked their lives saving others," the colour sergeant noted. "And a couple even gave their lives. Sadly, Her Majesty's government does not allow posthumous awards for bravery."

"Alright," Chard said with an assertive nod. "This is where I need you. I've only been here a few days and I simply don't know the men of B Company. Who were the survivors from the hospital defenders?"

Bourne fished out a pad of paper and pencil from one of his tunic pockets and began to write, as he and Bromhead recalled their names.

"John Williams, Henry Hook, Robert and William Jones. There was also Joseph Williams and 'Old King' Cole, but sadly they did not make it."

"Very good. What about those two who continued to carry ammunition to the line after they were wounded? I recall Corporal Allan, but who was the other man?"

"Private Fred Hitch," Bourne answered. "And they did more than just ferry cartridges to the line. They ran across the open compound after the outer wall had fallen and helped the lads in the hospital carry the wounded to safety. I watched Allan heave one crippled fellow onto his back using only his good arm. A pair of hard bastards, those two."

"Reynolds is working on Hitch, even as we speak," 'Gunny' Bromhead noted. "Had half his shoulder shot away, yet got right back up, used my pistol with his good hand, and continued to fight long after a lesser man would have fallen exhausted or dead."

Bourne's thoughts turned to the young soldier, who last he saw lying on Otto Witt's altar table while Surgeon Reynolds pulled slivers of shattered bone from his terrible wound. He hoped Fred would not succumb to his injuries or infection before he could be recommended for the Victoria Cross. He recalled something he had said to Bromhead the day prior.

"I did say I wanted to put Hitch in for a medal after he killed that deserter. At least now we can write up his citation for something a bit less scandalous."

"That deserter was killed by 'early enemy fire'," Bromhead remarked sternly, causing a moment of awkward silence.

"I would like to recommend the corporal with the injured foot from the Natal Mounted Police, as well," Chard said, getting the men back to the task at hand.

"Corporal Schiess," Bromhead recalled. "He's actually with the NNC, not the police. And that will be difficult. He's not even British, but Swiss."

"Regardless, he fought under British command and distinguished himself when he climbed over the ramparts and dispatched those fellows who were causing us much distress."

"I would bet my last shilling that he killed more men than any one of us left standing," Bourne added. "He held the line almost singlehandedly more than once. I personally watched him fell six men with six shots during one harrying engagement."

"Even if the GOC denies the recommendation, at least Schiess will know that we honour his bravery," Chard asserted.

"There's also Surgeon Reynolds," Bromhead added. "He not only saved a number of wounded, but exposed himself to enemy fire while bringing ammunition to the hospital."

"We should add Dick to the citation, as well," Bourne remarked with a chuckle, referring to Reynold's dog. This brought a much-needed laugh.

"And we're agreed that these men should all receive the Victoria Cross?" Gunny asked.

Chard nodded and looked to Bourne. "I think there is one senior NCO we should add to the list."

"Respectfully, sir, I would ask that you not put my name in for the VC," the colour sergeant said, lowering his eyes for a moment.

"What are you saying, colour sergeant?" Chard asked, utterly perplexed. "At our darkest hour, when every man thought we would never see another sunrise, you inspired them to keep fighting."

"All the same, sir, I feel that the Victoria Cross might actually hinder my future aspirations."

"Explain yourself, man."

"Our good colour sergeant wishes to become an officer someday," Bromhead said quickly. "If he is awarded the VC, he becomes an 'ornament' of the Regiment. They'll never let him take a commission outside of the 24th, which will limit his future prospects considerably."

"Then I will recommend you for the Distinguished Conduct Medal," Chard decided. "The annuity is the same as the Victoria Cross, and it is less likely to hinder your ambitions."

"Much obliged, sir," Bourne replied gratefully. "I think Corporal Atwood should receive the DCM as well. If not for his quick thinking and superb marksmanship, the Zulus might very well have set the storehouse on fire."

"In which case, we would not be having this conversation," Chard concurred. "Well, I think we have a good start. I will, of course, be writing an official report for the command staff. I'm certain other acts of valour worthy of distinction will come to light soon enough."

Having dispatched a trio of riders to Msinga, Lieutenant Colonel Russell was approached by Sergeant Naughton, the senior member of the Imperial Mounted Infantry to survive the Battle of Isandlwana.

"My report, sir," the NCO said, handing several pages of notes to his commanding officer.

Thirty-one men from the IMI had been left at Isandlwana. Ten survived. The colonel was anxious to learn the fates of the others, including the detachment's officer commanding, Lieutenant Francis Scott.

"Your report lists one man's name repeatedly," Russell observed.

In addition to the VCs and DCMs recommended for the defenders of Rorke's Drift, a lone award for valour was submitted for one of the survivors of Isandlwana. The British Army loathed rewarding anyone for actions that transpired during a defeat, no matter how brave or noteworthy. However, Sergeant Naughton was adamant in his report that Private Samuel Wassall be nominated for the Victoria Cross. Indeed, over half of Naughton's despatch detailed the young private's harrowing rescue of Private David Westwood.

Private Wassall crossed the uMzinyathi River no less than three times, at one point leaving his horse on the Zulu side to dive into the river and rescue Private Westwood. Returning to the Zulu side, he retrieved his horse and carried his comrade to safety. The entire time he was subjected to intense enemy musketry and flung assegais. It is, therefore, with the utmost emphasis that I recommend Private Wassall be awarded the Victoria Cross.

Though he felt it rather distasteful to bring public attention to what was clearly the most horrific disaster to affect the British Army in over a century, Lieutenant Colonel Russell agreed to endorse the recommendation and pass it on to Colonel Glyn. It would, ultimately, be up to the GOC to make the commendation, first to Whitehall and eventually to the Queen.

"That's all I ask, sir," the sergeant replied. "Her Majesty can decide if Private Wassall deserves the VC, so long as she knows about his selfless courage."

Russell then dismissed the NCO, who came to attention and saluted before leaving. Both men knew that the sacrifices of uncounted soldiers in Her Majesty's Forces would go unheralded, particularly given the extent of the disaster at Isandlwana. And because the British Empire *never* forgot her defeats, rare as they were, it was fitting that such a scene of epic tragedy should be accented by a single private soldier's act of noble bravery.

Later that afternoon, Arthur Russell brought the report to Henry Degacher. He was reviewing the recommendations he'd received from Lieutenant Chard.

"Ah, Arthur," Degacher said, waving his fellow officer to a nearby biscuit box. "Just reviewing the first batch of VC recommendations from Mister Chard."

"I suspect the GOC will endorse all of them," Russell conjectured. He handed Naughton's despatch to him. "I have one more to add to the list."

"On the face of it, Private Wassall has more than earned the Victoria Cross," Degacher said after reading the note. "A pity that it comes during a time of national tragedy and disgrace."

"Those were my thoughts, Henry. I also think that drawing attention to so many proposed VCs from Rorke's Drift will shine a rather glaring light on the disaster we've befallen."

"Yes. Lieutenant Chard made mention of a few others who, regrettably, he cannot recommend, as they did not survive."

"I imagine the same holds true for many of the lads still lying unburied, ten miles from here," Arthur speculated.

"One story has repeated itself numerous times over the past day," Degacher continued. "It seems Lieutenant Melvill retrieved the Queen's Colour and was attempting to take it to safety. An NNC officer, I can't recall his name, said he was with him and Lieutenant Coghill. The NNC fellow and Melvill were both swamped from their horses in the river, and sadly the Colour was lost. Coghill returned to save them only to have his horse shot out from under him. The NNC officer said when he last saw them, they were a few hundred yards from the river. He says he left to find horses but was chased away by Zulus."

"And what of Melvill and Coghill?"

Henry shook his head. "Still missing, though I have little doubts as to their fate."

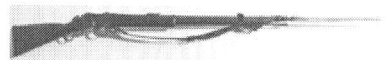

Harry Davies and Walter Stafford rode through Pietermaritzburg until they reached the residence of the high commissioner, Sir Henry Bartle-Frere. As they dismounted near the gate, they were surprised to see a trooper from the Newcastle Mounted Rifles emerging from the large house.

"Lieutenant," the man said with a salute, drawing baffled gazes from the two men.

"How the devil did you arrive before us?" Davies asked.

"No idea, sir. The past day or so has been a bit foggy. To be honest, I'm not altogether certain I even believed what I told the high commissioner. He at first accused me of being a deserter, looking to cause trouble. It was only when his native butler came in, frantically speaking something about a disaster that he appeared to believe me. All the same, sir, you might want to convey to him what you know. Might sound a bit more convincing coming from an officer."

Harry dismissed the trooper and told him to be at Fort Napier the following day. He and Stafford walked sombrely up to the large front door and knocked. They could hear some commotion from within. When no one came to answer, they decided to let themselves in.

They heard numerous voices arguing in the local dialect. Davies picked up talk of 'darkness' and 'pending doom'. Though Stafford did not speak a word of isiZulu, the tone and inflection alone was enough to let him know that the household staff of the high commissioner was in a state of panic. They saw light coming from a room upstairs, which they surmised was Frere's office. Harry knocked on the door.

"What is it now?" an irritated voice called from within.

Harry opened the door and saw Sir Henry Bartle-Frere pouring himself a drink from a crystal whiskey decanter.

"Lieutenant Davies, Edendale Troop, sir," he said by way of introduction.

"Come with more fictitious tales about how an entire column of British soldiers was massacred by filthy niggers carrying spears?" the high commissioner snapped. "I just sent one of your men away, and now my entire household has lost their blasted minds!"

"I'm afraid it's not a fictitious tale, sir," Davies replied. He went on to explain all that he knew regarding Chelmsford's departure with half the column the previous morning. He could give some details about the disposition of the men in the camp, as he had been part of Anthony Durnford's mounted column.

"So that idiot, Durnford, has brought tragedy and disgrace to the Empire once again." Frere's expression had calmed considerably, though his voice was like ice. "I warned Chelmsford not to give him a command!"

Davies did not reply to this, but simply finished telling the high commissioner all he knew. The GOC's whereabouts, as well as that of the rest of the column, were unknown. There was also the fear that Rorke's Drift had fallen.

"And what of the other columns?" Frere asked at last.

"Colonel Wood's No. 4 Column is only about twenty-five miles north of Isandlwana," the lieutenant recalled. "Last we knew, Colonel Pearson and No. 1 Column had crossed the Thukela and were headed for Eshowe."

"That's a hundred miles south of where we were," Stafford added.

The high commissioner did not reply, but sat behind his desk and began writing feverishly. After a few moments, he handed the message to Davies. "There is little chance of getting word to Colonel Wood in a timely fashion," he said. "We can only hope that Lord Chelmsford has managed to do so, provided he's still alive. This needs to be delivered to Colonel Pearson with all haste. He needs to be warned before those damned darkies surround and wipe out his command as well."

Harry took the message and the two officers excused themselves.

As they made their way out onto the street, Walter Stafford asked, "Does he think the Zulus can run a hundred miles in a couple days?"

"After what's happened, it would seem our adversaries are capable of superhuman feats," Davies remarked. "I imagine in the coming days, they'll become like gods in the eyes of the gullible populace."

"Well, they did smash a battalion of Her Majesty's finest," Stafford said. "What could be more godlike than that?"

Chapter XXV: One Hell of a Day

Rorke's Drift
23 January 1879
Nightfall

Major William Dunbar
Battalion Major, 2/24th Regiment

As evening fell upon the remnants of No. 3 Column at Rorke's Drift, the deprivations of the past two days finally began to overpower the battered survivors. Conditions were extremely cramped and uncomfortable. There simply was not enough room within the compound for the entire column. Due to the overcrowding, Chelmsford directed Major Upcher to return to Helpmekaar with his two companies the following morning. Meanwhile, NNC were ordered to sleep along the slope of Shiyane. This did not sit well with them. There was a great fear amongst them of the Zulus returning.

"Hell of a day, wasn't it?" John Williams asked. He sat with his back against the northern corner of the inner redoubt. He was wedged in between Henry Hook and Robert Jones. All three had cut holes in empty mealie sacks, which they used to protect themselves against the cold night. A stiff breeze blew in from the west, causing them to shiver.

"We should have let the damned Zulus have this cursed land," Jones growled. "Sweltering hot days, freezing rainy nights. It won't surprise me if half of us succumb to sodding fevers from this shit."

A raindrop splashed the private's forehead, causing him to pull his battered helmet over his eyes. Though the rains had been mercifully absent during the battle of the night prior, it seemed their reprieve would be short-lived.

"And the Zulus went and thrashed all our tents," Williams muttered.

"Was a bit rude of them, wasn't it?" Harry Hook forced a smile, despite the persistent pain from his scalp wound and the discomfort of the cold and squalid sleeping arrangements.

As the rains fell, compounding the misery of the horde of men crammed behind the barricades, they succumbed to overtiredness. All but the unfortunate souls on guard duty drifted off to sleep. For most of the shattered soldiers, it was enough that they were still alive. For some of the more cynical, they quietly thought that, perhaps, the dead were the fortunate ones.

The bugle sounding reveille reverberated around dawn. Henry Degacher was already awake. He rubbed his eyes and sat upright, quietly praying the past few days had all been a terrible dream. His neck was sore, as was his back. The hard floor in a corner of the storehouse had served as his bed, a half-empty mealie sack for a pillow. Next to him lay the hulking form of Major William Dunbar, still snoring loudly. Degacher let him be and pulled his stiff body to its feet. His mind was still numb, and he yawned loudly as he stepped out into the cool, damp air.

The morning stillness was accented by hundreds of men coughing and spitting up phlegm. With no shelter or greatcoats to keep out the rain and cold, the commander of 2nd Battalion rightly feared that illness and fever would become their greatest nemesis. The night had been one of utter misery. Frequent rain showers tormented them. Sheer exhaustion was the only reason anyone got any sleep. Something else he noticed was that Chelmsford was gone.

"Beastly morning, sir," his other battalion major, Wilsone Black, said. The Scottish officer had a kettle in his hand and was searching for straw and kindling that wasn't soaked from the night's rain. Normally, the officers' soldier-servants took care of menial tasks such as coffee and breakfast. That Major Black was searching for firewood to brew his kettle only reminded them of the harsh new reality. All soldier-servants for 2nd Battalion had remained at Isandlwana. Colonel Glyn's orderly, a young private named Williams, along with two bandsmen, were the only survivors. Black could only hope that his own servant, 17-year old Boy James Gurney, had died well.

"No sign of his lordship?" Degacher asked.

Wilsone shook his head. "The GOC roused himself and his staff two hours before dawn. I know because that git, Crealock, tripped over me twice. They're already well on their way to Pietermaritzburg to face the music, it would seem." He paused for a moment and apprised his battalion commander's pale and scruffy appearance. "How are you managing, sir?"

"Well enough, Wilsone, well enough. I wouldn't be honouring the memory of my brother, or the others, if I fell apart now. But I'm going to need you and Dunbar more than ever. To be perfectly candid, I am a touch concerned about Colonel Glyn."

Black understood. "He's scarcely said a word since we heard of the disaster. With Chelmsford's departure, the good colonel now has his command back. He's a tough bastard, so I'm certain he'll manage."

There was a trace of doubt in the major's voice. It betrayed Degacher's own feelings. Henry accepted that much of the daily responsibilities would fall on him. Not only was he the commanding officer for 2/24th, but as the lone substantive lieutenant colonel, he was the second ranking officer left at Rorke's Drift. Uncertain as to whether Colonel Glyn was making due, he steeled himself and decided to take the initiative. The first thing they needed was a thorough reconnaissance of the area. B Company may have repelled the Zulu onslaught, but that did not mean the enemy wasn't still out there. Lieutenant Chard had mentioned in his report seeing several hundred warriors on the ridgeline just prior to the column's return.

For all Degacher knew, this could be part of a much larger raiding force.

As he made his way over to the cattle kraals where the carbineers and mounted police had spent the night, the colonel heard a slew of shouted profanities coming from the calf pen.

"Oh, bloody piss, I stuck my hand in that!"

This was accompanied by a colourful series of curses, as well as laughter, from a gathering of carbineers. Degacher recognised one of the officers, Lieutenant Maxwell.

He was standing with his arms folded, shaking his head. "Well, that explains why it was lumpy and stank so bad," he said with a grin. He then composed himself and came to attention as Degacher approached. "Colonel, sir."

"A bit of a foul discovery, Mister Maxwell?"

"You could say that, sir. Some of the lads pulled down straw from the storehouse roof to make a bed. Well, it was after dark and they couldn't see a thing. Turns out they were sleeping on the corpse of a slain Zulu who got missed during the burial detail."

"Stuck me hand in his sodding guts," a trooper grumbled, wiping his hand off in the wet straw.

"Something we can do for you, sir?" the lieutenant asked.

Degacher pointed in the direction of the ponts. "I need a scouting party to search along the river and make certain the Zulus don't have spies or another assault force lurking about. I'll inform Colonel Russell of your orders."

"Very good, sir."

Returning to the storehouse, Degacher was approached by Surgeon James Reynolds. Given the number of wounded requiring surgery, he'd not allowed himself any sleep until the early hours of the morning.

With the hospital at Rorke's Drift destroyed, no protection from the elements for the sick and wounded, and his medical supplies nearing exhaustion, he explained his dilemma to the colonel.

"There's nothing for it, sir," he said. "The wounded and sick *must* be evacuated. Most of my stock of medicines and chloroform are either expended or were lost when the hospital burned. I'm all out of bandages. I've been using discarded tunics and undershirts. And then there's poor Corporal Lyons."

"How is he?" Degacher asked sympathetically.

"It's a miracle he's still alive," Reynolds stated. "The musket shot is buried in his neck and I simply cannot get to it. He's in terrible pain, especially in the arms and legs, which tells me the ball is wedged against the nerves of his spinal column. Poor fellow, I don't have anything left to dull his pain. And then there's Private Hitch. If we don't get something to disinfect his wounds, he'll die of gangrene."

"A more horrible death than a Zulu spear," Degacher remarked. "Not to worry, doctor. I'll inform Colonel Glyn that the patients need to be sent back to Helpmekaar and then to Ladysmith."

"Thank you, sir. Ladysmith has a proper hospital and is far more prepared to handle patients than we are here or at Helpmekaar. I worry about transporting Corporal Lyons in his state, but I simply do not have the tools necessary to work on him."

Surgeon Reynolds then went to write up a report with his recommendations for each of the wounded. Some, like Henry Hook, could return to duty. John Lyons and James Dalton would require additional surgery, which Reynolds hoped the doctors at Ladysmith could provide. In addition to Fred Hitch, he also recommended that Corporal William Allan be sent back to England. There was nothing left that either could hope to do to help the war effort. And as Lieutenant Bromhead told them, 'You've done your bit.'

One practical matter to be sorted was what to do with the 3rd Regiment of the Natal Native Contingent. Aside from the iziGqoza, their morale had been fragile even on the best of days. But now, having witnessed the defeat of the redcoats at Isandlwana and the death of the revered *inkosi*, Gabangaye, they were completely demoralised. Being forced to spend the rainy night exposed on the slopes of Shiyane had further crushed their spirits.

As the redcoats roused themselves and paraded before their officers and senior NCOs, Commandant Lonsdale ordered the 3rd NNC to gather near the base of the mountain. What was plain to him, 'Maori' Browne, and Charlie Harford was that a substantial number of their warriors were missing.

"Good riddance, cowardly shits," Browne swore.

Harford's feelings were decidedly mixed. While it had been an exacerbating experience, particularly trying to keep his picquets from abandoning their posts during the night at Mangeni, he could not help but feel a trace of pity for the Natal warriors. They had been levied into the ranks with almost no training, insufficiently armed and equipped, and led by officers and NCOs who were abusive and only marginally competent. That so many settlers had been given local commissions to lead these warriors without any sort of military background, nor being able to speak their language, was both insulting and impractical. Still, this did not excuse the mass defections and countless acts of cowardice. After all, these men were volunteers. No one had pressed them into service of Her Majesty.

The three officers stood in front of what remained of their regiment. Rupert Lonsdale, who did speak several local dialects, decided to address his regiment directly.

"Men of the Natal Native Contingent. The armies of the Great White Queen have suffered a setback, coupled with no shortage of personal tragedies for us all. However, this war will not be decided in a single engagement. We will invade again, and we will capture or kill our mutual enemy, Cetshwayo. Are you prepared to join the armies of the Queen and fight against the Zulus once more?"

There was a moment of uncomfortable silence. The warriors talked quickly amongst themselves. Most cast their eyes downward, shuffling their feet nervously. Only the iziGqoza showed any sort of inclination towards re-joining the fight. Even if they had lost faith in the invincibility of the white soldiers, their enmity towards their Zulu cousins could not be so easily extinguished. Finally, one of their *inkosi* stepped forward and spoke in heavily accented English.

"We will fight for the Great White Queen, Inkosi Lonsdale!"

Rupert gave a nod of appreciation and then ordered the iziGqoza, who numbered perhaps two hundred warriors, to fall out and stand off to the side. He then turned to 'Maori' Browne.

"Get these cowards out of my sight. Gather their weapons and headbands and dismiss the blasted lot of them."

"What of the iziGqoza?" Harford asked.

"We cannot maintain a regiment with a couple hundred warriors," Lonsdale explained. "Address them separately, and make certain they know that the shame does not fall on them. After all, we may need them again."

Lonsdale and Browne exchanged salutes. Rupert's last act as Commandant of the 3rd NNC was allowing his ill-tempered subordinate to disband the regiment.

As Lonsdale departed, 'Maori' summoned an English-speaking iziGqoza warrior to interpret for him. His hands on his hips, he shook his head and sneered at the assembled warriors.

"You yellow bastards!" he snarled at them. The interpreter gave him a confused look.

This lead to an embarrassing pause from Commandant Browne. "Cowards," he stressed. "Tell them they're a bunch of cowards."

The iziGqoza man began to berate the Natal warriors, gesturing wildly with his hands and showing his contempt. Though the Zulus were their kinsmen and bitter enemies, at least the iziGqoza could respect them as fighting men. These men from the Natal side of the uMzinyathi, he held nothing but contempt for. When the man finished, Browne added a few insults which he knew would strike deep at their collective manhood.

"The Great White Queen demands you return your weapons and red headbands. Instead, she offers you women's aprons, so that you might go dig in the fields with your wives!"

The interpreter could scarcely hide his glee at translating what was one of the most profound insults one could unleash upon a warrior. The men said nothing, but hung their heads in shame. They knew they had acted poorly and devoid of bravery in the face of the Zulus. At Harford's recommendation, Browne told the men they could keep their blankets, much to the warriors' delight. He also said they could take as much tinned beef as they could carry; after which he did not wish to see their shameful faces ever again. This promise of food buoyed their spirits. They no longer cared that their manhood had been questioned, or that their regiment was being disbanded in disgrace.

The European officers and NCOs gathered to collect their firearms, bandoliers, and headbands. Several boxes of bully beef were brought from the depot, and the men gathered as much as they could carry. It was a strange sight to Harford. The previously shamed mass of men were now bounding gaily towards their homes, laughing and carrying on as if they had just been out for a picnic.

"Let us hope the iziGqoza conduct themselves a little more manfully," Browne muttered.

"Shall I address them?" Harford asked.

Since he spoke Zulu and would not require an interpreter, Browne nodded his consent.

The young officer spoke at length about the courage and tenacity of the iziGqoza, that the Great White Queen would know well the tales of their bravery. He stated with much regret that they must now part, but that they should stand ever vigilant.

"This war does not end until Cetshwayo is overthrown, and the iziGqoza, the rightful sons of Zulu, return home victorious!" he concluded. This was met with a loud cheer from the two hundred warriors who remained. While they, too, were compelled to hand over their Martini-Henry rifles and red headbands, they did so with pride and their heads held high. They formed a circle around their officers and NCOs, chanting and beating their assegais against their shields. With a series of ovations and shields held over their backs in salute, they departed Rorke's Drift.

The assembled officers and NCOs were confused as to what would now happen to them. Browne told them to stand easy, while he and Harford sought out their commandant. Harford was one of the few who held a regular army commission. The rest were simply locally appointed. The officers found Rupert seated on the edge of the short cliff face which made up the north wall of the defences. He was scribbling away furiously on a note pad.

"Ah, gentlemen," he said, looking up at them. His headache from a recent injury had returned, and he was in a bitter temper. "I take it you sorted out those black devils."

"We did," Browne answered. "A pity we had to send off the iziGqoza. They were the only bastards worth a damn."

"Yes, well there was nothing for it." Rupert then handed a scribbled order to him. "Commandant Browne, you are now in charge of the European officers and NCOs until the GOC decides whether to discharge or reassign them."

"And what about you?" Browne asked.

"The 3rd NNC is no more," Rupert explained. "I have no further duties here. I'll ride for Helpmekaar to see if I might do some good there. Otherwise, I, too, will have to wait and see what use his lordship has for me. Captain Harford, as one of the few holding the

Queen's Commission, there will undoubtedly be work for you. As I understand it, your own regiment has arrived in Southern Africa."

"The 99th," Charlie replied.

"Then don't be surprised if Colonel Wellman asks his lordship to return you."

When he first sought to volunteer for the possibility of service in the Cape, Harford's regiment had been on Home Service and was not slated for an overseas posting. Had his commanding officer, Lieutenant Colonel Wellman, known that they, too, would be bound for South Africa, he never would have allowed Harford, his battalion adjutant, to run off seeking adventure with the indigenous forces.

It was midmorning when they watched Rupert Lonsdale ride away from the outpost. For Charlie Harford, his adventure as a colonial officer was now officially over. And because he held a regular army commission, he was not obligated to remain with Browne and the locally raised officers and NCOs; many of whom would likely elect to return home rather than seek a positing with whatever remained of the centre column. For Harford, he could not go home even if he wanted to. His regiment was now part of the No. 1 Column under Colonel Charles Pearson, headed for Eshowe.

With the crippling of No. 3 Column and no support readily available for the forces in the south, Harford was concerned for his regimental mates. Most likely, they did not know about the disaster that had befallen the centre column at Isandlwana. And depending on how far they managed to invade into Zululand, there was a very real danger they could be subsequently cut off and surrounded. A chill ran up the officer's spine. He feared his friends in the 99th would suffer the same fate as those poor souls from the 24th.

Chapter XXVI: Tears for the Dead

Ulundi
30 January 1879

Prince Dabulamanzi

Despite the lack of roads or infrastructure, news travelled exceptionally fast within the Zulu Kingdom. Runners passed the news, calling from hilltop to hilltop. Details were sparse with a greater emphasis placed on symbolism. *'The great branch of leaves has swatted away the locusts from the sea,'* being a commonly shouted phrase. Whatever flowering language was used, the message was clear; the white soldiers in red jackets had been roundly defeated. All throughout the kingdom, people gave thanks to the divines and their worldly messenger, King Cetshwayo, for delivering the nation from the armies of the Great White Queen. For the men who had won this great victory, however, the mood was one of both triumph and sorrow.

Simply put, the Zulus had never faced an adversary with such a fearsome ability to inflict death in massive numbers. The lead companies of the *amabutho*, particularly those in the 'Chest' and

'Left Horn' had paid a fearsome toll. The young *induna*, Mehlokazulu, was filled with immense pride in his warriors from the iNgobamakhosi Regiment. Their discipline and bravery was unmatched. They overran the British and Natal carbineers, as well as destroyed a mass of redcoats near the camp. And yet, he regretted there were so few left to share in the honours he was certain were forthcoming from the king. Of the 300 warriors under his charge, a hundred were either killed outright or died from their fearful wounds. A further 150 bore various wounds inflicted by grazing shots or thrusts of the bayonet. Mehlokazulu was among the fortunate few who survived the battle without serious injury.

"I fear the people will greet the news of our victory with mourning and not celebration." he said to some of his warriors on their second night at Mabaso.

The great *inkosi*, Ntshingwayo, had ordered the *amabutho* to rest for three days while they did what they were able with their numerous wounded. Gunshot wounds, slashes, shrapnel injuries, and bayonet gouges were bound with grass. Broken limbs were splinted, though it was understood that only the hardiest of those gravely wounded would survive before blood loss or infection claimed them. The chief reason for the three days' delay was so the majority of those who would perish might do so with some measure of dignity, surrounded by their friends.

Mehlokazulu's words were met with sombre nods and a few mumbled words from his fellow warriors. Having slain a British officer, Mehlokazulu had taken the man's jacket, which he would wear until their spirits could be properly cleansed. Any man who had personally killed was obligated to wear a piece of their victim's clothing. It was a mark of honour for those who now wore red infantry jackets, blue artillery tunics, or any of the various garments worn by the volunteers and carbineers. Those who had slain warriors from the NNC took their red headbands. Despite being a great honour, it was also a mark of spiritual contagion. Those who had killed, referred to as the *izinxweleha*, would need to be separated from the rest and purified by the *izinyanga*, or diviners.

As the army gathered its plunder of weapons and treasure taken from the field, Ntshingwayo met with the *amakhosi* to discuss their pending return to Ulundi. The old warrior was, naturally, relieved that the *amabutho* had emerged victorious, despite the ill omens and having rushed into battle without conducting a proper reconnaissance or the last of the protective rituals. However, he was also convinced that the tactical and spiritual failures had led to many needless deaths amongst his warriors.

"It was great misfortune, *inkosi*, that the whites discovered us before we could properly scout the British defences," a senior warrior named Mlambula said. "But this was a different enemy we faced. I don't think any manner of *izinyanga* charms could have defended our brave warriors from their bullets and bursts of great fire from the sky."

The warrior's face was ruddy, and he bore many nasty injuries about the body. He'd been grazed by rifle fire twice; once to the face, and another which had torn a hideous gash in his left thigh. He'd further been pierced in the hand and chest by enemy bayonets, yet still he stood. There was little doubt he would be named one of the *abaqawe*, or heroes of the Zulu people.

"The people will soon know of our victory," Ntshingwayo remarked. "We must rest, bind our wounds, and return to the king with all haste. Those bearing contagion from having killed must be purified. Then we will see what our divine ruler needs from us. Though great was our triumph, we can expect the armies of the Great White Queen to return."

Though they had destroyed a sizeable British force, Ntshingwayo was gravely disappointed to see an even larger number of red-jacketed soldiers returning to Isandlwana after the battle was over. He was also disturbed that there were no prisoners taken. Surely the king would want to question the enemy *izinduna*. And what a triumph for the people if they had captured the great *inkosi*, Chelmsford! Ntshingwayo, at first, thought the British commanding general had been slain; however, the sight of the redcoats coming from Mangeni made him question this. First off, none of the *amakhosi* even knew what Chelmsford looked like. Ntshingwayo now surmised that, not only did their chief adversary still live, but he had not been at Isandlwana at all.

And despite the magnitude of their triumph, there were no war cries, no music sang, no words of congratulations from the assembled regiments. One in every five warriors was either dead or injured, and Ntshingwayo knew that the wounded would slow their return march considerably. There was also much loot to be carried back; the most cherished being the newer firearms taken from the British dead. The heavy boxes of ammunition were loaded onto captured mule carts, as were many of the more seriously wounded. However, in their fury the Zulus had slain any draught animals they came upon, which meant they would have to carry their treasures back to Ulundi themselves. Most of the large wagons were left behind, due to their sheer weight and absence of beasts to haul them.

On the third day, with the impi ready to commence the long journey home, scores of warriors hefted the yokes and began the long, laborious trek back to the royal kraal. Inexplicably, the British cannon were left behind.

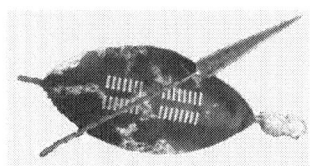

It took three days for the news of the *amabutho's* victory to reach Ulundi. However, the king's feelings of elation were soon tempered as rumours reached the Zulu capital regarding the fearful price paid in blood. It took more than a week for the regiments to return, though many of the wounded and exhausted warriors had elected to return to their homesteads.

"The *izinxweleha* have been separated from the rest, my king," a messenger said, bowing low and averting his eyes from Cetshwayo. "Once the evil influence has been cleansed from their bodies and spirits, the regiments will parade before you, *Ndabazitha*."

Just as the cleansing ceremonies before battle took several days to complete, so too did the purifying of those *'wet with yesterday's blood'*. The same diviners who had blessed them before marching off to war now met them at the stream. Still wearing the tunics of the dead, with spears and knobkerrie clubs covered in flakes of dried blood, the warriors from each *ibutho* who had taken a direct role in the killing were called forward. They removed the enemy tunics, bathing and washing the contagion from their bodies and weapons.

When physically washed, the warriors gathered around an *inyanga* who, just as before the battle, stood over a pot of burning medicines. A large bull was slaughtered, and the contents of its stomach added to the brew. Each warrior came forward, dipped his finger into the bubbling mixture, and sucked the foul-tasting liquids off. They gave a loud cry, leaping over the pot, as they were doused with the spiritually healing medicines, shouting for the spirits of evil to leave them. *'Come out, evil spirit, come out! Fall, evil spirit, fall!'*

On the fifth day of the post-battle cleansings, it was time for the *izinxweleha* to stand before the king. For Cetshwayo, there were his own rituals to undergo before he could meet with his warriors. Within the royal house, the king stood naked while a number of diviners rubbed his body down with oils and strong medicines. They chanted and blew incense into the king's face. His eyes were shut as he meditated, falling into a state of deep rage. For Cetshwayo, this sense of anger was heightened by his frustrations at not having personally led his armies into battle. He blamed himself for the loss of so many, for he should have stood tall with his men, like his uncle, the divine Shaka. Cetshwayo was no stranger to battle and had bloodied his spear many times. As king, it was no longer considered politic to stand in battle with one's warriors. He understood this from a practical standpoint, especially with his eldest son and heir being only a boy of ten. Cetshwayo's death in battle would create turmoil and chaos within the kingdom. And yet, his inner warrior spirit was filled with anger towards those who had compelled him to remain at Ulundi.

None of these feelings were known to any except the king. Outside, he could hear the first companies converging on the large enclosure where they would parade before him. The *amakhosi* would regale him with tales of bravery from their warriors, and if necessary, shame those who had proven cowardly in battle.

'Kuba impi!' the warriors shouted. *'It is war!'*

'Ngenxa kithi! Because of us!'

These were followed by many loud decrees. The converging regiments sought to proclaim themselves as the true heroes who won the Battle of Isandlwana. As they stamped their feet and waved their dancing sticks about—bringing weapons before the king was prohibited—there was a loud cry from an *inyanga* emerging from the royal house. The diviner fell onto his stomach, prostrating himself as the king emerged.

Cetshwayo was a fearsome sight to behold. Standing over six-and-a-half feet in height, and weighing in excess of 350 pounds, he towered over even the tallest of his warriors. His visage on this day was one of fearsome fury. His hulking mass was covered in medicines, and his expression betrayed his blinding wrath. His warriors dropped their shields and sticks, falling to their knees, unable to gaze upon their king. Cetshwayo strode down the wooden steps of his house and walked among his warriors. The royal throne was carried into the courtyard by a dozen attendants, all of whom prostrated themselves before the king.

"Bayede!" the warriors cheered, still on their knees with eyes averted. *"Hail the great elephant! You of the innermost circle, devourer of men! Hail the Black Lion!"*

"Hail, sons of Zulu!" the king boomed, raising his knobkerrie high in salute. He then sat upon his chair. "Speak now, and tell your king what you have experienced."

Cetshwayo's senior ministers, as well as the *amakhosi* who'd led the regiments into battle, knelt on either side of the royal throne. Ntshingwayo and the others remained silent, allowing the *izinduna* who'd participated in the actual fighting speak for their regiments. The proclamations were not just ceremonial, but the first factual information the king had received regarding the battle.

A common theme iterated from all the *izinduna* was how fiercely the British had fought. To some, this might have seemed like added posturing; making their enemy sound particularly ferocious to magnify the significance of their victory. Periodically, Cetshwayo, would glance down at Ntshingwayo, who would either nod or shake his head to confirm what he was hearing. What troubled the king deeply was hearing that the British rifles could cut down their warriors from as far as 800 paces. By the time they brought their own muskets to bear, the lead companies of the *amabutho* had suffered greatly, with hundreds of warriors giving up their spirits.

Mehlokazulu came forward as part of the iNgobamakhosi. He spoke of the butchery inflicted upon his companies before they finally closed the distance with their foes.

"Half my brothers fell before we could strike a single blow," he stated candidly. "Yet on we pressed forward, for we feared less the savage pain of death than disgracing our king and nation. We stand before you, *Ndabazitha*, deeply scarred but unbroken!"

Once it was made clear how ferocious an enemy the British were, the *izinduna* broke into voracious arguments over who were the first to close the distance and stab the enemy. The men waved willow sticks which, should the king single out their regiment, they would use to make a bead necklace, signifying their status as *abaqawe*, heroes of the Zulu people.

"We chased their horsemen for miles!" Mehlokazulu proclaimed. "When they formed a line in the donga, they cut down our warriors from hundreds-of-paces away, yet still on we came."

"You crawled on your bellies, like worms!" an *inkosi* named Ntuzwa retorted. Commander of the uMbonambi Regiment, his men led the left wing of the 'Chest' and had witnessed the struggles of the 'Left Horn', which Mehlokazulu's regiment had been a part of. "While you buckled beneath a paltry number of mounted whites and their cowardly Natal allies, we faced the might of the redcoats head-on! We battled not only their rifles, but their thunder guns that could kill twenty men with a single burst."

"We may have crawled to the donga, but you hid behind the ridge!" Mehlokazulu countered. "You would never have overrun their cannon had we not chased away their horsemen and flanked the redcoats."

Several *izinduna* from the uKhandempemvu Regiment, who led the right wing of the 'Chest', shouted indignantly at Mehlokazulu, stating that his men had taken the path of least resistance, while they bore the brunt of the British onslaught. Unfortunately for the warriors of the 'Right Horn', their mission of enveloping the enemy by encircling behind Isandlwana had taken them hours. By the time they closed the trap and engaged in the killing, the battle was mostly over. For them, there would be no *abaqawe* necklaces awarded. Like their British adversaries, rewards for valour among the Zulus were as much about opportunity as personal bravery.

Mehlokazulu was incensed that Ntuzwa and the other *izinduna* would dare question the valour of his men. The fact that so many of his brethren lay dead or horribly maimed, yet still they triumphed, spoke for itself. However, he knew the same could be said for the regiments of the 'Chest'. And while Mehlokazulu was a body servant and favourite of the king, he knew Cetshwayo would be conscious about showing unbiased fairness when it came to rewarding his bravest regiments.

His head bowed, Ntuzwa crawled up to the throne, presenting his willow stick to the king. "If it pleases you, *Ndabazitha*, I ask that you use my own stick to denote your *abaqawe*. If the suffering my warriors endured from the red soldiers with their rifles and cannon was not sufficient, then break the stick and let me return to my home in shame."

Mehlokazulu sneered at this bold move by the *inkosi*. There could be little doubt that every regiment who took part in the battle had fought bravely. Indeed, there had been no declarations of cowardice from any, which was an astounding feat in the face of such a fearsome adversary. Rather, it was a matter of which *ibutho* had shown the greatest courage and who had closed with and slain the redcoats first.

Cetshwayo stood and brandished Ntuzwa's willow stick. He waved it towards each of the three regiments which had proclaimed loudest their bravery. He thought, for a moment, to give the highest honour to the iNgobamakhosi, yet he stayed his hand. Mehlokazulu was a personal favourite. There was no doubting his courage or that of his men. But Ntuzwa had made a compelling case for the uMbonambi. They had, indeed, taken the brunt of the punishment from the British cannon. When the final charge came, they did not falter; even as swaths of their companions were ripped to pieces by the white soldiers' relentless volleys. With a nod towards Ntuzwa, he flung the willow stick in the direction of the *izinduna* from the uMbonambi. They leapt to their feet, shouting chants of victory coupled with ovations to their king, in whose name they had fought.

"Wear your *iziqu* with honour," the king said. He returned to his seat and called for Ntshingwayo. "Bring forward the spoils taken from the white soldiers so they might be divided among those most worthy."

Any plunder taken during battle was officially property of the king. Following a major victory, he would likely keep a few token possessions and distribute the rest among his best warriors. Hundreds of cattle had been taken from the British encampment; ironically, many of these belonged to Cetshwayo's loyal baron,

Sihayo, who was also Mehlokazulu's father. Others were from an *inkosi* named Gamdana, who had surrendered to Lord Chelmsford. Many would be added to the royal herd, including any with a white hide. Sihayo's were returned to him. The rest would be given to warriors who distinguished themselves.

Though cattle were the ultimate status symbol of the Zulus, of equal importance given their state of war, were the hundreds of modern firearms taken from the British dead. The king demanded that he be shown one of these terrifying weapons. An *induna* came forward, keeping himself low and his eyes averted, as he presented Cetshwayo with a Martini-Henry rifle. The king hefted the weapon, turning it over in his large hands and holding it up to his shoulder. It was very sturdy, more so than any of the archaic muskets in the royal arsenal. He knew not how it functioned, or that it used cartridges rather than powder and ball. What appeared to be a musket ramrod was in fact used to extract spent casings stuck in the breach. Still, he appreciated the robust quality of the rifle and hoped some of his warriors knew how they functioned. He suddenly regretted having sent away his white advisor, John Dunn, who no doubt knew how these weapons functioned!

"*Ndabazitha*," Ntshingwayo said in a low voice. "Though all captured weapons are, of course, yours to do with as you please, might I recommend that we allow those who captured these magnificent weapons to keep them? Surely all who did so placed themselves in danger and should be rewarded."

It was a diplomatic move on the commanding general's part. Both he and the king knew that such fantastic weapons would be jealously guarded by those who captured them, leading to much resentment should they be compelled to turn them over. Cetshwayo knew it would be prudent to allow this and declared any man who captured a gun would keep it as his personal treasure.

Other spoils were placed before the king. These included drums and other instruments which had belonged to the regimental bands of the 24th. Other weapons, such as pistols and officers' swords, were also laid in a pile.

While this pleased Cetshwayo, after a moment his appreciative smile turned into a scowl. "You mentioned the British cannon. Yet I do not see any. Why would you not bring your king such a mighty weapon that can kill many men in a single blast?" Before the *izinduna* could answer, he further berated them, "And where are the British officers? Where is their great *inkosi*, Chelmsford? Why are neither he nor his *izinduna* now my prisoners?"

One of the senior leaders, Mnyamana, elected to answer for the *izinduna* taken aback by their king's harsh words. "Forgive us, *Ndabazitha*, but the great guns were left on the battlefield. We had no means of bringing them back, and one had capsized and broken. As for prisoners, forgive us again, but the British fought to the last man. Even if we could have told officer from soldier, none were allowing themselves to be taken alive."

Cetshwayo scoffed. Though it was true that none of them knew what Chelmsford looked like, the king could readily tell the difference between British officers and enlisted ranks.

"Their officers fight with swords, their soldiers with rifles," he chastised. "Do none of you understand how useful it would be to have some of their *amakhosi* as prisoners? We could learn much from them, using them as hostages when it comes time to demand a truce with the Great White Queen."

It was a bitter blow to the *amakhosi*, as well as the assembled *izinduna*. While the king was certainly appreciative of their great victory, he possessed a much larger strategic view of the crisis. Cetshwayo understood that one battle, no matter how great a triumph, could not end the war. Had his warriors defeated the British and captured some of their senior officers, he would have been in a strong position to negotiate an end to hostilities. And if Chelmsford himself were captured, Cetshwayo had no doubt that his white sister, Queen Victoria, would capitulate to the Zulu overtures of peace. Instead, his warriors had proven short-sighted and failed to gain the greater prize. Without important prisoners to use for negotiations, there was nothing stopping the British from returning with an even larger army. The Zulus may have the current forces in the Cape greatly outnumbered, but Queen Victoria had a massive Empire to call upon for reinforcements. The king rightly concluded that he could not hope to win a war of attrition.

The price they paid for their triumph would soon become even more apparent as the king ordered the entire regiments to parade before him, not just the *izinduna* and those who'd shed the blood of their enemies.

The iNgobamakhosi were the first to come before the king, parading before him in company lines. Cetshwayo immediately noticed sizeable gaps. The three companies which Mehlokazulu led against the British cavalry were especially depleted. A lump formed in the king's throat.

"My brave warriors, where are your comrades? Why do they not join you?"

An *induna* knelt before the throne, his head bowed sombrely. "I am sorry, *Ndabazitha*, but this is all that remains. Our friends are either dead or so badly injured they cannot present themselves before you."

The king slumped into his chair. Cetshwayo felt like he'd been kicked in the guts by a bull. From the tales the *izinduna* had told of British tenacity, he knew the *amabutho* must have paid a high price. Now, seeing so many gaps within the ranks of a single regiment, he began to understand the true cost of triumph over the redcoats.

Despite his mighty visage, his voice cracked. He loudly proclaimed, *"A spear has been thrust into the belly of our nation. There are not enough tears to mourn the dead."*

The parade of regiments from the *amabutho* continued for two days. Noticeably absent were the regiments from the Undi Corps. They had taken their own path home rather than travel with the rest of the *impi*. Sooner or later they would have to face the shame and ignominy of their defeat.

Cetshwayo's sorrows were compounded by anger when he received news of his brother Dabulamanzi's defiance in the face of orders. He cursed Zibhebhu and his failure to maintain control over the indignant old warriors, including the king's personal regiment. The royal prince's personal invasion of Natal, and subsequent mauling at the hands of a few redcoats at the homestead of their late friend, Jim Rorke, was intolerable. Were this the age of Shaka, the king's younger brother could expect to be impaled for his reckless impudence.

On the day after the last of the *amabutho* parades, the wayward brother of the king returned. Prince Zibhebhu headed to his home many miles from Ulundi, allowing Dabulamanzi to deal with the king's wrath.

"The regiments of the Undi Corps have returned, *Ndabazitha*," a body servant said, as the king met with several of his councillors within the royal house.

The assembled *amakhosi* stared at each other, chancing the occasional glace upon the king's face,

Cetshwayo's expression remained impassive. He took a long, slow breath in through his nose before telling his advisors, "Leave me."

All bowed low as they quickly exited the king's royal hut. As the last of them left, none wished to so much as glance upon Prince Dabulamanzi, who swallowed hard before stooping low and entering the hut.

"So, my disobedient brother has returned," the king's voice boomed. "How many fathers of the Zulu nation did you leave across the river? And what have you to show for your impudence?"

"I assure you, my brother," Dabulamanzi implored, keeping low with his eyes averted from Cetshwayo's furious gaze. "We stormed and took the house at kwaJimu. But I must confess, our losses were heavy."

The prince assured himself it was not a lie, for the house belonging to Rorke had, indeed, been destroyed. As he knelt before his brother and king, he silently prayed Cetshwayo would not ask further questions.

"What am I to do with an insolent *inkosi* who directly defies my orders?" the king asked, his voice calm yet menacing. "What sentence would our father, or indeed our uncle, Shaka, pass onto you? You have broken my heart, dear brother. You, who stood by my side when so many of our brothers fought with the pretender all those years ago. You risked everything, fighting with me to win that which was rightfully mine from our father. Your loyalty has always been absolute, and you were the one man among our numerous siblings I could always rely upon. So, what now should I do, when my dearest kinsman so grotesquely disobeys me?"

"I ask that you give me a chance for redemption, my king." Dabulamanzi was devoid of his usual swagger and self-assurance in the presence of the king. He was grateful Cetshwayo remembered their long history of fighting together, and how he helped him secure his claim to the amaZulu throne. Yet he feared if he remained at the royal kraal, his brother's anger might cause him to seek retribution.

News of another British column to the south gave him the perfect opportunity to leave Ulundi and, hopefully, earn back his place within the royal court. This was Colonel Charles Pearson's No. 1 Column, who last the king had heard were crossing into Zululand at Thukela Drift. What neither he nor his brother knew was Pearson's men had won a victory over local *inkosi* on the same day as the battles at Isandlwana and kwaJimu.

"Another British force defiles our kingdom to the south, *Ndabazitha*," he explained. "Those are my lands, given to me in your name after we secured your place upon the amaZulu throne. It is only right that I return with my regiments, who also claim our southern territories as their home. Please, dear brother, let me drive these locusts from our kingdom, protect the lands you gave me, and bring glory to our house once more."

His words swayed the king. Cetshwayo felt sending Dabulamanzi away would serve two purposes. The first was the most obvious. This second British force had to be driven from their lands, and if the prince accomplished this, it would purge his shame from the family. The other was that it simply got Dabulamanzi away from the royal kraal. While the prince was still his favoured brother, Cetshwayo felt his continued presence at Ulundi would cause much scandal and disruption.

"Leave my house at once, and do not return until you have restored honour to the sons of Zulu."

"Ndabazitha."

Dabulamanzi's hasty departure may have proven fortuitous. It was soon after that Cetshwayo demanded his personal *ibutho*, the uThulwana, paraded before him. The most senior regiment in the entire *amabutho*, their warriors carried all white shields as a symbol of their status. At fifty-two to fifty-three years of age, they had served the Zulu Kingdom for thirty-six years. These were the same men who had borne the brunt of the fighting against the pretender, Mbuyazi, during the Zulu Civil War, twenty-three years earlier. Due to their age and losses sustained over the decades, their numbers were fewer than some of the younger regiments. Fifteen-hundred warriors bearing the king's shields had departed Ulundi several weeks before. As they sombrely paraded before Cetshwayo, there were less than a thousand gathered within the royal enclosure.

"My friends," he said to the solemn-faced warriors. His demeanour was one of comradery, in sharp contrast to the fierce rebukes he had given to some of the younger regiments. These men were not just warriors of the king, but his brothers. He loved each man more deeply than all but his closest kinsmen.

"Why don't the rest come in?" Cetshwayo persisted. "They have no reason to feel ashamed before their king. Please, summon the rest of my regiment!"

"If only we could, *Ndabazitha*," Mandlenkosi spoke, his head bowed, eyes wet with tears. The hideous gash to his shoulder had scabbed over and still caused him much discomfort. Making matters worse, he had just learned that his son, Kwanele, was among the slain left at Isandlwana. "The brave uThulwana cannot hear you, for they lie dead before the enemy barricades at Jim's homestead."

It was the final blow to Cetshwayo's heart. Though the losses suffered by the *amabutho* at Isandlwana had wounded him deeply, he knew by the number of rifles retrieved that they had faced at least a thousand British soldiers. The Undi Corps, the pride of the Zulu nation, had faced a much smaller force at kwaJimu. Cetshwayo would later learn from the brutal and honest reports from the corps' *izinduna* that, perhaps, a hundred redcoats had held the mission station. And far from winning a victory, as his brother implied, they had been thrown back in disgrace. Their dead numbered in the hundreds, most of their bodies left on the Natal side of the river. It was a bitter irony. His own warriors shared a similar fate to the redcoats at Isandlwana; left by their comrades, never to return home.

Chapter XXVII: Oaths of the Fallen

Rorke's Drift
3 February 1879

Sothondose's Drift, now known as Fugitives Drift, near where Melvill and Coghill were found. Note: The waters in January 1879 were much higher than depicted here

In the weeks following the battles, life at Rorke's Drift became one of abject misery. The feelings of devastated shock surrounding the slaughter at Isandlwana, followed by the profound relief that B Company, 2/24th had held the mission station, were beginning to fade. During the day, the survivors laboured intensely to improve the defence works of 'Fort Bromhead', as the men from B Company now called their stronghold. The mealie sacks and biscuit boxes were soon replaced by proper stone fortifications, with work details cutting and hauling rock from nearby Shiyane Mountain.

The summer rains continued to pummel the garrison, and with no shelter to be found, the fort quickly turned into a swamp. While work details laboured to erect the fort, others spent their days hauling buckets full of mud and water out of the quagmire where they were supposed to sleep. Each night, the battered soldiers of No. 3 Column went to bed filthy, with nothing but a soggy blanket and the clothes they wore to keep warm. Most difficult of all was keeping dry. On days when the burning sun beat down on them, they would hang their tunics out to dry only to have them become soaked again when the rains came.

Only B Company was given any sort of reprieve. As the heroes who defended Rorke's Drift, they were given the privilege of sleeping in the storehouse attic. The acrid stench from Lieutenant Adendorff, Second Corporal Atwood, and the other defenders' incessant rifle fire lingered.

The thatch roof was taken down and a series of large tarpaulins were placed over the rafters. These became bowed in the middle during the worst of the night-time rains, compelling the men to stand and empty the tarp. Charlie Harford and Surgeon Reynolds became the unfortunate recipients one evening, having evacuated their own flooded sleeping areas. Finding an unoccupied spot under the eaves of the building, they smiled at their good fortune. It provided just enough cover to keep most of the rains off. Having just drifted off to sleep, they were abruptly awoken when a horrific torrent of water crashed down on them as B Company emptied their tarpaulin.

With his posting as acting-captain with the NNC no longer relevant, Charlie Harford reverted to his substantive rank of lieutenant. For the time being, he was content to remain at Rorke's Drift, providing whatever assistance he could, until the army decided what to do with him. The most obvious was to send him back to his regiment. However, the 99th and the rest of No. 1 Column had far more pressing matters than what to do with their former adjutant. Most likely, they did not even know the 3rd NNC had been disbanded. And besides, a young subaltern had taken up Harford's responsibilities for the time being.

Early one morning, as he drank his coffee in silence, he observed a detail working to build the fort. Twenty men were pulling down the stack of heavy grain sacks from the north wall. Weighing two hundred pounds when dry, the incessant rains following the battle had left them waterlogged and even more difficult to move. Many were streaked with thick bands of blood, and the canvas was beginning to rot and tear itself apart as soldiers cleared them away.

The mealie grains were starting to decompose, and the stench was terrible. Harford's nose crinkled. He sniffed his armpit and reckoned none of them smelled any better.

"Mister Harford!"

Charlie grinned. He recognised the booming voice of the Wilsone Black. The two had formed a bond of sorts since the assault on the kraal at kwaSogekle. Barely three weeks had elapsed since that first action of the war, yet it felt as like three lifetimes.

"A fine morning to you, sir," Harford said. He lifted his kettle. It held a slosh or two of gritty liquid. "Coffee?"

"Would love to, but nay, I have no time at the moment. I'm forming a patrol to go have a look around a bit. I spoke with Colonel Degacher, and he agrees that it's time to stop hiding behind these walls and start scouting well beyond the borders of our little fortress. Would you care to join me?"

"I'd be delighted, sir."

He stood and quickly donned his tunic. As he was no longer actively serving with the NNC, he'd packed away his patrol jacket and returned to his imperial scarlet frock.

"There's a special purpose for this patrol," the major explained, as the men saddled their horses. "Ever since we caught wind of Lieutenant Higginson's tale about crossing the uMzinyathi with Melvill and Coghill, the lads have been anxious to find the missing Queen's Colour of 1st Battalion."

"And what of our fellow officers?"

Black shook his head sadly. "Had they survived, we would have seen them either here or at Helpmekaar. If Mister Higginson's story is true, and I see no reason why he would speak falsely, then we'll likely find our friends somewhere near Sothondose's Drift."

This initial patrol was venturing well away from the relative safety of Fort Bromhead. It was a small affair; no more than an initial scouting of the ground for any signs of enemy activity before returning with additional forces for a more robust patrol. Escorting the two officers were a few carbineers, as well as Privates James Trainer and Harry Grant from the ill-fated rocket battery of Durnford's column. Of the eight redcoats from 1/24th temporarily assigned to the battery, only they and one other had survived. This was more than could be said for their mates, as every man from their company had died at Isandlwana.

Both soldiers were in possession of the horses they acquired during the initial retreat of Durnford's column, and because no one had ordered them to turn them over, they continued to care for them as if they were their own.

Despite their relief at surviving, James Trainer was particularly wracked with guilt. He and Grant previously belonged to Captain Younghusband's C Company, 1/24th. Now they were all who remained. Eventually, they reported to Major Upcher, commanding officer of what remained of the battalion. As they still had their horses, and not knowing what else to do with them, Upcher allowed them to take part in patrols with the other mounted troops.

"We may have been detached to the rocket battery, but we are still 24th men," Trainer explained as he and Grant guided their mounts over to where Black and Harford were assembling their escorts.

Harford was glad to have the extra rifles with him. It was also a practical matter. The two redcoats had crossed near the southern drift and were more familiar with the terrain.

"I was in such an addled state, waiting to die, that I don't remember shit," Harry Grant confessed to his friend, as they accompanied the officers and half-a-dozen carbineers.

"We'll know we're close when we can start smelling the bodies," James reckoned morbidly.

It was approximately ten miles between the two drifts. The small patrol kept along the high ground, continuously scanning the far side of the uMzinyathi for any sings of the Zulus. Despite the complete lack of activity since the twin battles at Isandlwana and Rorke's Drift, many still feared a Zulu counter-invasion was imminent. The strength and fighting prowess of their enemies had taken on mythological proportions, in spite of the success of the defence of the mission station.

None of the men who followed the river to Sothondose's Drift knew that the Zulu *impi* was utterly exhausted after their ordeal and had returned home. Their casualties were appalling, and the king was compelled to disband his regiments to return home for the harvest. Occasionally the patrol would see small bands of fighting-age men roaming along the far bank, though these usually numbered no more than five to ten. Sometimes they were accompanied by their young sons.

"Not to worry lads," Harford explained when they spotted a group of seven men and about a dozen youths. "Those are probably just locals who've returned home. If the main *impi* was in any position to invade, they would have done so by now."

"You seem very sure of yourself, Mister Harford," Major Black said, a trace of doubt in his voice.

"I spent seven years of my youth in Natal, sir," Charlie explained.

"Hmm, I don't think I knew that," the major replied. "It explains why you speak their language so well."

"Well, it did take me a few weeks to brush up," Harford said. "And while I'd wager these are locals, it may simply be a matter of the Zulus taking in their harvest before continuing the war. The harvest has bought us time, but we still do not know Cetshwayo's intentions."

Black nodded appreciatively. He had little doubt that Lieutenant Harford had more practical experience within Southern Africa than any man in No. 3 Column, and quite possibly within all British Forces in the Cape. While most of the colonial officers were drawn from the settler community who called South Africa 'home', few had any sort of military experience. And almost none had bothered to learn any of the local languages or culture. Harford, conversely, was multilingual, as well as a highly-experienced military man.

"How long have you held your commission, Mister Harford?" Wilsone asked.

"Eight years, sir."

"I say, you should be earning your captaincy any day now," the major asserted.

"I hope so," Charlie remarked. "However, in this age of colonial wars and empire building, there never seem to be any vacancies. After Isandlwana, that's changed rather abruptly, regrettable as the circumstances may be."

"As officers we always toast *'to a bloody war or a great plague'*," Black recalled. "That seems to be the only way for young officers to get promoted. Of course, we say the toast partially tongue-in-cheek. Nothing dampens a promotion more than learning it was wrought on the bodies of one's dead friends."

Roughly two miles from the drift, the patrol saw the first body from the fugitives' plight; the bloated corpse of a horse lay half submerged in the river, up against a protruding rock. They next saw a terribly mutilated African man lying face down, washed ashore. His head was missing, making it impossible to tell if he was a Zulu or an allied NNC warrior. A shredded stump was all that remained of one of his legs, likely consumed by crocodiles. Harford said as much as they continued on.

"The beasts of the river had one hell of a feast," Black remarked.

The trees and thickets enveloped much of the high ground, compelling the patrol to go around, losing sight of the river and the far bank. By mid-afternoon they came upon a track in the tall grass. The ground was scored and churned up by the hooves of dozens of horses.

"This look familiar?" Harford asked the two privates from the 24th.

James Trainer nodded. "Vaguely, sir. Though I confess, we crossed before most of the fugitives, and the ground was not nearly as disturbed." He hung his head, feeling shamed by this confession.

The lieutenant said nothing.

"I believe it was here that we split off," Grant added. "James followed the river up to Rorke's Drift, while me, Bombardier Goff, and Private Johnson headed towards Helpmekaar."

Major Black gave an affirmative nod and waved for the men to follow him down towards the drift. As the river came into view, he raised his hand, bringing them to an abrupt halt. Off to the right, about 300 yards from the cliff, were two unmistakable red and blue forms lying next to each other. Wilson Black, being a Scottish catholic, made a quick 'sign of the cross' before riding down to where the bodies of the unfortunate Lieutenants Melvill and Coghill lay.

Wordlessly, the men dismounted, handing their horse reins to a pair of carbineers. The remainder spread out and kept a watchful eye on the far side of the river. Trainer and Grant followed the officers, though they kept a respectful distance. Teignmouth Melvill had been their battalion adjutant; and while as mere rankers they never had any personal dealings with the officer, they still felt the pain of loss. He was one of their own. Melvill lay at a right angle to the path, still in his red tunic. Neville Coghill was just a few feet away, lying parallel to the trodden track in his blue patrol jacket, his injured leg still heavily bandaged from a recent knee injury. As members of the patrol looked down the steep precipice which led to the river, they could see it was nothing short of a herculean feat that the two had gotten as far as they did. It gave an added sense of tragedy, that they had crossed the river, scaled the slope—likely with Melvill having to practically carry his hobbled friend—and then staggered a quarter mile further , only to die anyway.

"The Zulus must have been in a hurry," Black said quietly. "They've been assegaid but not disembowelled. And the men who slew them failed to take their jackets."

"I wonder if it was the Zulus," Harford stated. When the major shot him a quizzical look, he shrugged and explained. "There are plenty of indigenous people living close to the river on either side. We all know the Zulus are terrible swimmers. I find it difficult to believe that enough of them would attempt such a crossing, placing their own lives in mortal peril, just to slay a pair of officers."

"What are you saying? You think the locals on this side of the river killed them?"

"We'll never know, sir," Charlie said, raising his hands in resignation. "All I am saying is it would not surprise me if the Zulus called to the natives on this side and threatened to come and murder them in their homes if they did not kill them. As much as it turns my stomach, sir, I do not find it unexpected that the locals would slay a pair of white officers, who likely meant nothing to them, rather than risk incurring the wrath of the Zulus. It would explain why their uniforms weren't taken and why they were not disembowelled."

Wilsone scowled at the thought that the two might have been slain by Natal natives. As Harford pointed out, they would never know for certain. The official reports would state that it was the Zulus' doing. This was still true, in a sense, even if it had been others who did the actual killing. And though the bodies were in a state of decay with flies swarming about, they appeared to be otherwise unmolested.

"Now we shall see if they have the Colour on them," Major Black said hopefully.

Both Lieutenants Higginson and Smith-Dorrien had seen Melvill carrying the Queen's Colour. It was unknown if he removed it from its cumbersome staff and placed it in his jacket. What Higginson failed to mention, perhaps out of shame, was that Melvill had lost hold of the Colour in the torrential current, and he himself had failed to recover it. Black slowly undid the buttons on Melvill's tunic. Harford opened Coghill's patrol jacket.

"Nothing," he said with disappointment.

Wilson let out a sigh and hung his head for a moment. Had they found the Colour, it would have provided at least some respite from the sorrow he felt at seeing his friend slain and in such a terrible state.

Suddenly, he perked up. "I wonder if Melvill's watch is on him! He always carried it in the small waist-pocket of his breeches." Gingerly reaching into the pocket, Wilson gave a sad smile. He pulled out the gold pocket watch and gazed on it as it rested in the palm of his hand. "Poor Sarah, at least she'll have this to pass on to their sons."

As Black pocketed the watch, Harford went through Coghill's pockets, though he turned up nothing. He glanced down at the slain officer's heavily bandaged knee. He recalled how Coghill had injured himself while trying to retrieve a chicken for Lord Chelmsford's supper. Charlie walked the short distance to the cliff face they had scaled. It was very steep and strewn with large boulders. He shook his head, knowing Coghill would never have made the climb alone.

"We both will make it, or neither of us will," he muttered.

"What was that, Mister Harford?"

"Just something I recall Higginson saying Melvill told him when they were escaping. He and Coghill were determined to either survive with the Colour, or die together."

"They kept their oath," the major acknowledged. He spat on the ground. "Too bad Higginson proved to be a faithless coward." He then called out to their escorts, "Come on lads. We'll not leave our mates like this."

The ground was far too rocky to bury them, so Major Black directed them to cover the bodies with stones. He and Harford carefully laid the two next to each other, folded their arms across their chests, and then began the laborious task of covering them beneath a cairn of stones.

Trainer, Grant, and a pair of carbineers assisted the two officers, while the others kept watch. The men worked in silence, except for their grunts as they heaved the heavier stones into position. An hour later they finished, and Black made the 'sign of the cross' once more.

"Stand firm, 24th…"

Chapter XXVIII: The Queen's Colour

Near Sothondose's Drift
4 February 1879

Colonel Richard Glyn receiving the retrieved Queen's Colour of 1/24th

Word that Melvill and Coghill's bodies had been found spread quickly throughout the camp at Fort Bromhead. There was the natural grief, brought on by the confirmation that the two brave officers had fallen. And, there was a sense of fierce determination to find the missing Colour, which the men of the 24th refused to believe was lost forever.

"Well done, Wilson," Henry Degacher said, after listening to Black's report. This gave him the first real traces of closure, though he wondered if the horrific wounds to his soul left by the tragedy of Isandlwana would ever heal.

"With your permission, sir, I'll return tomorrow with a more sizeable patrol to scour the area," Black replied. "I'll also take that civilian chaplain; what's his name, Witt?"

"Smith," Degacher corrected. "Padre George 'Ammunition' Smith. Reverend Witt left the mission station to find his family before the attack on Rorke's Drift. Last I knew, they were still in Pietermaritzburg."

"Why do they call the padre 'Ammunition' Smith?"

"Just a name the lads in B Company gave him. Rather than simply praying, he did something useful and became a one-man ammunition detail over the course of the battle."

"A bit of a crisis-of-conscience," Wilson noted. "Being a man of God, yet providing the means for his companions to murder their fellow men. I suppose the Almighty understands killing to save one's friends. A pity the good padre is a civilian, otherwise I'd say put him in for the Victoria Cross or Distinguished Conduct Medal."

"As it is, we cannot even award him a campaign medal," Henry noted with regret. "Still, after this I am certain his lordship will see fit to bring him into the fold as an army chaplain."

"It's the least we can do," Black said.

There was no shortage of volunteers to accompany Major Black the following morning. However, as it was ten miles to the southern drift, they would have to be made up entirely of mounted men. This meant, aside from carbineers and those few with acquired mounts, such as James Trainer and Harry Grant, the patrol consisted almost entirely of officers. Colour Sergeant Bourne led a picquet detail to the top of Shiyane, where they would provide over-watch with their field glasses. Another colour sergeant from 2nd Battalion organised a ready-reserve force of a hundred men to advance towards the southern drift, should the patrol run into trouble and be compelled to retreat.

The patrol was again commanded by Major Wilson Black. Acting as his second was Commandant Cooper of the 2nd NNC. Most of the accompanying officers were NNC and local volunteers with the exception of Charlie Harford. A horse was requisitioned for Padre 'Ammunition' Smith. He was accompanied by the column's civilian interpreter, James Brickhill. Mr Brickhill had recently returned from Msinga, where he had ridden soon after escaping Isandlwana to warn the citizens. Thankfully, the much-feared Zulu invasion failed to materialise, and he returned to Rorke's Drift to see if he could be of further use to the British Army.

The mounted patrol waited until midmorning to depart, thereby giving Colour Sergeant Bourne and the picquets time to scale the heights of Shiyane. The officers rode in a column. The handful of other ranks and carbineers screened their advance. At the heights looking down on the drift, Major Black ordered the patrol to halt. With carbineers providing cover, he and most of the officers walked sombrely down to the pile of rocks that served as a temporary grave for Melvill and Coghill.

Once assembled around the cairn, the men removed their hats and helmets and bowed their heads. Chaplain Smith produced his Bible, which he had previously lost, and Harford later found. Though the pages were warped from being soaked in a puddle, they still turned and were legible. He opened to Psalm 46, which he found fitting; perhaps even written for a soldier.

"He maketh wars to cease unto the end of the earth; he breaketh the bow, and cutteth the spear in sunder; he burneth the chariot in the fire. I shall be exalted among the heathen, I will be exalted among the earth...the Lord of Hosts is with us."

He closed the Bible and spoke over the grave, "Oh Lord, accept now into thy loving embrace your sons, Teignmouth Melvill and Neville Coghill. Their duty to Queen and Country done, may they now rest in peace. Amen."

"Amen," the assembled officers echoed.

While grateful to have brought closure to Melvill and Coghill's unfortunate end, there was the unspoken anguish of knowing there were still a thousand poor souls left abandoned on the slopes of Isandlwana. The battlefield of tragedy was just ten miles from the river, but it may as well have been a thousand. For all the British knew, the ground was still swarming with Zulus. The region was dotted with kraals belonging to various families and *amakhosi*, and it was doubtful that they were feeling particularly charitable towards those who had burned their homes and slain many of their kinsmen. The wounds rendered by the great calamity could not begin to mend until the last of the fallen was properly laid to rest.

Having given a moment of silence out of respect to Melvill and Coghill, the officers donned their headgear.

Major Black turned to address Lieutenant Harford. "Mister Harford, you're the adventurous sort who has a knack for finding things. Take a couple of sure-footed men and begin your search of the riverbanks."

"Very good, sir." Harford rendered a salute before addressing the officers.

While there was no shortage of volunteers, it was decided that two of the battalion's staff officers, Captain Harber and Lieutenant Wainwright, were the most agile of the lot, as well as the best swimmers. Privates Trainer and Grant volunteered to follow the men, providing coverage with their rifles. The other officers and carbineers would conduct their own searches of the area.

"The river has fallen considerably," Mr Brickhill observed as the small band made ready to climb down the slope. He then pointed towards a large boulder which protruded six feet above the surface. "That massive rock was fully submerged just two weeks ago. I remember it well, because my horse struck it and nearly threw me off."

Given the nightly rains that pummelled them as they tried to sleep, it surprised the men greatly to see the river level had fallen rather than risen further. Walking through the tall grass, Harford stumbled over what he thought was a large rock. Unbeknownst to him, it was one of the Zulus slain by Melvill during his last moments of life. The search party then made its way down the sharp slope and onto the riverbank.

Near Brickhill's rock they saw uprooted bushes, driftwood, and various bits of natural flotsam. What they had not seen from atop the hill were the vast amounts of military debris strewn about. Most of it had sunk and snagged on rocks and submerged tree roots. Hats, helmets, bandoliers, ammunition pouches, broken carbines, and waterlogged pistols lay scattered about. Indistinguishable from most of the wreckage was Lieutenant Higginson's belt and ammunition pouches, as well as his carbine; its barrel was sunk into the thick clay.

With Harford in the lead, the three officers spread out, keeping an interval of about thirty yards between them. Trainer and Grant followed, their rifles at the ready, eyes scanning the far bank for marauding bands of Zulus. They followed the river downstream for a ways, until they came upon a vertical cliff on the Natal side. Here the water flowed between a large boulders.

Near the base of the cliff, Charlie began climbing over the rocks. He saw a rumpled mass floating and bumping lazily against the side of a flat boulder.

"Captain Harber! Come see this." The officer bounded over to him as quickly as he could on the uneven ground. His gaze followed Harford's pointing arm to the bobbing tube of mangled leather.

"There's the case!" Harford said excitedly. "The Colour can't be far off."

Lieutenant Wainwright soon joined them, an excited grin creasing his face as he, too, spotted the case. With the substantial drop in the river, the water was now less than waist deep and only a modest flow. Charlie stepped carefully into the rocky riverbed and waded over to the case, heaving it out of the water and placing it atop a large rock. The small band continued until Harford again halted them. Calling once more to Captain Harber, he pointed to a conspicuously straight pole that jutted straight up from the river.

"You see that straight piece of stick jutting up out of the water?"

"I see it," the captain acknowledged.

"Looks like a Colour pole."

"Wait here," Harber said. He removed his jacket and handed it to Harford before wading into the near chest deep waters. They were unusually calm, and he had little difficulty reaching the pole.

Like King Arthur grasping the hilt of Excalibur, Captain Harber pulled forth the Queen's Colour of 1/24th Regiment. The magnificent standard lurched from its watery grave with a splash. Holding the flag aloft, he made his way back, handing the Colour to Harford while he donned his tunic. As he did so, the embroidered crest in the centre of the flag fell loose; the silk threads having rotted away after two weeks of submerging.

"Here, catch that!" Harber exclaimed. Charlie snatched the crest from the water and placed it in his pocket, hoping some gentle hands could reattach it to the flag.

"Remarkable that it's still intact at all," he mused. Despite losing its centre crest, and with several holes torn throughout, it maintained a steadfast and defiant hold on its pole. The crown atop had snagged on the submerged river rocks. It was battered and bent, but otherwise intact.

From atop the ridge, just down the path from the graves of Melvill and Coghill, Major Wilsone Black waited impatiently for Harford's patrol to return. Every minute or so he scanned the Zulu side of the river, as well as the riverbed downstream, with his field glasses.

"Stand firm, 24th!" he heard from below. His heart soaring, the major scrambled down the slope towards the embankment just as Charlie Harford rounded a short bend, the Queen's Colour held high.

"Well done, Mister Harford, well done indeed!" Black gazed up at the tattered Colour, his heart filled with sadness and pride. Like most officers of the 24th, he had served with both battalions and, in fact, had spent much of his time as a company commander with the 1st. He beamed at Charlie. "As the man who retrieved the Colour, would you do us the honour of carrying it back to Rorke's Drift?"

"It would be an honour, sir, but I am not of the 24th. It is more fitting that one of her soldiers carry it home." He handed the standard back to a very grateful Major Black.

Two men filled with equal sadness and pride were James Trainer and Harry Grant. They looked on in silence. After all, it was their battalion's Colour; yet, they were simple enlisted soldiers who had merely been escorts to the search party. Right or wrong, all public honour and accolades would fall to the officers. Whatever history recorded of the incident, it was doubtful that their names, or those of anyone outside of Major Black and the three who found the Colour, would receive so much as a passing mention. It mattered not to them. The Queen's Colour of 1/24th, the very soul of the battalion and symbol of its undying fealty to Queen Victoria and the British Empire, was found.

During the ride back, Major Black carried the standard across his lap, fearful that if he rode too fast with it held aloft, the decayed fabric might tear away from the pole. It was only when they were within sight of Fort Bromhead that he hoisted the Colour high, bringing a loud cheer from the waiting garrison. Even from an extreme distance, Colour Sergeant Bourne's picquets had spotted the unmistakable flourish of red, white, and blue when Wilsone Black emerged from the riverbed at the drift.

Much to their surprise, a Guard of Honour was already formed, ready to receive the Colour. These were mostly mounted officers from the 24th. The companies from 2nd Battalion paraded along either side of the road leading into the compound. Leading the Guard of Honour were Colonel Glyn and Lieutenant Colonel Degacher. For Richard Glyn, it was a particularly emotional moment. He had commanded 1st Battalion when it received its Colour from Her Majesty, fourteen years before. For him, the tears in the ratted flag symbolised his fallen brothers; Henry Pulleine, William Degacher, Reginald Younghusband, George Wardell, Edward Bloomfield, Teignmouth Melvill, and of course the men they led. That the Colour still clung to its flagpole demonstrated that, no matter the depths of tragedy and the lives lost, the 24th would live on.

"Colonel, sir," Major Black said as the party halted before their column commander. "It is with honour and pride that I return the Queen's Colour to the Regiment."

Tears welled up in Glyn's eyes; the first sign of emotion since that terrible night they spent on the field of Isandlwana. He took the standard from Black and closed his eyes. "The Colour must be returned to 1st Battalion," he said at last. "The Guard of Honour will carry it to Helpmekaar and present it to the surviving companies."

The following day, Colonel Glyn and the Guard of Honour rode to Helpmekaar. At Major Black's recommendation, Charlie Harford accompanied them. And, as it was he who found the Colour, Glyn allowed him to carry it on the last leg of the journey into the garrison. Harford would write in his journal that evening,

It was the proudest moment of my life, and I shall ever consider it so. I very much doubt whether such another case has ever occurred, that an officer on duty and belonging to another Regiment has been given the honour of carrying its Queen's Colour.

D and G Companies from 1st Battalion under Major Upcher stood in parade formation, ready to receive the Colour. Regrettably absent was Captain Harrison's B Company, posted to the southern

Cape and therefore unable to join the remnants of their battalion. Lieutenant Colonel Arthur Harness, along with the survivors of N Battery, was also present. They kept a respectful distance, allowing the men of the 24th to have this moment. It was bittersweet for the officers and men. They still felt the stigma of not arriving in time to either stand with their mates at Isandlwana or, in the very least, aid in the defence of Rorke's Drift.

Major Upcher and Captain Rainforth sat astride their horses in front of their companies. The two men saluted Colonel Glyn as he and Lieutenant Harford approached them. Despite two weeks having passed since the disaster, Upcher noted that Glyn was still very pale and his eyes red, as if he had not slept. Given the column commander's broken state, Major Upcher was beginning to understand the full weight of responsibility that was now falling upon Henry Degacher at Rorke's Drift.

"Men of the 24th," Glyn said, his voice cracking. "Fourteen years ago, Major Upcher and I received the Queen's Colour from Her Majesty. As your battalion commander, this was the greatest honour of my tenure with the Regiment. It is with great sadness that as we receive the Colour once more, Major Upcher and I are two of the only ones from that auspicious day who remain."

Unable to speak anymore he nodded to Harford, who handed the Colour to Major Upcher.

"Battalion!" Captain Rainforth called over his shoulder.

"Company!" the colour sergeants responded.

"Present...arms!"

The men in the ranks first brought their rifles to port arms, then held them vertical in salute as Captain Rainforth and the subalterns saluted. The Queen's Colour had at last returned home.

Chapter XXIX: A Crucible of Honour

Pietermaritzburg
6 February 1879
***

Neither Elisa Wilkinson nor any of the other wives from the 24th had gotten a wink of sleep since first hearing about the disaster at a mountain whose name few of them could properly pronounce. Every night she prayed fervently that her beloved Arthur had somehow survived. He was as clever as he was brave. If anyone could have escaped the slaughter, it was him. Her prayers were combined with guilt. Why should God spare her husband and let others die in his place? Was his life any more precious than theirs? To Elisa, the answer was an emphatic 'yes'. However, this filled her with a further sense of shame.

She awoke one morning, her eyes bloodshot, mind befuddled, not even knowing what day it was. She was alerted by a muffled gasp coming from the next room. She walked in to find Eleanor sitting on the old sofa, a sheaf of papers clasped in her hands. Her face was pale, eyes distant. Wordlessly, she handed the sheet to Elisa. It was from a newspaper, *The Times of Natal*.

It is with deep regret that Lieutenant General Lord Chelmsford confirms the following were killed while making the heroic stand at Isandlwana, 22 January 1879.

1st Battalion, 24th Regiment of Foot

Brevet Lieutenant Colonel Henry Pulleine
Captain William Degacher
Captain George Wardell
Captain Reginald Younghusband

Elisa winced when she read the name of Arthur's officer commanding. As she continued through the list, the only other officer she recognised was the adjutant, Lieutenant Teignmouth Melvill.

"Poor Sarah," she murmured under her breath.

As an officer's wife, Sarah Melvill had taken it upon herself to act as a type of mother figure to the other wives in the regiment; even to ones such as Eleanor, who were older than she. Elisa had grown fond of her, even though the distinct differences between their social classes meant Sarah was often distant with the spouses of the enlisted soldiers. Elisa especially adored her two sons. The youngest, Charles, was just four months old. It saddened her to think that the boy would grow up never knowing his father.

Elisa's face tightened as she reached the names of the battalion's senior non-commissioned officers:

Sergeant Major Frederick Gapp
Quartermaster Sergeant Thomas Leitch
Sergeant-Instructor of Musketry Geoffrey Chambers
Colour Sergeant James Ballard
Colour Sergeant Thomas Brown

"Oh, Eleanor, I am so sorry," she said, placing a hand on her friend's shoulder.

"Keep reading," Eleanor said, before taking a long drink from the glass of water clutched in her left hand. In that moment, she wished she had something stronger. She was squeezing the glass so hard, it was a wonder it had not broken.

Elisa scrolled further down to the names of the other ranks, her heart tightening in her chest. Just seeing their names made them suddenly real to her. She stifled a sob when she saw the name of Arthur's best friend, Private Richard Lowe. The three had known each other since childhood. One of Elisa's friends, Molly, had been very sweet on Richard. She dreaded reading any further, yet knew she must. Her feelings of dread came to fruition at the very bottom of the list.

Private John Whelan
Private Thomas Whelan
Private Edward Whybrow
Private Arthur Wilkinson

Eleanor's intuition told her when Elisa found her beloved's name. Without even looking at her, she firmly but gently grabbed the young woman by the hand and guided her onto the couch next to her. Wordlessly, she placed an arm around Elisa, letting her head rest on her shoulder. For a few minutes neither moved; the only sound coming from their ragged breathing. Elisa let out a stifled sob, causing Eleanor to hold her tighter. This opened the floodgates. Elisa Wilkinson, left tragically widowed in Southern Africa at the age of nineteen, wept uncontrollably. Her body trembled, tears flowing freely down her face, as she cried into a blanket. In that terrible moment, life as she knew it ended.

The public relations campaign against Lieutenant Colonel Anthony Durnford began as soon as word of his death reached the Natal government. It started with Sir Henry Bartle-Frere sending a rather cryptic message to Colonel Charles Pearson, whose No. 1 Column was holding at Eshowe, a hundred miles south of Isandlwana and thirty-five miles into Zululand. The message was extremely vague and referred to the disaster as 'Durnford's defeat', giving no substantive details.

At Rorke's Drift and Helpmekaar, word had spread regarding the GOC's assertion that it was Lieutenant Colonel Anthony Durnford who bore responsibility for the Isandlwana disaster. While waiting at Helpmekaar for a hospital wagon that would take him to Ladysmith, Private Fred Hitch overheard Major Upcher and Captain Rainforth discussing the matter.

"It doesn't feel right," Fred protested. He walked over to where Corporal William Allan sat on a camp stool, a pipe clutched in his teeth as he admired the sun setting slowly. His arm was in a sling and he, too, was being sent to Ladysmith.

"What doesn't feel right?" the NCO asked.

"Just something I overheard the officers talking about, what with his lordship trying to blame Colonel Durnford and all. I'm sorry, but it doesn't sit well, him trampling on the dead like that. What do you think?"

"What do I think?" Allan raised his eyebrows. He pondered for a moment, removed his pipe, and shook his head. "It doesn't matter what I think, Brickie. All this political talk and bickering amongst the officers, is completely fucking bollocks. Doesn't mean shit to the likes of you and me. We're soldiers of the Queen, and that's all."

"You may still be, but how much longer do you think Her Majesty will have use for a cripple like me?" Fred asked.

His right arm was slung, with both the front and back of his shoulder heavily bandaged. Both men's tunics had been torn and bloodied by their injuries, and they only had their tattered shirtsleeves to wear. This suited Hitch just fine, as he was tired of incessantly sweating beneath a jacket of wool every day.

"It is true, I may eventually return to duty," the corporal said, nodding his head and apprising the young soldier, whose injuries he knew were far worse than his own.

"Even if I don't catch an infection and die horribly," Fred continued, "Surgeon Reynolds rather bluntly told me I'll never regain full use of my arm. To think, I was once considered one of the best shots in B Company."

"Except for me," Allan countered with a grin. He then asked, "And how could you expect to gain full use of your arm, when half your shoulder and scapula's been shot away? I will say this, Brickie, if it were up to me, the Queen would personally give you a medal for being the toughest bastard who ever wore the uniform. How in the bleeding fuck you're not dead is beyond me, let alone continuing to fight the way you did."

This was as close to a compliment as Fred Hitch had ever gotten from any NCO since he joined the Army, and he found himself grinning as his face turned a shade of red.

"Well, you didn't do so bad yourself," Hitch replied. "You got hit much earlier in the fight, yet you continued to bring ammunition to the lads for several hours." He furrowed his brow for a moment. "So, do they have a 'toughest bastard' medal?"

"No, you'll probably just have to make do with the Victoria Cross."

Hitch laughed, though the corporal's expression was unchanged.

"I'm serious, Fred. I know that Mister Bromhead recommended you for the VC. Won't surprise me if the Queen herself presents it to you."

"Bugger me," the private swore quietly. They sat in silence for a few minutes, watching the red glow on the horizon. Out of modesty, Allan did not mention that he, too, was on the list of recommendations for the Victoria Cross.

"You know, it still bothers me," Hitch said, returning to their original conversation. "As you say, I'm just a private soldier from the gutter who can't even read. Grand strategy and politics are beyond my care or understanding. Yet I have this nagging in the back of my mind, that Lieutenant Colonel Durnford is somehow being used as a convenient scapegoat by the GOC."

"Damn it all, man, you're still going on about that?" Allan said in exasperation. "You never even met Durnford. Why in the sodding hell do you care who his lordship pins the blame on? The war is over for us, old boy. Fifty miles from here to Ladysmith, where I reckon they'll leave me for the time being, in the hope that I might recover to be of some use to the war effort. You, my lad, will be headed home. A hundred and fifty miles from Ladysmith to Port Natal, where hopefully a ship will be waiting to take you back to England. I imagine they'll let you convalesce at Netley Hospital. You know, springtime can be quite lovely at Southampton."

There was a tinge of jealousy in the corporal's voice. For him, the absolute worst fate was being left to linger in Ladysmith, neither returning to the regiment with his mates nor able to go home. Still, he was grateful he would be able to see his family. Unable to pen a letter with his crippled arm, he had dictated a message to his wife, Sarah Anne. She was currently staying in Pietermaritzburg, and had feared the worst when the list of casualties was printed in the local paper. After reassuring her in his letter that he was still alive, he told her he would send word to her once he arrived at Ladysmith.

For Private Fred Hitch, the war, and for all intents and purposes his military career, was over. He had served with the Colours for just shy of two years, having enlisted after working as a bricklayer. Gazing down at his stricken arm, he knew that returning to his former profession was out of the question. He would likely require several months of convalescing. It was just a matter of time before the army discharged him as unfit for continued service. And then what?

He'd just celebrated his twenty-second birthday a couple of months prior. It was a serious blow to be partially disabled at such a young age. He was illiterate and now unable to perform manual labour. His future prospects greatly concerned him. The Army might give him a small disability pension, which could be enough to keep him from starving in the gutter, but that was not guaranteed. Though currently a bachelor, Fred knew he would eventually like to marry and have a family. He recalled young Emily Meurisse. He'd always been rather fond of her. Yet how could he provide for her, as well as any children they might have, if he was unable to find work?

He shook his head and quietly chastised himself. After all, he should be overjoyed that he was still alive! He had witnessed and battled through horrors that no one should ever experience. His terrible injuries would have broken less men, and still he remained. Not only had he survived, he continued to fight beside his mates long after most men would have given up and perished. And if he did receive the Victoria Cross, the highest honour a British soldier could ever receive, it also came with a small annuity. That the years to come would be difficult, he had no doubt. However, nothing could ever compare to what he had already been through.

As the sun finally set behind the hills to the west, Frederick Hitch was filled with the simple joy which came from being alive. That alone made the future hopeful, and he would face it with the same relish with which he'd fought to protect his mates at Rorke's Drift.

After about a week, the shock and disbelief eventually subsided within Elisa Wilkinson. An unsettling sense of reality slowly came over her. There was no sense in denying it any longer. Her husband was dead. Worse still, his body, like the rest of the unfortunate fallen at Isandlwana, remained where he was slain. Weeks had passed, and the Zulus still controlled the far side of the uMzinyathi. It was not safe to send a detail over to bury the dead. She often found herself staring at her wedding ring, which had belonged to Arthur's late mother. It broke her heart that she would never recover her husband's ring, that had once been his father's. Elisa frequently thought about their wedding day. Arthur's father had spoken to her privately, giving her his own ring to place on his son's finger. She further recalled that the elder Wilkinson had, at first, greatly opposed the idea of his son joining the Army. Later, he told Arthur he was proud of him, and that the uniform suited him. Elisa could only imagine how great his sorrows would be, once he learned Arthur was killed in battle.

"What will I do now?" Elisa asked quietly.

She and Eleanor took a walk along the dirt path that ran from Fort Napier to one of the drill fields, where half-rotted sacks of dirt hung suspended from rickety scaffolds. A handful of soldiers were practicing bayonet drill. Their corporal shouted at them to, *'Bloody well get it right, unless you want to wind up gutted by the sodding Zulus!'*

Hearing this made both women wince. Elisa longed to get away from the fort, and from the Army in general. Though she'd been treated kindly by the soldiers at Fort Napier, especially after receiving news of Arthur's death, she hated seeing the red jackets they all wore. More than anything, she wanted to know *why* her husband was sent to die. It was maddening that no one could explain why exactly the British Empire had gone to war against the Zulus in the first place.

The ever-growing city of Pietermaritzburg lay sprawled out below them, white colonists and indigenous Africans going about their daily business. Volunteer militia, supported by some of the redcoats from the fort's garrison, laboured with shovels and pickaxes to build defensive earthworks around the city. Despite the victory at Rorke's Drift, the centre column was severely depleted of both manpower and resources. There was now the ever-present fear that the Zulus would unleash their full might against the people of Natal. Elisa had often wondered about this perceived threat, yet she felt nothing. If anything, she would welcome death on a Zulu spear as a reprieve from her sorrow and the pitiful state she'd suddenly found herself in.

"A shame that Sergeant Roberts is married," Eleanor remarked offhandedly. "He's very attractive, even if he is a few years younger than me."

Elisa gave her a horrified look, her eyes wide and mouth twisted in disgust. "How can you even say that? We've only just learned that our husbands are dead! You already seek another?"

The older woman's expression was hard and seemingly devoid of emotion. "Be glad you still have it in you to be an idealist, my dear. Do not let idealism become naivety. It is a harsh and unforgiving world we live in. Just what do you think happens to the widows and families of Her Majesty's fallen 'heroes'? There is no pension for us, only what few pennies remained from our husbands' stoppages and outstanding pay. If we're lucky, they'll offer us passage aboard the next steamship bound for England. And then what?"

"I don't know." Elisa shook her head, her endless anguish slowly giving way to fear. "What does happen to those like us?"

"If we were married to officers, we'd probably be alright," Eleanor answered. "After all, the gentry class always takes care of its own. But for the common dregs like us, there are only three options. The first is finding another soldier to marry. Believe me, my dear, this is more common than you realise. When a soldier dies, it is not uncommon for his widow to be immediately propositioned."

There was a short pause while Eleanor thought back to some of her earlier memories. "I recall a story my father once told me, when I first spoke of marrying Thomas. Many years ago, when he was a sergeant, he came from the funeral of one of his men where he overheard the widow being propositioned by the soldier's colour sergeant. The poor lass burst into tears; not because another asked for her hand while she still wore mourning black, but because a corporal had already asked her at the funeral and she'd said 'yes'. It was a step up for her, going from being a private's wife to a corporal's. But, she would have been far better taken care of had she married a colour sergeant. I never knew why my father told me that story until now."

"I should never have accepted Arthur's proposition," Elisa said, suddenly feeling sick to her stomach. "But I loved him...I loved him with all of my soul!"

"Please don't think that I didn't love my husband. Thomas was my world. I fully intended to grow old with him, perhaps raise children, and hopefully later watch our grandchildren grow. But now he is gone, never to return. As much as it pains me to say this, it is, perhaps, a blessing we never had children. In my heart, I will always love him. Now I must look to my own survival, lest I wind up starving in the gutter. Sadly, marrying one of Thomas' friends is no longer an option, since all of them are dead, too. My heart breaks for those who left behind wives and children."

Elisa began to understand. She thought back to Mary Edwards and the handful of other enlisted wives who were now widows. Then there were the poor children, who not only would grow up without their fathers, but their very futures had suddenly become imperiled. It was barbaric that the Army had no provision for families of those who gave their lives for the Empire!

As they walked towards a large tree grove, Eleanor continued. "The second choice we have is to consign ourselves to the workhouses, where we can spend the remainder of our years as spinsters or factory workers until consumption or decrepit old age renders us useless and we waste away. If we're lucky, some other poor dreg will take pity on us and ask for our hands. You're young enough that might still be possible. I'm just a few years removed from being beyond child-bearing, which makes me far less desirable."

Elisa shuddered. While she knew she could return home to Stratford-upon-Avon, she would still be a widow with little prospects and would have to either find another husband or become a spinster.

"And the third?" she asked, suspecting she already knew the answer.

"Become a 'lady of the night'. It's more common than you think, especially in the colonies. If one strolls through certain neighbourhoods of Pietermaritzburg, Cape Town, or Port Natal, they will find ample company from young, fair-skinned women, available for a price. And where do you think most of them came from? They most certainly were not shipped over here from Blighty as a commodity! Oh, a few of the madams may have been enterprising women who knew how to make their fortunes in the far-flung corners of the Empire. As for most of the 'workings girls', I'd wager my very soul that most were once wed to young men in red jackets."

"That's terrible," Elisa said, after taking a few moments to digest it all.

"As I said, it is a terrible and unforgiving world we live in, my dear."

For the past two weeks, the strategic situation had remained precarious for Lord Chelmsford and the British forces in Southern Africa. Having returned to Pietermaritzburg to confer with Sir Henry Bartle-Frere, the GOC was compelled to officially notify Her Majesty's government in London. No doubt both Whitehall and Horse Guards would be furious that Bartle-Frere and Chelmsford had invaded the Zulu Kingdom and started a war against their expressed wishes. What was more intolerable was that they had suffered an ignoble defeat; 1,300 British soldiers killed in the name of the Queen, in a war she had neither sanctioned nor even known about. No doubt recriminations would be coming. Even if Chelmsford could somehow pin responsibility for the defeat on Anthony Durnford, there was no avoiding that it was he, and not Durnford, who launched an illegal war. But whether Her Majesty, the prime minister, and the senior generals at Horse Guards liked it or not, the British Empire was now at war. And once at war, there was no turning back until total victory was achieved. There was no doubt Chelmsford would at last receive the crucial reinforcements he'd been asking for over the past year, even if he was eventually sacked in the process. His task now was to stabilise the border and hopefully win the war before he could be replaced. Thankfully, with the conflict in Afghanistan, coupled with incessant troubles around the British Empire, it was likely that there were not any general officers available to replace him. He said as much to his secretary, who was also his closest confidant, Lieutenant Colonel John Crealock.

"Horse Guards will have my head if we don't sort this out," the GOC said plainly.

"The remnants of No. 3 Column have sufficiently fortified the crossing at Rorke's Drift," Crealock noted. "And Colonel Wood's No. 4 Column has crossed back into Natal at Utrecht. They are still operational and able to prosecute the war in the north. Captain Cherry's NNC battalion still holds Middle Drift. The high waters there make a Zulu incursion from that point unlikely." He placed his finger on a map Chelmsford had been pouring over every day since they'd arrived at Pietermaritzburg. "It's the southern border at Thukela Drift, where we are most vulnerable."

"Colonel Pearson established a pair of forts on either side of the river," the GOC recalled. "These are manned by a naval detachment, mounted volunteers, and two companies of regular infantry from The Buffs Regiment. What is more distressing is that he's allowed himself to get trapped, along with 1,500 infantrymen at Eshowe, thirty-five miles into Zulu country! We've already suffered one catastrophe. To lose the core of Pearson's column, including most of the 2nd Buffs Battalion, will be ruinous." He took a deep breath and found his resolve. "The next phase of this war will take place in the south. Right now, Colonel Wood's column is the only one that is still combat effective. However, they are too few in number to prosecute the war on their own."

"Colonel Rowland's No. 5 Column is still at full strength," Crealock noted, referring to the scattered British forces that were left to garrison the Cape Colony. Given the recent troubles they'd had with various little rebellions, not to mention the recent war against the Xhosa, a robust force was still required to maintain order throughout Southern Africa.

"His men are stretched thin as it is," Chelmsford noted. "But, I will need him to make ready to cede control of those regiments nearest Utrecht to Colonel Wood. It means accepting additional risk within the colony, though at the moment we have little choice."

"And in the meantime, we need to focus our efforts on relieving Colonel Pearson," his military secretary remarked.

"Precisely. Get ready to pen a despatch to Wood. We will need him to harry the Zulus and keep pressure off what remains of the centre column, while we rally what forces we can to relieve Pearson. Once No. 1 Column has re-established itself near Thukela Drift, and if we can get Horse Guards to finally send us some damned reinforcements, we can see about bringing this war to a successful conclusion."

"Very good, my lord."

Having taken down the general's dictated message, which Chelmsford then signed, Crealock brought his attention to a handful of despatches and general orders that had arrived from London. These were older, some dating back to mid-December, and he was only now catching up with them. The usually impassive Crealock's face winced as he read through one particular page that he knew would soon be republished in the *Times of Natal*. He had read it through several times already. But, given the current circumstances, it felt as if it were pouring salt on an already deep, fresh wound.

"Distressing old news?" Chelmsford asked.

"Under normal circumstances, I would say 'no'," his military secretary remarked. "But these are not normal circumstances, my lord." He then handed the single page to Chelmsford:

Local General Order No. 196, (undated), Times of Natal, 6th February 1879

Extract from London Gazette
BREVET – the following promotion to take place:
Lieutenant Colonel Anthony William Durnford, Royal Engineers, to be Colonel, dated 15th of December 1878.

His lordship managed to remain impassive as he read the order, though he felt its biting sting, as if the fates were mocking him.

"So, history will remember him as *Colonel* Durnford," he remarked.

"Quite the paradox to his rather disreputable end," Crealock added. Chelmsford said nothing but shifted his gaze to the colonel, who shrugged dismissively. "You know it is necessary, general, if we are to save ourselves from disgrace. I don't like the idea of trampling on the graves of the dead any more than you, believe me."

The GOC nodded. Privately, he was filled with conflicted feelings. As general officer commanding of all forces in Natal, he was ultimately responsible for everything that transpired, regardless of whether he was present or not. He also felt pangs of regret about having recently been so harsh with Colonel Durnford, who he was actually quite fond of.

That said, he was filled with anger at the late colonel for acting so recklessly. Though he had little knowledge of what had happened except for the few scant reports from survivors, it was clear Durnford had acted rashly. Otherwise, how could one explain over a thousand professional soldiers, armed with modern rifles, being overrun and killed by an army of barbarians carrying spears? At the same time, it did feel rather unfair, particularly as Durnford's body still lay exposed on the battlefield, and he was in no position to defend himself. He said as much to Crealock.

"What is there to defend, my lord? Colonel Durnford was an affable fellow and a true gentleman. However, that does not change the facts. You and I know he acted irresponsibly, and a thousand of our men paid the price for it. It is now up to us to make certain the public, and more importantly Her Majesty's government, understand this. And once you've defeated the Zulus soundly, it will be clear that it was Durnford who committed such a grave folly, and not you."

Chelmsford nodded and let out a sigh of resignation. Expecting a quick and decisive victory, before anyone in London could protest, he now found himself fighting two separate wars. The first, and most crucial, was defeating Cetshwayo. His immediate task therein was relieving Colonel Pearson's besieged column at Eshowe. Only then, and after receiving his much-needed reinforcements from around the Empire, could he prosecute the war once more in earnest.

The second conflict was salvaging his personal honour and reputation. And for that, he needed to ultimately defeat the Zulus, while deflecting the responsibility for Isandlwana from himself onto Colonel Anthony Durnford.

"Hateful, but necessary," Crealock noted when the GOC made mention of it.

"A crucible of honour," Chelmsford added darkly.

Historical Afterward

At Rorke's Drift and all along the uMzinyathi River, the much-feared Zulu counter-invasion never materialised. Cetshwayo was still determined to fight a purely defensive war, in hopes of eventually reaching a negotiated end to hostilities. The British newspapers loudly proclaimed that B Company, 2/24th had repelled the Zulu invasion, thereby saving Natal; an exaggeration, though understandable. After all, no one on the British side knew what Cetshwayo's intentions were or that Prince Dabulamanzi had, in fact, defied his brother's expressed orders not to cross into Natal.

The war, however, had only just begun. To the north, Colonel Sir Henry Evelyn Wood's No. 4 Column withdrew to the border, yet continued to actively engage Zulu forces in the region. As the only combat-effective element remaining from the initial invasion force, various garrison troops in the region of Utrecht were reassigned under his command.

A significant crisis developed in the south when 1,500 imperial soldiers from Colonel Charles Pearson's No. 1 Column became trapped at their stronghold near Eshowe. Cut off from the rest of the British Army in Natal, and unable to retreat back towards Thukela Drift, Lord Chelmsford feared they would face a fate similar to the poor souls at Isandlwana.

Leaving Colonel Wood to continue the fight in the north and Colonel Glyn to hold the border at Rorke's Drift, the GOC set about forming an expedition to relieve Pearson's beleaguered column. Having requested reinforcements, yet with the shadow of repercussions from London hanging over his head, Lord Chelmsford urgently set about bringing an end to the Siege of Eshowe. Only then could he look to the next phase of the war, in hopes of snatching final victory from the crushing maw of his early defeats.

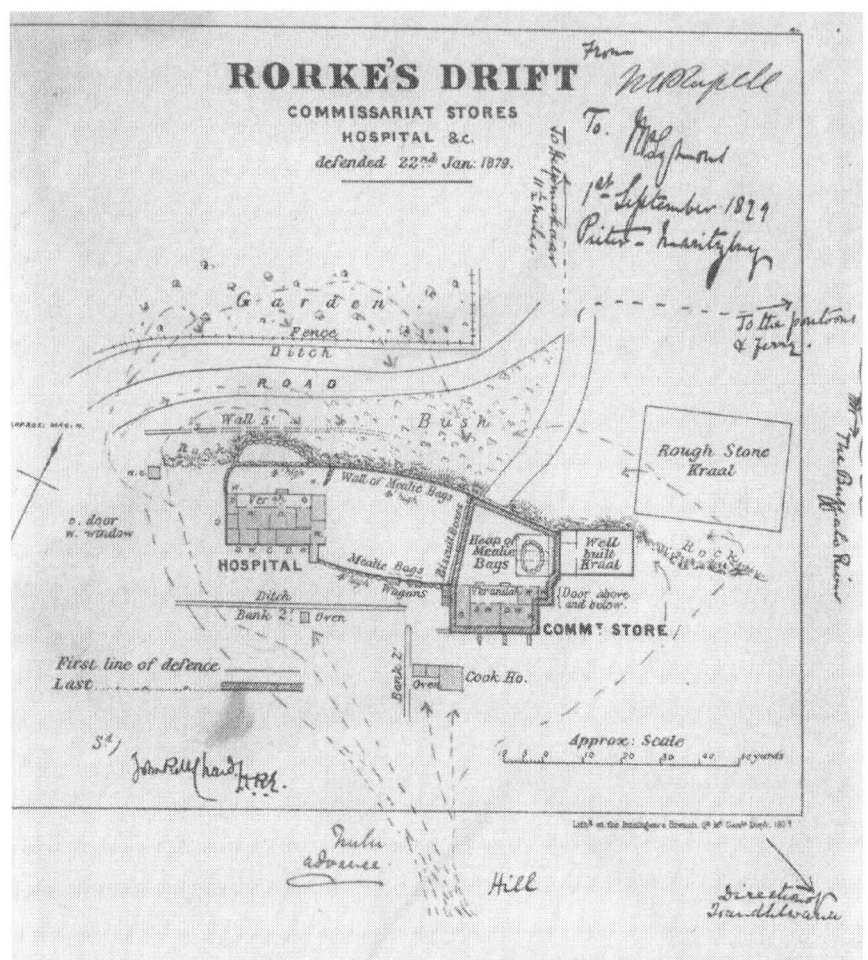

The official sketching of Rorke's Drift by Lieutenant John Chard
Arrows denote the approach of the Zulus

Appendix A: Historical Requiem – B Company, 2nd Battalion, 24th Regiment

The Survivors of Rorke's Drift
B Company, 2/24th Regiment, at the end of the Anglo-Zulu War

For the survivors of B Company, 2/24th Regiment, there was nothing in the way of glory, just months of squalor and misery, following the Battle of Rorke's Drift. With their tents destroyed, the terrible conditions at Fort Bromhead took their toll, and many were evacuated to Ladysmith with dysentery or fever. While their valiant defence had won the praise of both Queen Victoria and the British public, there were those within the military establishment who viewed the survivors with scorn. Later in the war, General Sir Garnet Wolseley was not shy about his resentment at having to present the Victoria Cross to numerous men whom he described as, *'Little more than trapped rats in a hole'*. Even today, there are those who criticise the awarding of so many VCs (the most for an entire regiment in a single action), yet when one looks at the heroic deeds of each soldier, it is plain to see that every Victoria Cross and Distinguished Conduct Medal was well-earned.

Unbeknownst to any of the survivors, their names would echo down through history, greater than any company of fighting men in the history of the British Empire. Eighty-five years after the battle, B Company was immortalised in the film, *Zulu*, starring Sir Stanley

Baker and Sir Michael Caine. And one hundred years after the war, the tragedy and sacrifice of 1/24th at Isandlwana was captured in the 1979 prequel film, *Zulu Dawn*, starring Peter O'Toole, Burt Lancaster, and Bob Hoskins. In further tribute to their forbearers, B Company, 2nd Battalion of the Royal Welsh—the current embodiment of the 24th—was renamed B (Rorke's Drift) Company. Most recently, they served in the Helmand Province during the Afghanistan War.

Every year on the anniversary of the Battle of Rorke's Drift, companies throughout the Regiment gather to watch the film *Zulu*. Officers and NCOs disseminate truth from fiction for the younger soldiers, teaching them the real stories of heroism and sacrifice; a legacy which they carry on to this day.

Appendix B: Historical Requiem – The Defenders of Rorke's Drift

Lieutenant John Chard was promoted to captain, with an immediate brevet to major, several months after the Battle of Rorke's Drift. He remained to assist with the building of the defences in anticipation of a Zulu counter-invasion; however, the squalid conditions and poor weather took their toll, and he was evacuated with a fever to Ladysmith. Following his recovery, he was attached to Brigadier General Wood's division for the second invasion of Zululand. Wood, however, took an immediate dislike to Chard, questioning his heroism, and disparaging him as a useless officer. Despite this, as well as earning the ire of Lord Chelmsford's eventual replacement, General Sir Garnet Wolseley, Chard's valour and extreme courage at Rorke's Drift had won him the adulation of Queen Victoria, as well as the British public. He was awarded the Victoria Cross for his bravery which was presented, albeit reluctantly, by Wolseley on 16 July 1879, soon after the final battle of the Anglo-Zulu War at Ulundi.

Upon his return home, he was invited to dine with the Queen at Balmoral Castle. He then went on to spend six years in Cyprus, where his brevet to major was made substantive in 1886. He spent the next five years on Home Service in England, before being dispatched to Singapore. In 1892, he was promoted to lieutenant colonel. Four years later, he returned to Britain and took up what would be his final posting as Commanding Royal Engineer in Perth, Scotland. In January 1897, he was promoted to full colonel and invited once again to visit Queen Victoria. However, he was having severe health issues and was compelled to decline. A lifelong smoker, Chard was diagnosed with tongue cancer. Despite having part of his tongue surgically removed, the cancer proved fatal. Colonel John Chard, VC, died at his brother's home in Somerset on 1 November 1897 at the age of forty-nine. He never married nor had children.

In 1972, Sir Stanley Baker, who portrayed Chard in the 1964 film, *Zulu*, purchased Chard's medals, including his Victoria Cross. Sir Stanley thought the VC was a replica and that the original had been lost. It was only in 1996—twenty years after his own death—that it was discovered to, in fact, be the original. Lord Ashcroft acquired the medals which are now on display at the Imperial War Museum in London.

General Sir Garnet Wolseley presenting the Victoria Cross to Major John Chard, 16 July 1879, by Godefroy Durand

Lieutenant Gonville Bromhead was promoted substantively to captain, for there was no longer a shortage of vacancies following the tragic loss of life at Isandlwana. In recognition for his actions during the defence of Rorke's Drift, he was given an immediate brevet to major. He remained at Rorke's Drift with the other survivors who built up the stone fortifications which they named 'Fort Bromhead'. He suffered from severe psychological trauma, which today we know as Post-Traumatic Stress Disorder (PTSD). However, he met with little sympathy from his fellow officers. Sir Garnet Wolseley had little good to say about him and, indeed, both Major Francis Clery and Lieutenant Henry Curling wrote some rather damning assessments of the man whose company saved the depot. However, he retained the loyalty and affection of his soldiers, who praised his courage and leadership under extreme duress. He was gazetted the Victoria Cross, which he received from General Wolseley at Utrecht on 22 August 1879.

Upon his return to England, the citizens of his native Thurlby in Lincolnshire presented him with a revolver and a special ceremonial sword. Like Chard, he was also invited to dine with Queen Victoria in Balmoral; however, he was on a fishing trip to Ireland at the time and missed the invitation. He never received another, though the Queen did send him a portrait of herself. He was posted to Gibraltar with the 24th Regiment for a brief time in 1880 before they were dispatched to India. He returned to England and attended the School of Musketry in Hythe from October to December 1882 before returning to India. His brevet to major was made substantive in April 1883, three years before his Rorke's Drift counterpart, John Chard. From October 1886 to May 1888, he served with his battalion in Burma during the Third Anglo-Burmese War. They were subsequently posted to Allahabad, India. It was there Major Gonville Bromhead, VC, died of typhoid fever on 9 February 1891 at the age of forty-five. He never married nor had children.

Bromhead's Victoria Cross is held at the Regimental Museum of the Royal Welsh in Brecon. Due to its extreme value (estimated at around £750,000), a copy is displayed, while the original is kept in a bank vault. Bromhead was portrayed by Sir Michael Caine in the 1964 film, *Zulu*, in what would be his first starring role.

Major Gonville Bromhead's original Victoria Cross (front and back), which the author was fortunate enough to have seen and photographed during a visit to Brecon in 2011

Colour Sergeant Frank Bourne remained with B Company for the duration of the war. For his valour and cool-headed leadership he was awarded the Distinguished Conduct Medal. Many have questioned why he was not awarded the Victoria Cross, as his gallantry was widely regarded as being equal to that of Lieutenants Chard and Bromhead. One speculation is that Bourne himself declined being recommended for the VC. He was, however, offered a direct commission after the battle, though in his own words, *"Being an eighth son, with the family exchequer empty…"* he was compelled to decline for the time being.

In 1880, he was appointed battalion instructor of musketry and was later posted to both India and Burma with the 24th. While in Bombay he married Eliza Fincham, with whom he would have five children. He was promoted to quartermaster-sergeant in 1884, and finally received his long-awaited commission in 1890. In 1893 he was appointed Adjutant to the School of Musketry in Hythe, where he remained until retiring in 1907 at the rank of major. Of Rorke's Drift he always said, "I considered myself lucky to have been there." He commemorated the battle with a dinner on each anniversary, yet he discouraged his family from discussing it otherwise.

In 1914, Major Bourne returned to active service at the outbreak of the Great War. He became Adjutant to the School of Musketry in Dublin where he remained for the duration. He retired once more in 1919, this time as a lieutenant colonel. That same year he was appointed an *Officer of the Most Excellent Order of the British Empire* (OBE).

He proved to be one of the longest-lived veterans of the Anglo-Zulu War, serving as a mourner at the funerals for many of his old comrades. In 1936 he made a radio broadcast for the BBC about the Defence of Rorke's Drift. Sadly, the audio has been lost, though the transcript survives. A reading of the transcript was recorded by his grandson, Charlie Bourne, in 2004. Lieutenant Colonel Frank Bourne, OBE, DCM, outlived every other survivor of Rorke's Drift, finally passing away on VE Day, 8 May 1945, at the age of ninety-one. His medals are on display at the Regimental Museum of the Royal Welsh in Brecon.

In the film, *Zulu*, Bourne was portrayed by Nigel Green. Though Green's performance was one of the most acclaimed in the film, at forty years of age and standing 6'2", his appearance was in stark contrast to the 24-year-old, 5'6" Bourne at Rorke's Drift.

Lieutenant Colonel Frank Bourne's medals
(L to R): Order of the British Empire, Distinguished Conduct Medal, South Africa Campaign Medal, Burma Campaign Medal

Sergeant Henry Gallagher moved to Utrecht with the rest of B Company, although they took no further part in the war. He spent most of 1880 in Gibraltar before returning to Home Service. The following year he was promoted to colour sergeant. Over the next fourteen years, he and his wife, Caroline, would have six children together.

In 1883, he and his family were sent with the 24th Regiment—now known as the *South Wales Borderers*—to India and later to Burma. In 1889, at just thirty-three years of age, he was promoted to sergeant major. This meant that for a short time he outranked his former colour sergeant, Frank Bourne, before the latter's commissioning the following year. He and his family returned to Britain in 1893 after being away for ten years. However, they would spend less than two years in England before being sent overseas once more, this time to Egypt. While in Cairo, Henry was promoted to garrison sergeant major, the very pinnacle of the non-commissioned officer's career path. While serving as GSM, every morning he would undergo a thorough inspection of his uniform, conducted by his eldest daughter, Carolin. The Gallaghers finally returned home in 1897, where Henry retired after serving twenty-three years in the British Army. Though now a civilian, he spent the next fourteen years as Barrack Warden at Coleworth Barracks, Hilsea and Alexandria Hospital.

Following his permanent retirement, Henry and Caroline moved to Drayton near Portsmouth Harbour. He never lost touch with his Irish roots and each year around Saint Patrick's Day his sons, and later grandsons, would send him a small box of clover from Ireland. He maintained a lifelong friendship with Fred Hitch, VC, who would come to visit, often around the anniversary of Rorke's Drift. This was one of the few occasions that the otherwise jovial Irishman became sombre and withdrawn.

Garrison Sergeant Major Henry Gallagher died in December 1931 at the age of seventy-five. His beloved Caroline followed soon after. All three of his sons went on to have distinguished military careers of their own. The youngest, Lawrence Stanley Gallagher, rose to the rank of colonel in the Royal Artillery. To this day, the descendants of Henry Gallagher continue to serve in the British Armed Forces.

Caroline and Henry Gallagher, prior to the Anglo-Zulu War

Sergeant Joseph Windridge continued to be haunted by his want of drink and was found 'absent without leave' on 6 July 1879, for which he had to forfeit his good conduct pay. On 16 November he was arrested for drunken behaviour and reduced in rank to private. It is reasonable to assume that his return to the bottle was brought on by severe psychological trauma as a form of 'self-medicating', as it is sometimes referred.

The following January, Private Windridge accompanied 2/24th to Gibralter and then to India. He eventually managed to sobre himself up. Regarded as an exceptional NCO, he began to climb back up the ranks once more. He was promoted to lance corporal that September, and then full corporal a month later. Though he would never reach his former rank of quartermaster sergeant, he did manage to rise back to sergeant in 1882. The following August, Sergeant Windridge retired from the ranks, having served with the Colours for twenty-four years. Despite the numerous problems brought on by his drinking, including eight admissions to hospitals during the course of his career, he was still entitled to four good conduct badges with his discharge papers denoting his conduct as 'very good'.

Upon his return to England, Joseph found employment as clerk to a lamp maker in Birmingham. His employer paid him well and with his pension from the Army, the Windridge family could afford to live very comfortably. In all, he and his wife, Helena, would have twelve children together. However, the years were fraught with terrible calamity, and only three would survive to adulthood. In 1896, a most heartbreaking tragedy ruptured the family. Six of their children, between five months and eight years of age, all died within two weeks from an accute form of tuberculosis. To numb his grief, Joseph returned to his old nemesis, the bottle, which contributed to his marriage failing in 1900 after twenty-three years. While staying with his sister, Sergeant Joseph Windridge died of a stroke on 30 August 1902 at the age of sixty. In the film, *Zulu*, he was portrayed by veteran stuntman, Joe Powell.

Corporal William Allan was one of the first recommended for the Victoria Cross by Lieutenant Bromhead and Colour Sergeant Bourne. The award was gazetted on 2 May 1879, though he would not receive it until that December. His injuries required his being invalided home in August, and on 9 December he was presented the

VC by Queen Victoria in a ceremony at Windsor Castle. By this point, his sergeant stripes had been returned to him.

Despite the lingering effects of his injuries, he remained with the Army as a reservist, transferring to the 3rd (Militia) Battalion, South Wales Borderers in October 1881. He was later promoted to colour sergeant and appointed Battalion Instructor of Musketry. He and his wife, Sarah Ann, whom he married in 1876, had eight children together.

Colour Sergeant William Allan, VC, died suddenly from influenza on 12 March 1890 at the age of forty-six. His VC is held by the Regimental Museum of the Royal Welsh in Brecon. In the film, *Zulu*, he was portrayed by Glynn Edwards.

Sergeant William Allan receiving the Victoria Cross from Her Majesty at Windsor Castle, from the London Gazette

Memorial to Corporal John Lyons, erected in 1996
(No known photographs of him exist)

Corporal John Lyons survived his terrible injury, though the musket ball remained lodged in his neck. Several attempts by Surgeon Reynolds to extract the shot proved unsuccessful, and he was evacuated to Ladysmith on 26 January. The bullet had lodged against his spinal column, leaving him in horrific pain, especially in the arms. His right arm lay limp and dead. With the terrible pain, he asked that his limbs be amputated though this request was denied. He lingered in agony for a full month before the bullet worked its way out, forming a large lump beneath the skin. On the advice of the Surgeon-General of the Forces, an attempt was once again made to extract the shot, this time proving successful. The pain in his arms was almost immediately relieved, and he would eventually regain use of both. In his weakened state and having been exposed to the rain and cold, he came down with Bright's Disease, though he miraculously managed to survive this as well. Lyons would keep the musket ball as a souvenir, attaching a shard to a watch chain that he wore for the rest of his life.

He was invalided back to England where he spent several months at Netley Hospital. A medical review board found him to be, *'Suffering from general debility at the Cape, 1879. A very clear and honest case of a worn-out soldier, scarcely able to earn anything for his family'*. He was discharged as being unfit for further service 4 August 1879, after which, he settled in Manchester for a short time. The family later relocated to Newport, Wales. Little is known about the remainder of his life, except that one of his daughters preceded him in death. Corporal John Lyons died in 1923 at the age of seventy-eight. His widow gave the watch chain and musket ball shard to the regimental museum, where it is on display to this day.

Shard of the musket ball that struck Corporal Lyons in the neck

Reputedly Corporal Christian Ferdinand Schiess
From the Alphonse de Neuville painting, 'The Defence of Rorke's Drift'
(No known photographs of Schiess exist)

Corporal Christian Ferdinand Schiess was recommended for the Victoria Cross for gallantry and indomitable bravery at Rorke's Drift. Despite there being no precedent for a foreign national to receive the VC, the award was approved, as Schiess had been serving under British command. According to John Chard, in addition to dislodging enemy combatants from the defences and possibly saving them from being overrun, the sheer number of men Schiess killed was enough to warrant the VC.

After the war, he worked for a brief time at the telegraph office in Cape Town. For reasons unknown, he lost his job and failed to find subsequent employment, even from the British authorities. He soon fell into poverty, and in 1884 was found living homeless on the streets of Cape Town. Members of the Royal Navy, recognising who he was, took him in, gave him food, and offered him passage to England. He accepted, and was bound for Britain aboard the HMS

Serapis. However, his condition was already too far gone, having suffered extensively from malnutrition and exposure.

Corporal Christian Ferdinand Schiess, VC, never made it to England and died on 14 December 1884 at the age of twenty-eight. He was buried at sea, and his Victoria Cross, which was found in his pocket, is now displayed at the National Army Museum in London. In the film, *Zulu*, he was portrayed by British actor, Dickie Owen, who at thirty-seven was substantially older than the 22-year old Ferdinand Schiess at Rorke's Drift.

Second Corporal Francis Atwood was promoted to sergeant soon after the battle. For his distinguished heroism in defending the storehouse, thereby preventing the Zulus from setting its thatched roof on fire, he was awarded the Distinguished Conduct Medal. He returned to England after the war and was first posted to the Army Service Corps South Camp, Aldershot before taking a posting in Plymouth as sergeant in charge of the military bakery. He took in a live-in partner named Amy Jane with whom he had a daughter, also named Amy. To retain an air of respectability and avoid scandal, Francis and Amy Jane declared themselves as married. Wishing to no longer live with such deception, they formally wed in a private ceremony in London on 25 September 1883 before returning to

Plymouth. Their happiness was short lived, and Sergeant Atwood died suddenly of an epileptic convulsion five months later, on 20 February 1884 at the age of thirty-nine. He was buried at Milehouse Cemetery with full military honours.

During World War II a German bomb destroyed much of the cemetery, including Sergeant Atwood's tombstone. The graves were exhumed in the 1960s, and he was re-interred at Efford Cemetery in an unmarked grave. In 2009, Corporal Tim Needham of the Royal Marines, in conjunction with the Royal Army Service Corps and Royal Corps of Transport, Plymouth Association, erected a new memorial plaque at a special ceremony honouring Sergeant Atwood.

Private Alfred Henry Hook was among the first nominated for the Victoria Cross by Lieutenant Bromhead for his bravery and for saving the lives of numerous patients when the hospital was overrun. He received his VC from General Sir Garnet Wolseley at Rorke's Drift on 3 August 1879, making him the only defender to receive his award at the actual site of the battle.

Having grown tired of army life, he purchased an early discharge the following June and returned to England. However, he soon found himself missing the comradery and went on to serve twenty years in the reserves with the 1st Volunteer Battalion, Royal Fusiliers. His reputation and demonstrated competency helped him rise to the rank of sergeant-instructor.

In the 1881 census he is listed as a servant in the house of a Doctor George Owen Willis in Monmouth. However, he soon moved to London, settling at Sydenham Hill, where he found employment at the British Museum. There is much mystery surrounding his first wife, who is alluded to in the film, *Zulu*. Some rumours stated that she thought he had been killed in South Africa and ran off with another man. This appears to be little more than gossip, albeit their marriage soon failed and the couple divorced not long after his return. They never had children. Hook eventually remarried, though much later in life. On 10 April 1897, he and Ada Taylor were wed in London. They would have two daughters together.

He retired from the British Museum in January 1905 due to ill health brought on by tuberculosis. Sergeant-Instructor Alfred Henry Hook, VC, died just three months later, on 12 March 1905 at the age of fifty-four. He is buried at St Andrew's Parish in Churcham, just outside of Gloucester.

In the film, *Zulu*, he was portrayed by James Booth. While one of the most memorable characters in the film, Hook is depicted as a drunken malingerer who is in the hospital under arrest and only redeems himself during the battle; in other words, nothing like the actual Henry Hook. His daughters, now in their sixties, went to the premier and were so upset by how the film makers character-assassinated their father that they left midway through in disgust. It is unfortunate that the film adaptation is how Hook is remembered; an unfitting legacy to an exemplary soldier.

Sergeant-Instructor Henry Hook (right) with Sergeant John Williams (Fielding) in later life

Private John Williams was recommended for the Victoria Cross by Lieutenant Bromhead for heroically saving numerous wounded patients along with Henry Hook. However, he would not see his award until a year later in Gibraltar, when he received his VC from Major General Anderson. He spent the next three years with the Regiment in India before taking his discharge from the regular army. He went on to serve in the reserves with the 3rd Volunteer Battalion, South Wales Borderers, where he rose to the rank of sergeant.

In civilian life, he went by his birth surname of Fielding, and it is unknown why he enlisted in the army as Williams. He later married Elizabeth Murphy by whom he had three sons and two daughters. His children all went by the surname Fielding. Tragically, one of his sons was killed in 1914, during the Retreat from Mons at the start of the Great War. Williams went to the recruiting depot in Brecon and asked to re-enlist. Due to his age, fifty-seven at the time, he would only be accepted if he could prove his prior service. Not knowing who he was, the recruiting sergeant asked him if he had any other awards or commendations, besides his South Africa Campaign Medal. Williams, being rather unassuming and non-boastful, hesitated before giving his answer, which almost caused the recruiting sergeant to fall out of his chair. "Yes, the Victoria Cross at Rorke's Drift."

Because of his age and status as a VC recipient, he was not allowed to deploy to France, but instead remained at the depot in Brecon for the duration of the war. Sergeant John Williams (Fielding), VC, was the last surviving Victoria Cross recipient from Rorke's Drift. He died of heart failure on 24 November 1932 at the age of seventy-five. His family later donated his Victoria Cross to the Regiment of Wales Museum in Brecon. In the film, *Zulu*, he was portrayed by Peter Gill. Contrasting the controversial depiction of Henry Hook, Williams is portrayed with reasonable accuracy.

Sergeant John Williams (Fielding) during the Great War

Private Frederick Hitch underwent excruciatingly painful surgery following the battle. Surgeon Reynolds removed numerous bone splinters from his shattered shoulder and scapula. His injuries were so severe that he was immediately invalided home. Lieutenant Bromhead recommended him for the Victoria Cross, which he received from Queen Victoria while convalescing at Netley Hospital on 12 August 1879.

Hitch's wounds left him partially disabled, and he was unable to reach his right arm over his head. Two weeks after receiving his VC, the Army discharged him as medically unfit for continued service. He received a small disability pension of £10 per year, in addition to the £10 annuity from his Victoria Cross. This was barely enough to keep his family out of poverty, and he struggled to find work. He was unable to perform manual labour due to his injuries, and he had few other skills. Hitch finally managed to find employment with the Commissionaire at the Imperial Institute and later spent a career as a London Cab Driver. He started with horse-drawn hackneys before moving up to a motorised taxi.

In 1881, he married Emily Matilda Meurisse with whom he had eleven children, three who died young. Hitch always proudly wore his VC and in 1901, while still working for the Commissionaire, he was rendered unconscious after falling from a ladder, after which a thief stole his medal. His sons petitioned the government for a replacement, which was finally presented by Lord Roberts in 1908. Private Frederick Hitch, VC, died of pleuropneumonia and heart failure on 13 January 1913 at the age of fifty-six. He was buried with full military honours and his funeral was attended by over a thousand London cabbies. In the film, *Zulu*, he was portrayed by David Kernan. Kernan gave a solid depiction of Hitch, though oddly enough, the film shows him being shot in the leg rather than the shoulder.

Private Frederick Hitch, while convalescing at Netley Hospital

Private Robert Jones suffered numerous injuries during the Battle of Rorke's Drift, including several assegai stabs, being struck by a stray bullet, and various burns. Along with William Jones, he saved the lives of six patients from the burning hospital for which he was recommended for the Victoria Cross. His award was gazetted in May 1879 and presented to him by General Sir Garnet Wolseley on 11 September. He served with the battalion in Gibraltar and India before returning to England in November 1881. He transferred into the reserves soon after, was recalled for a time in 1882, and finally discharged in 1888.

In 1885, he married Elizabeth Hopkins with whom he had five children. They lived in Herefordshire where Jones found work as a groundskeeper. He suffered terrible nightmares and flashbacks from the war, especially the harrowing night in the burning hospital at Rorke's Drift. He later complained of headaches, yet whether they were caused by an old injury or more recent illness was never known. By today's standards, he likely would have been diagnosed with severe PTSD; however, this was unknown at the time and would have been unaccepted during the age of the 'stiff upper lip'.

Private Robert Jones, VC, took his own life on 6 September 1898 by shooting himself in the mouth with his employer's shotgun. He was forty-one years old. In the film, *Zulu*, he is portrayed by Denys Graham.

Private William Jones was invalided back to England due to severe rheumatism. Along with Robert Jones, he was recognised for having saved six patients from the burning hospital at Rorke's Drift. He was retired from the Army as medically unfit for further service at Netley Hospital on 2 February 1880, having served with the Colours for twenty-two years. He received the Victoria Cross from Her Majesty in a special ceremony at Windsor Castle.

He married a widow named Elizabeth Frodsham with whom he had two children in addition to her five from her previous marriage. They settled in Manchester, though work proved difficult to find. Jones took part-time jobs as an actor and even toured with Buffalo Bill's Wild West Show when it came to Britain. Those who came to the shows knew of the great hero from Rorke's Drift and urged him to tell tales of his adventures during his years in the ranks. Despite the modest level of fame, he fell on hard times and in 1893 pawned his Victoria Cross. It later ended up with the Royal Welsh Museum in Brecon.

Like Robert Jones, he suffered greatly from the psychological trauma brought on by their terrible experiences. In later years, he also suffered from dementia, at one time being found out on the street in the middle of the night, carrying his infant granddaughter in his arms, 'to save her from the Zulus', completely unaware of what was happening. He was later admitted to a local workhouse and died on 15 April 1913 at the age of seventy-three. In the film, *Zulu*, he is portrayed by Welsh actor, Richard Davies, where he delivers the famous (albeit inaccurate) line, *"This is a Welsh Regiment..."*

Heroes of the Victoria Cross
At the Depot in Brecon, during the unveiling of the Anglo-Zulu War Memorial Plaque. Robert Jones, Henry Hook, and William Jones are standing, while Fred Hitch and John Williams are seated on the right. Seated on the left are retired Sergeant David Bell and Brigadier General Edward Browne. This was taken after William Jones had pawned his VC, and just a few months before Robert Jones took his own life.

Driver Charles Robson remained as John Chard's batman for the duration of the war. He returned to England on 4 October 1879, joining now-Major Chard on an unofficial tour of Britain. He took his discharge from active service in June 1881, though he continued to serve as a reservist for a short time before re-joining the colours the following year.

In 1883, he married Jane Farrand with whom he had one daughter. Robson retired from the Army in April 1894, having served twenty-one years in the ranks. The family settled in the Plumstead district of London, and during the Great War both Charles and Jane worked in the munitions factory at Woolwich Arsenal. He permanently retired in 1919, keeping to his garden with chickens, a dog, and an enormous cat that he named after General Redvers Buller.

Driver Charles Robson died on 19 July 1933 at the age of seventy-eight. He was buried in an unmarked grave at Woolwich Cemetery, and it wasn't until 1993 that he was given any sort of proper headstone.

In March 2017, his South Africa Campaign Medal sold at auction for £132,000, shattering the record for a non-Victoria Cross from the Anglo-Zulu War.

Memorial to Driver Charles Robson

Surgeon James Henry Reynolds toiled tirelessly with saving the more seriously wounded following the battle. His gallantry at saving numerous lives, as well as ferrying ammunition to the line, all while under intense enemy fire, earned him the Victoria Cross. His Jack Russell terrier, Dick, was even mentioned in the citation for his, *'Constant attention to the wounded under fire where they fell'*. In further recognition of his service, Reynolds was promoted to surgeon-major. He soon fell ill from dysentery and was evacuated to Ladysmith. He recovered in time to cross into Zululand during the second invasion and was present for the final battle at Ulundi. He received his VC from Colonel Richard Glyn at a special parade in Pinetown for the remnants of 1/24th. Soon after, he returned to Ireland, remaining with the Army Hospital Corps, and accompanying British forces during the disturbances of 1879-1881.

On 22 September 1880, he married Elizabeth McCormick. He was later posted to Gibraltar, where he was promoted to lieutenant colonel in April 1887. In December 1892, he was appointed brigade-surgeon lieutenant colonel. He retired three years later and took up part-time employment with the Royal Army Clothing Factory, and as Medical Officer to the Cadet Company of the King's Royal Rifle Corps. Tragically, two of his sons were killed during the Great War.

Brigade-Surgeon Lieutenant Colonel James Reynolds, VC, died on 4 March 1932 at the age of eighty-eight. In the film, *Zulu*, he was portrayed by Northern Irish actor, Patrick McGee. His VC is on display at the Army Medical Services Museum in Aldershot.

Acting Assistant Commissary James Langley Dalton was sent to Pietermaritzburg for treatment of his injuries. At the end of the war, when B Company, 2/24th paraded through the city, he stood with the cheering crowds. However, the men in the ranks pulled Dalton from the crowd and compelled him to march with them, with many loudly proclaiming him as *'the bravest man we ever knew'*. He was at first not properly recognised for his role in the Battle of Rorke's Drift, even though many of the defenders conceded that it was in fact he, and not Chard or Bromhead, who organised the defence. This was rectified a year later, and he was finally presented with the Victoria Cross by General Hugh Clifford, VC, at Fort Napier on 16 January 1880. A month later, he was appointed to the permanent rank of sub-assistant commissary, roughly equivalent to a lieutenant. As he was already a military retiree, he was immediately sent home to England and placed on half-pay.

In 1886, he returned to South Africa, working the goldfields at Barberton in Transvaal. He went to visit an old friend in Port Elizabeth during the Christmas holidays, where he soon took ill. Sub-assistant Commissary James Dalton, VC, died in his sleep on 7 January 1887 at the age of fifty-four. He never married nor had children. In the film, *Zulu*, he is portrayed, rather bizarrely, by Dennis Folbigge. He is depicted as a rather weak and effete character; a far cry from the battle-hardened former senior NCO that he was. His actions that earned him the Victoria Cross are completely ignored, making the mention of his receiving the VC at the end of the film rather confusing.

Padre George 'Ammunition' Smith accompanied the 2nd Division during the second invasion of Zululand, but because he was technically a civilian, he could not be awarded the South Africa Campaign Medal. Instead, he was given a permanent appointment to the Army Chaplain's Department as Chaplain to the Forces, making him eligible for future campaign medals and awards. He served in Egypt from 1882 to 1884 and was present at the Battle of Ginniss. Most of the remainder of his career was spent in England, apart from a year at Harrismith, Natal, in 1903. He never married nor had children, and died on 27 November 1918 at the age of seventy-three.

Lieutenant Gert Adendorff was singled out by Lieutenant Chard as the only Isandlwana survivor to remain and fight at Rorke's Drift. Since no one at the post knew him, and because he had fought the entire battle from a firing position inside the storehouse, there were many who expressed doubts as to his presence during the battle. However, there were others from Chelmsford's command, including Charlie Harford, who verified his presence at the Drift on the morning of 23 January.

He resigned his commission when the 3rd NNC was disbanded rather than trying to find another posting with the second invasion force. He spent the next several years working for the Gold Commission in Newcastle, Natal, before moving to Pretoria, where he met his wife, Hester Grobler. During the wars between the Boers and the British, the Adendorff family found itself deeply divided with members fighting for both sides. Gert remained a civilian, refusing to become involved. He later wrote an account of the battles of Isandlwana and Rorke's Drift, which met with fierce backlash from the other settlers. The rest of his life is rather obscure, as was common for members of the settler community in South Africa. Lieutenant Gert Adendorff died around 1914, at the age of sixty-six. In the film, *Zulu*, he was portrayed by South African actor, Gert van den Bergh. In the film, he was used as a plot device to explain the Zulu tactic of the 'Horns of the Beast'. Historically, the British were already aware of the Zulu battle strategies, plus Adendorff's grasp of the English language was very poor.

Reverend Otto Witt departed Rorke's Drift just prior to the first Zulu attack. He lost his way during the night, and an unnamed local African had told his wife, Elin, that he had been killed during the fighting. Fearing for her own safety, and that of her children, she fled to Pietermaritzburg. Otto eventually arrived at Msinga to find his wife had left; however, the family was reunited a few days later, when he arrived in Pietermaritzburg. Upon hearing that, despite the defenders repelling the Zulu attack, the mission station had been destroyed, the Witts left Natal in February. They spent two weeks in England before returning to their native Sweden.

The following year, Witt decided to return to Natal; however, upon his arrival in Durban, he found himself an extremely unpopular figure. While he had supported the British invasion and was staunchly in favour of overthrowing King Cetshwayo, he had also expressed much sympathy towards the Zulu warriors, who were simply defending their homeland. This, combined with his sharp criticisms towards the settler community regarding their treatment of the indigenous Africans, brought much hostility towards the reverend. The Witts returned to Rorke's Drift on 21 August 1880, only to find their house burned to the ground and the church converted into a now abandoned fortress. Otto petitioned the British government for compensation; however, he was rebuffed with the explanation that the damage had been caused by the Zulus rather than British soldiers. With financial aid from the Church of Sweden, he demolished both structures and had a new house and proper church rebuilt on the foundations. These are the buildings that exist at Rorke's Drift today.

Eleven years later, having achieved lacklustre success as a missionary, and with a growing rift between himself and the Church of Sweden, Witt decided to leave South Africa for good. The family returned to Sweden where Otto spent many years as a pastor in and around Stockholm. He published his memoirs in 1922 and died the following year at the age of seventy-three. In the film, *Zulu*, he was depicted by Jack Hawkins as a much older pacifist widow with an adult daughter (portrayed by Ulla Jacobson). They are shown leaving Ulundi in a horse carriage and making their way fifty miles to Rorke's Drift before the attack; a physical impossibility, even today. It is doubtful that Witt ever visited Ulundi or even met Cetshwayo, who had expelled missionaries from the Zulu Kingdom several years earlier.

The ruins of Rorke's Drift, following the Anglo-Zulu War

Appendix C: List of Casualties

Of the 156 soldiers listed on the rolls (compiled by Lieutenant Chard and Colour Sergeant Bourne)*, the following gave their lives in defence of the mission station at Rorke's Drift, 22 to 23 January 1879:

Sergeant Robert Maxfield
Lance Sergeant Thomas Williams (died of wounds)
Private Robert Adams
Private James Chick
Private Thomas Cole
Private John Fagan
Private Garret Hayden
Private William Horrigan
Private James Jenkins
Private Edward Nicholas
Private John Scanlon
Private Joseph Williams
Private William Beckett (died of wounds)
Trooper Sydney Hunter
Storekeeper Louis Byrne
An iziGqoza warrior from the NNC (name unknown)

Seriously wounded:

Acting Assistant Commissary James Dalton, VC
Corporal William Allan, VC
Corporal John Lyons
Corporal Carl Scammell
Corporal Christian Schiess, VC
Private Frederick Hitch, VC
Private John Waters
Private James Bushe
Private Patrick Desmond
Private Robert Jones, VC
Private Henry Hook, VC

Private John Smith
Private William Tasker
Trooper Robert Green
Drummer James Keefe

*Note: Deserters, such as Captain Stevenson and his NNC detachment, were excluded from the roll. Hence why the slain Corporal Anderson does not appear on the casualty list.

Zulu casualties are difficult to know exactly, though 351 bodies were found in the immediate vicinity of the station and buried in mass graves. A substantial number of bloody drag marks were also discovered, where slain or badly wounded warriors had been taken from the field. Numerous additional bodies were also found hidden in the grass and along the slopes of Shiyane, over the coming weeks. Modern estimates place the toll at least 600 Zulu warriors either killed or died of their injuries, with perhaps twice as many wounded.

In April 1879, a former stonemason within the regiment named Private Mellsop carved an obelisk memorial at the cemetery at Rorke's Drift, inscribed with the names of the British dead. It was not until 2005 when a bronze sculpture was unveiled, honouring the Zulu dead. The leopard represents the king, who is lying protectively over the shields of his fallen warriors. The tree growing in the centre is called an Mphafa. Planted over graves, as well as near battlefields, it is said to be able to capture the spirits of those who've fallen so far from home. According to local guide and historian, Dalton Ngobese (who is also the great-grandson of Mehlokazulu), this particular Mphafa also symbolises reconciliation between British and Zulu.

Memorial to the British fallen

Memorial to the Zulu fallen

Appendix D: Glossary of Terms

Note: All terms from the isiZulu language will appear in italics

Assegai – Term used to describe a Zulu spear, though it does not appear in the isiZulu language. Their actual name for the short stabbing spear is *iklwa*. Assegais usually referred to the throwing spears, though it was often used to describe all spears carried by the Zulus.

Battalion – British Army unit designation, consisting of eight line companies, plus battalion staff officers. Commanded by a lieutenant colonel, with the sergeant major as the senior non-commissioned officer.

Boer – From the Dutch term meaning 'farmer', refers to all Dutch-speaking settlers in South Africa.

Bombardier – An artilleryman, roughly equivalent to an infantry lance corporal, except a bombardier was rated as a full non-commissioned officer, while a lance corporal was not. They wore a single gold chevron on their right shoulder.

Boy – British army rank given to those who were underage. The minimum age was fourteen, and they served as buglers, bandsmen, and officers' servants. Upon reaching the age of eighteen, they were given the option of enlisting onto the roles as a private. Contrary to the myths depicted in both art and film, the youngest boy at Isandlwana was sixteen.

Brevet – A temporary promotion given to officers who were filling a billet above their substantive rank, as well a reward to those who had performed exceptional service. Though they would wear the insignia and be addressed by their brevet rank, they were still paid at their substantive grade, and were always subordinate to substantive officers of the same rank. Example: Henry Pulleine was a brevet lieutenant colonel, yet he was still paid as a major, and was subordinate to Antony Durnford, who was a substantive lieutenant colonel.

Captain – Commissioned officer, just above lieutenant and below major. Most often given command of line companies, and in some cases used as battalion staff officers.

Colour Sergeant – The senior non-commissioned officer within a company, responsible for day-to-day training, drill, discipline, and logistics. He was the equivalent to a modern Company Sergeant Major (British Army) or First Sergeant (U.S. Army). He wore an insignia of three gold chevrons, with two crossed flags and a crown above, on his right shoulder.

Company – British Army unit, consisting of up to a hundred soldiers, including officers and other ranks. Commanded by a captain, with a colour sergeant as the senior non-commissioned officer. Note: Companies on overseas service were notoriously understrength, with seventy to eighty total soldiers being the norm.

Corporal – First of the non-commissioned officer ranks in the British Army. They acted as assistants to the sergeants, and were sometimes given command of their own sections or specialty units, such as company sharp-shooters. They wore two white chevrons on their right shoulder.

Drift – A natural river crossing, more commonly known as a 'ford' in modern times.

Ibutho **(plural *amabutho*)** – A term used to describe a Zulu regiment. Each *ibutho* was age-based, with the king raising new regiments around the time young Zulu males turned seventeen to twenty, based on the needs of the kingdom. They served as the chief labour force, at the king's pleasure, in addition to their military responsibilities in defence of the kingdom. Zulu men were considered youths until they were allowed to marry, usually around the age of thirty. At which time, and with the king's permission, they would take wives-often marrying en mass together-and be allowed to take charge of their own households. Married regiments were exempt from labour and menial details, and were only assembled during times of war or national emergency.

Impi – The name given to a large Zulu army consisting of numerous *amabutho*.

Induna **(plural *izinduna*)** – An officer within the ibutho, selected by his peers. Most often given charge of roughly a hundred warriors, they were roughly the equivalent to a captain in the British Army.

Inkosi **(plural *amakhosi*)** – A Zulu chieftain, sometimes referred to as a 'baron' by the British, for their titles came by birth right, rather than appointment. In war, they commanded the *amabutho*, with the older and more experienced *amakhosi* placed in charge of the younger regiments.

***Inyanga* (plural *izinyanga*)** – Diviners, also derogatorily referred to by Europeans as 'witchdoctors'. They oversaw all spiritual ceremonies for the Zulu *impi*, as well as serving as herbalists and healers.

***Iqawe* (plural *abaqawe*)** – Zulu warriors of great renown, who had shown extreme bravery and prowess in battle. Those elevated to the *abaqawe* were regarded as the most valiant heroes of the Zulu Kingdom.

Koppie – Comes from the Dutch term, 'kop', which literally means 'head'. It is used to describe a small, stony hill that stands out on an otherwise flat landscape.

Kraal – Though not a Zulu term, it came to describe local African homesteads. Typically, they consisted of several huts surrounding a central cattle pen. Kraals that belonged to the nobles of the *amakhosi* could hold dozens or even hundreds of huts, with thousands of residents. The Royal Kraal at Ulundi is said to have had several thousand huts with numerous cattle pens and arena pits.

Laager – A term used by the Dutch to describe encircling wagons as a means of defence. Can also be used to describe temporary wood or stone fortifications.

Lance Corporal – An uncommon British Army rank just above private. Though not officially a non-commissioned officer (a status which changed in 1961), they are often given leadership responsibilities and used to assist the sergeants and corporals. They wore a single white chevron on their right shoulder.

Lance Sergeant – Another uncommon British Army rank, lance sergeants were corporals who were either temporarily appointed to a sergeant's billet, or who had displayed great leadership potential and were waiting for promotion to full sergeant. They wore three white chevrons on the right shoulder.

Lieutenant – Junior commissioned officer, most often used as a subaltern within a company, or staff officer at the battalion. Because promotions were so painfully slow during most of the Victorian Era, they tended to vary considerably in age, with older lieutenants often given command of companies while waiting for an eventual promotion to captain.

Note: While the U.S. Armed Forces pronounce the rank as it is spelled "lew-tenant", in British and Commonwealth Forces it is pronounced "left-tenant".

Lieutenant Colonel – A commissioned officer above major and below colonel, it is the rank used by commanding officers at the battalion level.

Major – A commissioned officer above captain and below lieutenant colonel. Most often used as staff officers, there are two per battalion, each of whom can assume overall command if needed.

Ndabazitha – A Zulu term of reverence to their king, equivalent to 'your majesty'.

Nek – Refers to the lower ground between two high points. In modern times, this has been mostly replaced by the term 'saddle'.

Private – Most common rank in the British Army, outnumbering all other combined ranks approximately eight-to-one, and given to all other ranks upon their enlistment and completion of basic recruit training. In a company, between seventy and ninety of the soldiers will be privates. They wear no rank insignia.

Quartermaster – A commissioned officer, tasked with overseeing all supply and logistics for the battalion. Though the equivalent of a major, because they are in the Support Arms (i.e. Commissariat / Transport / Medical) they technically cannot give orders to combat soldiers (i.e. infantry, cavalry, artillery). They are, however, given the respect of their rank and referred to as 'sir' by subordinates.

Quartermaster Sergeant – A senior non-commissioned officer, acting as chief assistant to the battalion quartermaster. Though nominally equivalent to a colour sergeant in terms of rank, they were considered to be senior, due to their position being a regimental appointment. They wore four gold chevrons on the right sleeve.

Sergeant – A non-commissioned officer, given command of a section, consisting of up to twenty soldiers. They answered directly to the colour sergeant, and oversaw the daily drill, discipline, and welfare of their soldiers. Each sergeant usually had at least one corporal or lance corporal to assist him. They wore three gold chevrons on the right shoulder.

Sergeant Major – The senior non-commissioned officer within the battalion, he is responsible for the overall training, standards, and discipline. He also acts as a mentor to the younger lieutenants, even though they technically outrank him.

Subaltern – Term to describe the junior commissioned officers of a company, usually lieutenants, who were tasked with aiding the officer commanding. The senior subaltern would assume command in the captain's absence.

Usuthu **(sometimes spelled *uSuthu* or *uZulu*)** – Refers to the uSuthu faction, who fought for Cetshwayo during the Zulu civil war of 1856. Following Cetshwayo's victory, it became the battle cry of all Zulus who fought for the king.

Voorlooper – An African boy used to guide the teams of oxen and draught animals.

Author's Final Thoughts

Upon finishing my story about the tragedy that was the Battle of Isandlwana in *Brutal Valour*, it was only natural that I continue with the heroic stand at Rorke's Drift. Those familiar with the 1964 film, *Zulu*, starring Sir Michael Caine, will undoubtedly notice a number of rather drastic differences between the big-screen depiction and my story. This is because the film took a vast number of historical liberties; far more than its 1979 prequel, *Zulu Dawn*. Many of these have been addressed in the appendices above. Mind you, *Zulu* is still one of my favourite films of all-time, and like many, it is what got me interested in the era in the first place. As a dear friend and fellow historian once told me, "If not for the films, the Zulu War would be completely forgotten". For that, we owe both *Zulu* and *Zulu Dawn* a debt of gratitude.

My primary motivation in writing this series is to both renew interest in the Anglo-Zulu War, while presenting it to a new generation. While the films are a fantastic introduction to the time, they are beginning to show their age, particularly in the U.S., where they are mostly forgotten. Sir Michael Caine remains an extremely popular figure on both sides of the Atlantic, yet many of his American fans, even those old enough to remember his early works, have never even heard of Zulu.

While working on this volume, I was fortunate enough to accompany famed Zulu War historian, Ian Knight, on one of his tours of the battlefields in South Africa. Ian once again served as the primary historical reviewer for this work, having previously reviewed and penned the forward to *Brutal Valour*. Tapping into his decades of knowledge, while also walking the ground at Isandlwana, Rorke's Drift, and the slew of other Zulu War battlefields that will be covered in future volumes, was invaluable. In recent years, these tours have been taken over by a company called The Cultural Experience, who have done a fantastic job of continuing to utilise Ian's knowledge and historical expertise. The groups are kept small (less than twenty), which adds a more 'personal' feel. If one has even the slightest interest in the Anglo-Zulu War, or just wants an enriching experience in the heart of Southern Africa, I highly recommend it.

http://www.theculturalexperience.com/tour10084/battlefield-tours/the-zulu-war-battlefield-tour.html

In addition to Ian's instrumental assistance, I continue to receive guidance and support from the former curator at the Royal Welsh Museum in Brecon, retired Sergeant Major Bill Cainan. Though Bill has retired from the museum, he is still very much involved in keeping the history of the Regiment alive. I am also indebted to him for so openly sharing his knowledge of the Victorian Army, and for helping me gain access to countless first-hand accounts and resources.

My recent experiences, both in Britain and South Africa, have inspired me to continue this series, beyond what was covered in the films; to tell the entire saga through to the bitter end. Though savage and harrowing, the Battles of Isandlwana and Rorke's Drift were only the opening salvoes of the Anglo-Zulu War. It would be an injustice to those who continued to sacrifice all in the ongoing conflict, if I were to stop now. Indeed, the next chapter in this story will depict what has often been referred to as 'The Forgotten Column'.

I must also take a moment to express my love and gratitude to my beloved wife, Tracy. When I first mentioned going to South Africa with Ian Knight, I at first thought she would cringe at the cost. Yet, without missing a beat, she said, "You need to do this!" She has been an endless source of inspiration and support in this, and all my literary endeavours.

And finally, this work is dedicated in memory of both the British defenders, as well as the gallant warriors of the Undi Corps, who gave their lives during the Battle of Rorke's Drift. *Requiesce in Pace,*

James Mace
July 2017

The author with Zulu War author and historian, Ian Knight, and fellow historian, Alex Haimann, atop Nyoni Ridge, overlooking Isandlwana
April 2017

Further Reading / Bibliography:

Bibliography

Castle, Ian and Knight, Ian. 1992. *Zulu War 1879, Twilight of a Warrior Nation.* Oxford: Osprey.

Harford, Henry Charles. 2015 (first edition 1881). *The Zulu War Journal.* Barnsley: Pen and Sword Books.

Horse Guards War Office. 1873. *Queen's Regulations and Orders for the Army - 1873.* London: Her Majesty's Stationary Office.

Knight, Ian. 2011. *Zulu Rising.* London: Pan MacMillan.

Knight, Ian. 1992. *Zulu, Isandlwana and Rorke's Drift 22-23 January 1879.* London: Windrow and Greene.

Payne, David and Payne, Emma. 2006. *Harford: The Writings, Photographs, and Sketches of Henry Charles Harford.* Llandysul: Gomer Press.

Snook, Lt Col Mike. 2010. *Like Wolves on the Fold: The Defence of Rorke's Drift.* London: Frontline Books.

The story of the Anglo-Zulu War continues with the saga of Colonel Charles Pearson and the No. 1 Column.

Lost Souls: The Forgotten Heroes of Eshowe

Printed in Great Britain
by Amazon